Henry Miller

New Perspectives

Henry Miller

New Perspectives

Edited by
James M. Decker and Indrek Männiste

Bloomsbury Academic
An imprint of Bloomsbury Publishing Inc

BLOOMSBURY
NEW YORK · LONDON · NEW DELHI · SYDNEY

Bloomsbury Academic
An imprint of Bloomsbury Publishing Inc

1385 Broadway	50 Bedford Square
New York	London
NY 10018	WC1B 3DP
USA	UK

www.bloomsbury.com

BLOOMSBURY and the Diana logo are trademarks of Bloomsbury Publishing Plc

First published 2015

© James M. Decker, Indrek Männiste, and Contributors, 2015

All rights reserved. No part of this publication may be reproduced or transmitted in any form or by any means, electronic or mechanical, including photocopying, recording, or any information storage or retrieval system, without prior permission in writing from the publishers.

No responsibility for loss caused to any individual or organization acting on or refraining from action as a result of the material in this publication can be accepted by Bloomsbury or the author.

Library of Congress Cataloging-in-Publication Data
Henry Miller : new perspectives / edited by James M. Decker, Indrek Manniste ; foreword by Louis A. Renza.
pages cm
Includes bibliographical references and index.
ISBN 978-1-62892-123-6 (hardback)
1. Miller, Henry, 1891—Criticism and interpretation.
I. Decker, James M., 1967- editor. II. Manniste, Indrek. III. Title.
PS3525.I5454Z694 2015
818'.5209–dc23
2014043624

ISBN: HB: 978-1-6289-2123-6
ePub: 978-1-6289-2125-0
ePDF: 978-1-6289-2126-7

Typeset by Integra Software Services Pvt. Ltd.
Printed and bound in the United States of America

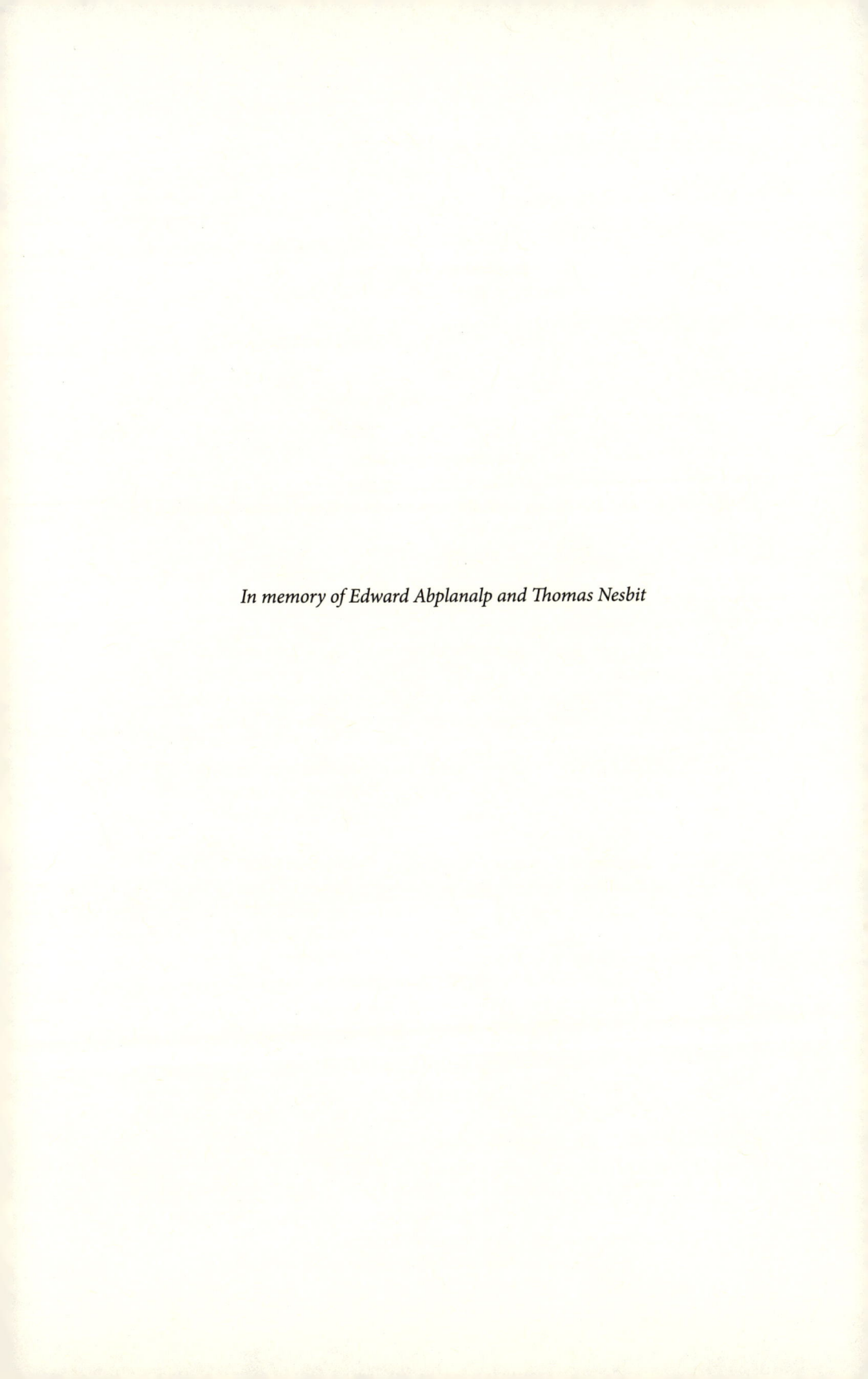

In memory of Edward Abplanalp and Thomas Nesbit

Contents

Notes on Contributors — viii
Foreword *Louis A. Renza* — xi
Acknowledgments — xiv
Chronology — xv
Abbreviations — xviii

Introduction — 1

1 Henry Miller's Inhuman Philosophy *Indrek Männiste* — 9
2 "The agonizing gutter of my past": Henry Miller, Conversion, and the Trauma of the Modern *James M. Decker* — 21
3 When Henry Miller Left for Tibet *Paul Jahshan* — 33
4 The Religiosity of Henry Miller *Edward Abplanalp* — 45
5 Henry Miller and Morality *Guy Stevenson* — 63
6 *Tropic of Cancer*: Word Becoming Flesh *Ondřej Skovajsa* — 75
7 "A dirty book worth reading": Henry Miller's *Tropic of Cancer* and the Feminist Backlash *Anna Lillios* — 85
8 Henry Miller: Obscene Other of the Law *Rob Herian* — 95
9 The Ecstatic Psychotic: Henry Miller via Jacques Lacan *Hamish Dale Mercer Jackson* — 109
10 *Big Sur* and *Walden*: Henry Miller's Practical Transcendentalism *Eric D. Lehman* — 127
11 A Surrealist Duet: Word and Image in *Into the Night Life* with Henry Miller and Bezalel Schatz *Sarah Garland* — 137
12 Cartography of the Obscene *Jeff Bursey* — 159
13 Dispossessed Sexual Politics: Henry Miller's Anarchism Qua Kate Millett and Ursula K. Le Guin *James Gifford* — 173
14 Miller's Paris *Finn Jensen* — 187
15 Henry Miller's Titillating Words *Katy Masuga* — 199

Bibliography — 215
Index — 225

Notes on Contributors

Edward Abplanalp was Professor of Philosophy and Comparative Religion at Illinois Central College. His work focused on social justice, particularly with respect to the environment and appeared in journals such as *International Dialogue*. In addition to his academic pursuits, Ed loved to play guitar and travel. He passed away in June 2014.

Jeff Bursey is a Canadian literary critic whose works have appeared in a variety of publications, including *Nexus: The International Henry Miller Journal*. He is also the author of *Verbatim: A Novel* (2010).

James M. Decker is Professor of English, Humanities, and Language Studies at Illinois Central College. He is the author of *Henry Miller: Constructing the Self, Rejecting Modernity* (2005) and *Ideology* (2003), and he edits *Nexus: The International Henry Miller Journal*.

Sarah Garland is a lecturer in American literature and culture at the University of East Anglia. She is an interdisciplinary scholar of literature, film, and art history. Her research interests include transatlantic modernism; the American avant-garde; taste, consumption, the body and the everyday aesthetic; canonical and noncanonical American literature of the 1920s and 1930s (particularly expatriate writing); collaboration across the arts, and image-text intersections, juxtapositions, and configurations. She has had a longtime interest in Miller's work.

James Gifford is Associate Professor of English and director of the University Core at Fairleigh Dickinson University, Vancouver. His book *Personal Modernisms* appeared in 2014, and he has published broadly on modernism, postcolonial literatures, popular culture, and cultural theory.

Rob Herian is a lecturer in law at the Open University in the United Kingdom. Aside from a long-held interest in the work of Henry Miller, on which he has published in *Nexus: The International Henry Miller Journal*, Rob is also writing a PhD on the law of equity and works as a musician.

Hamish Dale Mercer Jackson received his B.A. in American and English literature from the University of East Anglia, where he was awarded first-class honors. His dissertation on Henry Miller and Jacques Lacan received distinction. He has also written articles on Miller for *Nexus: The International Henry Miller Journal*. A native of England, Hamish now lives with his wife in Brooklyn, New York, and is a glass-blower and ceramicist.

Paul Jahshan is Professor of American Studies at Notre Dame University, Lebanon. Author of *Henry Miller and the Surrealist Discourse of Excess: A Post-Structuralist Reading* (2001), his research interests include twentieth-century American fiction, the postmodern detective, cyber-theory, and Arab–American studies.

Finn Jensen graduated from the University of Copenhagen with an M.A. and PhD in literature. He has written a number of articles and two books about Miller: *The Angel from Brooklyn* (1993) and *The Age of Liberation* (2006). He is now retired from his teaching posts and is working on a major book about Miller's writing in Paris from 1930 to 1939.

Eric D. Lehman teaches literature and creative writing at the University of Bridgeport, and has published essays, reviews, and stories in dozens of journals and magazines, including *Nexus: The International Henry Miller Journal*. He is also the author of ten history and travel books, including *Becoming Tom Thumb: Charles Stratton, P.T. Barnum, and the Dawn of American Celebrity*, and *Homegrown Terror: Benedict Arnold and the Burning of New London*.

Anna Lillios is a professor of English at the University of Central Florida. Her research interests center on literature of place, particularly Mediterranean studies (focusing on the work of Lawrence Durrell) and Florida studies (focusing on the work of Zora Neale Hurston and Marjorie Kinnan Rawlings). She is the author of *Crossing the Creek: The Literary Friendship of Zora Neale Hurston and Marjorie Kinnan Rawlings* (2010). *Crossing the Creek* received a 2011 Florida Book Award for nonfiction and was the subject of a commentary on the editorial page of *The Wall Street Journal*. She edited the collection of essays, *Lawrence Durrell and the Greek World* (2004). She directs the Zora Neale Hurston Electronic Archive at http://pegasus.cc.ucf.edu/~zoraneal and is the editor of *Deus Loci: The Lawrence Durrell Journal* and *The Marjorie Kinnan Rawlings Journal of Florida Literature*. She is an ex-president of the International Lawrence Durrell Society and is currently a member of its executive board. She is an ex-president of the Florida College English Association and has received its 2008 Distinguished Colleague Award. She's currently the executive director and a trustee of the Marjorie Kinnan Rawlings Society.

Indrek Männiste works as a lecturer at Estonian Academy of Arts. He received his PhD in philosophy from the University of Auckland, New Zealand. In the past, he has worked as a Visiting Fellow in the Department of English and Comparative Literature in The University of Warwick, United Kingdom. He is the author of *Henry*

Miller: The Inhuman Artist (2013) and a contributor to *Nexus: The International Henry Miller Journal*. His main research interests besides Henry Miller are D.H. Lawrence, modernism, and modern technology.

Katy Masuga holds a PhD in comparative literature and a joint PhD in literary theory and criticism. Her first book, *Henry Miller and How He Got That Way* (2011), sets Miller in relation to his major sources of influence: Walt Whitman, Fyodor Dostoevsky, Arthur Rimbaud, Lewis Carroll, Marcel Proust, and D.H. Lawrence. Her second work, *The Secret Violence of Henry Miller* (2011), is a treatment of Miller's experimental and ekphrastic language in relation to the work of Maurice Blanchot, with comparisons drawn between James Joyce, Franz Kafka, and Marcel Proust via Félix Guattari and Gilles Deleuze's theory of a minor literature. Masuga has also published numerous articles and chapters on Miller and on topics including Ludwig Wittgenstein, Maurice Blanchot, Samuel Beckett, D.H. Lawrence, Shakespeare and Company in Paris, contemporary art, image and text relations, Frankenstein's Creature, and half a dozen short stories. She teaches comparative literature at Skidmore College in Paris.

Ondřej Skovajsa defended his doctoral dissertation *Written Voice: Leaves of Grass* (1855) *and Tropic of Cancer* in the Department of Comparative Literature at Charles University, Prague, in 2014. The dissertation re-conceptualizes oral composition theory to discuss modernist works. He translated and prepared a Czech edition Henry Miller's *Essays* (Dauphin 2011) and is currently working on a Czech translation of Whitman's first *Leaves* (1855). He spent a year 2011/2012 as Fulbright Scholar at University of California, Santa Cruz, and works as an assistant professor of English at Purkyně University, Ústí nad Labem, Czech Republic.

Guy Stevenson is an associate lecturer of English and American literature at Goldsmiths College, University of London. His principal areas of research are Henry Miller, early twentieth-century modernism and countercultural American literature of the 1950s and 1960s. He has contributed reviews and essays to a range of publications, including London's *Times Literary Supplement* and Toronto's *National Post*.

Foreword

You would be hard pressed to find any serious representation—most often you would find none—of Henry Miller's works in the present U.S. academic world. For instance, he remains conspicuously absent from the most notable anthologies of American literature. Beyond that, refereed academic articles on his works come few and far between in today's well-known U.S. critical journals, which in effect both reflect and help constitute the zeitgeist of American literary studies. Perhaps, most telling of all is Miller's notable absence from pedagogical arenas. I seriously doubt if any of his works (not just *Tropic of Cancer*, *Tropic of Capricorn*, and *Sexus*, but relatively noncontroversial ones like *Black Spring*, or even the topically innocuous "travel" work, *The Colossus of Maroussi*) makes its way into regular syllabi of college and university courses in American literature and/or American studies. Indeed, I am fairly certain I was the first and possibly the last instructor to assign *Tropic of Cancer* and *Tropic of Capricorn* in a course I taught at Dartmouth College for close to forty years.[1]

Why this *miss*-representation? As with Mark Twain's major novel but without his canonical credentials, Miller's major self-referential works recurrently get censored for different reasons in different periods. George Orwell, for example, defended Miller early on but questioned his anarchic (i.e., nonreformist) politics. In former times, U.S. censorship of Miller's *Tropic* narratives mainly stemmed from how their "obscene" language and representational materials violated middle-class American moral standards. Miller himself anticipated this contemporary reception while writing *Tropic of Cancer*: "Sometimes I would lie abed till noon. There was nothing pressing, except to finish the book, and that didn't worry me much because I was already convinced that nobody would accept it anyway" (CAN, 223).

Today, his texts run into a different kind of moral censor. The "cultural studies" paradigm that dominates the current American academy openly judges written works mostly according to their propagation of liberal social values. In this politically charged context, Miller's writings get cited if at all as pejorative demos of politically incorrect views: sexism, racism, ethnic stereotypes, and even anti-Semitism.[2] This devalued view of Miller more or less gets summarized by Salman Rushdie's elitist dismissal of Miller's work on the grounds of his apoliticism: "Miller's reputation has more or less completely evaporated, and he now looks to be very little more than the happy pornographer beneath whose scatological surface Orwell saw such improbable depths." Indeed, few so-called "creative" writers before the Beats have felt beholden in some way to Miller's literary precedent.[3]

One can complicate if not entirely rebut the aforementioned charges,[4] but to what end given academic reliance on a categorical imperative defined by one or another version of identity politics? Yet, why even take a defensive posture with Miller's works at all? He himself (again) anticipated such a future reception and, eschewing programmatic political alternatives of every kind, in effect set down the terms for interrogating beforehand his present academic censorship: " ... to be human seems like a poor, sorry, miserable affair, limited by the senses, restricted by moralities and codes, defined by platitudes and isms" (CAN, 259). Put another way, Miller's works put in question the unquestioned axioms behind such academic mala-judgments. At the very least, literary-critical studies would do well to follow the principle that Fang Lizhi remarked as a sine qua non of scientific investigation: to begin its own formulation about any subject with a good measure of methodological self-doubt. In fact, why not try suspending the hermeneutics of suspicion with works like Miller's and adopt a "second naïveté" so as to find a new, positive relation to them?[5]

The following collection attempts to do just that and from an impressive variety of disciplinary angles. The chapters in this book allow for a critically aware double reflection on these works, including how they concern at least one favorite subject of recent American studies: a transnational tableaux. Nonetheless, Miller's *bête noire* was and remains "identity politics" itself, whatever its avatar. A spiritual pragmatist, as it were, his writing instead constitutes a project precisely to deracinate his civilized self—its succumbing to one or another identitarian category—in order to engage a cosmic anonymity of self, as much as he could realize it in and through his writing: "What is war, disease, cruelty, terror, when night presents the ecstasy of myriad blazing suns? What is this chaff we chew in our sleep if it is not the remembrance of fang-whorl and star cluster" (CAN, 254). This book defines Miller's relation to writing from beginning to end. His works therefore request dialectical critical responses, the better to register his *post*-hedonist relation to sex (*pace* Rushdie) and other basic appetites, particularly as recorded in the two *Tropic* narratives and *The Rosy Crucifixion*.

Among other things, viewing Miller's writing as enacting symbolic strategies, to adopt a Kenneth Burkean term, would also allow us to re-view his loud deployments of ethnic stereotypes as purposeful signifiers of social–cultural formations into which one—he too—tends to fall, and which therefore require the deconstructions afforded by rhetorical modes of "obscenity." Such critical formulations show Miller's writing to be a kind of spiritual experiment. In that sense, another Henry, one whom he considered an authorial precursor, might very well have situated Miller's works within the paradoxically marginal mainstream of U.S. antinomian writing and living: "Books, not which afford us a cowering enjoyment, but in which each thought is of unusual daring; such as an idle man cannot read, and a timid one would not be entertained by, which even make us dangerous to existing institutions—such call I good books."[6]

Louis A. Renza
Emeritus Professor of English, Dartmouth College

Notes

1. Herbert West, a Dartmouth professor of Comparative Literature at Dartmouth College, was one of the first to write a "serious" academic review of *Tropic of Cancer* in the *Dartmouth Alumni Magazine* (1937). See Robert Ferguson, *Henry Miller: A Life* (New York: Norton, 1991), 270, 291.
2. See, for example, the by now familiar charges again deployed by Jeanette Winterson in a review of Frederick Turner's book on Miller's writing of *Tropic of Cancer*: "The Male Mystique of Henry Miller," *The New York Times Sunday Book Review* (January 26, 2012).
3. Rushdie's remark occurs in his essay taking Orwell to task for not maintaining the "political" standard entailed in literary work; hence the latter's wrong-minded defense of Miller in his 1940 essay "Inside the Whale." Rushdie, "Outside the Whale," *Granta 11* (1984), http://www.granta.com/Archive/11/Outside-the-Whale/Page-4. To a query in 1958 about his opinion of Miller, William Faulkner—one of the very few modernist American writers whom Miller had ever praised—responded: "Sorry, I don't know him. Should I?" *Faulkner in the University*, ed. Frederick L. Gwynn and Joseph Blotner (Charlottesville: University of Virginia Press, 1959), 282. Even hyperbolic hawkers of Miller's "genius" by early and late peers like Karl Shapiro and Norman Mailer failed to inspire any academic-critical reopening *chez* Miller.
4. For example, the Miller narrator arguably exposes (and so tries to separate himself from) a nihilistic, reductive male sexism in his *self-evidently* burlesque caricature of Van Norden in *Tropic of Cancer*. As for Miller's use of ethnic stereotypes, if nothing else, he was an equal-opportunity stereotyper, and not least of his own German-immigrant relatives about whom he remained caustically critical throughout his autobiographical works.
5. Paul Ricoeur makes this proposal in *The Symbolism of Evil* (Boston: Beacon Press, 1986). Cf. Wendy Doniger's heuristic suggestion in a 2008 Convocation talk at the University of Chicago where she applies Ricoeur's notion of a "second naïveté" specifically to contemporary academic subjects: "We need to balance what literary critics call a hermeneutics of suspicion—a method of reading that ferrets out submerged agendas—with a hermeneutics of retrieval, or even of reconciliation.... [W]here in our first naïveté, we did not notice the racism, and in our subsequent hypercritical reading we couldn't see anything else, in our second naïveté we can see how good some writers are despite the inhumanity of their underlying world views." http://divinity.uchicago.edu/sites/default/files/imce/pdfs/publications/criterion/winter_09.pdf. My thanks to Jed Dobson for pointing me to these references.
6. Henry David Thoreau, *A Week on the Concord and Merrimack Rivers*, A Penn State Electronic Classics Series Publication, ed. Jim Manis (Philadelphia: Pennsylvania State University Press, 2003), 73.

Acknowledgments

The authors would like to thank Haaris Naqvi of Bloomsbury for shepherding the project along and for his gracious assistance and unwavering wisdom. The authors also are thankful for the editorial assistance of Rajakumari Ganessin, Avinash Singh, and James Tupper. They would also like to show appreciation to Laura Murray for her help on the early stages of the book.

James Decker would like to thank his coeditor, Indrek Männiste, for pursuing a wonderful idea with aplomb and acumen. I also wish to pay tribute to Roger Jackson, whose tireless efforts on behalf of Henry Miller paved the road. The combined efforts of the contributors to *Nexus: The International Henry Miller Journal* have proven invaluable not only to me but also to all of the contributors in this book. Thanks as well are due Kenneth Womack and D.A. Pratt, whose curiosity and skill always spur me on. I also can't say enough about Karl Orend, whose groundbreaking scholarly work continues to stimulate. I would also like to acknowledge the amazing Henry Miller symposium hosted by Guy Stevenson, Dominic Jaeckle, and Caroline Blinder of Goldsmiths, University of London. I learned so much! Thanks to Megan Ames, Stuart Boyd, Josh Butler, Trevor Crawford, Ethan Hedman, Alexis Maloof, and Zac Maloof for so ably distracting me from deadlines with parties and trivia nights at Blue: Go Cloppers! Of course, no list of acknowledgments would be complete without thanking my amazing and talented children, Siobhan, Anastazia, and Evan. You make me proud. Finally, no words can do justice to Stephanie Guedet, the astonishing dynamo who inspires my every moment and owns my heart. Thank you for all of our remarkable verbal duets—whether fueled by glasses of wine or water—and, most of all, for your love.

Indrek Männiste is enormously grateful to James Decker for coming behind the project and filling, what in the beginning was a rather abstract idea, with his years of experience, hard work, and unparalleled Miller expertise. He would also like to thank his ever-supporting friends Andreas Ventsel, Toomas Lott, and Mari-Liis Madisson for offering, by way of their wonderful company, a soft cushion in the days when needed the most. A special thanks goes to Angela Pollard-Pantoja and Robin Willens for their help and friendship, be it in Luang Prabang, Phu Quoc, or London. Last but not least, Männiste would like to thank Maarja Uuspõld for seeing him through the most difficult days of the project by providing unwavering support and kindness.

Chronology

1891   Henry Valentine Miller was born on 26 December in New York to Heinrich and Louise Miller (née Nieting)

1906   Miller attends Eastern District High School in Williamsburg

1908   Miller and his friends found the Xerxes Society

1909   Miller graduates from Eastern District; Miller wins a scholarship to study German at Cornell University but even with the scholarship, his family could not afford it; in September Miller enrolls in to the tuition-free City College of New York but leaves the college after six weeks and later takes a job as a clerk at the Atlas Portland Cement Company; begins an affair with Pauline Chouteau (née Laura May), a thirty-seven-year-old divorcée

1912   Pauline becomes pregnant but loses her baby in the fall; in March, Miller goes to New Mexico to work as a cattle herder but due to the lack of need is forced to work as a picker on a lemon ranch in Chula Vista; attends a talk by the notorious anarchist Emma Goldman in California and becomes fascinated by anarchist ideas; Miller grudgingly agrees to take an apprenticeship at his father's tailor shop in Manhattan

1915   Miller has vague ideas about becoming a writer; in October, Miller meets and falls in love with Beatrice Sylvas Wickens

1917   Miller leaves the tailor shop and marries Beatrice, partly to avoid the draft

1919   Henry and Beatrice's daughter, Barbara Sylvas, is born on 30 September

1920   Miller is hired as an employment manager at Western Union Telegraph Company

1922   Miller writes his first book *Clipped Wings* on a three-week vacation from Western Union

1923   Miller meets and falls in love with June Mansfield (born, according to Ellis Island records, Julia Smerth); on 21 December, Beatrice divorces Miller

1924   on 1 June, Miller and June get married; in September, Miller quits his job at Western Union to live the life of a writer

1927   Miller writes his second book *Moloch*; June abandons him for Europe but returns a few months later

1928   Henry and June visit Europe for the first time

1929	Miller and June return to New York
1930	on June's insistence, Miller returns to Paris alone to continue his literary career; Miller reacquaints with Alfred Perlès (whom he had first met in 1928)
1931	Miller meets Walter Lowenfels and Michael Fraenkel; Miller works as a proofreader for Paris's *Chicago Tribune*; starts working on his "Paris book" that would eventually become *Tropic of Cancer*; meets Anaïs Nin, with whom he starts both a literary and love affair
1932	Miller's first Paris-based short story "Mademoiselle Claude" was accepted for publication in the anthology *Americans Abroad*
1934	*Tropic of Cancer* is published by Obelisk Press and immediately banned in the United States and Great Britain; divorces June by proxy in Mexico
1935	Miller briefly visits New York
1936	*Black Spring* is published in June by Obelisk Press
1937	Lawrence Durrell visits Miller in Paris
1938	*Max and the White Phagocytes* is published by Obelisk Press after having been turned down by Alfred A. Knopf in the United States and Faber and Faber in Britain
1939	*Tropic of Capricorn* is published by Obelisk Press. James Laughlin's new firm New Directions brings out *The Cosmological Eye* in the United States; travels in South of France and, with the war impending, goes to Corfu to stay with Lawrence Durrell and his wife
1940	Miller returns to New York in mid-January. In late October he begins a road-trip around the United States with Abe Rattner in order to write *The Air-Conditioned Nightmare*; publishes *The World of Sex*
1941	Colt Press publishes Miller's Greek book, *The Colossus of Maroussi*
1942	in June, Miller settles in Beverly Glen in California; starts to work on volume one of the *Rosy Crucifixion* trilogy, *Sexus*
1944	Miller moves to Big Sur. Marries Janina Martha Lepska
1945	*The Air-Conditioned Nightmare* is finally published. In October, Miller and Lepska's daughter, Valentine Lepska, is born
1948	in August, Lepska gives birth to their son, Henry Tony
1949	*Sexus* is published in Paris
1952	Miller and Lepska divorce; *Books in My Life* is published
1953	in December, Miller marries Eve McClure; *Plexus* is published in Paris

1954 Miller and Eve visit Europe for the first time after the war

1955 *Big Sur and the Oranges of Hieronymus Bosch* is published

1959 Miller and Eve travel around Europe; *Nexus* is published in Denmark

1960 Miller and Eve divorce

1961 on 24 June, Grove Press publishes *Tropic of Cancer* for the first time in the United States. (68, 000 copies were sold in the first week); In July the book is banned in Massachusetts; a series of court cases begins; *Tropic of Capricorn* is published to circumvent piracy

1964 The United States Supreme Court (case Grove Press Inc. v. Gerstein) overrules the state court charges of obscenity in *Tropic of Cancer*

1965 Grove publishes the *Rosy Crucifixion* trilogy

1967 Miller marries Hiroko Tokuda

1969 Kate Millett's *Sexual Politics* attacks Miller's works as chauvinistic and misogynous

1977 Miller and Hoki divorce

1980 *The World of Lawrence* is published; Miller dies of cardiovascular failure on 7 June

Abbreviations

ACN   *Air-Conditioned Nightmare* (New York: New Directions, 1945).

BIML *The Books in My Life* (New York: New Directions, 1952).

BS   *Black Spring* (New York: Grove Press, 1963).

BSOHB *Big Sur and the Oranges of Hieronymus Bosch.* (New York: New Directions, 1957).

C   *Capricorne—Ebauche de Tropique du Capricorne* (Paris: Blanche, 2013).

CAN *Tropic of Cancer* (New York: Grove Press, 1961).

CAP *Tropic of Capricorn* (New York: Grove Press, 1961).

CBF *Complete Book of Friends* (London: Allison and Busby, 1987).

CC   *Crazy Cock* (New York: Grove Weidenfeld, 1991).

CE   *The Cosmological Eye* (Norfolk: New Directions, 1939).

CHM *Conversations with Henry Miller*, ed. Frank L. Kersnowski and Alice Hughes (Jackson: University Press of Mississippi, 1994).

COM *The Colossus of Maroussi* (New York: New Directions, 1941).

DB   A Dream of a Book (Big Sur: H Miller, 1958).

HAM *Hamlet* (with Michael Fraenkel) (London: Carrefour, 1962).

HMC *Henry Miller in Conversation* (with Georges Belmont) (Chicago: Quadrangle, 1972).

HMJL *Henry Miller and James Laughlin: Selected Letters* (with James Laughlin) (New York: Norton, 1996).

HMW *Henry Miller on Writing* (New York: New Directions, 1964).

INL *Into the Night Life* (with Bezalel Schatz) (Berkeley: H. Miller, 1947).

LAN Henry Miller (with Anaïs Nin) *Henry Miller: Letters to Anaïs Nin* (edited by Gunther Stuhlmann) (New York: Putnam, 1965).

LE   *Letters to Emil* (New York: New Directions, 1989).

LKM	"Letter to Kate Millet, May 27, 1969" *Nexus: The International Henry Miller Journal* 8 (2011): 3–4.
LP	*A Literate Passion: Letters of Anaïs Nin and Henry Miller 1932–1953* (New York: Harcourt Brace Company, 1987).
MOL	*Moloch or, This Gentile World* (New York: Grove Press, 1992).
NEX	*Nexus: Book Three of "The Rosy Crucifixion" Trilogy* (New York: Grove Press, 1965).
NI	The New Instinctivism (A Creative Duet) (With Alfred Perlès) *Nexus: The International Henry Miller Journal* 4 (2007): 3–56.
PLEX	*Plexus: Book Two of "The Rosy Crucifixion" Trilogy* (New York: Grove Press, 1965).
R	*Reflections* (edited by Twinka Thiebaud) (Santa Barbara: Capra Press, 1981).
RTR	*Remember to Remember* (New York: New Directions, 1947).
SAW	*Sunday After the War* (Norfolk, CT: New Directions, 1944).
SEX	*Sexus: Book One of the "The Rosy Crucifixion" Trilogy* (New York: Grove Press, 1965).
SMF	*The Smile at the Foot of the Ladder* (New York: Duell, Sloan, and Pearce, 1948).
SSLH	*Stand Still Like the Hummingbird* (New York: New Directions, 1962).
TNR	Letter to the Editor (re: Dreiser's Style) (*The New Republic*, 28 April 1926: 308).
TOA	*The Time of the Assassins: A Study of Rimbaud* (New York: New Directions, 1956).
WOH	*The Wisdom of the Heart* (New York: New Directions, 1941).
WOL	*The World of Lawrence: A Passionate Appreciation* (Santa Barbara: Capra Press, 1980).
WOS	*The World of Sex* (Chicago: J.H.N. [Ben Abramson], 1941).
WR	*The Waters Reglitterized: The Subject of Water Color in Some of Its More Liquid Phases* (London: Village Press, 1973).

Introduction

In 1976, Norman Mailer observed that "Literary criticism has left a space around Henry Miller."[1] Nearly forty years later, Arthur Hoyle ends his biography of Miller by drawing attention to the writer's "continuing [academic] exile,"[2] and an essay in *The Guardian* remarks that Miller holds "more influence on other writers than mainstream audiences."[3] Indeed, it seems almost obligatory for writers on Miller to lament the critical wasteland in which Miller apparently exists. Nevertheless, if one peruses the secondary literature prior to the 2000s, one will discover a narrow but steady stream of articles and books that explore Miller's importance as a writer. With a few important exceptions, however, this criticism may have harmed Miller more than it advanced his case within academe. Broadly, the earlier analyses of Miller focused on four principal areas: biography, self-liberation, sexuality, and sexism.[4]

Often, critics in all four categories made little attempt to distinguish between Miller and his narrator and tended to trust Miller's own comments and timelines with little question. As Karl Orend's pioneering biographical work demonstrates, however, correspondence between the biographical Henry Miller and the "Henry Miller" who populates the narratives is problematic at best.[5] The actions and attitudes of "Henry" differ in significant ways from those of Miller and, as Katy Masuga convincingly argues, an uncritical acceptance of the biographical similarities between Miller and his narrator, while encouraged by Miller himself, reduces the scope of both the text and the critical approach.[6] Such conflation of narrator and writer also tends to elicit commentary that assumes a moralistic tone (either celebratory or reproving) and suggests that not only does Miller qua author/man endorse the actions and beliefs of his character, but also that he *is* his protagonist.

Commencing with the new millennium, however, critics started to engage Miller in a more theoretically informed way, fulfilling the promise of Ihab Hassan, Gilles Delueze and Félix Guatarri, and other pioneers who saw the narratives as more dynamic and challenging than many early readers.[7] Miller studies have never seen a richer, more varied critical practice than that of the last decade or so. In addition to an academic journal devoted to Miller and his circle,[8] numerous monographs addressing the writer have appeared in the last fifteen years, none of which are "general" studies of the type that typified early scholarship. Miller's critics are also achieving success in significant journals and making some inroads in more general studies of American modernism and the novel. Unlike the past, moreover, when scholars of Miller—as suggested by

Louis Renza in his foreword—worked in isolation and rarely had the opportunity to form the community of researchers necessary to build a writer's critical reputation, a rich dialogue replete with diverse theoretical convictions has commenced. In September 2014, for instance, Goldsmiths, University of London hosted a lively international symposium on Henry Miller that revealed tremendous new insights about little studied aspects of Miller's work. Arthur Hoyle is also helping Miller reach a new generation via his articles for *The Huffington Post*. Miller's critics, furthermore, are citing, helping, and challenging one another in ways that strengthen their praxis and generate wider interest in the author.

All of this, of course, begs the question of why readers should study Miller in the first place. Beyond the obvious answers—his groundbreaking representation of sex; his influence on writers such as Philip Roth, Thomas Pynchon, Jack Kerouac, and Lawrence Durrell; his connection to the European avant-garde; his delirious use of language; his critique of American materialism; his relentless self-examination; his spiritual mysticism—a key reason that readers need to investigate Miller closely involves his ability to generate discomfort in his audience. As many of the contributors to this book note, this uneasiness embodies many forms, wears many masks. Both in the 1930s and now, readers of Miller respond viscerally to his narratives, for his words touch exposed nerves, bring anxieties to the surface. His Whitmanesque contradictions decenter readers, unsettle them in a way that many more famous books no longer have the power to achieve.

In Miller's books, such contradictions occur at the anecdotal level, to be sure: anti-Semitism and philo-Semitism; misogyny and philogyny; wisdom and ignorance; materialism and asceticism; arrogance and doubt; beauty and ugliness; good and evil. Miller's more perceptive readers, such as Michael Fraenkel, Anaïs Nin, and Lawrence Durrell, noted and applauded such incongruities from the start, although many others accepted or rejected his work based on only one side of the equation.[9] As with his hero Whitman, indeed as with many of the writers and traditions that attracted him, Miller does not attempt to explain away such contradictory impulses or treat them separately. For many of his Western readers, used to comfortable binaries, such acceptance breeds anxiety, discomposure.

Beyond the level of "plot," however, Miller reveals (ostensible) inconsistencies at the level of tone, style, and form. Miller's words explode off the page in a hate-filled jeremiad only to float back to earth with a tender disquisition. Sprawling lists, indignant diatribes, tributes to other writers, and micro-essays on music, art, and love sit adjacent to sexual encounters, bizarre fantasies, hallucinatory reveries, burlesque slapstick, and anecdotes about boyhood or corporate America. As Miller wrote to Emil Schnellock, "The hell with form, style, expression, and all those pseudo-paramount things which beguile the critics" (LE, 72). Miller was anathema to formalists, to put it mildly. Readers, even sympathetic ones, often lament Miller's lack of plot, criticize his "uneven" prose, lose track of his digressions within digressions, fret over his amalgamation of genres.

Eighty-plus years after the publication of *Tropic of Cancer*, Miller exists on the margins of academe, yet his power to stir readers, to frustrate them and engage them, is undeniable. Far from merely personifying Kingsley Widmer's "rebel buffoon"[10] "revel[ing] in the degradation of women,"[11] as Jeanette Winterson accuses, or even exemplifying Karl Shapiro's "wisdom writer,"[12] Miller epitomizes Claude Lévi-Strauss's "bricoleur," "speak[ing] not only *with* things ... but also through the medium of things."[13] As Lévi-Strauss conceives it, bricoleurs employ a kind of "mythical thought" wherein they "build up structures by fitting together events, or rather the remains of events."[14] In this way, the bricoleur uses the same material as "ends or means."[15] Miller's use of fragments and repetition, his problematization of photographic realism, his systematic rejection of system, all point toward the metaphoric and the metaphysical even in his most seemingly truthful and mimetic passages. His medium *is* his message, and it is a message designed to coimplicate the reader in language's failure to communicate shared experience and external "fact," much less the essence of identity or spiritual energy.

Miller argued that the most interesting and successful writers possess the "ability to 'exploit' the vast silence which enwraps us all" (BIML, 38). In continuing to produce such strong and varied responses within his audience, Miller reveals his own facility for exploiting this vast silence—whether or not readers want to listen. Such an aptitude warrants interrogation. Such a capacity merits moving beyond initial impressions, received opinions, and theoretical prejudices regarding Miller's work. The present book offers the first collection of chapters on Miller in over thirty years.[16] Additionally, unlike the previous three collections, which relied heavily on reprinted articles, *Henry Miller: New Perspectives* consists of entirely new chapters and attempts to investigate the various ways in which Miller's narratives function. Additionally, the various chapters within *Henry Miller: New Perspectives* typify the more nuanced methodologies the current generation of critics are applying to Miller's narratives.

In the first chapter, "Henry Miller's Inhuman Philosophy," Indrek Männiste explores the relationship between philosophy and Miller's ideas. Against the critics, who have habitually denied that Miller's theoretical insights form a coherent philosophical system, Männiste argues that by focusing on Miller's key concepts such as the *traditional* and the *full present*, as well as his notion of the *inhuman artist*, Miller's thinking does indeed form a systematic set of ideas that he labels as Miller's metaphysical sense of life or his *inhuman philosophy*. By disclosing these two oppositional realms—*traditional* and *full present*—as the very source of the conflict between Miller's *inhuman artist* and the modern Western world, he demonstrates that Miller's philosophical dispositions were directed against the most dominant features of the progress-oriented modern age: linear conception of history, time, technology, and the aesthetic notion of art.

In the next chapter, "'The agonizing gutter of my past': Henry Miller, Conversion, and the Trauma of the Modern," James M. Decker explores the twinned concepts of conversion and trauma as they relate to Miller's narratives. Decker demonstrates that the narrator's dissatisfaction parallels the alienation often experienced by those on the verge of conversion. The roots of this profound disconnection lie in the narrator's traumatic relationship with modernity, particularly in terms of material success. Through an examination of the conversion tradition as it applies to the secular, Decker identifies a deep concern for conversion and rebirth within Miller's texts.

Paul Jashan, in his chapter "When Henry Miller Left for Tibet," examines in depth Miller's life-long fascination with Asian cultures and ideas. He demonstrates how Miller's journey from America to France, and then to Greece, before going back to his native country, helped him develop a theory of ethnocultural differences culminating in the vision of a perfect race of individuals, that of the artists.

In his chapter titled "The Religiosity of Henry Miller," Edward Abplanalp examines Miller's views on the topics of religion and religiosity. He discusses Miller's conceptions of God, salvation, heaven and hell, the meaning of life, spirit, the symbols of angels and demons, death, crucifixion, and similar ideas. He also scrutinizes Miller's ideas of birth and rebirth, the Bible, as well as his views on certain religious figures, and organized religion in general. He also offers an insight into Miller's engagements with astrology and how numerous philosophical–theological traditions shaped his overall religious motif.

Guy Stevenson, in his chapter "Henry Miller and Morality," outlines Miller's moral approach by engaging with the 1930s' European milieu; a cultural atmosphere disturbed by the First World War, the economic depression, and the frightening but exhilarating rise of political and philosophical extremism. Through the commentaries of Ezra Pound and George Bataille, two reviewers from the 1930s, who approached Miller's *Tropic of Cancer* from opposite ends of the political spectrum (radical right and left, respectively), Stevenson offers an analysis of the tension and conflicts that these insights reveal regarding Miller's views on morality.

In his chapter, "*Tropic of Cancer*: Word Becoming Flesh," Ondřej Skovajsa offers a compelling reading of *Tropic of Cancer*. He argues that *Cancer* breaks in radical fashion with literature in order to question the linear and meager narrative of modernity with the purpose of resurrecting the readers' bodies, emotions, and dignity. Furthermore, he shows that Miller's textual *I* ventures to *kill* the reader to a more courageous and perceptive life. He examines how this is achieved by drawing on linguistic, anthropological, and theological aspects of oral theory and moving from the *paratextual* level to *style, genesis, ethos*, and, finally, to the *story* of the *I*.

Anna Lillios, in her chapter "'A dirty book worth reading': Henry Miller's *Tropic of Cancer* and the Feminist Backlash," tackles heated debates Miller's works caused in the feminist theories from the late 1960s and 1970s to the contemporary era. While Miller, Lillios argues, did not quite satisfy the contemporary feminist requirement of "de-idealizing" the woman in order to celebrate the "human," he did indeed celebrate the human connection between the sexes.

Rob Herian, in "Henry Miller: Obscene Other of the Law," offers a Žižekian reading of the notion of law and how Henry Miller's works and their reception exemplify it. His chapter draws on the aspects born in the psychic space of the subject, as elucidated by psychoanalysis, which are in dialogue with the external sociojuridical structure called "law," and which strive to better understand affective and culturally engrained notions of obscenity.

In his chapter, "The Ecstatic Psychotic: Henry Miller via Jacques Lacan," Hamish Dale Mercer Jackson explores the "form of formlessness" of Miller's surrealistic texts with a view to reveal, through Lacanian analysis, his *psychosis* or what is hidden in his unconsciousness. Jackson's analysis is expected to shed an important light to a central paradox in Miller's writings: the intention to express himself, as a self-realized man, despite being psychologically unsure of whom he is. This paradox lies behind much of the critics' confusion surrounding the reliability of Miller's narrator.

In his chapter, "*Big Sur* and *Walden*: Henry Miller's Practical Transcendentalism," Eric D. Lehman revisits Miller's connection with American Transcendentalism. He argues that by focusing on Miller's early novels many critics have missed deeper and more profound similarities found in *Big Sur and the Oranges of Hieronymus Bosch*. The latter book, Lehman argues, parallels Thoreau's *Walden* in many ways. It explores transcendental values, and shows where Miller diverges from them regarding the relationship of the individual to community. In it, Miller particularly challenges the Transcendentalists' idealistic and utopian thinking, exploring the positive and negative sides of it. This inevitably leads to a struggle with his established philosophy of creative individualism.

Sarah Garland, in her chapter, "A Surrealist Duet: Word and Image in *Into the Night Life* with Henry Miller and Bezalel Schatz," argues that in his collaboration with Schatz on the large illustrated edition of "Into the Night Life," and in a general approach to writing that in *Tropic of Cancer* he calls "collaborating with myself," Miller both draws on the idea of the image as a figure for the unconscious and uses the idea of the image as representing a trace of ungoverned creation in conjunction with a set of symbols for death and rebirth of the self in order to resurrect the self by remaking it as other.

Jeff Bursey's chapter, "Cartography of the Obscene," analyzes the ever-intriguing question of the obscenity of Miller's works as reawakened by some of the more contemporary Miller-critics (notably Jeanette Winterson). Bursey finds that what is obscene is a topic that contains competing definitions, distinctions, biases, and judgments and that literature loses when discussion is closed off because of indignation and repulsion.

James Gifford, in his chapter "Dispossessed Sexual Politics: Henry Miller's Anarchism *Qua* Kate Millett and Ursula K. Le Guin," argues that Kate Millett's *Sexual Politics*, with its extensive critique of misogyny in *Tropic of Cancer*, surprisingly misunderstood Henry Miller's anarchist praxis for writing. Gifford reveals an interesting interplay between Miller's works, Millet's critique, and Le Guin's allusive response. The sequence of their works, Gifford argues, illustrates both Miller's sexual politics and his relational anarchism, or his sexual anarchism and relational politics.

Finn Jensen's chapter, "Miller's Paris," untangles Miller's deeply rooted but varied inclinations toward modern cities, especially Paris. While Miller usually describes cities as places of degradation and destruction, Paris plays very different roles for Miller. Jensen explores Miller's three-layered notion of "real," historic, and symbolic Paris through *Tropic of Cancer* and other texts as well as provides illustrative material of Miller's life in Paris.

Katy Masuga, in her chapter "Henry Miller's Titillating Words," argues that Miller's lifetime of writing relies on a use of the erotic that is oriented toward greater ends—to explore the limits of language, which has been often overlooked. She demonstrates that Miller uses the erotic experience as one of the most crucial gestures for attempting to express the interminable chaos that exists beyond the borders of cultural complacency.

The chapters in *Henry Miller: New Perspectives* thus approach Miller from a variety of contexts and start a renewed dialogue over his literary contributions. In addition to employing diverse theoretical methodologies, the chapters investigate a wide range of Miller's texts. While Miller was quite prolific, most of the previous criticism has focused on a single book, *Tropic of Cancer*. This book begins to fill in this critical space and demonstrates that Miller's artistic vision evolved over his career. Toward this end, many of the chapters explore the background of Miller's writing and demonstrate how he synthesized his influences, be they literary, philosophical, religious, cinematic, artistic, or otherwise. Hopefully, these provocative chapters will spark a more nuanced and productive dialogue about an author whose reputation too often hinges on stereotypes or facile biographical correspondences.

Notes

1. Norman Mailer, *Genius and Lust: A Journey through the Major Writings of Henry Miller* (New York: Grove, 1976), 3.
2. Arthur Hoyle, *The Unknown Henry Miller: A Seeker in Big Sur* (New York: Arcade, 2014), 329.
3. Huw Nesbitt, "Why Henry Miller and Louis-Ferdinand Céline Deserve Success as well as Scandal," *The Guardian* 19 Feb. 2014. url: http://www.theguardian.com/books/booksblog/2014/feb/19/henry-miller-louis-ferdinand-celine-scandal In an interesting pairing of style and content, Nesbitt also suggests that Miller's "occasionally overwrought and misogynistic" passages have harmed his reputation.
4. On occasion, critics would deviate from these foci and discuss Miller's influences (Romanticism, Transcendentalism, etc.).
5. See, for instance, Karl Orend *Brotherhood of Fools and Simpletons: Gods and Devils in Henry Miller's Utopia* (Paris: Alyscamps, 2005). Orend's work in general overturns many of the assumptions about the alleged equivalence between Miller's life and work.
6. Katy Masuga, *The Secret Violence of Henry Miller* (Rochester: Camden House, 2011), 27.
7. See Ihab Hassan, *The Literature of Silence: Henry Miller and Samuel Beckett* (New York: Knopf, 1967); Gilles Deleuze and Félix Guattari, *Anti-Oedipus: Capitalism and Schizophrenia,* trans. Robert Hurley, et al. (Minneapolis: University of Minnesota Press, 1983); and *A Thousand Plateaus: Capitalism and Schizophrenia,* trans. Brian Massumi (Minneapolis: University of Minnesota Press, 1987).
8. *Nexus: The International Henry Miller Journal* began appearing annually in 2004. *A Café in Space: The Anaïs Nin Literary Journal and Deus Loci: The Lawrence Durrell Journal* are other important outlets for work pertaining to Miller and his circle.
9. One thinks here of the various district attorneys who seized upon the paean to Tania's cunt as evidence of *Tropic of Cancer*'s obscenity yet ignored the painterly scene that immediately follows. See Earl R. Hutchinson, Tropic of Cancer, *on Trial: A Case Study of Censorship* (New York: Grove Press, 1968).
10. See Kingsley Widmer, *Henry Miller,* rev. ed. (Boston: Twayne, 1990), 96–117.

11 Jeanette Winterson, "The Male Mystique of Henry Miller." Review of *Renegade: Henry Miller and the Making of* Tropic of Cancer. *The New York Times Sunday Book Review*. 26 Jan. 2012.
12 Karl Shapiro, "The Greatest Living Author," in *Tropic of Cancer*, by Henry Miller (New York: Grove, 1961), v.
13 Claude Lévi-Strauss, *The Savage Mind* (Chicago: University of Chicago Press, 1966), 21.
14 Lévi-Strauss, *The Savage Mind*, 22.
15 Lévi-Strauss, *The Savage Mind*, 33.
16 Previous essay collections include George Wickes, ed., *Henry Miller and the Critics* (Carbondale: Southern Illinois University Press, 1963); Edward B. Mitchell, ed., *Henry Miller: Three Decades of Criticism* (New York: New York University Press, 1971); and Ronald Gottesman, ed., *Critical Essays on Henry Miller* (New York: G.K. Hall, 1992).

1

Henry Miller's Inhuman Philosophy

Indrek Männiste

If we believe D.H. Lawrence, then every novelist "who amounts to anything has a philosophy."[1] Indeed, philosophy is something that writers *have* rather than something that they *do* as opposed to professional philosophers. Philosophy, in this largely hidden and often unexplainable sense, is ultimately to do with one's life as lived day to day. It is existential by nature. It guides and permeates one's life and thinking and manifests itself in the writer's works mostly indistinctly, not explicitly. We could call this literary *lebensphilosophie*, a metaphysical sense of life. Metaphysics, however, can be experienced and voiced both as a professional doctrine and as an "intuitive relation to reality."[2] It is precisely in this latter sense, and the frame of thinking, that, I think, we should approach to reflect on Henry Miller's relationship with philosophy.

Miller's association with philosophy is an ambivalent one, to say the very least. While he found academic philosophy, as a seemingly endless study of doctrines and never-ending quarrels, to be dull and lifeless, he, at the same time, was greatly fascinated and influenced by philosophers like Friedrich Nietzsche, Oswald Spengler, Henri Bergson, Lao-Tzu, and several others, in whose ideas he saw a creative and vigorous response to his time and its human condition, including very much his own. If it were to have any practical use at all, philosophy would have to serve as a catalyst for both artistic and everyday rejuvenation for Miller. Ideas, always, have to be "wedded to action," he said (CAN, 246).

Concerning the issue of Miller's own philosophy, or the question whether he does in fact have one, the commentators have so far remained fairly skeptical, if not outright dismissive. It has been argued, for example, that "no explicit or systematic philosophical approach" could possibly be drawn from Miller's works[3] and that he has *feelings* rather than "*a* philosophy" (LP, 194). However, since states of feeling are in essence "inseparable from the states of being,"[4] the latter observation alone does not at all exclude Miller from philosophical discussions. On the contrary, *being* is one of the fundamental questions of metaphysics; the one that is asked both "in moments of rejoicing" and "boredom"[5] and Miller, in his own way, *lived* this question throughout his peculiar auto-novel genre. It's not, then, a question of *whether* but *how* Miller's ideas and concepts relate to a wider realm of philosophical ideas. Indeed, regardless of the supposed ambiguities, thinkers like Paul Weiss and Count von Keyserling have claimed to see "a philosophical position" in Miller's work.[6] Also, prominent French thinkers like Gilles Deleuze, Félix Guattari, and Maurice Blanchot have found value and originality in Miller's thinking.[7]

While the prevailing skepticism is often warranted in the face of Miller's tendency to convolute different or even opposing philosophical ideas into his texts and regularly contradict himself, the critics, perhaps, have expected too much from a novelist. Indeed, taking once again D.H. Lawrence's advice, I take his thought that metaphysics must always "subserve the artistic purpose beyond the artist's conscious aim. Otherwise the novel becomes a treatise,"[8] to be a sound suggestion in tracing down the role of philosophy in any writer's works. It would seem that a writer's unique metaphysics, in the sense I we qualified above, can be approached successfully only from the inside of his text and *lebenswelt*, from his own conceptual array, and not by evaluating the philosophical worth of a literary work by its clear-cut compatibility and consistency (or lack thereof) to well-known philosophical systems.

Here, I argue against skeptics that Miller does indeed have a kind of philosophy, which underpins most of his texts. Furthermore, I demonstrate that this philosophy, as a metaphysical sense of life, can be seen as forming a pervading theoretical structure the understanding of which is necessary to explain even some of the most basics of Miller's ideas. I argue that by repudiating some of the most potent elements of late modernity such as the linear sense of time and history, Miller paves the way for overcoming the decidedly positivist stance of Western thinking. By drawing attention to his distinction between the *traditional* and *full present*, I unveil an important philosophical demarcation line for Miller's thinking. In addition, building upon his notion of the *inhuman artist*, as a kind of redeemer of the "destitute times" of the *traditional present*, I view Miller's literary-artistic journey as that of transcendental passing over from *human* to *inhuman*, from *traditional* to *full present*. Finally, I show that the *inhuman*'s aspirations are finalized in Miller's transcendental *China*-concept, which is to be read as the climax of the *full present* whereupon one has overcome the metaphysics of the *traditional present* in its overpowering entirety.

Nightmare of history

Much like with several other modernist writers, Miller's philosophical sympathies grow out from his reactionary sensitivity to the modern age. Modernists' dialectical visions of concurrent destruction and renovation, the decreation and creation of modern man and society express an essentially crises-centered view of their reality[9] and Miller is no exception to it. Wallace Fowlie quite rightly suggests that Miller, as a visionary, "daily lives the metaphysical problems of his age."[10] The main concern of Miller's "daily metaphysics" always remains the same: the question of the possibility of the life of the modern artist in the "destitute times" [*dürftiger Zeit*] of the "early winter of Western Civilization," to borrow Hölderlin's and Spengler's well-known descriptions.[11] Indeed, it seems that the ever-present confrontation between the horror of the present day, the times of need in the deepest sense for many, and the envisioned freedom of the artist's life becomes an underlying yet conflicting tension for Miller, which he sets out to resolve throughout his oeuvre. More particularly, it is precisely his rejection of the most dominant ideas of modernity—a linear notion of time and history, progress, modern technology, and an aesthetic view of art—that form the center of Miller's philosophical avenues.

We find Miller intently voicing discontent regarding the modern era in his *Tropic of Cancer*. "The cancer of time is eating us away. Our heroes have killed themselves, or are killing themselves. The hero, then, is not Time, but Timelessness," wrote Miller in the very first page of the book (CAN, 1). While "time" can be read here both historically and as a temporal category in a metaphysical sense, in either case the failure is evident for Miller. Historically, modern times have failed to produce the better man and world that "our heroes" of the Enlightenment era dreamt about. Miller is fighting against a notion of time that is embedded in the very metaphysics of the age, a metaphysics that is commonly taken to support the linear concept of history. Time's role, commonly construed as rigid, it seemed to Miller, served to a great extent merely for the purpose of justifying historical developments as necessary and inevitable. Since this very notion of history has produced only madness, Miller reasons, the exact opposite of time and history is needed: namely *timelessness* and *ahistoricity*.

With this view Miller did not position himself against any particular individual or view but rather against a general trend of the modern Western world, which saw its main purpose in human progress. The idea of progress, in turn, is often based on an interpretation of history "which regards men as slowly advancing in a definite and desirable direction, and infers that this progress will continue indefinitely."[12] Accordingly, it was believed that a condition of "general happiness will ultimately be enjoyed."[13] For Miller, however, this type of "happiness" is merely a "statistical happiness" (CAP, 4) for it omits the artists' kind.

While Miller was not directly exposed to the views of the defenders of this "progressive view," he learned them via the works of later critical commentators of modernity (Max Stirner, Friedrich Nietzsche, Oswald Spengler, and others) and of the actual results the ideas described above had on the modern society of his day. We see throughout Miller's works that, for example, Auguste Comte's (the founding father of positivism) vigorous insistence on scientific descriptions of the human condition is one of the fundamental errors of the modern day for Miller since it completely disregards the artist's perspective and well-being. In like manner, Miller considers Friedrich Hegel's linear account and the universal notion of freedom not as a victory, but indeed as the defeat of humanity.

How, then, does Miller come to reject the linear notion of history and why? Miller declares in *Tropic of Capricorn* that "the world I knew is no more, it is dead, finished, cleaned up. And everything that I was is cleaned up with it. I am a carcass getting an injection of new life..." (CAP, 220). In this decidedly apocalyptical description, he seems to fix the past, construed historically, as dead. He also marks the end of his past self understood within the limits of the wardship of history. Yet, this Miller sees as a thoroughly positive event. He welcomes the discontinuation of his life from the indifferent flow of time, which seems not to bother most of the people around him. Miller distances himself, as it were, from the general human history altogether. It is, it seems, precisely with the help of Spengler's distinctions between "two possibilities of world formation" that Miller saw the potential for rejecting the historical and time-bound view of himself. In asking "for whom is there History?" Spengler concedes that while "history is obviously for everyone" it makes a great difference

> ... whether anyone lives under the constant impression that his life is an element in a far wider life-course that goes on for hundreds and thousands of years, or conceives of himself as something rounded off and self-contained. For the latter type of consciousness there is certainly no world-history, no world-as-history.[14]

We notice that Spengler directly opposes himself to the "progressive view" of the history of Enlightenment. In his quest for "timelessness," both in its metaphysical and ahistorical meaning, Miller exhibits similar anxieties to Spengler. Miller, being an individualist, and greatly sympathizing with Spengler's view of ahistorical nature of certain cultures (Classical, Indian, etc.) clearly saw himself as being "self-contained" and, as noted above, rejected the idea of "world-history." Miller seems to echo Spengler's distinction even more distinctly when he separates the "objective" time that people ("historical men" in Spengler's terms) measure with clocks and calendars from the time of one's own "inside chronometer." In a letter to Michael Fraenkel he elaborates this view

> Are times out of joint? Then look to the clock! Not the clock on the mantelpiece, but the chronometer inside which tells when you are living and when you are not.... Now we are swamped with time—Western Union time, sidereal time, Einsteinian time, reading time, bedtime, all kinds of time which tell us nothing about what is passing inside us, or even outside us. We are moving on the escalator of time... (HAM, 19–20)

Consequently, Miller moves toward the establishment of his own notion of time, based on his individual experiences, not on natural laws and science. He steps off, as it were, from the "escalator of time" because it has nothing to do with his personal life and feelings. Since time is now measured, or rather directed, by his own "inside chronometer," Miller can, it seems, uphold certain moments and sustain their aura as long as he pleases. The moment is over when one no longer wishes to dwell in it, not when the clock or calendar says it's another minute or day. Time for Miller becomes something essentially psychological or phenomenological, it seems. Capitalizing on David Hoy's insight, it could be even argued that Miller makes a salient distinction between time and temporality. Time, according to Hoy, refers to "universal time, clock time, or objective time," whereas temporality is "time insofar as it manifests itself in human experience."[15] Temporality is "lived time" and thus, Hoy suggests, quite literally, "time of our lives." It is this personal view of time as temporality that Miller draws our attention to. Tacitly adopting the distinction between time and temporality,

Miller seems to come very close to Spengler's conjecture that "we ourselves are Time, inasmuch as we live."[16]

Evidently, Spengler's discussions of time and history had an enormous effect on Miller. He, in a true modernist spirit, refused to dance "to the cracked tune that Chronos sings,"[17] that is, to the music of the "progressive view" of time, which, among other things, is susceptible to Spengler's charge of being "mechanical" in nature. If one continues to be moved by physicalistically construed time, nothing can change. Similar to James Joyce's Stephen Dedalus, it seems, Miller wants to awake from the "nightmare of history."[18]

Miller's two presents

Having seen how Miller abandoned progressive notions of time and history, we can move on to a crucial distinction that he makes, based on this very idea. Very much under influence of Carl Gustav Jung, who insisted that modern man "becomes unhistorical,"[19] Miller invoked the Jungian notion of the present, reading it both into Hamlet's relationship with his time and into his own (and Michael Fraenkel's) relationship to the modern era in his *Hamlet* letters: "... we stand to Hamlet," Miller wrote,

> ... as Hamlet stood to his age. It was the very exactitude of his relation to the age which permitted Hamlet as a "projection" of the modern man ... he was so neatly socketed in time that he burns eternally. The ghost, then, becomes the *traditional present* [my italic]; that dead slag of the past which refuses to stay buried, which burrows into the present and corrodes it like a cancer. (HAM, 73–74)

On Miller's reading the main enemy, then, both for Hamlet and for himself becomes the *traditional present*. For him personally, as for others who also shared the emerging modernist consciousness, the *traditional present* was to be understood as the "progressive" present, which started with the Enlightenment and had developed, with the help of the Industrial Revolution and its multiple mutated manifestations (positivism, totalitarianism), to his day. The *traditional present* has brought about by the very same "historical men" of Spengler's that saw history as ever evolving and progressing. It sees history as being necessary, linear, and teleological. However, this "delusion of historical destiny," Miller responds, "is merely the counterpart of our picture of scientific planetary destinies" (61). He thus rejects this view of present describing it as "... a vacuum, a painful frozen state, a sort of gloomy vestibule in which we lie suspended" (50). With this reality Miller has "no concern."

The opposite of the *traditional present*, for Miller, seems to be something that he calls the *full present*. The *full present* is "the eternal here and now, the expanding infinite moment which is flame and song" (63). The important line of distinction here is that while the *traditional present* is bound to the historical view of time and thus, for Miller, covers only a "short span of human behavior, human evolution" (123), the *full present* seems to accord with what Miller labels the "anarchic" view "in which we move not within definite cultural limits but within unlimited human ones based on the realization of our own potentialities" (123). The *full present* is not the highest point of man historically; it is also not betwixt past and future: it is whereupon man can be and do anything. The *full present* for Miller is fundamentally a possibility, a beginning. It is the absolution of time and the salvation of the modern artist. He explains:

> ... And finally, it is not the past which matters at all, because when we come into the *full present* [my italic] the past is there and future too and neither are frightening or bewildering. In the full present which is the living moment, we join forces with past and future... we forget and enjoy, and remember everything. (112)

Together with Walt Whitman, Miller thus rejects the time qua historical time, but, as an artist, welcomes it universally, or "accepts it absolutely" (63). Like Whitman, Miller participates in all the three tenses simultaneously; or rather the distinction is rendered meaningless in the *full present*. Miller's *full present* bears also remarkable resemblance to Spengler's "Pure present"; an ahistorical and timeless mode, in which Classical and Indian cultures, having no concern for the past and future as "arraying perspectives," allegedly lived.[20]

Miller's distinction between the *traditional* and *full present* importantly enabled him to localize and then deal, in his own way, with the unbearable present. The ills of the epoch for Miller were always first manifested in relation to his own life. He as an individual represented the ongoing doom. "The world is the mirror of myself dying ...," he said (BS, 26). In this, Miller once again reflects a disposition common to modern artistic types who "carry within themselves profound anxieties (as a mirror of their 'civilization'), yet have the power to transform, to transmute them into symbols of spiritual strength, integrity, and plenitude."[21] Since Miller has importantly qualified his understanding of the present, it is clear that he was "dying" only in so far as he construed himself to be part of the *traditional present*. The *full present* is where he would be reborn. What Miller is trying to convey, it seems, is that if we continue to think in terms of past, present, and future, we will never get out of the web of history; we will be stuck in the *traditional present* and will be at the mercy of its historical dictates (whatever happens to be in fashion at the moment). Thus, we have to "kill" the past and future, and embrace ourselves in the "present never ending," which is the *full present*; an ahistorical state of being. This liberates us to being reborn in the current moment. It frees us from the foot race with time. "There is never anything but the present," declares Miller proudly (WOL, 81).

The inhuman artist

In *Tropic of Cancer*, Miller introduces his idiosyncratic term *inhuman*. It seems that it is precisely his *inhuman*, which stands for a new type of creative artist, who carries in him the metaphysical essence of Miller's philosophy. Indeed, it is only in the light of Miller's *inhuman* theme through which our previous distinctions between the *traditional* and *full present*, as well as his *China*-notion, unveil conclusively.

In *Tropic of Cancer* Miller announces

> Once I thought that to be human was the highest aim a man could have, but I see now that it was meant to destroy me. Today I am proud to say that I am inhuman, that I belong not to men and governments, that I have nothing to do with the creaking machinery of humanity—I belong to earth! (CAN, 257)

It seems that for Miller the *inhuman* is meant to represent the exact opposite of the *human* of the day. The passage clearly signals the failed ideals of humanism in modernity, which were evidently never realized. Moreover, we can now say that these false hopes in certain ideals that were taken to promote humanism or human life have resulted precisely in the "creaking machinery" of the *traditional present* as described above. *Human* for Miller, then, becomes an essentially derogatory notion much the same way as *last man* is for Nietzsche. In fact, Miller's *human* and Nietzsche's *last man* denote exactly the same kind of person: a degraded, weak-willed individual of the Western civilization.[22] It is also distinct that in terms of our ongoing categorization, *humans* for Miller seem to occupy the sphere of the *traditional present* and the *inhumans* that of the *full present*.

Miller qualifies the notion of the *inhuman* further and reveals that he is, in effect, a certain type of artist, who "side by side with the human race," takes "the lifeless mass of humanity," and turns it "into bread and the bread into wine and the wine into song" (CAN, 258). The *inhumans* Miller then equates with a breed of artists who, while living together with *humans*, pursue an entirely different life. The passage importantly also reveals the twofold nature of the *inhuman artist*. While on the one hand he is "turning upside down" (CAN, 258) the life of the *humans* in the *traditional present* and therefore moves "in blood and tears," on the other hand the *inhuman* "sings" and "grasps for the beyond" (CAN, 258). To anticipate, it is precisely in the latter that the *inhuman artist* manifests his striving toward the ahistorical *full present*.

By invoking the *inhuman*, Miller, in addition to his former *traditional* and *full present* dichotomy, has now importantly qualified the sense of the inhabitants of these respective realms. Establishing the *inhuman* enables Miller to distance himself and the artist kind firmly from the *traditional present* and the *humans*. The *inhuman* is now importantly defined against the human as the "other." We saw before that the *inhuman*'s task is largely twofold: he should wreak havoc on the *traditional present* but also build up a new world—the *full present*. The *inhuman* then has both negative and positive qualities. The duality of this peculiar essentia of the *inhuman* is perhaps best captured when we find Miller writing that he has "St. Anthony on one side of me, Beelzebub on the other" (BS, 202). The symbiosis of these two apparently contradictory figures—a religious hermit and "the prince of the devils," then, is how Miller seems to construe the antagonistic nature of the *inhuman artist*. He seems to refer to this opposing combination also in *Tropic of Capricorn* when he says that he is "most suave silky, cunning animal—and at the same time what might be called a holy man" (CAP, 224). Through *inhuman artist* as Beelzebub, it seems, Miller was able to bespeak the destructive component of his philosophy and to deal unceremoniously with all the superfluities of *human* life in the *traditional present*. It is Miller himself as the *inhuman* qua Beelzebub who walks in "blood and tears" and who seeks to bring the "life of illusion" to an end. In this regard the *inhuman artist*, Miller seems to indicate, is "a maggot in the corpse which is the world" (HAM, 152). The *inhuman artist*, qua Beelzebub, "feasts on the death" of the *traditional present*, as it were: "the more death there is the stronger I become," Miller writes (HAM, 152). The Beelzebub side of the *inhuman artist* is then an authoritarian one; he gives orders and punishes. It is Miller's hands-on approach to the *human* problem. Although the two are intimately related, St Anthony side of the *inhuman artist* Miller associates predominantly with building up and nurturing of the *full present*.

Inhuman and China

In his *Hamlet* letters, Miller writes that an artist, such as himself, "must escape this death which is engulfing the world in order to protect and preserve his magic role. He flees to imaginary China" (HAM, 70). Miller's readers are well aware of how prominent the *China* theme is for Miller: it comes up throughout his works and letters (especially to Michael Fraenkel but also Lawrence Durrell) and finds its strongest theoretical expression in *Hamlet* letters and, perhaps, the most surrealistic one in "Walking Up and Down in China" in *Black Spring*. What is Miller's *China* and how does it relates to his *inhuman artist* and the division between the *traditional* and *full present*?

China, evidently, is not so much a physical place, as it is a condition, or state, of being. Leon Lewis has suggested that "China was as good a name as any for a 'place' where a certain spirituality replaced the greed and lust of the West."[23] Robert Ferguson qualifies this by saying that *China* was "a personal shorthand term he [Miller] used to denote the admiration and sympathy he felt for the Taoist philosophy of Lao-Tzu and Chuang Tzu."[24] William Gordon calls *China* a "symbolic realm"[25] and J.D. Brown "a realm of pure being."[26] While they all are right, I think we have the means to unpack this highly idiosyncratic concept in even more detail.

While the *China* theme may have had certain significance to Miller already in his youth, the context in which it becomes theoretically most relevant is (as always) Miller's vision of life of the modern, or as we can now say, the *inhuman artist*. In this sense and context, *China* evolved into an important conceptual marker through Miller's reading of Havelock Ellis's *The Dance of Life* (1923), which he quoted extensively to Michael Fraenkel in his *Hamlet* letters (without ever referring to him directly though). Miller wanted to explain his view of the art and artist life, and by citing the admiring passages of Chinese culture and its artistic practices to Fraenkel, he admitted that he is "coming eventually to the Chinese conception of art and life with which I am in complete sympathy and which, I believe, for the moment marks the quality of difference in our approach to life" (HAM, 32). While Miller, writing that letter, presumably did not yet have the full grasp of the eminence of the *China* concept as it would evolve later, the germ of the important ideas was now irreversibly planted. To his long awaited joy, Miller seems to have discovered that there was indeed a place and nation in the world that, contrary to the *traditional present* qua corrupted Western culture, still had their "creative powers." Moreover, these "powers" had enabled the Chinese to enjoy a joyous and healthy life far longer than any other culture. It also must have appealed to Miller that their success in preserving their lifestyle derived not from association with neighboring countries, least of all the Western world, but, quite literally, by bricking themselves into their own country. It is precisely this distinction between encircled China and the rest of the world in which the *full* and *traditional present* make their first adumbrative appearance. Indeed, in a passage from *The World of Lawrence*, a book that at least in part coincides with the period of the Fraenkel letters, Miller says that "everything Chinese is the extreme opposite of all that we feel, think, do, believe ... China, I repeat, seems indeed the antithesis of all that we regard the human world to be" (WOL, 138). *China*, then, is the antithesis of world in the same way the *inhuman* is the antithesis of *human*. *China*, to Miller, marked the absolute remoteness and incommensurability of the modern artist in relation to his age: the true artist was as far from *human* and contemporary society as China was from the Western world.

Miller's "Walking Up and Down in China," can be interpreted as Miller's detailed narration of the birth of the *inhuman* as he is about to enter or be born into the realm of *China*. Before that can happen, however, he must let go of the past time and these former selves with which he identified himself in the former life of the *traditional present*. "Now I am walking to the grave, marching to my own funeral," Miller writes (BS, 192). In several passages, Miller draws a parallel to the Great Wall of China as a symbolic demarcation line which separates his former life from what's ahead: the *traditional present* from the *full present* and *human* from *inhuman*. Nonsymbolically, the demarcation is that between dream and reality, consciousness and unconsciousness. Walking physically on the street of Paris, Miller is effectively "walking inside the Great Chinese Wall" (211). Sitting in a café over an aperitif Miller is in fact "in communication with the whole earth" and in the "womb of time" (198). It is evident that Paris offered a physical location fitting for Miller's plunge into his own unconsciousness in a way that no place had done before. What he calls "obsessional walks" carried out in the streets of Paris are, symbolically, trips into unconsciousness, each of which carries him ever so closer to *China*, as yet another false notion of himself, or "bloody corpse," is left behind during the walk. We notice how the individual parts of Miller's *inhuman* philosophy come together when he writes

> According to the map I am in Paris; according to the calendar I am living in the third decade of the twentieth century. But I am neither in Paris nor in the twentieth century. I am in China and there are no clocks or calendars here. (197)

The "timelessness" of one's true being and the essential requirement of the *full present*, which we saw him defend before, are now firmly incorporated into *China*. The ultimate self qua *inhuman artist* is necessarily atemporal and ahistorical for Miller.

Inhuman revolution finished?

Let us now summarize Miller's complex view using his entire conceptual arsenal. First Miller distinguished between the *traditional* and *full present*. The former stands for the historical, science-oriented modern society but also for the common reality as such. *Traditional present* stands for being, which needs to be surpassed. "To be," Miller asserts, "is to have mortal shape, mortal conditions, to struggle, evolve" (WOH, 4). As an artist type is unable to "adapt himself to [this particular type of] reality," he creates "a reality of his own," that is, the *full present* or *China*: which is "a projection into the spiritual domain of his biologic condition of non-being" (WOH, 4). In the *full present*, man, according to Miller, "triumphs over reality, over becoming" (WOH, 4). The *full present* started out as a response to the *traditional present* claiming to provide an ahistorical, atemporal but also amoral dimension for the artist. *China* is the further qualification, the climax, of that idea. *China* seems to be this "final reality which the artist comes to recognize in his maturity," Miller writes (3). *China* is where the artist can live out "his unconscious desires, wishes, dreams" (3). These opposite realms, *traditional present* and *full present* (or *China*), have, according to my reading of Miller, their respective representatives in *human* and *inhuman* where the latter is the antithesis of the former: the *inhuman* becomes a "traitor to the human race" (BS, 160). The *inhuman's* "betrayal" takes a twofold form. With his more destructive Beelzebub side he must reveal and destroy various manifestations of the *traditional present* (history, technology, progress, science but also false kinds of art). With his more lenient St. Anthony side he pleads for a creative approach to life, which ultimately leads to *China*. *China* is only attainable when one has a proper relationship with art. "By living into his art," Miller explains, "he adopts for his world an intermediary realm in which he is all-powerful, a world which he dominates and rules" (WOH, 7). The art's role is thus essentially intermediary.

> Art is only a means to life, to the life more abundant. It is not in itself the life more abundant. It merely points the way... (BSOHB, 349)

Art for Miller does not usually mean works of art but rather what the artist does or feels when he creates a work of art. Art is a creative activity that helps one to get in touch with "non-being" as opposed to the "being" granted by the illusory means and the reality of the *traditional present*. In fact, art should lead toward the death of all the false selves obtained in the *traditional present*. Moreover, art should make one "willing to die" (WOH, 12) voluntarily in order to be reborn. By "becoming an end" art and artist "defeat itself" (8). If the artist chooses to live, then, he defeats his own nature, according to Miller. The artist's goal is the ultimate self-discovery and a better life, but as he occupies the realm of *China* he must "live" only metaphorically or "vicariously."

One of the best examples of how Miller construed this sort of artist's life qua *Chinaman* we find in his descriptions of his painter friend Hans Reichel, whom he visited during his Paris years. In Reichel, Miller saw what art really can do to a person. For Miller, Reichel was a personified *Chinaman*, one who "every day... paints a fragment of the universe" (HAM, 124). Reichel's universe was that of the "singing" *full present* and not of the "synthetic" *traditional present*. In the presence of Reichel, Miller claimed to have felt "the eternality of things," which, without a doubt, reminded Miller of Ellis's eternal here and now. Reichel represented to Miller the artist's ability to transcend the age. His most vexing anxieties: the crisis of man, art, and the modern age seemed to have found a solution in Reichel's artistic life. "He is living with us in our time under the same conditions," Miller writes, but "he is not in despair" because "this man is really in communication with life …" (125). In Reichel the plight of the modern artist had finally come to an end for Miller. The art had given way to the *inhuman life*, to *China*.

Notes

1. D.H. Lawrence, "The Novel," in *Complete Works of D.H. Lawrence* [Kindle Edition] (Delphi Classics, 2011).
2. Julian Young, *Heidegger's Philosophy of Art* (Cambridge: Cambridge University Press, 2011), 123.
3. John Parkin, *Henry Miller: The Modern Rabelais* (Lewiston: Edwin Mellen Press, 1990), 183.
4. Michael Bell, *D.H. Lawrence: Language and Being* (Cambridge: Cambridge University Press, 1991), 6.
5. Martin Heidegger, *An Introduction to Metaphysics*, trans. Ralph Manhein (New Haven and London: Yale University Press, 1959), 1.
6. Jay Martin, *Always Merry and Bright: An Unauthorized Biography* (Santa Barbara: Capra Press, 1978), 414.
7. See Katy Masuga, *Henry Miller and How He Got That Way* (Edinburgh: Edinburgh University Press, 2011) for the vivid analysis of Miller's engagement with these thinkers.
8. Cited in Frank Kermode, *Lawrence* (London: Fontana/Collins, 1973), 26.
9. Malcolm Bradbury, "The Name and Nature of Modernism," in *Modernism: 1890–1930*, eds James Walter McFarlane and Malcolm Bradbury (New York: Penguin, 1976), 20.
10. Wallace Fowlie, "Henry Miller as a Visionary," *Critical Essays on Henry Miller*, ed. Ronald Gottesman, (New York: G.K. Hall, 1992), 186.
11. Friedrich Hölderlin, "Brot und Wein," in *Sämtliche Gedichte und Hyperion*, ed. Jochen Schmidt (Leipzig: Insel-Verlag, 1999), 285–91. Oswald Spengler, *The Decline of the West*, trans. Charles Francis Atkinson (New York: Knopf, 1926), 44.
12. John Bagnell Bury, *The Idea of Progress: An Inquiry into Its Origin and Growth* (Charleston: Bibliobazaar, 2007), 17.
13. Bury, *The Idea of Progress*, 17.
14. Spengler, *The Decline of the West*, 8.
15. David Couzens Hoy, *The Times of Our Lives: A Critical History of Temporality* (Cambridge, MA: MIT Press, 2009), xiii.
16. Spengler, *The Decline of the West*, 122.
17. William Butler Yeats, "The Song of the Happy Shepherd," in *Collected Poems of W.B. Yeats* (London: Macmillan, 1958), 7.

18 See the further analysis of Nietzsche's and Jung's influences on Miller's notion of time and history in my book *Henry Miller: The Inhuman Artist—A Philosophical Inquiry* (New York: Bloomsbury, 2013), 34–36.
19 Carl Gustav Jung, *Modern Man in Search of a Soul* (London: Routledge, 1961), 227.
20 Spengler, *The Decline of the West*, 9.
21 David Stephen Calonne, "Euphoria in Paris: Henry Miller Meets D.H. Lawrence," *Library Chronicle of the University of Texas* 34 (1986): 95.
22 See my extensive analysis of the affinities between Miller and Nietzsche in my *Henry Miller: The Inhuman Artist*, 85–95.
23 Leon Lewis, *Henry Miller: The Major Writings* (New York: Schocken, 1986), 129.
24 Robert Ferguson, *Henry Miller: A Life* (New York: Norton, 1991), 215.
25 William A. Gordon, *The Mind and Art of Henry Miller* (Baton Rouge: Louisiana State University Press, 1967), 57.
26 J.D. Brown, *Henry Miller*. (New York: Ungar, 1986), 33.

"The agonizing gutter of my past": Henry Miller, Conversion, and the Trauma of the Modern[1]

James M. Decker

Speaking of Miller's oeuvre, Amy M. Flaxman observes that "Miller reaches out beyond tragedy to redemption."[2] Flaxman further contends that Miller's writing, which investigates emotionally contradictory impulses, "reminds us of our own humanity" and functions as a way to disrupt complacency and allow readers to "know their own capacity for love" (115). The absence of this capacity to love, a lack predicated on a paucity of self-awareness and a misguided sense of duty, represents for Miller the nadir of modernity and manifests itself repeatedly in his works via characters such as Van Norden, Maude, and Karen. For Miller, modernity's emphasis on rationality and productivity tended to reduce humanity to a conformist mass in mindless pursuit of material comforts and spiritual platitudes. Instilled and enforced by stultifying institutions, such as schools and churches, the concept of external obligation (and the concomitant deferral of self-fulfillment) created a psychic fissure within most individuals, which resulted in profound alienation.

The Henry Miller represented in Miller's narratives reveals such psychological trauma through the "sordid memories" of his life (ACN, 12). Only partially aware of a gnawing emptiness in his life, Henry drifts through a series of sexual trysts, creative false starts, and petty rebellions that provide temporary diversion from his external demands but that never allow him to overcome his spiritual hollowness and realize what he calls his "potential being" (WOS, 25). Once Mona abandons him, however, Henry's trauma shocks him to the core, a phenomenon that allows him to experience a conversion of the soul. Writing of the conversion tradition, Peter A. Dorsey notes that "although physical discomfort and calamity were typically received as punishments, they were also the means by which God brought about repentance—considered essential for conversion."[3] In Henry's case, such calamity spurs on the all-night session in which he hypnotically transcribes the notes that become Miller's ur-text and serve as the almost mystical wellspring of both his self-reflection and creative output:

> About five that afternoon, in a mood of utter despair, I sat down at the typewriter to outline the book I told myself I must write one day. My Domesday Book. It was like writing my own epitaph.

> I wrote rapidly, in telegraphic style...for some inexplicable reason I found myself recording chronologically, *and without effort*....Page after page I turned out, and there was always more to put down...if these telegraphic notes were to be expanded into a book, would it not require several volumes to do it justice? The very thought of the immensity of this task staggered me. When would I ever have the courage to tackle a work of such dimensions? (NEX, 165–166)

Miller returns again and again to this moment of conversion, and the bulk of his writing operates as an exegesis of his narrator's awakening, the mythic genesis both of his self-acceptance and artistic voice. In telling his narrator's conversion stor(ies), Miller rejects the linear, eschews the rational, denies the modern. While his conversion is the "structural center" of these texts, Miller abandons the chronological organization that he alludes to above and employs an alinear, spiral form that shares affinities with many premodern spiritual traditions as well as with those esoteric and avant-garde movements intent on exploding the scientific rationalism of the Enlightenment.[4] Mingling what Raymond Williams describes as residual, dominant, and emerging modes of discourse,[5] Miller establishes his narrator's life and inner struggle as an exemplary one that might jar his audience out of spiritual inertia and thus start to address its own sublimated desires, and, in Katy Masuga's words, "overcome passive indifference."[6]

Originally associated with St. Augustine's *Confessions* and its concomitant spiritual tradition, the conversion narrative now frequently represents secular transformations.[7] As Patrick Riley explains, "God's place in the narrative of conversion is increasingly occupied by the author's *intellectual, philosophical*, or *authorial* vocation, and these three are often inextricably linked."[8] For Miller, who repeatedly examines the events leading up to his narrator's liberating discovery of an authentic voice, the implications of such a flexible genre seem clear. Indeed, Miller himself directly mentions conversion in *The World of Sex*: "There was a period in Paris, after I had experienced a conversion, when I could visualize the whole pattern of my past life...everything that had happened to me took on significance" (14). In describing this semimystical moment and the "tremendous evolution of...being" it leads to, Miller emphasizes the hermeneutic aspect of the conversion, the investment of memory with self-meaning, an interpretation shared discursively (BIML, 26). Gerald Peters observes that "the self is a fiction, a mirage produced by language," and he notes that the "narrative of conversion becomes both a means by which individualized identities undermine traditional forms of authority and a means by which conflicting ideological communities attempt to impose their order."[9] Peters's comments have a direct bearing on Miller's approach to narrative form, for, as Karl Orend astutely points out, "Miller loves that which flows because water has no consciousness or ego."[10] While the convert may experience a single, overwhelming epiphany,[11] Dorsey reports that "conversion narratives often contain a cyclic pattern of conversion and reconversion, as if the converted are predisposed to repeat and reinforce this fundamental experience over and over."[12] As numerous of Miller's critics—both hostile and sympathetic—have charged, Miller's narratives investigate certain episodes repeatedly, and Miller's own characterization of spiral form parallels the type of recursive experience Dorsey describes.

As Sarah Garland, Masuga, and others have contended, Miller writes in an extraordinarily intertextual fashion, with overt and covert allusions running in a constant stream throughout the narratives.[13] Certain writers hold for the narrator an almost mystical quality and are integrally related to his episodic conversion from a disaffected, directionless malcontent into a writer confident enough to compose in his own voice and style, a style that, ironically enough, liberally cites his artistic kindred. Dorsey argues that such a phenomenon commonly occurs in conversion narrative: "By interacting with one form of sacred literature, the successful believer was able to construct another."[14] Miller's literature, of course, runs the gamut from the sacred to the profane, but Dorsey's larger point suggests that many, if not most, conversion narratives are highly aware of their place in a larger tradition and cite like-minded spirits frequently. Chana Ullman, in a study of the psychology of the religious convert, reveals that "conversion stories often rested upon an infatuation with a powerful authority figure" and that the convert also prized forming a "relationship with a group of peers who lavished acceptance and love."[15]

For Miller's narrator, totemic names such as Whitman, Dreiser, Spengler, Rimbaud, and Nietzsche function in a dual role, first as authority figures who both inspire and paralyze the narrator and later, when the narrator gains more confidence in his powers, as peers. One such moment occurs in "The Fourteenth Ward," a sketch concerned with the "great fragmentation of maturity" and affiliated sorrow experienced by the narrator (BS, 10). The narrator juxtaposes his soulless, mechanical existence as he "walks round and round in a circular cage to the roll of drum-fire [as] the theater burns and the actors go on mouthing their line" with the day he first hears of Dostoevsky: "one day, as if suddenly the flesh came undone and the blood beneath the flesh had coalesced with the air, suddenly the whole world roars again and the very skeleton of the body melts like wax" (BS, 14). As Maria Bloshteyn convincingly argues, the narrator's Dostoevsky bears little resemblance to the writer and that he "picked *a la carte* those ideas ... that bolstered [his] own perspectives and furthered [his] own agendas."[16] Dostoevsky's personal meaning to the narrator—his ability to transport the narrator to the realm of art—functions similarly to a conversion experience. The god-like Dostoevsky, like the other authors the narrator admires—holds a key to unlocking the narrator's prison and enabling him to pursue the life of the writer. As Caroline Blinder remarks, "For Miller, the artist ... is a visionary, and the desire to search for something above and beyond reality is the crucial denominator in the creative process."[17]

In his rejection of the "half-human, half-celluloid" individuals who seem to be "walking in their coffins," Miller's narrator locates in modern progress neither freedom nor truth (BS, 195). His "enviable" job in the Cosmodemonic Telegraph Company teaches him that material success comes with a severe psychic and spiritual price. The rhetorical promise of the American Experiment—boundless freedom and opportunity—has dissolved into vacuity and mechanization. As Michel Foucault presciently discerns:

liberty, far from putting man in possession of himself, ceaselessly alienates him from his essence and his world; it fascinates him in the absolute exteriority of other people and of money, in the irreversible interiority of passion and unfulfilled desire.[18]

Outwardly, the narrator is "lucky" to possess a well-paying job especially in comparison to the messengers he hires and considering the New York poverty he describes. Nevertheless, his liberty and his money leave him, as Foucault describes, "abandoned to [his] own anxiety, in which the passions surrender time to unconcern or to repetition in which, finally, madness can function freely."[19] Contemplating his American society, the narrator declares, "Alphabetically, numerically, statistically, it made sense. But ... when you examined one lone individual ... you saw something so foul and degrading, so low, so miserable, so utterly hopeless and senseless, that it was worse than looking into a volcano" (CAP, 12). In *Tropic of Cancer* the narrator, speaking of his fellow humans, opines that "They move in apparent freedom, but they have nowhere to go. In one realm only are they free and there they may roam at will—but they have not yet learned to take wing" (249).[20] Ultimately, the narrator will experience a conversion, a "changing reality for which no language has yet been invented" (BS, 197). He continues: "I believe, as I walk through the horror of the present, that only those who have the courage to close their eyes, only those whose permanent absence from the condition known as reality can affect our fate" (BS, 199). In this way, the converted narrator will deliriously reject liberalism, along with its institutions and its scientific progress, for an alternative reality that starts with art but that ends with what Foucault terms "that threatening space of absolute freedom," the "madness" of unreason and passion, the "potential being" of which Miller speaks in *The World of Sex* (14).[21]

Prior to conversion, however, a convert typically experiences what D. Bruce Hindmarsh terms "self-despair,"[22] and Ullman's research indicates that 80% of converts undergo "considerable distress prior to conversion."[23] Peters further suggests that conversion narratives often function to reorient a "sick soul,"[24] and Dorsey claims that in most such discourse "conversions occur at the depths of the greatest despair and after periods of greatest affliction."[25] Estranged and confused, the preconverted individual wallows in self-pity and pursues momentary, but fruitless, escapes and wanders aimlessly through life. For Miller's narrator, of course, the central moment of "rebirth" happens at precisely such a moment, when Mona and Stasia have abandoned him for Europe and he is left "barking in the night" in misery (NEX, 7). This personal loss is compounded by the narrator's return to the frustrating and alienating world of drudgery from which Mona had helped him escape, the life that he likens to a "grand chancre on a worn-out cock" (CAP, 12) and where the "new men made of stovepipes and cylinders mov[e] according to chart and diagram" (BS, 245). The resultant psychic trauma sends the narrator into the depths of depression until he spends all night manically recording thirty odd pages about his life with Mona, notes that will form the locus of his work as a writer.

In addition to the trauma caused by his relationship with Mona, the narrator endures continuing anxiety over the stultifying effects of modernity. In characterizing and denouncing the dehumanizing aspects of modern life, what he deems the "cesspool of the spirit in which everything is sucked down and drained away to everlasting shit" (CAP, 4), the narrator at once reveals the ideological context for his despair and represents the means by which he managed to reject his role among the alienated masses, for, as Srila Roy points out, the act of telling one's story "transforms traumatic memory into narrative memory, thereby remaking the survivor's sense of self and her relation to the world."[26] Part of the narrator's conversion involves his refusal to participate in a system that harnesses empiricism and reason to the yoke of materialism and its attendant violence. Born at the height of progressive optimism, the narrator becomes distressed at the mindless quest for "security" ("statistical wealth, statistical happiness" [CAP, 4]) and the violence—both figurative and literal—that ensues from it. The narrator, before his conversion, laments this state, frankly declaring, "There are days when the return to life is painful and distressing."[27]

Leigh Gilmore argues that "language fails in the face of trauma" and that writers who speak of such events must inevitably metaphorize them, a contention that dovetails well with Peters's earlier claim about the constructed nature of conversion narratives.[28] In both types of narrative naïve audiences expect literal truth—what Mark Freeman calls the "fetishization of accuracy"[29]—yet both rely on provisional, figurative means. Repeatedly, Miller and his narrator distance themselves from a literal notion of truth, stating that the so-called realism is but a "surface"[30] and they are "guilty of altering, distorting, and disguising the facts—if 'facts' there be" (BIML, 13) in order to achieve a "greater reality" (CE, 371) through the use of "creative memory" (HAM, 27). The narrator's representation of the trauma that stimulated his (repeated) conversion can only be approximate, a standing-for-truth and the "broken parts" of his identity rather than Truth itself (SSLH, 84). Alluding to his conversion-to-come, the narrator remarks in *Tropic of Capricorn*:

> I didn't dare to think of anything then except the "facts." To get beneath the facts I would have had to be an artist, and one doesn't become an artist overnight. First you have to be crushed, to have your conflicting points of view annihilated. You have to be wiped out as a human being in order to be born again as an individual. (28)

For the narrator, "getting beneath the facts" involves tapping into the "greater reality," grappling with essence rather than substance. The narrator must metaphorize his memories and interpret them for himself and his audience in order to discover the truth "beneath the facts." As Nanci Adler and Selma Leydesdorff remind us, "No matter how true, each story is an edited version of the personal truth."[31]

Miller's narrator recognizes this personal truth, and, rejecting the "perennial jackass" of form (BIML, 67), claims that one must "wade through rivers of shit to find a germ of reality"; he constantly subverts his own anecdotes via verbal excess, digression, catalogue rhetoric, and other strategies (NEX, 100). Riley calls the preconversion self "fragmentary and contingent," and this is the self on which the narrator focuses and spirals around.[32] The narrator explains his inability to communicate directly about his preconverted state: "For years now I have been trying to tell this story; each time I have started out I have chosen a different route. I am like an explorer who, wishing to circumnavigate the globe, deems it unnecessary to carry a compass" (CAP, 330). Unable to capture the "untransmissable events" (SEX, 20) once and for all, the narrator endlessly defers the lessons of the conversion, retreats to his preconverted states, veers toward the gates of what he calls China, but never enters, offering instead a "self-portrait which yields only the missing parts" (BS, 29). Such a progression calls to mind Dorsey's idea that conversion narratives speak to "progressive selves... rather than ultimate knowledge or truth,"[33] and it reflects the apparently improvised or automatic style used in much of Miller's work. Indeed, in his study of American Modernism, Rob Wallace suggests that literary ad-libbing has much to do with the trauma of the modern: "Faced with the vicissitudes of modernity, improvisation became an increasingly important tool for making art because it could itself change and adapt."[34] The "spontaneous," urgent feel of the narratives thus functions as a psychic buffer of sorts, as the narrator may revise (erase, distort, emphasize, etc.) the "facts" as he frantically heaps contingent interpretation upon contingent interpretation.

The narrator's memories thus function not as discrete, finished "truths," but as malleable and provisional impressions, simultaneous echoes of the past and bellwethers of an uncertain present. The narratives grasp at the truth yet never finally obtain it. Julia Straub, noting the expectation of truth in narratives of trauma, asserts that "The decision aspect is not the authorial act of putting experiences onto paper, but the act of interconnecting memories, the weaving of a web of unforeseeable, unheard correspondences."[35] Such "unforeseeable, unheard of correspondences" function as the narrator's "anecdotal life" (CAN, 3) and result in the apparently formless and chaotic narrative decried by critics such as Kingsley Widmer.[36] Miller and his narrator frequently point out the "vanity of resurrecting the past" (BIML, 97) and claim that the past "lives in symbols" (TOA, 55).[37] In his various redactions, however, Miller's narrator includes new details, subtracts others, and fashions stunningly different juxtapositions, and Masuga suggests that in doing so the narrator stresses the "disconnection between reality and words," an interpretation that relies on the narrator's self-consciousness about his incapacity to relay his unadulterated experience to his audience.[38] Overwhelmed—or perhaps amused—by his inability to replicate experience, the narrator, pointing out that overelaboration equals struggle (CAN, 256), generates metaphor after metaphor, mask after mask, that can only intimate (imitate?) his trauma and stand for his conversion.[39] Hindmarsh, in calling for more sophisticated readings of conversion narratives, points out "how creative and significant is the act of interpretation in selecting, arranging, and presenting events—even the events of one's own life."[40] The spiral form at play in the narratives underscores precisely this interpretation as well as its ultimate failure.

The "rebirth" ostensibly at the heart of the *Rosy Crucifixion* trilogy never fully materializes. While, as already shown, the narrator does cite the pivotal moment in which he attempts to transcribe his life with Mona, he fails to describe the effects of that moment, the "death of the little self" that is necessary so "the real self may emerge" (TOA, 37). Instead, he enacts it through the very process of telling the tale(s); the narratives themselves bear witness that the narrator ultimately finds his voice and his vocation as a writer.[41] Stephanie Guedet observes that "the effects of the conversion happen not only through the reconstruction of the self in narrative, but via the retelling of the story that accompanies this process."[42] As the narrator declares, "the man who is reborn is always the same man, more and more himself with each rebirth" (CAP, 226). The details of the narrative, though, finally matter less than the existence of the narrative itself and the conversion that it represents. Nevertheless, the anecdotes, allusions, rants, reveries, dreams, and desires that overflow the trilogy's pages embody one version of the events that lead up to the mystical all-night session and the turning point it represents.[43] Starting with an allusion to a key step on the narrator's multi-staged conversion—meeting Mara—the trilogy brims with symbols and signs of the elite fraternity the narrator desperately wishes to join. Still, while the narrator can *think* about writing and, more important, *talk* about writing, even with hours of writing time he cannot produce even a scrap of text. He despairs. In multiple anecdotes, however, strangers tell the narrator that he is destined for greatness, and others advise him to "write like he talks." In *Sexus*, for instance, Ulric chastises the narrator, declaring, "You don't write like you talk.... If you ever open up and tell the truth it will be like Niagara Falls" (SEX, 46). The trilogy, some 1,500 pages long, clearly represents the result of the narrator's conversion and subsequent ability to use his own voice and "open up."

The concept of voice is crucial for understanding the narrator's conversion to writing. Throughout the trilogy and *Tropic of Capricorn*, the narrator describes his writing as bearing the too obvious marks of his masters. Most notably in *Clipped Wings*, where he imperfectly mimics Dreiser's style in *Twelve Men*, the narrator allows his influences to subsume his writerly identity and cause him to produce stilted "literary" prose of the type he excoriates in the opening pages of *Tropic of Cancer* when he declares, "Everything that is literature has fallen from me" (CAN, 1–2). In these works—as well as in *Moloch* and *Crazy Cock*—the narrator seeks his style everywhere but within. He reads the words of his heroes yet he fails to comprehend their secret, the code that will allow him to enter the realm of China and move beyond mere art: be yourself. Eventually, the narrator will stand with such writers instead of kneeling before them.

Essential to the narrator's artistic self-discovery are the reveries that allow him, like Emerson, to tap into the cosmic energy and transcend the quotidian realities of modern life and the cosmodemonic world that keeps him in thrall. In these "marked" passages, as Paul Jahshan describes them, the narrator interrupts his anecdotes, diatribes, fantasies, and other modes of discourse in favor of rhetorical pyrotechnics that blast off the page and substitute sound and texture for reason and denotation. Masuga contends that such passages "disrupt the structure of conventional forms of writing."[44] Additionally, the verbal deluges function to isolate the narrator and embody the "antisocialization" that Dorsey finds essential to conversion.[45] Such antisocialization is premised on a turning away from the convert's original state and toward the new. As such, the convert simultaneously rejects the old life—and the denizens who fail to hear the calling—and embraces the new. Riley identifies this as the central paradox of conversion, a process wherein "identity is both coagulated and dissolved by radical subjective change."[46] Via this paradox, the narrator both describes the preartistic self that Indrek Männiste associates with the "traditional present"[47] and establishes the conditions whereby his rebirth to the "full present"[48] will occur: "I walked about like a ghost in their midst.... Something had killed me, and yet I was still alive" (CAP, 225). Another such moment occurs in *Tropic of Cancer*: "If I was a truly great human being ... then what was the meaning of this slavering idiocy about me? ... I had moments of ecstasy and I sang with burning sparks. I sang of the equator, her red-feathered legs and the islands dropping out of sight. But nobody heard" (254). In both passages, the narrator perceives his difference, his alienation, yet in the second the narrator has begun his conversion and responds joyously.

In sharp contrast with these verbal flights, the "unmarked" passages that they interrupt frequently take the form of anecdotes that show the narrator attempting to resist—however feebly—the social strictures that he vaguely perceives as holding him back from his potential self. As Eneken Laanes maintains, the "anecdote reworks experience in the process of remembering," and such an anecdotal strategy allows the narrator to substitute multiple subjective truths for mimesis bent on reflecting a single, static Truth.[49] With respect to trauma, Laanes argues, "Anecdotal remembering restores agency and dignity through remembering where the events themselves can no longer be changed."[50] In this way, the narrator can recontextualize the episodes of his life and invest them with significance, particularly in the way that they prepare him for his conversion to writing.

While it is important not to approach a polyvalent writer such as Miller solely through a monovalent lens, the concept of conversion aids readers in understanding the texts' use of both despair and joy, particularly in the context of the narrator's rebirth. In applying theories of conversion and trauma to the works, it becomes clear that the narrator stands on the other side of a divide looking back on his preconversion self. Sensing his difference but not yet an artist, the narrator must wander in vague despair before his abandonment sets him on the path to conversion: "Outside their world as a cannibal is outside the bounds of civilized society" (CAP, 47). Ultimately, though, the narrator joins the ranks of his idols, the writers. While he has crossed over, however, his conversion never truly ends, and his fight against the "malnutrition of the soul" (SAW, 76) never sees a "final draft" (TOA, 131).

Notes

1   (CAN, 177).
2   Amy M. Flaxman, *New Anatomies: Tracing Emotions in Henry Miller's Writings* (Belfast, ME: Bern Porter, 2000), 115.
3   Peter A. Dorsey, *Sacred Estrangement: The Rhetoric of Conversion in Modern Autobiography* (University Park: Pennsylvania State University Press, 1993), 33.
4   Dorsey, *Sacred*, 36.
5   Raymond Williams, *Marxism and Literature* (Oxford: Oxford University Press, 1977), 122.

6 Masuga, *Secret*, 4.
7 Miller, who in the *Hamlet* letters describes his rereading of *City of God*, refers to Augustine as an "idiot" (HAM, 386). In *The Books in My Life*, he affirms this impression by suggesting that *City of God* is "monstrously ridiculous," but he also claims that the *Confessions* "made a deep impression" on him (BIML, 31). Miller parodies the Augustinian meaning of conversion when he describes when Moloch "almost got converted" (MOL, 109). Miller presents a less jaded view of traditional conversion in *Tropic of Capricorn* when the narrator describes Grover Watrous, who "suddenly took to God with such a passion that there was no blowing your nose before him without asking God's permission" (CAP, 164). The narrator describes Grover's fundamental change, including his "bright new language" (CAP, 167) and "illumination" (CAP, 168). What the narrator finds especially fascinating is how "alive" Grover is in contrast to average person (CAP, 168). This clearly parallels the narrator's own transformation.
8 Patrick Riley, *Character and Conversion in Autobiography* (Charlottesville: University of Virginia Press, 2004), 2.
9 Gerald Peters, *The Mutilating God: Authorship and Authority in the Narrative of Conversion* (Amherst: Amherst University Press, 1993), 9, 11.
10 Orend, *The Brotherhood of Simpletons and Fools*, 139.
11 Koral Ward investigates such flashes of insight in *Augenblick: The Concept of the "Decisive Moment" in 19th- and 20th-Century Western Philosophy* (Burlington: Ashgate, 2008). Ward defines *Augenblick* as "a fleeting but momentous event, an occurrence usually accompanied by an altered perception of time, either as condensed and swiftly passing or slow and drawn out" (xi). Miller's narrator experiences such flashes at intervals rather than only once. One example appears in "Reunion in Brooklyn": "we stood apart in silence for another fleeting moment during which I comprehended in a flash the appalling tragedy of their life and of my life …" (SAW, 67).
12 Dorsey, *Sacred*, 3.
13 See, for example, Sarah Garland, "'The Dearest of Cemeteries': European Intertexts in Henry Miller's *Tropic of Cancer*," *The European Journal of American Studies* 23, 3 (2010): 197–215; Masuga, *Henry Miller and How He Got That Way*.
14 Dorsey, *Sacred*, 22.
15 Chana Ullman, *The Transformed Self: The Psychology of Religious Conversion* (New York: Plenum, 1989), xvii; xviii.
16 Maria Bloshteyn, *The Making of a Counter-Culture Icon: Henry Miller's Dostoevsky* (Toronto: Toronto University Press, 2007), 138.
17 Caroline Blinder, *A Self-Made Surrealist: Ideology and Aesthetics in the Works of Henry Miller* (Rochester: Camden House, 2000), 16.
18 Michel Foucault, *Madness and Civilization: A History of Insanity in the Age of Reason*, trans. by Richard Howard (New York: Vintage, 1965), 214.
19 Foucault, *Madness*, 217.
20 The narrator also likens the modern Western world to a prison: "Behind these gray walls there are human sparks, and yet never a conflagration" (CAN, 249). The use of prison imagery again calls to mind Foucault, who writes that "confinement represents … the myth of social happiness." Foucault, *Madness*, 63.
21 Foucault, *Madness*, 84.

22 D. Bruce Hindmarsh, *The Evangelical Conversion Narrative: Spiritual Autobiography in Early Modern England* (Oxford: Oxford University Press, 2005), 56.
23 Ullman, *Transformed*, 18.
24 Peters, *Mutilating*, 3.
25 Dorsey, *Sacred*, 34.
26 Srila Roy, "On Testimony: The Pain of Speaking and the Speaking of Pain," in *Tapestry of Memory: Evidence and Testimony in Life-Story Narratives*, eds Nanci Adler and Sema Leydesdorff (New Brunswick: Transaction, 2013), 97.
27 The narrator is referring to waking from a dream here, but the point stands, for the reality to which he is reluctant to return is one "whose solution for everything is death" (SEX, 291).
28 Leigh Gilmore, *The Limits of Autobiography: Trauma and Testimony* (Ithaca: Cornell University Press, 2001), 6.
29 Mark Freeman, "Too Late: The Temporality of Memory and the Challenge of a Moral Life," *Journal für Psychologie* 11 (2003): 69–70.
30 Miller continues, "Their realism never takes one right into the truth of reality. You're just served up facts, and for my part I believe that these facts say nothing in themselves. What is important is the interpretation of the facts" (HMC, 39). He also writes Nin, "The reality is void of interest. Flat" (LP, 197).
31 Nanci Adler and Selma Leydesdorff, eds, *Tapestry of Memory: Evidence and Testimony in Life-Story Narratives* (New Brunswick: Transaction, 2013), vi.
32 Riley, *Character*, 16.
33 Dorsey, *Sacred*, 75.
34 Rob Wallace, *Improvisation and the Making of American Literary Modernism* (New York: Continuum, 2010), 2. Miller's "automatic" writing, of course, was anything but spontaneous. Miller revised his work thoroughly and cut mercilessly. For discussion of Miller's use of automatic writing, see Blinder, *Self-Made*, 13–41.
35 Julia Straub, "Richard Wollheim's *Germs*: Life Writing as Therapy, Despite Theory," in *Haunted Narratives: Life Writing in an Age of Trauma*, ed. Gabrielle Rippl, et al. (Toronto: Toronto University Press, 2013), 93.
36 Widmer, claiming that Miller rejects "craft" and its concomitant "ordering," argues that Miller employs "purely personal associations" and offers an "onanistic" approach to art. *Henry Miller*, revised edition (Boston: Twayne, 1990), 107.
37 Miller refers to the mixture of fact and fiction as a "deepening of the truth" (BIML, 169).
38 Masuga, *Secret*, 48.
39 In a recent presentation, Dominic Jaeckle likens this phenomenon to translation, wherein legend and myth represent a self-destructive "transmutation of memory." See: "Thoreau Was an Atlas, or Responding to the Hummingbird: Antagonizing a Diurnal Real in Henry Miller's Literary Reflections." Unpublished MS.
40 Hindmarsh, *Evangelical*, 3.
41 One might also, of course, view *Tropic of Cancer* as showing the narrator's postconversion life: "A year ago, six months ago, I thought I was an artist. I no longer think about it, I *am*" (CAN, 1). In this passage, the narrator confidently declares that he has fulfilled the promise of his conversion. Note, though, that the action presented here takes places years after the action in *Nexus*, demonstrating Dorsey's point about conversion as representing a process rather than a single epiphany.
42 Stephanie Guedet, "Transformations of Self: Narrating Conversions, Constructing Identities." Unpublished MS.

43 Conversion, Dorsey reminds us, literally means a turning. *Sacred*, 18.
44 Masuga, *Secret*, 137.
45 Dorsey, *Sacred*, 10.
46 Riley, *Character*, 3–4. As James Gifford points out, Miller is well aware of this paradox: "for Miller, this 'true self' is unstable, undefinable, and subject to radical transformation, yet it is still his own." *Personal Modernisms: Anarchist Networks and the Later Avant-Gardes* (Edmonton: University of Alberta Press, 2014), 195.
47 Indrek Männiste, *Henry Miller: The Inhuman Artist* (New York: Bloomsbury, 2013), 68.
48 Männiste, *Henry*, 102.
49 Eneken Laanes, "Anecdotalization of Memory in Jaan Kross's *Paigallend*" in *Haunted Narratives: Life Writing in an Age of Trauma*, ed. Gabrielle Rippl, et al. (Toronto: University of Toronto Press, 2013), 199.
50 Laanes, "Anecdotalization," 196.

3

When Henry Miller Left for Tibet

Paul Jahshan

In Tom Schiller's 1975 documentary *Henry Miller Asleep & Awake*, the viewer is taken on a rare tour of Miller's bathroom, the walls of which are covered with photos, magazine pages, newspaper clippings, drawings, and various other inscriptions. Miller comments on his favorite selections, which include Junichiro Tanizaki, his fifth wife Hoki, Tony Yoma San, Blaise Cendrars, Hieronymus Bosch, Roshi Bobo, Herman Hesse, Carl Jung, a Chinese wine advertisement, advice from General Nogi's wife, Gurdjieff, Floriano Steiner, Chinese and Japanese actresses (with a surprise live appearance from an Asian female coming out of the shower), various Buddha photos from Cambodia, "Siam," and Burma, and Gauguin paintings. What is striking is the predominantly Far-Eastern and, to a lesser extent, European nature of the items Miller chooses to describe. The collection, as he explains at the beginning of the documentary, is "a sort of voyage ... a voyage of ideas; we're traveling not around the world but around my bathroom, which is a little microcosm like the world."

Miller was part of the expatriate population of American writers visiting Europe—mainly Paris—and running away from the intellectual and cultural stultification they saw in their home country, but few of these writers embraced, so whole-heartedly, ethnic differences as Miller, who ended up incorporating the "non-Western" into his writings, his philosophy, and his personal life. Harold T. McCarthy wrote that when Miller "settled down in Paris in 1930, it was with no mere sense of being an expatriate. He believed he had died and been reborn."[1] Miller was unique on more than one level, and this may account for his late acceptance by critics and for the difficulty in placing his works within an existing literary tradition. In 1959, Don Kleine wondered about Miller's position vis-à-vis his compatriots in Europe, writing that "by the time he starts to write these expatriate novels his contemporaries are already back in Brooklyn.... Why be ten years behind, why seem so indifferent to the external history of your era?"[2] and frustratingly asking "But who then is Henry Miller?" Steven Foster also wondered about Miller's so-called "Patagonian insights," which he described as his ability to separate "the self from the society in order to be at the bottom looking up."[3]

Miller was equally baffled, in *Tropic of Capricorn*, about his American life: "What race of men is this, I asked myself. What does it mean? ... I was looking upon a strange and incomprehensible world, a world so removed from me that I had the sensation of belonging to another planet" (CAP, 62–63). Yet Miller was also aware that the alienation was reciprocal, and was candid enough to write: "I ask myself if there isn't something wrong with me. The only conclusion I can come to is *that I am different*" (CAP, 96). In *Black Spring*, he goes much further: "I remember that just as I was about to cross the border they asked me what I had to declare and, like an idiot, I answered: '*I want to declare that I am a traitor to the human race*'" (BS, 160). Such pronouncements were unlikely to please his critics. Czeslaw Milosz, for one, decried Miller's posturing: "His violent gestures, vulgarities, and floods of invective are clearly directed against some enemy, though his yammerings make it impossible to decide who or what that enemy is. The twentieth century? America? New York?... Something disturbing happens when Americans throw themselves on European authors, especially Nietzsche,"[4] and described Miller as a "Martian" (126).[5]

Miller liked to portray himself as a "Mongol," unreachable, primary, rugged, and standing at the edge of civilization: "*Mongol blood!* Of course I had heard it before!... Whenever the word Mongol came up it registered on me like a password" (PLEX, 569). He believed that this "Mongol" in him "represents the root being whose sap runs back to some ageless ancestral limb of the genealogical tree," in which his American identity has been "swallowed up as the ocean swallows the rivers which empty into it" (NEX, 19). Miller categorically renounced his roots; his "people were entirely Nordic, which is to say *idiots*. Every wrong idea which has ever been expounded was theirs" (CAP, 3), and by trying to distance himself as much as possible from any Anglo-Saxon ancestry, he was eager to explore racial possibilities, however far-fetched: "I'd like to know more about my ancestors. Maybe they weren't all German" (NEX, 98). Indeed, Miller's willful estrangement from his Americanness and his embracing of other ethnicities was, by and large, a unique combination of firsthand experience and readings. As Indrek Männiste accurately points out, Miller's philosophy is the result of four currents, the European, the American, the Indian, and the Chinese.[6]

I will show, in this chapter, how Henry Miller's journey from America to France, and then to Greece before going back to his native country, helped him develop a theory of ethno-cultural differences culminating in the vision of a perfect race of individuals, that of the artists.

To say that Miller was drunk with language is an understatement. Aside from his list of new words that he kept next to his typewriter, he was particularly thrilled with exotic tongues. In a synaesthetic recollection of his childhood days, Miller described the fascination of names:

> For us there was something grotesque about the name Santos Dumont. About his exploits we were not much concerned—just the name... Santos Dumont, then, was something delightfully foreign... a magical word which suggested a beautiful flowing moustache, a sombrero, spurs, something airy, delicate, humorous, quixotic. Sometimes it brought up the aroma of coffee beans and of straw mats... it was so thoroughly outlandish and quixotic. (CAP, 137)

Miller was attracted to a name, Santos Dumont, half-Spanish/Portuguese half-French, as if the possibility of acquiring a double ethnic nature was evident. This disjointedness

Miller tried to nurture as when an artist drew him at the antipodes of his Anglo-Saxon origins: "In less than no time Stasia had made a recognizable portrait of me.... It was in the image of a Chinese mandarin, garbed in a Chinese blue jacket, which emphasized the austere, sage-like expression I had evidently assumed" (NEX, 55). In *Plexus*, Miller wrote: "All anyone had to do in those days were merely to mention China, Java or Borneo, and I was all ears. Mention anything foreign and remote and I was a willing victim" (PLEX, 96), and the names of Italian figures and cities had an almost hypnotic effect on him: "The mere sound of their names put me in ecstasy: Taddeo Gaddi, Signorelli, Fra Lippo Lippi, Piero della Francesca, Mantegna, Uccello, Cimabue, Piranesi, Fra Angelico, and such like. The names of towns and cities were of equal fascination: Ravenna, Mantua, Siena, Pisa, Bologna, Tiepolo, Firenze, Milano, Torino" (PLEX, 67).

Miller's yearning for a nonexistent past placed him as both a helpless—and late—romantic and a self-made Orientalist who was only too happy to voraciously gobble whatever came his way: "To love Oriental art. Who does not? But which Orient, the near or the far? I loved them all" (NEX, 266). The journeys were, of course, mainly imaginary, a representation Edward Said would describe as a stage, a theater,[7] and in this case the re-construction of a construction, as Miller himself lucidly realized: "We [himself and O'Mara] would live as vividly in the books we devoured together as in our imaginary peregrinations through China, India, Africa" (PLEX, 96). By transforming himself and his writings into beautifully exotic objects, Miller was building an artistic, literary sphere, which was meant to radiate outward and change everything around it the way it changed him.

Probably the most relevant incident in Miller's childhood, in this context, was the urban transformations taking place near Williamsburg, in Brooklyn, especially the arrival of different ethnicities that would problematize relations between them and the earlier inhabitants:

> I lived then, as a boy, close to the boundary between the north and the south side.... The actual boundary was Grand Street, which led to Broadway Ferry, but this street meant nothing to me, except that it was already beginning to be filled with Jews... I was living, therefore, between two boundaries, the one real, the other imaginary—as I have lived all my life. (CAP, 210)

Miller's world was, like that of most children, a mini-cosmos complete in itself, "containing just such representatives of the human race, each one a world unto himself and all living together harmoniously and inharmoniously, *but together*, a solid corporation, a close-knit human spore which could not disintegrate unless the street itself disintegrated" (CAP, 211). With the opening, in 1903, of the Williamsburg Bridge that connected Brooklyn to the Lower East Side of Manhattan, Miller's world expanded considerably with "the disintegration of our little world, of the little street called Fillmore Place" (CAP, 211), caused by what Miller called the "invasion of the Jews" (CAP, 211) coming from Delancey Street in New York. The arrival of the Jews also signaled the onset of a mixing of languages, an auditory experience that may account for Miller's fascination with non-Anglo-Saxon tongues, for "with the change the English language also disappeared; one heard nothing but Yiddish" (CAP, 211). The new demarcation line "neatly divides the Gentile world that I knew from the ledger from the Jewish world that I am about to know from life" (BS, 118). It is a line he will cross, never turning back.

Crossing the border line, going to the "other side," be it on the level of erotic descriptions, of linguistic rant, or physically on a street, has been one of Miller's hallmark traits. He recounts a recurrent dream that haunts him,

> a dream which I have had over and over, which I still dream now and then, and which I hope to dream as long as I live. It was the dream of passing the boundary line.... Across the line I am unknown and absolutely alone. Even the language has changed. In fact, I am always regarded as a stranger, a foreigner. (CAP, 213–214)

While living for a time near Fort Green Park, not far from Manhattan Bridge on the Brooklyn side, Miller recalls the feelings associated with going over to the "slums":

> After strolling through the sedate quarters it was a thrill to cross the line, to mingle with Italians, Filipinos, Chinese and other "undesirables." A pungent odour invested the poor quarters: it was compounded of cheese, salami, wine, punk, incense, cork, dried fish skins, spices, coffee, stale horse piss, sweat and bad plumbing.... It was like passing from a cool, immaculate mausoleum into the thick of life. (PLEX, 365)

But the crossing was salutary, as "[t]here were no longer the stereotyped wooden faces of the born American but racial types, all saturated with character" (PLEX, 365).

Incidentally, Miller's literary journey started with his encounter with the non-American, non-Anglo-Saxon, Russian Fyodor Dostoevsky, for, as Katy Masuga wrote, Miller had "a very fervent interest in the Russian writer, and he credits his personal philosophical awakening to his discovery of Dostoevsky's work";[8] it is interesting to read how even this haphazard, almost Surrealist, fortuitous encounter is framed within the ethnic sphere of the "undesirables" of his white society: "It was exactly five minutes past seven, at the corner of Broadway and Kosciusko Street, when Dostoevski first flashed across my horizon.... The Jew who pronounced his name for me had thick lips; he could not say Vladivostok, for instance, nor Carpathians—but he could say Dostoevski divinely" (BS, 15). Most of Miller's friends and acquaintances in New York and in Paris are Jews, and this is relevant because, as he says, "I already speak like a Jew" (CAN, 3).

But was Miller really able to make himself a Jew, or a Chinese sage, or a Mongol? He knew that he could only emulate them, and his "rosy crucifixion," however grand he may look at it, paled in comparison to the suffering of the great races: "I am a Gentile, and Gentiles have a different way of suffering" (CAN, 9). It is this suffering which makes Jews, according to Miller, "the first people to turn to when you're down and out" (CAN, 192), capable of genuinely empathizing with their fellow humans, for when a Jew "sees a man in distress, hungry, abused, despised, he sees himself. He identifies immediately with the other fellow. *Not us.* We haven't tasted enough poverty, misfortune, disgrace, humiliation. We've never been pariahs. We're sitting pretty, we are, lording it over the rest of the world" (NEX, 298). The Jews in Miller's world are heirs to a long lineage of spiritual luminosity linked to an almost other-worldly "undue reverence for the written word," which he describes as "their weakness, as with the Chinese"; for them, "the Word has a significance almost unknown to the Gentiles. Whey they become exalted they glow like letters of fire" (SEX, 342). Letters and spirituality come together to produce a race where the head and the heart complement each other:

> I couldn't help remarking ... how typical it was of Jewish physicians to behave thus. Never had a Jewish doctor pressed me to pay my bill. Never had I met one who was not interested in the arts and sciences. Nearly all of them were musicians, painters or writers on the side. What's more, they all held out the hand of friendship. How different from the run of Gentile physicians! (PLEX, 209)

Arabs were an ethnic group visible enough in the New York of the late nineteenth and early twentieth centuries; immigrating in droves from Syria (the term applied then to Syrians and Lebanese), they constituted a sizeable diaspora. Miller found them pleasant, "friendly people," and their "women were ravishingly beautiful" (PLEX, 296). Together with the other non-Anglo-Saxon ethnicities, Arabs made up a large proportion of the messenger force under Miller's tragi-comic management at the "Cosmodemonic" Western Union company. Miller takes pains to give his readers, assumedly verbatim, a letter he received from one of his boys, an Egyptian named Mohamed Ali Sarwat, who decided to leave the company and who had found himself, in America "lost among the crowds of the Materialistic rush in the very busy streets of the Western Metropolice [sic] ... Capitalism is enslaving Labour in the midst daylight of the twentieth century, and Democracy is but a word of no meaning" (BSOHB, 258–259).[9]

It was the dehumanization and materialism of the American enterprise, a far cry from Walt Whitman's dreams of democracy and humanism that veered Miller away from his birthplace in a never-ending search for a superior race of humans. In a Marcusian and Foucauldian vein, Western civilization, "rotting now like the toenails of the saints" (CAN, 248), is a giant carceral place of confinement, a one-dimensional universe where genius is doomed never to develop, and in which Miller could only see "the figures of men and women moving listlessly behind their prison walls, sheltered, secluded for a few brief hours" (CAN, 249). Oswald Spengler's *The Decline of the West* was to influence Miller's views and to haunt him "for many a year"; he is "fully aware that the study of this great work represents another momentous event" in his life (PLEX, 618). What Spengler was presenting, Miller had felt before: "For many years I had been aware that I was participating in a general decline. We all knew it, all felt it.... What we hadn't understood so clearly, most of us, was that we were part of this very 'West,' that the West included not only Europe but North America" (PLEX, 620). What Spengler had prophesied about Europe, Miller took and instead applied, ruthlessly, to America.[10]

Miller evinces a visceral reaction toward his native country; what he feared most, after living in France, was "to be put in double harness again, to work the treadmill," preferring to be "a poor man of Europe" (CAN, 73). To him, America was "further lost than a lost continent, because with the lost continents I felt some mysterious attachment, whereas with America I felt nothing at all" (CAN, 181), wondering in the process whether it would be for the better "to keep America just like that, always in the background, a sort of picture post card, which you look at in a weak moment" (CAN, 212). America, indeed, "doesn't exist.... It's a name you give to an abstract idea" (CAN, 212). Yet Miller cannot leave his American past behind; the pain he experienced before leaving for Europe was to mark him throughout his life:

> I can think of no street in America, or of people inhabiting such a street, capable of leading one on towards the discovery of the self. I have walked the streets in many countries of the world but nowhere have I felt so degraded and humiliated as in America. I think of all the streets in America combined as forming a huge cesspool, a cesspool of the spirit in which everything is sucked down and drained away to everlasting shit. (CAP, 4)

The Anglo-Saxon race in America has made of a once beautiful continent a "grand chancre on a worn-out cock. It looked worse than that, really, because you couldn't even see anything resembling a cock any more" (CAP, 12–13). The country had become a "whorehouse run by women, with the native sons acting as pimps and the bloody foreigners selling their flesh" (CAP, 35), a country where Miller found himself *persona non grata* because he refused to conform: "To be accepted and appreciated you must nullify yourself, make yourself indistinguishable from the herd.... But if you dream something different you are not in America, of America American, but a Hottentot in Africa, or a Kalmuck, or a chimpanzee" (CAP, 49).

Americans are, despite all appearances, a "lonely people, a morbid, crazed herd thrashing about in zealous frenzy, trying to forget that we are not what we think we are, not really united, not really devoted to one another, not really listening, not really anything, just digits shuffled about by some unseen hand in a calculation which doesn't concern us" (SEX, 127), and it would be much better if the white population were to leave and hand the country back to its rightful owners: "Empty this vast wilderness called America, drain it of all its pale faces, halt the meaningless hustle and bustle... hand the continent back to the Indians" (NEX, 101). Miller, however, is "grateful to America for having made me realize my needs. I served my sentence there. At present I have no needs" (BS, 23), a lesson he learned the hard way when, for the reasons mentioned earlier, he decided to leave his homeland and head for Paris.

One of Miller's boyhood reminiscences includes a friend, Claude de Lorraine, a French boy who, despite being set apart by the other boys for his strange language and manners, "always smiled very charmingly before replying and he was very cool, collected, employing an irony and a mockery which was beyond us" (CAP, 134). When Claude left the neighborhood, Miller felt that he had blundered by not reciprocating the friendship offered by the French boy: "At the time I thought of this incident it suddenly dawned on me that Claude de Lorraine must have seen something different in me and that he had meant to honor me by extending the hand of friendship" (CAP, 135). The two words that Henry remembers marking him most, during the Claude de Lorraine episode, were *gentleman* and *reasonable*.

If, writes Miller, in America "you think of nothing but becoming President of the United States some day" because every American is "Presidential timber," in France "every man is potentially a zero" (CAN, 153–154), which is not necessarily a bad thing, as it helps create, and maintain, a "world without hope, but no despair" (CAN, 155). Paris does not have to be good to everybody, but "when you've suffered and endured things here it's then that Paris takes hold of you, grabs you by the balls, you might say, like some lovesick bitch who'd rather die than let you get out of her hands" (CAN, 175–176), and Miller can hardly hold his enthusiasm among the Parisians as they remind him of his childhood days when the "undesirables" invaded the old neighborhoods: "In New York what I like best is the ghetto. It gives me a sense of life. The people of the ghetto are foreigners; when I am in their midst I am no longer in New York but amidst the peoples of Europe. It is that which excites me" (ACN, 24). The French are reasonable and gentlemanly even in war:

> They never talked about licking the enemy, they never showed any real hatred for the Germans; they spoke of it as a job which had to be performed, a disagreeable one, which they would do without question because they were citizens of France.... To me their attitude always seemed to reveal the highest form of courage: always it was eminently pacifistic. They would fight out of a sense of duty and without hatred. (ACN, 71)

Surrounded by a bevy of French and European prostitutes, Miller found himself free to observe the female in what he believed was her pristine nature: uncivilized, unspoiled, in other words fundamentally *human*. On the one hand, Germaine, although "she was ignorant and lusty," was "a whore all the way through—and that was her virtue!" (CAN, 49); on the other hand, Claude "had a soul and a conscience; she had refinement, too, which is bad—in a whore" (CAN, 46). In France, Miller assures his readers, the moment "a woman loses a front tooth or an eye or a leg she goes on the loose. In America she'd starve to death if she had nothing to recommend her but a mutilation. Here it is different" (CAN, 165).

The French are impulsive but *bons vivants*, and at Jimmie's Bar, in Le Havre, Miller and his friends meet the owner, his face "red as a beet," and his wife Yvette, "a fine buxom Frenchwoman with glittering eyes" (CAN, 205). That the evening ends with a terrible fight does not change Miller's admiration of the French *façon de vivre*, and when, years later, he looks back at his beloved France under German occupation, he is in no doubt that it is the French spirit that will ultimately conquer, for "even if everything is demolished, even if every city of importance is destroyed, levelled to the ground, the France I speak of will live. If the great flame of the spirit be extinguished the little flames are unquenchable; they will burst through the earth in millions of tiny tongues" (ACN, 75).

In June 1939, Miller was ready to leave France for Greece at the invitation of fellow-writer and friend Lawrence Durrell. What struck him first was the Greeks' ability to work with what is already available, to create out of existing materials, and to love their creations. Akin to Claude Lévi-Strauss's *bricoleur*, a Greek's concern is not with *engineering*, but with *bricolage*, and for a Greek, "every event, no matter how stale, is always unique. He is always doing the same thing for the first time: he is curious, avidly curious, and experimental. He experiments for the sake of experimenting, not to establish a better or more efficient way of doing things. He likes to do things with his hands, with his whole body, with his soul (COM, 14); Miller himself, as James M. Decker points out, "ever the bricoleur... extracts whatever anecdotes he can from the substance of his own life in fashioning the narratives."[11] The Greek character gave Miller a second opinion of his fellow English-speaking British, who now appear as "torpid, unimaginative, lacking in resiliency" (COM, 36) compared to the Greeks who have remained undaunted in the face of the "cruelest enemy a people could have—the Turks" (COM, 36). Reverting to his usual benchmark of the Far East, Miller sees that Greece "is a little like China or India... the Greek himself is everywhere, like the Chinaman again," and respects, like the fabled American India, nature: "He does not leave little particles of himself distributed all over the lot, as the American does, for example. When the Greek leaves a place he leaves a hole. The American leaves behind him a litter of junk—shoe laces, collar buttons, razor blades, petroleum tins, vaseline jars and so on" (COM, 49). Greece's contemporary poets exemplify this attitude of reverence for the most mundane creations of nature, and marvel about them the way the French Surrealists marveled about *objets trouvés*. The poet Yannopoulos's description of rocks, the refuse of nature, touches Miller to the core: "I'll read you what he says about the rocks—just the rocks, nothing more. You can't know what a rock is until you've heard what Yannopoulos has written. He talks about rocks for pages and pages; he *invents* rocks, by God, when he can't find any to rave about" (COM, 68). Yannopoulos was "out of proportion," for again, in tune with Lévi-Strauss, the "human proportions which the Greek extolled were superhuman. They weren't *French* proportions. They were divine, because the true Greek is a god, not a cautious, precise, calculating being with the soul of an engineer" (COM, 68). Building toward his later theory of the universal artist, Miller advocated a cross-fertilization of hybrid ethnicities: in the Greek, one "feels the influence of Egypt, the homely human immediacy of the Etruscan world, the wise, communal organizing spirit of Inca days" (COM, 121).

It is an immediacy that Miller had been looking for all his life, and that he will try to re-create later in Big Sur, California, a coordination between human and land: "I became deflated, restored to proper human proportions, ready to accept my lot and prepared to give of all that I have received" (COM, 237). His short stay in Greece was suddenly cut by the beginning of the war, but his *Colossus of Maroussi* contains an appendix, written in August 1940 by Durrell after Miller's departure. It contains the unforgettable account of Miller's Greek hero-writer, George Katsimbalis, crowing, in almost unbelievable crescendo fashion, with the "Cocks of Attica" responding to him from every side:

> He screamed himself hysterical and his audience in the valley increased until all over Athens like bugles they were calling and calling, answering him.... The whole night was alive with cockcrows—all Athens, all Attica, all Greece, it seemed, until I almost imagined you being woken at your desk late in New York to hear these terrific silver peals: Katsimbaline cockcrow in Attica. (COM, 244)

After his return to the United States, Miller tried to come to terms with the unavoidable fact that he is an American, and was recognized as such wherever he went. Unable to renounce his native ethnicity, he rationalizes the import of his travels by superimposing his gained experience onto a project to tour the country and write his impressions:

> There was a reason, however, for making the physical journey, fruitless though it proved to be. I felt the need to effect a reconciliation with my native land ... I didn't want to run away from it, as I had originally. I wanted to embrace it, to feel that the old wounds were really healed, and set out for the unknown with a blessing on my lips. (ACN, 10)

America, he discovered, was "magnificent—*and* terrifying. Why terrifying? Because nowhere else in the world is the divorce between man and nature so complete" (ACN, 20), with a rupture not only between Americans and their land but also between Americans and everybody else. Because of the white man's propensity for cruelty, a once peaceful continent has witnessed the most horrible persecutions: "One of the curious things about these progenitors of ours is that though avowedly searching for peace and happiness, for political and religious freedom, they began by robbing, poisoning, murdering, almost exterminating the race to whom this vast continent belonged. Later, when the gold rush started, they did the same to the Mexicans as they had to the Indians" (ACN, 28). Most importantly for Miller, America is at war with the creative genius, the writer, the artist, the nonconformist; this North American continent "is no place for an artist: to be an artist is to be a moral leper, an economic misfit, a social liability. A corn-fed hog enjoys a better life than a creative writer, painter or musician. To be a rabbit is better still" (ACN, 16).

This is all the more unfortunate because despite the huge opportunities and the vast resources, the white Anglo-Saxon has managed to live a life of misery. This contradiction is brought to light by an African-American woman:

> I remember a conversation with a colored maid in the home of one of my friends. She said, "I do think we have more love for you than you have for us." "You don't hate us ever?" I asked. "Lord no!" she answered, "we just feel sorry for you. You has [sic] all the power and the wealth but you ain't happy." (ACN, 55)

Yet, it would be a mistake to think that Miller put all white, Anglo-Saxon Americans in the same basket. The Amish people in Lancaster County, Pennsylvania, for example, hold on "stubbornly to the ways of their ancestors in comportment, dress, beliefs and customs," and, contrary to their compatriots who have decimated everything they could lay their hands on, they "have converted the land into a veritable garden of peace and plenty... [and] live a life in direct opposition to that of the majority of the American people" (ACN, 37). In addition, the two halves of the United States are, to Miller, sharply different. The South is "full of eccentric characters; it still fosters individuality.... When you go through a sparsely settled state like South Carolina you do meet men, interesting men—jovial, cantankerous, disputative, pleasure-loving, independent-thinking creatures who disagree with everything, on principle, but who make life charming and gracious. There can hardly be any greater contrast between two regions in these United States, in my mind, than between a state like Ohio and a state like South Carolina" (ACN, 45–46). What is more, Southerners to Miller acquire an elevated status precisely because they hail back to an ancient tradition which they have learned to preserve against all odds, and most often by isolating themselves from the rest: "When he [the Southerner] elects to retire from the world it is not because of defeatism but because, as with the French and the Chinese, his very love of life instills him with a wisdom which expresses itself in renunciation" (ACN, 108–109). This is why Miller himself adopted a philosophy mixing Whitman's love of crowds with the nineteenth-century flâneur's detached observation of human nature and with the serene Far-Eastern contemplation of change from within a stable center. This center, Miller chose to be America, but an America of his creation, from which he could re-create the lost Eden that was supposed to be the New World. The difference is clear: "I say Big Sur, not America. For, however much a part of America Big Sur may be, and it is American through and through, what distinguishes it is something more than the word America conveys" (BSOHB, 32–33).

It is in Big Sur that Miller met Howard Welch, a neighbor, the ideal, "lone-American type" who possesses in him all the qualities Henry had been searching for. He is the type Whitman would have admired, the "democratic man our poets sang of but who, alas, is being rapidly exterminated," an American who "never starts a war, never raises a feud, never draws the color line, never tries to lord it over his fellow-man, never yearns for a higher education, never holds a grudge against his neighbor, never treats an artist shabbily and never turns a beggar away" (BSOHB, 254). As Edward B. Mitchell remarked in 1966, Miller and Plato shared the same concern about the nature of the poet, but the difference was that the former was against banishing the artist from society,[12] for it is the artists, to Miller, who will inherit the earth, because all races and all ethnicities are joined in them. As such, they become *inhuman*, "nothing to do with creeds and principles" for, "side by side with the human race... [runs] the race of artists who, goaded by unknown impulses, take the lifeless mass of humanity and by the fever and ferment with which they imbue it turn this soggy dough into bread and the bread into wine and the wine into song" (CAN, 258–259). Männiste explains that the *inhuman* "is meant to be read as the antithesis of the *human* of the *traditional present*,"[13] and artists, as Decker adds, "may rise deliriously above the fray," with the ethnic subcultures working as "a catalyst for Miller's literary outpourings."[14]

Artists are the new breed indeed, a "race of individuals ransacking the universe, turning everything upside down... always clutching and grasping for the beyond, for the god out of reach" (CAN, 258); they belong to the "X root race of man" (CAP, 317). As Miller found out through his own life, artists belong to no specific race, but embrace all ethnicities: "I'm not an American any more, nor a New Yorker, and even less a European, or a Parisian. I haven't any allegiance, any responsibilities, any hatreds, any worries, any prejudices, any passion. I'm neither for nor against. I'm a neutral" (CAN, 156). Emulating his arch-hero Whitman, Miller sings of the "absolute impersonality" that allows one to "become automatically the personification of the whole human race, shaking hands with a thousand human hands, cackling with a thousand different human tongues" (CAP, 91). The great races of humanity will form one great ethnicity in harmony with the earth, the "great sentient being," which will not be "the home of the white race or the black race or the yellow race or the lost blue race," but "the home of *man* and all men are equal before God and will have their chance, if not now then a million years hence" (CAP, 26).

The old artificial line dividing the races, which frightened Henry as a child, must disappear and humanity in its entirety must be one: "My home? Why it is the world—the whole world! I am at home everywhere, only I did not know it before. But I know now. There is no boundary line any more. There never was a boundary line: it was I who made it" (CAP, 222). Miller as artist energizes his vision of life by rediscovering the universal genetic legacy inside of him: "We carry the ancient peoples in our souls and when the later acquired reason is relaxed, as in the dream or in drunkenness, they emerge with their rites, their pre-logical mentality, and grant us an hour of mystic participation" (PLEX, 384), and this universalism Miller gives as the reason why he always felt "so disjointed": "When I read about the Renaissance I feel like a man of the Renaissance; when I read about one of the Chinese dynasties I feel exactly like a Chinese of that epoch. Whatever the race, the period, the people, Egyptian, Aztec, Hindu or Chaldean, I'm thoroughly in it, and it's always a rich, tapestried world whose wonders are inexhaustible" (NEX, 214). Reflecting upon his rich journeys, Miller wrote that though "born American, though I became what is called an expatriate, I look upon the world not as a partisan of this country or that but as an inhabitant of the globe" (ACN, 17); he knew that he had sprung "from the mythological founders of the race" (CAN, 259) who created all humans alike.

In a typical moment of candidness, Miller recalled when a Hungarian friend, after having heard him rant against his own country, responded by telling him that he "had probably loved America too much" (ACN, 23). Maybe this is the clue to Miller's love-hate relationship with his country; an idealist and a romantic, a starry-eyed reader of Whitman, a staunch believer in the American Dream, he would not accept the limitations imposed on humans, whether social, religious, or racial. Always the traveler, he announced: "The ancestral spirits are calling me; I can't put them off much longer," and in a mystical vision saw himself disappearing from sight, maybe to Tibet, to "come back again one day, in another suit of flesh" (ACN, 188–189), perhaps reincarnated in one of the ethnicities he loved so much or, better, in the all-encompassing New Human he hoped one day would rule the world.

Notes

1. Harold T. McCarthy, "Henry Miller's Democratic Vistas," *American Quarterly* 23, 2 (1971): 221.
2. Don Kleine, "Innocence Forbidden: Henry Miller in the Tropics," *Prairie Schooner* 33, 2 (1959): 125–126.
3. Steven Foster, "A Critical Appraisal of Henry Miller's *Tropic of Cancer*," *Twentieth Century Literature* 9, 4 (1964): 199.
4. Czeslaw Milosz and Richard Lourie, "Henry Miller," *Grand Street* 1, 3 (1982): 124–125.
5. Milosz and Lourie, "Henry Miller," 126.
6. Männiste, *Henry*, xiii.
7. Edward W. Said, *Orientalism: Western Conceptions of the Orient*. (London: Penguin, 1995), 63.
8. Katy Masuga, "Henry Miller and the Book of Life," *Texas Studies in Literature and Language* 52, 2 (2010): 193.
9. It is interesting to note that the first novel in English written by an Arab named Ameen Rihani in 1911 was *The Book of Khalid* (Dodd, Mead, & Co.). Rihani, a Lebanese-American, recounts in semiautobiographical fashion the tribulations of his eponymous hero in New York as an immigrant and his subsequent disillusionment and return to his native country. Many scenes from Rihani's novel mirror Miller's own experience a few years later.
10. See Männiste for an in-depth coverage of Miller's Splenglerian dimension, 32–35.
11. James M. Decker, *Henry Miller and Narrative Form: Constructing the Self, Rejecting Modernity* (New York: Routledge, 2005), 5.
12. Edward B. Mitchell, "Artists and Artists: The 'Aesthetics' of Henry Miller," *Texas Studies in Literature and Language* 8, 1 (1966): 103.
13. Männiste, *Henry*, 79.
14. James M. Decker, "Literary Text, Cinematic 'Edition': Adaptation, Textual Authority, and the Filming of 'Tropic of Cancer,'" *College Literature* 34, 3 (2007): 153.

4

The Religiosity of Henry Miller

Edward Abplanalp

The following is a roughly consistent description of Miller's religiosity. Many of the key elements that will be discussed include his conceptions of God, salvation, heaven and hell, the meaning of life, spirit, the symbols of angels and demons, death, crucifixion, the womb, and artists and saints. I will also examine his ideas of birth and rebirth, the Bible, as well as his views on certain religious figures, and organized religion in general. I will also touch upon his view of astrology and how numerous philosophical-theological traditions shaped his overall religious motif. Admittedly, the present work is incomplete. But besides reading Miller's own works, readers with a keen interest in Miller's religiosity should also consider Thomas Nesbit's *Henry Miller and Religion* (2007), Karl Orend's *The Brotherhood of Fools and Simpletons: Gods and Devils in Henry Miller's Utopia* (2005), as well as William A. Gordon's *The Mind and Art of Henry Miller* (1967).

There are numerous problems to consider when one begins to first think about Miller's religiosity. For one thing, Miller did not approach religion and God the way most academics or theologians do today. For instance, were Miller alive today, he might have had a mild interest in the squabbles between contemporary apologists (such as William Lane Craig and Alvin Plantinga), and the New Atheists—that is, Christopher Hitchens, Richard Dawkins, Sam Harris, and Daniel Dennett. But Miller was not in the least bit interested in the traditional arguments for God's existence. He never critiqued Paley's "Divine Watchmaker." He never attempted in print to defend (or refute) Anselm's ontological proof. The cosmological arguments given by Aquinas were of no concern to Miller. Miller did not engage the rationality of religious belief in the way one might by contemplating Pascal's infamous wager. In a word, Miller's religiosity is not predicated upon the Western logic of natural theology or atheology, both of which employ rigorous philosophical argumentation.

Furthermore, it could be biased recruitment of evidence to select only particular passages that comport with a particular religious paradigm and then say "Because of what Miller wrote here, his religion was (or was not) such and such." Consider the Miller protagonist claiming in the beginning of *Tropic of Capricorn*, that if there were a God, "...I would meet Him calmly and spit in His face" (CAP, 2). Clearly, no fundamentalist Jew, Christian, or Muslim would say such a thing. However, one cannot simply consider a passage like this in isolation and legitimately infer anything about the author's religiosity. By saying that he would spit in God's face, is Miller's character supposed to represent the way the historical Miller thought in his younger years? Did such a thought even occur to the historical Miller (in his youth)? As we all know, a writer's beliefs change over time. Moreover, as James M. Decker has explained in *Henry Miller and Narrative Form: Constructing the Self, Rejecting Modernity* (2005), Miller did not employ a linear conception of time in his writings. Instead he used what Miller called "spiral form."[1] Miller says: "In telling the story of my life I have frequently disregarded the chronological sequence in favor of the spiral form of progression. The time sequence which relates one event to another in linear fashion strikes me as falsely imitative of the true rhythm of life" (WOS, 53–54). Moreover, a writer's personal views can also be different than what he or she writes. Authors express nonliteral views for various reasons. In terms of religion, a novelist might use his or her writings as a vehicle to explore a certain set of religious beliefs that he or she finds fascinating. Moreover, it would be a false dichotomy to think that a person can subscribe to one—and only—religious paradigm. All these concerns apply in the case of Henry Miller.

Of course, Miller is probably most well known for his semiautobiographical novels, several of which were famously censored for indecency. When he wrote them, these works did not conform to any sort of writing style hitherto known to humanity. Thus, they defy easy categorization. But Miller also wrote travelogues, pamphlets, and essays on a wide variety of topics. He has been thought of as a literary product of the Transcendentalists. His works have been considered surrealist, pornographic, and mystical. One might say that they are Dadaesque. One might also say that they are poetic. Karl Shapiro notes, "I do not call him a poet because he has never written a poem; he even dislikes poetry, I think. But everything he has written is a poem in the best as well as in the broadest sense of the word."[2] Furthermore, many of Miller's works can be described as autobiographical narratives. *Perhaps*. Shapiro also observes: "Every word he has ever written is autobiographical, but only in the way *Leaves of Grass* is autobiographical."[3] At any rate, in terms of understanding his religiosity, it would be a serious mistake to attempt to read Miller as one would read theologians such as Augustine, Aquinas, Maimonides, or Luther.

Perhaps, for present purposes, what makes Miller somewhat of an enigma is the fact that his first-person character is often inscrutable and sometimes makes the most inconsistent remarks—including contradictory ideas about religion. The inner voice of his protagonist even seems to embrace contradictions. He wrote, "Between subjective and objective there is no vital difference" (WOH, 25). Also, "One can be absolutely truthful and sincere even though admittedly the most outrageous liar" (WOH, 25). In "The Universe of Death" he also said, "Life can be more deadly than death, and death on the other hand can open up the road to life" (CE, 109). This sort of narrative cannot be seriously embraced by most Western intellectuals—for as all logicians know, anything follows from a contradiction. But perhaps Miller's inconsistencies and hyperbole should not be viewed as inherently problematic. While inscrutable if taken literally, Miller is readable—indeed, to the point where the reader often feels like she or he is making some sort of sense out of his syntactic, allegorical, and hyperbolic "nonsense."

One might initially wonder whether Miller was really a religious writer at all. His religious metaphors, for example, are sometimes really a bit much. He sometimes compares himself to a messiah, to Christ, or to God. Or, for another example, he said, "For two thousand years we have been using Jesus-Christ as a mouthwash ..." (NI, 3). In *Henry Miller on Writing*, he said "Serenity is when you get above all this, when it doesn't matter what they think, say or want, but when you do as you are, and see God and Devil as one" (HMW, 157). In *Tropic of Cancer* he also said "I have found God, but he is insufficient" (CAN, 103). And would a truly religious person write the anti-Semitic things that Miller did? Perhaps not.

Moreover, would a truly religious person objectify women the way Miller does? One might further ask: if the aim of Miller's writings was to convey a religious message, then why so much smut? There are several things to be said with respect to this question. First, Miller's books are not merely about religion. That is, Miller did not intend *only* to express religiosity through his texts. Because of the amount of gratuitous sex, it must be that Miller's ambition was not *merely* to produce purely religiously didactic narratives—that is, books written solely to teach a religious lesson, or make a spiritual point. However, it does not follow that Miller was not attempting to convey *any* sort of religiosity through his writings.

Moreover, asking why a religious writer would employ sexuality in his or her art form makes sense only if one finds religion and sexuality incongruous, which Miller did not. Toward the beginning of *The World of Sex*, Miller claims:

> The question might arise, in the minds of some, as to whether there is a conflict between the sexual and the religious. In my opinion there is none. Conflict there is, but only because life is essentially that. Every aspect of life is necessary and inevitable, and capable of conversion to different levels.... To live out one's desires, and in doing so to subtly alter the quality of desire, is, it seems to me, the great purpose of living. (WOS, 6)

So, not only did Miller think that there is no inconsistency in the sexual and the religious, he might also have been using sex in his writings to express a spiritual aim. In fact, in his "Obscenity and the Law of Reflection," Miller said that the aim of his sex scenes "is to awaken, so to usher in a new sense of reality" (RTR, 287).

In this vein, recall that in Hinduism there are many paths to enlightenment, many of which embrace sexuality. Similarly, Miller thought that for some individuals, religion and sex can be entwined. But perhaps other individuals have a spiritual path that does not include sex. In *The World of Sex*, Miller says, "For some sex leads to sainthood: for others it is the road to hell" (WOS, 51). But more generally, Miller thought that the modern world has practically eviscerated the meaningfulness of sex. That is, for most people sex no longer has any aesthetic or spiritual meaning. In *The World of Sex*, Miller writes:

> The sexual life, it seems to me, is at its best in the purely physical world of the pagan, or again, or again in the religious world, when coupled with devotion, or finally in the primitive world, where it is expressed through magic and ritual. (48)

Thus, in a truly religious world, for Miller, sex would no longer function "in a void." Instead, sex would exist on a "spiritual plane." And, as we shall soon see, to the extent that Miller's religiosity contains the concept of sin. Sin, for Miller, would roughly amount to doing something that contravenes one's pursuit of self-liberation. Writing about himself as the author of *Tropic of Cancer*, in *The World of Sex* Miller states: "Liberally dosed with a sexual content as was that book, the problem of its author was never one of sex, nor even with religion, but of self-liberation" (8). So, according to Miller's religiosity, sex is not necessarily a sin. Perhaps it becomes sinful only when it detracts from self-liberation.

Thus, the amount of sex contained within Miller's writings should not prevent one from viewing Miller as a religious writer. Consider that in *The World of Sex* Miller said, "It goes then without saying that I am essentially a religious person" (WOS, 6). Also, in "Reunion in Brooklyn" Miller said, "I answer to God, and not to the Chief Executive, whoever he may be" (SAW, 106). Orend relates that Miller viewed *Tropic of Capricorn* and the *Rosy Crucifixion* trilogy as "deeply religious and metaphysical books."[4] Recall, also, Miller's interview in the *Paris Review* in which the interviewer says "… you yourself have been called a very religious man." Miller replies:

> Yes, but without espousing any religion. What does that mean? That means simply having a reverence for life, being on the side of life instead of death. Again, the word "civilization" to my mind is coupled with death. When I use the word, I see civilization as a crippling, thwarting thing, a stultifying thing. For me it was always so. I don't believe in the golden ages, you see. What I mean is that it was a golden age for a very few people, for a select few, but the masses were always in misery, they were superstitious, they were ignorant, they were downtrodden, they were strangled by Church and State ….[5]

By saying he was a religious person who did not espouse a religion, was Miller being serious? Being for life instead of death? Most secular humanists would agree. But associating civilization with death and claiming that the bulk of humanity is ignorant, superstitious, and "strangled" by the Church and the state? Many would take this as pure hubris. Was Miller a snide atheist? Admittedly, Miller did make absurd religious proclamations. Still, let us strive to view Miller as some sort of religious writer, and make an effort to describe, at least roughly, his overall religiosity.

Consider what Miller's religiosity might indicate about the meaning of life. Recall that Christianity is a religion of salvation. In fact, for Christians and Muslims, the purpose of life is basically to reside in the present physical world in a manner so as to ensure an eternal life a heaven. Nonetheless, this view of the ultimate *telos* of life is not shared by all the world's religions. For instance, the locus of Judaism is a covenant between God and his special people. Buddhism aims at *nirvana*. So, how did Miller view the meaning of life, and how did it connect with his overall religiosity? For example, one might initially view Miller as a hedonistic Epicurean—especially if one only focused on the Dionysian sex, food, alcohol, and so on, scenes in Miller's works.

If this were the case, then the meaning of life for Miller would be for one to have as many pleasant experiences as one can before dying. This is not the case.

In his "Creative Death," Miller states, "Strange as it may seem today to say, the aim of life is to live, and to live means to be aware, joyously, drunkenly, serenely, divinely *aware*" (WOH, 2). Also, in *The World of Sex*, Miller notes that D.H. Lawrence thought that there were "two great modes of life, the religious and the sexual." Miller continues: "To me it seems that there is only one great way and that is the way of truth" (8). So, Miller's religiosity is not fixated on salvation (at least as it is usually understood—e.g., eternal salvation). Rather, as we shall see, a focal goal of Miller's religious paradigm is enlightened self-liberation. Instead of flowing with the status quo and merely addicting oneself to animalistic pleasures, the meaning of life, for Miller, is to find one's identity and to live in accord with one's true nature.

But what does that mean? Miller, like many other thinkers, writers, and artists, held that our true nature, or true identity, has been corrupted or hidden by modern society. In *Black Spring* Miller writes:

> The plague of modern progress: colonization, trade, free Bibles, war, disease, artificial limbs, factories, slaves, insanity, neuroses, psychoses, cancer, syphilis, tuberculosis, anemia, strikes, lock-outs, starvation, nullity, vacuity, restlessness, striving, despair, ennui, suicide, bankruptcy, arteriosclerosis, megalomania, schizophrenia, hernia, cocaine, prussic acid, stink bombs, tear gas, mad dogs, auto-suggestion, auto-intoxication, psychotherapy, hydrotherapy, electric massages, vacuum cleaners, pemmican, grapenuts, hemorrhoids, gangrene. No desert isles. No Paradise. Not even *relative* happiness. Men running away from themselves so frantically that they look for salvation under the ice floes or in tropical swamps, or else they climb the Himalayas or asphyxiate themselves in the stratosphere. (46)

Here, Miller is suggesting that what was called "modern progress" might not be progress at all. Rather, for Miller, the modern world—and especially America—is literally dehumanizing, in that it destroys much of what makes us uniquely human. As a result, many people do not know who they are, or how to really live. This is a key point to which we shall later return.

What is clear is that throughout his works Miller liberally employed a host of religious terms, analogies, symbols, metaphors, and ideas. Consider his use of the term "God." Miller wrote a variety of contradictory ideas. As an illustration, at one point Miller compares money to God. In his "Money and How it Gets That Way" he says:

> In a profound sense money may resemble God Almighty. Indeed this is neither an original thought nor a sacrilegious one, for in the century preceding that of Thomas Aquinas there appeared in the lowlands of Scotland a monk of the Dominican order who preached the divine transvaluation of money, or to put it in everyday language, that God and Money are One. Nor did the good Fathers of the Church at that time find anything blasphemous in such preachings. (SSLH, 123)

How curious. What sort of religious writer would say such a thing?[6] Is it not *sacrilegious* to say that money resembles God? Of course, here Miller did not say that money *is* God. He claimed that money *resembles* God. Miller did not really think that money is God. Consider, also, Miller's use of "God" in his treatment of the Moldorf character in *Tropic of Cancer*. Miller writes: "I am trying ineffectually to approach Moldorf. It is like trying to approach God, for Moldorf *is* God—he has never been anything else" (8). What could this mean? When Miller writes that "Moldorf is God," does the idea tell Moldorf is identical to God? Perhaps the notion is that Moldorf possesses some of God's qualities? But Miller does not adumbrate many of Moldorf's qualities. Furthermore, Moldorf is married and lacks the great-making qualities theists typically attribute to God. For Miller, then, what was God?

Miller was raised Lutheran, but was not formally trained in any religion. Nonetheless, Miller was familiar with the basics of most of the world's religions, and he was especially fascinated by Hinduism, Zen Buddhism, and the occult. He was interested in the avant-garde East Coast religions of his day, which in a radical ecumenical sense blended together esoteric elements of ancient spirituality, Eastern and Western religions, telepathy, psychology, and science.[7] By outward appearances, Miller was not actually a practicing Hindu, Buddhist, Jew, Christian, or Muslim. He was, however, heavily influenced by the writings of Madame Blavatsky and was active in the Theosophical Society both in America and France.[8] And infused into Miller's religious mixture are certain elements of the philosophies of Nietzsche, Bergson, and Spencer, as well as the theory of Jung. So, it is probably best to view Miller as a clever and creative self-made intellectual who, in a certain sense, created his own "religious universe."[9] That is to say, Miller is best seen as an open-minded and well-read Rosicrucian or Theosophical synthesizer who selected beliefs and tenets from a wide variety of traditional and esoteric religions and pragmatically blended them together.

Now, Miller certainly was not consistent in his use of "God," "Godhead," "divine," and so forth. Nonetheless, according to Nesbit (and others), Miller assembled " ... a religious world in which the self is God."[10] But what could it mean to say that the self is God? It certainly does not mean that Miller viewed every person as being identical to an undesigned and uncaused Abrahamic God who designed and caused the entire cosmos and who possesses the divine properties of classical theism— that is, omnipotence, omniscience, and omnibenevolence. It is not clear that Miller believed in *that* sort of God. In his essay on Blaise Cendrars Miller writes: "What a writer learns from Cendrars is to follow his nose, to obey life's commands, to worship no other god but life" (BIML, 68). However, what irony for Miller to say that one should "worship no other god but life." Again, Miller is sounding like a person who does not believe in God. But remember that it is only from certain religious perspectives, say those of traditional Christianity or Islam, that many serious Hindus, Buddhists, or Baha'is are not really considered theists.

A theme that runs throughout Miller's corpus is the notion that everyone has the potential to be divine. This is not to say that Miller believed that everyone can actually become the God of Abraham. According to Orend, "Miller was profoundly religious and saw evidence of the Divine spirit everywhere ...."[11] In his *The Colossus of Maroussi*

Miller writes, "As for clinging to God, God long ago abandoned us in order that we might realize the joy of attaining godhead through our own efforts" (COM, 78). But what could it be for a person to attain "godhead?" As we will see, Miller uses a number of religious metaphors in describing how the individual *qua* artist transcends conventional values (in the Nietzschean sense) and pursues liberated self-identity. For example, Miller's *Tropic of Cancer* describes a liberating journey from being spiritually dead to becoming spiritually alive in Paris, and eventually connecting with the crucial spiritual flow, or élan vital.[12] Perhaps it is when the individual completes this liberating process that she has approached "attaining godhead." For instance, in *Plexus*, Miller writes through the character Claude:

> There will come a time when man will no longer distinguish between man and god. When the human being is raised to his full powers he will be divine—his human consciousness will have fallen away. What is called death will have disappeared.... Man will be free, that's what I mean. Once he becomes that god which he is, he will have realized his destiny—which is freedom.... Freedom converts everything to its basic nature, which is perfection.... There is only one thing, *spirit*. It's all, everything, and when you realize it you're it. (571–572)

So, while a passage like this is virtually incomprehensible for many devout Christians, it might make a certain amount of sense from the perspective of Eastern religions. For example, in Hinduism God is in everything, and everyone is God. That is, once illusion (*maya*) is removed, the metaphysical truth is that the self (*atman*) and the divine (*Brahman*) are really one. Along these lines, if Orend is correct, "... Miller's notion of God is not one solely of goodness and perfection, but a deity encompassing all aspects of creation as in Hindu or Baha'i faith."[13] But for Miller, as the aforementioned passage suggests, becoming divine is connected with freedom, and becoming one with spirit. And the opposite—living within certain sorts of constraints—is associated with death. This is a theme to which we shall return shortly.

It is fairly clear that Miller thought that one does not become a liberated person by following mainstream organized religions within the Western tradition.[14] In fact, it does not appear that Miller thought much of most institutionalized forms of religion. Miller adored Henri Bergson. Perhaps Miller agrees with Bergson's dichotomy between static (organized) religions, and dynamic religions (which operate outside the status-quo).[15] For example, Miller said "... the 'real men of God' are outside the church."[16] Consider, also, his interview with the *Paris Review*. Miller said, "Whenever a taboo is broken, something good happens, something vitalizing." After the interviewer asks whether all taboos are bad, Miller replies:

> Not among primitive peoples. There is reason for the taboo in primitive life, but not in our life, not in civilized communities. The taboo then is dangerous and unhealthy. You see, civilized peoples don't live according to moral codes or principles of any kind. We speak about them, we pay lip service to them, but nobody believes in them. Nobody practices these rules, they have no place in

our lives. Taboos after all are only hangovers, the product of diseased minds, you might say, of fearsome people who hadn't the courage to live and who under the guise of morality and religion have imposed these things upon us. I see the world, the civilized world, as largely irreligious. The religion in force among civilized people is always false and hypocritical, the very opposite of what the initiators of any religion really meant.[17]

It seems, then, Miller thought (similar to Nietzsche) that most people involved in organized religion do not have the "courage to live." He also suggests (like Kierkegaard) that most professed believers seeped in routine organized religion are not really religious at all.

Nonetheless, one must distinguish between the tenets of a particular religion—as, say, found in its sacred texts—and the official (and pseudo-authoritative) doctrines that are articulated by the leaders and prominent pundits of a religion. One could easily describe oneself as being Christian, for example, while at the same time eschewing the sort of organized Christianity that appeals uniquely to the mainstream provincial values of an uneducated populace. Ironically, however, Miller said he was for the Church. In "New Instinctivism" he writes, "We are for the Church because being for it does more harm than being against it" (7). Later in the chapter, we will observe more problems that Miller saw with institutional religion. But now let's turn our attention to whether Miller's religious universe has a sacred text from which we can learn more about his notion of God or the divine.

The most beloved religious text in Islam is the *Quran*. Judaism has its *Tanakh*, and Christians have a number of versions of their holy Bible. One might ask: what was Miller's central sacred text? Such a question would be loaded: it presupposes that Miller had a central sacred text. What did Miller think about the Bible? Unlike many fundamentalist and evangelical Christians, Miller did not think that the Christian Bible is literal. In a section of *Black Spring* devoted to discussing toilets, Miller says the following about the King James Version of the Christian Bible:

> The King James Version was created by a race of bone-crushers. It revives the primitive mysteries, revives rape, murder, incest, revives epilepsy, sadism, megalomania, revives demons, angels, dragons, leviathans, revives magic, exorcism, contagion, incantation, revives fratricide, regicide, patricide, suicides, revives hypnotism, anarchism, somnambulism, revives the song, the dance, the act, revives the mantic, the chthonian, the arcane, the mysterious, revives the power, the evil and glory that is God … (51)

How ironic that an author who so frequently quotes or alludes to passages from the Bible would say such a thing. We must suppose, then, that while Miller did not take the Bible to be factually true, within it he must have thought that there was something of value to be found.

In "The New Instinctivism" Miller says that he is against the 23rd Psalm, and that he has plans for a new bible (7). And in *Tropic of Cancer*, the Miller character asserts that he and his roommate Boris will write *The Last Book*, which is to be a "new Bible" (27). What is this "new Bible?" According to Nesbit, Miller thought that books in general can be "portals to the divine."[18] But in *Tropic of Capricorn* the Miller character suggests that Bergson's *Creative Evolution* is a new Bible (CAP, 214, 216). But how could Bergson's *Creative Evolution* be the new Bible if the Miller character in *Tropic of Cancer* claims that he will write a new Bible? Perhaps there will be numerous new Bibles? Whitman held such a thought. And Orend contends that "... people like Cendrars, Durrell and Colette Roberts recognized *Tropic of Cancer* as a religious book (one of the new Bibles that Whitman had heralded) ...."[19] At any rate, in "The New Instinctivism" Miller claims that the new Bible—"... a vessel in which to pour the vital fluid"—will be "a new cosmogony of literature," in which "(a)ll those who have anything to say will say it... —*anonymously*" (26). However, beyond that, it is far from clear what Miller thought such a book would look like.

So far we have seen that it is reasonable to conjecture that Miller was influenced by many religions, including Hinduism and Buddhism, and that he thought the aim of life is to discover one's true identity, and that it is possible for a person to become a godhead/God by undergoing some sort of liberating process. Moreover, this process—which will then allow one to become one with spirit—is not to be found in mainstream organized religions, or by having faith in the infallibility of the Bible. But before delving deeper into these aspects of Miller's religiosity, it will be instructive to next consider Miller's conceptions of heaven and death. To begin with, then, did Miller believe in heaven? And what role, if any, does the notion of heaven play in his overall religiosity.

It is not clear that Miller believed in a heavenly "afterlife" of the sort in which a typical Christian or Muslim might believe. Still, Miller writes of a new heaven. In his "Children of the Earth," Miller writes:

> A new heaven and a new earth! Can they not be ushered in without slaughter and destruction? Can we not bring the senseless machine to a halt, declare a moral holiday, as it were, and with a fresh new vision establish order, harmony, justice, peace? How much that is rotten and useless can be done away with by merely letting go! (SSLH, 20)

Here, Miller identifies his "new heaven" as a "new earth" and intimates that it will be brought about with "slaughter and destruction." Miller's use of death as a symbol will be discussed in more detail later. But for now, what could Miller possibly mean by a new earth? And at what sort of destruction was Miller hinting? For a clearer insight into Miller's vision of this "new heaven" and the sort of destruction which must precede it, we must note the role that astrology played in Miller's overall religiosity.

It is well known that Miller believed in astrology, and routinely used horoscopes. On the other hand, Miller wrote, "... the only way I get astrology or anything else... is as poetry, as music. If the astrological view brings out new notes, new harmonies, new vibrations, it has served its purpose—for me."[20] Still, based on astrology, it appears Miller thought that a great artist must act like "God at the dawn of creation."[21] (Miller's notion of art as a means to his idea of salvation will be discussed later.) But one must ask: the creation of what? Not the literal creation of the cosmos. Rather, Miller thought that he was living in a schizophrenic world that was cracking like an egg. To be more precise, he believed that it was "written in the planets" that the world was being split between life and death.[22] Moreover, Dostoevsky and Balzac were two of Miller's favorite writers, and both of them believed "in a dawn of a New World."[23] So, it is likely that the fissure about which Miller was concerned was the old world that would have to be destroyed, and out of which a new world would be born. In *The World of Sex* Miller says:

> A new world is being born, a new type of man is in the bud. The great mass of men, destined now to suffer more cruelly perhaps than man has ever suffered before, have become paralyzed with fear, have withdrawn into their own shell-shocked souls.... The body, which was once the temple, has become a living tomb. (9–10)

In the old world—which is the present world—most people are suffering in their "living tomb." In such a state, their bodies cannot be "temples," and so people are in some sense dead. In contrast, the new world presumably will be a world in which it will be much easier for individuals to attain their potential powers of divinity. In this sort of condition, individuals can attain Miller's ideal of self-liberation. Perhaps when this occurs, there is no distinction between self and God.

This, then, leads us to Miller's notion of death. Actually, there are several senses of death found in Miller's writings. One is simply the biological death of one's physical body. There is no evidence that Miller thought one can escape this sort of medical death. That being said, Miller was interested in the Hindu and Buddhist idea that death is part of Maya (illusion). In that vein, Hindus believe that the physical body dies a medical death. Buddhists do, as well. (The Buddha, himself, died a physical death.) Nonetheless, within such traditions our normal sense of death is a sort of chimera.

But as we are seeing, there is another sense of death contained within Miller's religiosity that reflects the notion that there are many people who, while not being medically dead, are not alive in Miller's sense of truly living, or not being connected to spirit. Miller applied this sense of death not only to people, but also to the world in which he lived. In "Stand Still Like the Hummingbird" Miller wrote:

> Buddha gave us the eight-fold path. Jesus showed us the perfect life. Lao-Tzu rode off on a water buffalo, having condensed his vast and joyous wisdom into a few imperishable words. That they tried to convey to us, these luminaries, was that there is no need for all these laws of ours, these codes and conventions, the books of learning, these armies and navies, these rockets and spaceships, these thousand and one impedimenta which weigh us down, keep us apart, and bring us sickness and death. We need only to behave as brothers and sisters, follow our hearts not our minds, play not work, create and not add invention upon invention. Though we realize it not, they demolished the props which sustain our world of make-believe. True, the world still stands or spins, but the meaning has gone out of it. It is more dead, this illusory, everyday world, than if it had been shattered by a million atom bombs. We live as ghosts amid a world of ruins. All is senseless repetition. (190–191)

This passage conveys the idea that the tedious "everyday world" of modern society is dead. Moreover, Miller's living "as ghosts amid a world of ruins" also conveys the sense of death that is expressed when Miller intimates that most people already are dead. These might be individuals who, lacking self-identity and not being connected to spirit (or élan vital), live rather hum-drum existences. Having not attained self-liberation, then, their actions and projects become prosaic, with no genuine meaning.

Along these lines, there are many examples one might choose from throughout the Miller corpus that might assist in contradistinguishing Miller's view of being genuinely alive and being dead. But for the purpose of brevity consider the case of Grover Watrous, of whom the Miller character says in *Tropic of Capricorn*, " ... I have met thousands of people and none of them were alive in the way that Grover was" (168). Miller claims that it was not Grover's energy that made him alive—America is full of energetic people. Rather, unlike the Miller character's father, overnight Grover rejected all his "preconceived values" and "ceased moving as other people move" (CAP, 168). What precipitated such a spiritual change? Miller says that "(c)onvinced of the dead certainty of death Grover suddenly became tremendously and overwhelmingly alive" (CAP, 169). And Miller writes that by being alive and empty, Grover approached "Godhood" (CAP, 167).

But there is one more sense of death that is instrumental to Miller's overall religiosity. This is the sense of death connoted by Miller when he contends that in the process of becoming an individual (a writer, an artist, etc.) one must die in order to live. And it is this sense of death that connects with his concept of crucifixion, as well as his idea of the artist as a savior. Note that Miller also used "death", "dead", "dying", "tomb", and so on, to praise (or criticize) other writers. In his "The Universe of Death," for example, Miller harshly disparages James Joyce (and to a certain extent Proust). When Miller describes Lawrence (whom he viewed as a sort-of prophet/savior), he says:

> Lawrence's life and works represent a drama which centers about the attempt to escape a living death, a death which, if it were understood, would bring about a revolution in our way of living. Lawrence experienced this death creatively, and it is because of his unique experience that his "failure" is of a wholly different order from that of Proust or Joyce. His aborted efforts towards self-realization speak of heroic struggle, and the results are fecundating—for those, at any rate, who may be called the "aristocrats of the spirit." (CE, 108)

Here, Miller is suggesting that Lawrence's "creative death" was not really a failure. So, this sort of death, which can be experienced by an individual many times over a lifetime, is not a bad thing in the end. Of course, it might seem horrific to the individual as she progressively loses parts of her false identity. Gordon describes this sort of creative death as a "fertilizing process."[24] As opposed to people who are dead simply in the sense that they lack any sort of self-identity or spirit, the artist who suffers a creative death ultimately ends up with a healthier spiritual outlook.

So, when describing Joyce again in "The Universe of Death," Miller says " ... Joyce, though still alive, seems even more dead than Proust ever was" (CE, 108). So, unlike

Lawrence, Miller must have thought that Joyce's "death" was not a positive creative death. Miller says:

> In Joyce the soul deterioration may be traced even more definitely, for if Proust may be said to have provided the tomb of art, in Joyce we can witness the full process of decomposition. "Whoso," says Nietzsche, "not only comprehends the word Dionysian, but also grasps his *self* in this world, requires no refutation of Plato or of Christianity or of Schopenhauer—he smells the *putrefaction*." *Ulysses* is a paean to "the late-city man," a thanatopsis inspired by the ugly tomb in which the soul of the civilized man lies embalmed. (CE, 110)

Again, note in this passage Miller uses expressions like "soul deterioration," "tomb of art," "decomposition," and "the ugly tomb in which the soul of the civilized man lies embalmed." Remember that Miller thought that most people live far below their potential. Perhaps Miller is complaining that the works of Joyce (and perhaps Proust) do little to assist individuals in living their lives closer to their potential; and, thus, that the works of such writers do not assist in the attainment of self-liberation.

So, what did Miller mean by "crucifixion?" Miller's crucifixion, of course, is not literally a crucifixion like that done to Jesus or Peter. Rather, it is a *process* through which a person suffers. But what sort of suffering did Miller have in mind? Christians believe that Jesus qua "Lamb of God" was crucified to atone for "original sin" and to defeat death, thus making possible eternal salvation. For Miller, however, the crucifixion of the person brings about the possibility of a new life as an artist or a true individual. Moreover, for Miller, an individual can undergo "crucifixion" many times. In *Tropic of Capricorn* Miller wrote: "All my Calvaries were rosy crucifixions, pseudo-tragedies to keep the fires of hell burning brightly for the real sinners who are in danger of being forgotten" (322–323). Again, Miller thought that the bulk of humanity in the modern world live meaningless lives. By becoming mere cogs in "the machine," people forget their true nature and their actions have no inherent value.

Thus, according to Miller's religiosity, when what a person does really has no meaning, then that person has lost spirit and has become "dead." But Miller was not a nihilist. In fact, in a certain sense, Miller's religiosity might be seen as a mixed religious–secular solution to the problem of nihilism. In "Creative Death" Miller says "Life has to be given a meaning because of the obvious fact that it has no meaning" (WOH, 5). Trapped in the world that must be destroyed, Miller's ideal would be for the individual to undergo a sort of "crucifixion" that enables her to unshackle herself from the "brainwashing" of modern culture (including a good part of status-quo moral and religious values) and to then freely live a Nietzschean-Dionysian life of art, which involves living in a sort of Buddhist present "now"—not in the future or the past. But this sort of "creative death" or "crucifixion" is a beginning, or a sort of birth/rebirth. But before exploring Miller's sense of birth, let us note Miller's idea of a savior/messiah, and what he thought of Jesus.

Jews, Christians, and Muslims believe in a messiah (a Christos). While Jews do not believe that the messiah has come, Christians and Muslims take Jesus to be the Christos. But many religions do not place a premium on salvation. Judaism, for example, is not a religion of salvation. Buddhism—to the extent that it involves salvation at all—maintains that refuge can only be found in oneself. And, of course, Christians believe that Jesus is their savior. Now, at a certain level, Miller thought that everyone is his or her own savior. In *The World of Sex* Miller said, "Like every man, I am my own worst enemy, but unlike most men, I know too that I am my own savior" (11). But on another level, Miller viewed the artist as a messiah/savior.[25] And, more generally, Miller viewed art as a means to salvation (HMW, 205).

However, if Miller associates the artist with a messiah, then according to his religiosity there can be a great number of messiahs/Christos. Consider Miller's comparison of Walt Whitman to a Christós in his "Walt Whitman."

> ... From the moment of his awakening—for it was truly an awakening and not a mere development of creative talent—he marches on, calm, steady, sure of himself, certain of ultimate victory. Without effort he enlists the aid of willing disciples who serve as buffers to the blows of fate. He concentrates entirely on the deliverance of his message. He talks little, reads little, but speculates much. It is not, however, the life of a contemplative which he leads. He is definitely in and of the world. He is worldly through and through, yet serine, detached, the enemy of no man, the friend of all. He possesses a magic armor against wanton intrusion, against violation of his being. In many ways he reminds one of the "resurrected" Christ. (SSLH, 108)

Although Miller thought that there could be multiple saviors, one should not think that Miller was opposed to Jesus. While Miller was not a Christian in the normal way of speaking, he did not despise what he took to be Jesus's message. It appears that what Miller liked about Jesus was that Jesus was a radical, an individual who defied the status-quo religious authorities of his day. In "Open Sesame!" he writes, "Jesus set about to destroy the old way of life, reminding us that the only true guide is the Spirit within us" (SSLH, 21). Did Miller believe in the Trinity? Well, sort of. In his "Creative Death" Miller states: "The trinal division of body, mind, and soul becomes a unity, a holy trinity" (WOH, 9).

Thus, to be an artist, a true artist—one who has painfully struggled to become a living soul full of spirit or élan vital—is to be a savior or a messiah. And, according to Miller's religiosity, salvation is associated with self-liberation. Correspondingly, saints are basically those writers who assisted Miller in becoming an artist, and more generally the community of saints is a "community of artists."[26] Why art? The reason must be that because (good) art liberates, and because the artist conveys a vision of the new world. In *The World of Sex*, Miller writes: "the artist ... is obsessed, admittedly or not, with the idea of recreating the world in order, as I see it, to re-establish man's innocence. This innocence, he knows, is achieved only through freedom" (7). Moreover, Miller thought that a sense of death is an indelible part of good art. In the "Universe of Death," Miller says:

> If there is any solution of life's problems for the mass of mankind, in this biological continuum which we have entered upon, there is certainly little hope of any for the individual, i.e., the artist. For him the problem is not how to identify himself with the mass about, for in that lies his *real* death, but how to fecundate the masses by his dying.... This he can do only by establishing a new relationship with the world, by seizing anew the sense of death on which all art is founded, and reacting creatively to it. (CE, 108–109)

So, "the sense of death" that Miller thought grounds good art is not a morbid fascination with the normal sense of biological death. Rather, it is more like a creative reaction to the destruction of the artist's prior conception of the world—for example, producing art that transcends conventional morality. It also could be a creative response to one's situation in life—especially if one is in a situation that is preventing self-liberation.

This, then, leads to Miller's notion of birth/rebirth. By "birth" Miller was not concerned with biological childbearing. And by "rebirth" Miller did not literally mean for to be physically dead in a tomb for three days, say, and then to be resurrected to ascend to heaven. Rather, the idea is that a person who has lost his or her identity (and thus spirit) has the potential to be reborn as a writer, an individual, an artist. One finds this, for example, in Miller's *Nexus* and *Capricorn*, where the symbol of "birth" connotes the "birth of the artist."[27] No longer subscribing to a Nietzschean "slave morality," the true artist can become reborn as an "inhuman."[28] However, if birth/rebirth is a key notion within Miller's religiosity, then it is also natural for the womb to be an important metaphorical symbol, as well. For instance, the theme of *Tropic of Cancer* is Miller's trials and tribulations as a writer in Paris. Notice, then, how miller describes *Tropic of Cancer* in his *The World of Sex*. "The *Tropic of Cancer* is a sort of human document, written in blood, recording the struggle in the womb of death" (10). But why did Miller employ the metaphor of the womb? In "The Enormous Womb," Miller says, "... the womb is the place where anything is engendered or brought to life. As far as I can make out, there is never anything but womb" (WOH, 94).

For Miller, the modern world frequently does not allow a person to find her natural identity. Most people's true natures have been corrupted by the heteronomy of modern life and conformist values, beliefs, and so on, and as a result they have failed to become authentic individuals who lead a genuinely spiritual life. These people are "dead" in Miller's negative sense. And Miller speaks of such individuals as people who view the world as a "tomb." However, some individuals (e.g., artists) have the ability to attain some degree of self-liberation. But as we have seen, the process of self-liberation can be painful, and is consequently dubbed by Miller as a "crucifixion." And if one's crucifixion is "rosy," that is, if one has experienced creative deaths, then one can eventually be connected to spirit, and proceed in the process of creating a new world. Such individuals, for Miller, have "... accepted the world as a womb, and not as a tomb. For they seem neither to regret what has passed nor to fear what is to come. They live in an intense state of awareness and yet are apparently without fear" (WOH, 95). In terms of Miller's auto-novels, recall that *Tropic of Capricorn* is a poetic semiautobiographical story of the growth of the artist. Thus, as birth is freedom from the womb, this most likely explains the frequent uses of "ovaries," "ovarian," and so on, within the work.

Finally, let's consider the role of hell, demons, and angels within Miller's religiosity. There are some connections between Miller's works and Dante's *Inferno*. And perhaps Miller agreed with Blake in that the individual can only gain entrance to heaven by passing through hell. In *Tropic of Capricorn* Miller writes: "Dear reader, you must see Myrtle Avenue before you die, if only to realize how far into the future Dante saw" (295). Moreover, one can view *Tropic of Capricorn* as the Miller character's journey through hell.[29] But while Miller identifies hell as New York (i.e., Brooklyn and Manhattan), this is not meant literally. Rather, Brooklyn is where Miller grew up, and Manhattan is where Miller worked. But what would make a place a "hell" for Miller? Again, Miller felt that he was living in a world that annihilates much of what is good for allowing a person to be an individual—creativity, imagination, autonomy, and so on. In principle, then, hell could be any place or situation that deprives one of her autonomy.

In *Tropic of Capricorn*, for example, it is his job at Western Union that prevents the Miller character from achieving his potential as an individual/artist. Recall, then, that the Western Union Telegraph Company (where Miller worked) becomes the "Cosmodemonic Telegraph Company of North America." In *Tropic of Capricorn* Miller writes:

> Wait, you cosmococcic telegraphic shits, you demons on high waiting for the plumbing to be repaired, wait, you dirty white conquerors who have sullied the earth with your cloven hoofs, your instruments, your weapons, your disease germs, wait, all you who are sitting in clover and counting your coppers, it is not the end. The last man will have his say before it is finished. Down to the last sentient molecule justice must be done—*and will be done!* Nobody is getting away with anything, least of all the cosmococcic shits of North America. (26)

Here, Miller is using expressions like "demons" and "cloven hoofs." But members of upper-level management do not become demons simply because of their greed, or because they exploit other people. Rather, people "sin" or become demons when they participate in the blocking of the power of the individual to be divine. That is, Miller's demons are those who deprive persons of their capability to ensure that what they do has some sort of intrinsic meaning.

But what about angels? Miller frequently used the angel symbol throughout his writings. However, Miller's use of angels is slightly different than the Bible's use, say, of the angel Gabriel to let Mary know that she will give birth to Jesus. In the story of the Annunciation (Luke 1:26–39), Gabriel is acting in the capacity of a holy messenger. Perhaps *part* of Miller's use of angels is to intimate the idea of Miller (or the Miller character) functioning as a spiritual messenger. Orend writes how Miller told his close friend, Moricand, how he "identified with Angels, with messengers of God, and as such a messenger his mission was one of Divine expression."[30]

But there is more to Miller's use of the angel symbol than to express the idea of a religious messenger. For instance, Miller uses an angel metaphor in *Tropic of Capricorn* to describe the moment the Miller character leaves his old zestless life to begin anew.

> At such a moment what a man *does* is of no great importance, it's what he *is* that counts. It's at such a moment that a man becomes an angel. This is precisely what happened to me: *I became an angel*. It is not the purity of an angel which is so valuable, as the fact it can fly. An angel can break the pattern anywhere at any moment and find its heaven; it has the power to descend into the lowest matter and to extricate itself at will. The night in question I understood this perfectly. I was pure and inhuman, I was detached, I had wings. I was dispossessed of the past and I had no concern about the future. I was beyond ecstasy. When I left the office I folded my wings and hid them beneath my coat. (336)

Note that being "dispossessed of the past" and having "no concern about the future" sounds like the goal of "awakening" in Buddhism—that is, a moment of *satori* in Zen Buddhism. Thus, by suffering through crucifixion, by reclaiming his autonomy, and being reborn into a new life, the Miller character became "awake" in the Buddhist sense. At that instant, the Miller character recognized self-liberation, and became aware of what it is to live with the spirit. And at that precise moment the Miller character became an angel.

In sum, Miller's worldview is constituted by beliefs and tenets from a number of philosophies and religions, especially Eastern religions such as Buddhism and Hinduism. Miller's use of religious expressions and symbolism is not consistent. Still, it is clear that Miller thought that he was living in a world that was spiritually dead, and in which most people are not connected to spirit, and instead live in self-created tombs. Miller's religiosity is grounded in a reverence for authentic life, and the idea that everyone can be divine. Miller thought that the self is God, and he maintained that one's ultimate purpose is self-identity and self-liberation, which is his conception of salvation. For Miller, hell is comprised of situations that prevent self-liberation. And instead of believing in heaven in the traditional sense, he maintained that a "new heaven" or "new earth" would eventually be actualized. For Miller, social criticism, art, sex, and other aspects of living an authentic liberated life are all part of religion. He thought that everyone is his or her own savior—meaning that it is up to every person to ensure that what he or she does has some sort of meaning. He also viewed artists as saviors *qua* re-creators of the world, and he thought that saints are artists who create art that helps others with self-liberation. However, to become a genuine artist one must sometimes suffer a "creative death," which removes parts of his or her inauthentic self. Moreover, one might have to suffer numerous "crucifixions" that enable him or her to become reborn as an artist. By undergoing this sort of liberating process, which does not involve organized mainstream religions or the Bible, one can connect with spirit, and live in the Buddhist sense of the present. When this is accomplished, one views the world as a womb—a beautiful place for creation.

Notes

1. See Decker, *Henry Miller and Narrative Form*.
2. Shapiro, "The Greatest Living Author," v.
3. Shapiro, "The Greatest Living Author," vi.
4. Orend, *Brotherhood of Fools and Simpletons*, 92.
5. George Wickes, "Henry Miller, the Art of Fiction No. 28," *Paris Review* VII (1962): 23.
6. Miller, of course, is parodying Ezra Pound's idea of social credit in this essay.
7. See Thomas Nesbit, *Henry Miller and Religion* (New York: Routledge, 2007), 27–31.
8. Nesbit, *Henry Miller and Religion*, 29.
9. Nesbit, *Henry Miller and Religion*, 5.
10. Nesbit, *Henry Miller and Religion*, 127.
11. Orend, *Brotherhood of Fools and Simpletons*, 88.
12. See Nesbit, *Henry Miller and Religion*, 41–61.
13. Orend, *Brotherhood of Fools and Simpletons*, 7.
14. See James M. Decker, "Choking on My Own Saliva: Henry Miller's Bourgeois Family Christmas in *Nexus*," *Style* 31 (1997): 270–289 for a discussion of Miller's distaste for the hollow rituals of organized religion.
15. See Nesbit, *Henry Miller and Religion*, 75–76.
16. Shapiro, "The Greatest Living Author," xxiv–xxv.
17. Wickes, "Henry Miller, The Art of Fiction No. 28," 23.
18. Nesbit, *Henry Miller and Religion*, 100.
19. Orend, *Brotherhood of Fools and Simpletons*, 91.
20. Orend, *Brotherhood of Fools and Simpletons*, 89.
21. Orend, *Brotherhood of Fools and Simpletons*, 13.
22. Orend, *Brotherhood of Fools and Simpletons*, 13.
23. Orend, *Brotherhood of Fools and Simpletons*, 18.
24. Gordon, *The Mind and Art of Henry Miller*, 68.
25. Nesbit, *Henry Miller and Religion*, 34.
26. See Nesbit, *Henry Miller and Religion*, 102–105.
27. Gordon, *The Mind and Art of Henry Miller*, 54.
28. See Nesbit, *Henry Miller and Religion*, 59–60.
29. Nesbit, *Henry Miller and Religion*, 67.
30. Orend, *Brotherhood of Fools and Simpletons*, 6.

5

Henry Miller and Morality

Guy Stevenson

For a hundred and fifty pages the reader not having started to think very hard, might suppose the book is amoral, its ethical discrimination seems about that of a healthy pup nosing succulent "poubelles," but that estimate can't really hold. Miller has, and has very strongly, a hierarchy of values. And in the present chaos, this question of hierarchy has become almost as important as having values at all.

Ezra Pound[1]

Today I awoke from a sound sleep with curses of joy on my lips, with gibberish on my tongue, repeating to myself like a litany—"Fay ce que vouldras! ... fay ce que vouldras!" Do anything, but let it produce joy. Do anything, but let it yield ecstasy.

Tropic of Cancer (CAN, 255–256)

Since the 1934 publication and subsequent banning of his first novel, *Tropic of Cancer*, Henry Miller has widely been characterized either as an immoral dilettante or an amoral iconoclast. The possibility that there might be a serious, coherent set of values behind his explicit, rebellious voice was entertained by very few of the early critics—either approving or disapproving—most tending to agree with Edmund Wilson, who called *Cancer* "the lowest book of any merit I have ever read"[2] or George Orwell, whose essay "Inside the Whale" saw no difference between Miller the author and Miller the narrator and labeled him "the ordinary, non-political, non-moral, passive man."[3] With Miller's unbanning in the 1960s, however, a body of scholarship began to emerge that sought to understand him in the context of a unified antiestablishment ideology. More interestingly, in the past fifteen years Caroline Blinder (*A Self-Made Surrealist*, 2000), James Decker (*Henry Miller and Narrative Form*, 2005), Sarah Garland (*Rhetoric and Excess*, 2005), Thomas Nesbit (*Henry Miller and Religion*, 2007), Katy Masuga (*The Secret Violence of Henry Miller*, 2011), and Indrek Männiste (*Henry Miller: The Inhuman Artist*, 2013) have moved beyond reductive ideas of Miller as sexual or spiritual prophet, highlighting a complex and often self-contradictory system of aesthetics and morality that relates intriguingly to the dominant artistic and political innovations of the early-twentieth-century.

This chapter is an attempt to outline Miller's moral approach by engaging with the 1930s European milieu out of which *Tropic of Cancer* emerged; a cultural atmosphere still deeply disturbed by the First World War, the ensuing economic depression, and the frightening but exhilarating rise of political and philosophical extremism. As well as the scholars mentioned above—particularly Sarah Garland, whose essay "Dearest of Cemeteries" posits Miller as a "parodic and syncretic" appropriator of European literary ideas[4]—I take my lead from Ezra Pound and George Bataille, two reviewers from the thirties and forties who prospected beneath what Salman Rushdie would dismiss as *Cancer*'s "scatological surface"[5] and struck upon—in Pound's words—"a strongly felt hierarchy of values." That Pound and Bataille approached the text from opposite ends of the political spectrum (radical right and left, respectively) should give some clue as to the kinds of contradictions that will come to light.

Ezra Pound's unlikely interest in Miller, I would argue, points to a fundamental paradox at the heart of the latter's moral code: that he was motivated by radically humanist and universalist impulses—toward unconditional tolerance and compassion, individual self-autonomy, and sexual and spiritual freedom—but expressed and explored them using deliberately brutal and ostensibly antihumanist language. Miller desires a world in which people have "no feeling of class, caste, color or country ... no need of possessions, no use for money, no archaic prejudices about the sanctity of the home or marriage" yet fiercely and systematically refuses the moral logic of social consciousness and day-to-day compassion (SAW, 150). He is opposed politically and economically to capitalism—a "crazy system of exploitation (SAW, 153)" built on a "pitiful, ignominious spiritual shambles"—but couches his solutions in totalizing and intolerant terms (SAW, 159). Moreover, these terms are common to earlier modernist writers—like Pound but also his literary collaborators T.E. Hulme and Wyndham Lewis—who leaned toward radical conservatism and fascism in the twenties and thirties rather than the progressive and zealously inclusive philosophy Miller espoused. Indeed, Pound's identification of a moral code in *Tropic of Cancer* will be read against an ideological migration by English and American experimentalists in the 1910s and 20s toward reactionary political and artistic positions, a trend pithily summed up by Lewis in his 1928 essay "Fashion:" " ... against sentimentality people of course reacted. So the brutal tap was turned on. For fifty years it will be the thing to be brutal, 'unemotional.' "[6]

Bataille, a social and literary theorist with a background as much in Marxism as in Surrealism, sheds a different and equally interesting light on Lewis' "brutal tap." His 1947 essay "La Morale de Miller" both elucidates and complicates the paradox between antisentimentality and compassion by exploring a concomitant conflict between desires toward control and excess in *Cancer*.

Among the first of many high-profile writers to praise Miller's debut, Pound based his review on the conviction that it embodied a "sense of good and evil" and "eminent fairness" in an age bereft of both.[7] Miller counters, he believes, "a slump towards the impoverishment of values [and] towards the cheapening of every mental activity whatsoever" that has been going on since the turn of the century.[8] By this Pound implies a corroboration of his own elaborate theory on morality in art—a system that connects the literary evil of "abstract,"[9] "slushy"[10] linguistic expression to the social, political, and economic evils of "liberal government," a "bought press," "usury" and military conflict.[11] As we shall see, it is possible to read between the lines of this apparently straightforward co-option to identify certain unexpected overlaps with Miller's hatred of bourgeois, "Lutheran" manners (CAP, 191), and "the absence of any relationship between ideas and living" (CAN, 157). It is also possible to identify points of even less likely crossover between Miller's narrative and what T.E. Hulme identified as an emerging "antihumanist" artistic age, grounded in "the subordination of man to certain absolute values."[12] For the moment, however, it is important to note Pound's deliberately provocative denial of the immediate textual evidence.

Far from "eminently fair," Miller's semiautobiographical narrator is consistently and explicitly antagonistic toward traditional definitions of reasonable and "virtuous" behavior. Indeed, *Cancer*, as well as the short story "Max" (1938) and *Cancer*'s New York-based prequel *Tropic of Capricorn* (1939), are permeated by consciously unjust diatribes against the undeserving, from the comfortable expatriates who feed and shelter him while he is living rough in Paris to fellow down-and-outs who rely on him for advice and financial aid. Eating supper at the house of the playwright Sylvester, with whose wife he is having an affair, Miller rages internally at his host:

> To think that a poor, withered bastard with those cheap Broadway plays up his sleeve should be pissing on the woman I love…. The cheek of him!… My God, man, you ought to get down on your knees and thank me. Don't you see that you have a *woman* in your house now? (CAN, 61)

Similarly, after securing a job at an expatriate newspaper, he responds with brazen indifference to the announcement that his colleague Peckover has fallen down the office elevator shaft and died: it was "pathetic and ludicrous at the same time" (141) since Peckover—whose name conspicuously implies "pecker"—"was a zero, and even the fact that he was dead wouldn't add a cipher to his name" (142).

This antipathy toward inoffensive, helpful, and often helpless people is integral to his wider exploration into the true nature of empathy and compassion, a fact that the majority of critics have either missed altogether or underestimated. Kate Millett, who famously read Miller as a "counterrevolutionary sexual politician" in 1969,[13] and George Orwell—mentioned earlier as someone who was convinced of Miller's amorality—both took his crassness in *Cancer* at autobiographical face value. If Miller the narrator expressed objectionable feelings about women, Millett argued, Miller the human being must also be morally objectionable, a "compendium of American sexual neuroses" emblematic of his gender and age.[14] In Orwell's case, Miller's abnegation of moral responsibility, when it came to squalor and sexuality, was an equally convenient sign of his parity with the common man. At the other extreme, various late 1950s and 60s critics correctly interpreted Miller as a profoundly compassionate writer but ignored the strategy at work in his excessive attacks on conventional approaches to compassion. Left-wing literary scholars Kenneth Rexroth ("The Reality of Henry

Miller," 1959) and Karl Shapiro ("The Greatest Living Author," 1960), for example, praised Miller's radically progressive approach to sexuality and human relations but chose to gloss over his cruelty in order to argue the case for his humanism. As Rexroth puts it, "absolute freedom from...the sense of guilt, implication and compromise, makes Miller humane, maybe even humanistic."[15]

Intent on appropriating him as a messenger of libertarian, antipuritanical ideals, readings like Rexroth's and Shapiro's, make little use of the complex resonances that arise from Miller's experiments into the human reaction to suffering. More recent works by Bertrand Mathieu (*Orpheus in Brooklyn*, 1976), Gilles Mayné (*Eroticism in Georges Bataille and Henry Miller*, 1993), and James Decker (*Henry Miller and Narrative Form*, 2005) engage more seriously and subtly with Miller's approach to suffering but do not fully recognize his use of cruelty as a deliberate ploy to expose the discrepancy between peoples' complex reactions to misery and the spectacle they stage for the outside world.

The apparent antihumanism, I argue, masks an emphatic attempt to understand and improve the human condition to redefine "sympathy," "empathy," and "compassion" in a way that takes count of the full complexity of human experience. As Miller's friend Lawrence Durrell recognized in one of his many letters to him, this was a method designed to "do down...the dreadful sentimentality which disguises brutality."[16] It is at its most extreme and most effective when applied to the various homeless characters that populate the texts. In "Max", Miller's account of his friendship in Paris with a near-suicidal American beggar, he tests the social pressure to display compassion toward destitute and marginalized people against the actual feelings induced by direct contact with them. Indeed, in a retrospective preface to "Max" in 1959's *The Best of Henry Miller*, he claims that "it was from the despised and neglected ones that I learned about life, about God, and about futility of 'doing good'" (134). "There are some people," he goes on "to whom you feel immediately attracted, not because you like them, but because you detest them. You detest them so heartily that your curiosity is aroused; you come back to them again and again to study them, to arouse in yourself a feeling of compassion which is really absent" (CE, 8). As with the unfortunate Peckover in *Cancer*, Miller relishes his sadistic use of Max for experimental artistic purposes: "Today I'm going to listen to you, you bugger" he goes on, again in an aside to the reader rather than to his subject's face, "listen to every nuance. I'll extract the last drop of juice—and then, *overboard you go!*" (CE, 18).

For Miller, the catchall principle of "doing good" is futile because it denies the visceral repulsion that materially and psychologically comfortable people inevitably experience in the presence of the materially and psychologically destitute. He is fascinated by the disjunction between what he regards as an irrepressible physical rejection of the sight and smell of the poor and the respectable face of pity ordinarily presented to the world. Passing a group of homeless people sleeping by a metro station in *Cancer*, he expresses this in terms that call to mind "A Modest Proposal," Jonathan Swift's eighteenth-century satire, in which Swift famously proposes feeding the poor on the meat of their own children:

Even the dead horses and the cows and sheep hanging from the greasy hooks look more inviting ... these filthy beggars lying in the rain, what purpose do they serve? What good can they do us? They make us bleed for five minutes, that's all. (CAN, 245-246)

By the use of extreme and provocative irony, pity is posited as superficial and self-serving, not a genuine attempt to sympathize with or help the poor but a compulsive, temporary distraction from the feelings of disgust, anxiety, and powerlessness that overwhelm the observer.

This is presumably one of the reasons for George Bataille's positive appraisal in "La Morale de Miller," written in 1946 for the "Comité de défense d'Henry Miller," a group to protect their American peer against an impending obscenity charge. Bataille proposes reading *Cancer* and *Capricorn* "as though the author wanted them to be 'a search for moral values lost.'"[17] Miller is, Bataille argues, the rare example of an adult artist "in exile from childhood," able to "maintain the shifty attitude of the child" by upholding the "dangerously inconvenient" premise that "life's meaning is intrinsically linked to the negation of restraint." In line with this, Bataille's essay "The Psychological Structure of Fascism" (1938) posits "charitable pity" as a "shameless evasion" of the true excessive repulsion felt in the presence of absolute dejection: "The nauseating forms of dejection provoke a feeling of disgust so *unbearable* that it is improper to express or even to make allusion to it."[18] Like Bataille, Miller understands "material poverty" and "abjection" as excessively truthful states that somehow supersede moral judgment. These aspects of human experience belong, in Bataille's view, to "the heterogeneous world," a sphere of existence separate from and unclassifiable within conventional societal definitions of virtue and vice, good and evil.[19] "The impoverished classes," he goes on to say are one of "numerous elements or social forms that *homogeneous* society is powerless to assimilate."[20]

Heterogeneity is, Bataille writes, "everything rejected by *homogeneous* society as waste or as superior transcendent value."[21] He envisions society as a body that deems itself healthy as long as it can exclude the heterogeneous, and material poverty as foreign matter it cannot physically accept or incorporate. Conditions of destitution are rejected by homogeneous society, Bataille suggests, because they carry with them the warning of "*excessive* consequences"; namely the terrifying prospect that established structures of thought, morality, and government might be overthrown.[22] Indeed, because of the "abjection" experienced and represented by the materially and socially destitute, contact with them is as overpowering as contact with symbols of the divine:

The theme of sacred poverty—impure and untouchable—constitutes precisely the negative pole of a region characterized by the opposition of two extreme forms ... an identity of opposites between glory and dejection, between exalted and imperative (higher) forms and impoverished (lower) forms.[23]

The ordinary, materially and socially functional human being is therefore as distanced from the materially and socially defunct human being as he is from the heroic and "exalted" figures represented in myth and religion. "Exalted" and "impoverished" forms of life impose an equally "insuperable gap" between themselves and the rest of humanity—the cause of unparalleled terror in the nonabject, nondivine ordinary human being.[24]

Miller shares Bataille's belief that the "excessive consequences" of material poverty are a source of disgust but also desire. To him, the feeling of "disgust" comes from the destitute figure's externalization of all that we fear—in particular, our own mortality. The homeless person's totemic representation of truths beyond the realms of conventional moral judgment forces the viewer to confront his or her own limitations and fears. "Everything [Max] said," Miller writes:

> was true, horribly true.... People don't want to hear these truths. They *can't* hear them, for the reason that they're all talking to themselves in the same way. The only difference is that Max said them aloud, and saying them aloud he made them seem objective. (CE, 11)

In this instance, Miller refers to Max's compulsive vocalization of his neuroses—a mode of involuntary expression that, in many ways, reflects Miller's own creative method—but the same is also true for the latter's physical appearance. Indeed, Max's prematurely aged face and ill-fitting suit are active symbols, Miller says, for all the "woes...miseries...disease...unemployment" in the world (10). Physically and psychologically dysfunctional characters are terrifying, Miller suggests, because they denote the frightened, unhinged private selves concealed by those who—in Bataille's words—"consider themselves the expression of normal man."[25] These characters also symbolize a series of genuine reasons to be frightened. By accepting and expressing his own fear, hatred, disgust, and attraction rather than suppressing and masking these with the neutral language of charitable pity, Miller posits himself as liberated from the collective lies of moral certainty, respectability, and altruism.

Another related collective illusion he intends to challenge is the premise that all intellectual and moral positions are equally valid, an intention that apparently conflicts with his larger interest in the pluralist theories popularized by French philosopher Henri Bergson in the 1910s and 20s. The narcissism of Miller's infantile, explosive invectives—summed up when he says to Sylvester, "Fuck your two way of looking at things! Fuck your pluralistic universe..." (CAN, 61)—appears anathematic to his Bergsonian faith in what he describes, in the 1933 essay "Un Etre Etoilique," as "the multiplicity of things" (CE, 282) and refers to later in *Cancer* as the understanding "that everything was justified, supremely justified" (100). Indeed, as I mentioned at the beginning of this chapter, Miller's absolute tolerance exists side-by-side with a pronounced refusal to tolerate any contradictory point of view. Both Sarah Garland and Caroline Blinder note that Bergson's 1911 text *Creative Evolution*—in which he asserts subjective reality as continually evolving and human beings as universally capable of liberating themselves psychologically and emotionally by accepting "the intuitive nature of the human consciousness"—had a profound impact on Miller's worldview. In *Tropic of Capricorn*, he describes the moment he discovered Bergson's book as one of perceptual and emotional epiphany:

> Everything which before I thought I had understood crumbled, and I was left with a clean slate... everything the brain has labored for a lifetime to assimilate, categorize and synthesize has to be taken apart and reordered. Moving day for the soul! (CAP, 215–216)

This paradox of Miller's aggressive egotism and his simultaneous attraction to philosophically pluralist ideas is connected to a deeper political paradox surrounding Bergson's influence on art at this time. As Henry Mead points out in his 2008 study "T.E. Hulme, Bergson, and the New Philosophy," "Bergson appealed to readers on both the right and the left, those seeking a return to religious certainties on one hand, and those seeking a more radical progressivism on the other."[26] Indeed, T.E. Hulme, Ezra Pound's great friend and philosophical mentor in the 1910s, is exemplary of the incongruous and tense marriage between Bergsonian pluralism and politically radical conservatism during that decade. Hulme's antirenaissance, antihumanist, and antiromantic convictions are curiously relevant to Miller, because both writers embodied a Bergsonian skepticism about the effectiveness of thought structures to capture subjective experience while at the same time used Bergson's philosophy to promote what Hulme, in his essay "Humanism and the Religious Attitude," calls "the breaking up of the humanist attitude" and its replacement by a set of "absolute values."

Next to Hulme, who admired Bergson for his "exploration of... the opposition between immediate experience and organizing concepts," but also believed in order and absolute moral positions, Miller embodies and critiques a very particular early modernist paradox.[27] Hulme opposes humanism on the grounds that when "the reality of... absolute values is lacking, you get a refusal to believe any longer in the radical imperfection of either Man or Nature. This develops logically into the belief that life is the source and measure of all values, and that man is fundamentally good."[28] As a result, he goes on, "the problem of evil disappears, the conception of sin loses all meaning" and people regard "order [as] merely a negative conception."[29] The irony in Hulme's appropriation of Bergson—whose "creative evolution" theory was employed by philosophers like William James to disprove absolute religious moral positions—elucidates the regressive and progressive paradox as well as the simultaneous acceptance of disorder and admiration for hierarchy that lie at the center of Miller's aesthetics. While demonstrating his faith in certain universal values, Miller adhered to the humanist worldview that Hulme attacked, consistently agreeing with the notion that "life is the source and measure of all values, and that man is fundamentally good."[30]

Bataille, once again, offers useful insight into these contradictions, writing that "Miller calls God the Father 'the worm-eaten son of a bitch' [and] 'old goat!' However, if there does exist a God it is Henry Miller."[31] While attempting to denigrate the very principal of fixed systems of moral order, he himself imposes his own particular moral authority on his text. In place of the limited ideas of sympathy critiqued in "Max", he envisions an improved approach to suffering that is founded on the Bergsonian premise of existence as infinitely various and interpenetrating, with contrasting elements that are all equally justifiable, but he presents this in terms of a *religious conversion*. Indeed, in a 1933 letter to his then lover and literary ally Anaïs Nin, intended to justify his recent indifference to her feelings of depression, he writes:

> It's a very human condition which lifts you, temporarily at least, above so many useless problems and vexations. You just can't be made wretched, sorrowful, miserable. You live there for a while, at the apex of clarity, and you see things with the naked eye and everything looks good, *is* good. It's almost like getting religion— only so much better, so much more sane. (LP, 159)

"Compulsive" morality—determined, Miller claims by "that great sympathy which makes men like Guatama and Jesus seem divine" (CAN, 100)—can be productively replaced by a code that is both more and less tolerant, a way of reacting to suffering that sympathizes with all behavior and experience and therefore gives the appearance of sympathizing with none. Like his claim that "everything was ... supremely justified," Miller's ideas about "sympathy" are permeated by the presumption of absolute authority and the refusal to consider the person he addresses. By assuming his own position at the "apex of clarity" and dismissing Nin's emotional issues as "useless problems and vexations," he suggests a state of omniscience and benevolence that is presented as wholly compassionate and also entirely self-fixated.

According to this scheme, objective distance leads to a stronger sense of communion between people. Rather than reacting under societal, psychological conditioning to other peoples' pain, the enlightened observer perceives that pain clearly, "sanely" in the context of the multiplicity of experience and is able to respond with humor and genuine compassion. This is manifested in *Cancer* through outpourings of laughter and tears that propel the individual beyond rational moral judgment and demonstrate the futility of struggling against suffering. In *Cancer*, while counseling his American friend Fillmore about his turbulent relationship with a French woman, Miller presents crying as a process of pure, unmitigated emotional release, a way of neutralizing anguish:

> He just let everything gush forth. Jesus, I thought to myself, that's fine to have a release like that. Fine to be a complete coward at least once in your life. To let go that way. Great! Great! It did me so much good to see him break down that way that I felt as though I could solve any problem. I felt courageous and resolute. (CAN, 311)

Surrendering the body to the true extremity of negative emotions is posited as natural and incontestably good; like Miller's refusal to pity Max, it is an antidote to the collective lie of mental and moral robustness. Laughter, he claims, is valuable for a similar reason: it is instinctive rather than cerebral, a spontaneous physical reaction that demonstrates the acceptance of tragedy, suffering, guilt, and humiliation as integral parts of life. In the moment of laughter, the mind—so used to searching for reasons as to why something has happened, what the self truly feels, how the self should respond—is relieved of the desire to make these connections:

> ... when you laugh until the tears flow and your belly aches, you are really opening the skylight and ventilating the brains. Nobody can persuade you at that moment to take a gun and kill your enemy; neither can anybody persuade you to open a fat tome containing the metaphysical truths of the world and read it. (CAP, 302)

This progressive, pacifistic attempt to free the mind and body from the restrictions of intellect and conscience also carries with it exactly the totalitarian implications that Ezra Pound was attracted to in Miller. Just as Hulme used Bergson's intuition theory to validate moral religious absolutes, Pound appropriated Miller's faith in the liberating power of instinct to corroborate his own deeply suspect aspirations for "A New Era"[32] that would replace "the present chaos."[33] A brilliant and sensitive poet who turned to Mussolini's fascism as a "constructive"[34] foil for what he saw as "the running sore" of weak literature, venal "Semitic" capitalism, and "cow-towing" corrupt liberal democracy, Pound's admiration for Miller's "incurably healthy" prose demonstrates the dangers implicit in *Cancer*'s brutal attack on limiting bourgeois values. This unlikely and unintended meeting of minds is perfectly illustrated by the fact that Miller ridiculed Pound's attempt—via their mutual acquaintance James Laughlin—to get him "to swing the bat for his crazy economic theories." Regardless of these misgivings, Miller shares Pound's (and Italian fascism's) rage at the futility of cerebral ideas—and particularly the "Lutheran" "... doctrine of cleanliness, to say nothing of righteousness" (CAP, 3)— to truly reflect and improve the human condition, opting instead for solutions residing physically in the body. While Pound regards "belief" and "doctrine"—religious, political, and social—as "a cramp"[35] and calls for the reinstatement of "ideas which are in one's stomach or liver,"[36] Miller writes that man "will debauch himself with ideas" (CAN, 101), claiming that genuine "ideas are related to living: live ideas, kidney ideas, intestinal ideas" (246).

Miller's positioning within this gray area between early twentieth-century extreme right-wing ideologies and avant-garde artistic movements is comprehensively dealt with by Caroline Blinder in her study *A Self-Made Surrealist* and Paul Jahshan in *Henry Miller and the Surrealist Discourse of Excess* (2001). Miller was part, Blinder suggests, of a wider "totalizing attempt—especially 'metaphysical'—to define what is mystical and universal."[37] A more extreme but equally helpful analysis can be found in Gilles Mayné's 1993 study *Eroticism in Georges Bataille and Henry Miller*:

> Under the guise of liberalism, Miller's universe hides the most cynical, dangerous realities. His transforming evil into a good does not make evil a "lesser" entity but, on the contrary... the "worst" evil: evil not felt as an evil and just performed without the awareness of it (although with a certain pleasure); the icy evil of brutal force; evil legitimated, legalized and institutionalized—made a totalitarian system.[38]

Miller is condemned here for overthrowing the tyranny of bourgeois taboo and "fearful" conceptions of right and wrong only to inadvertently replace them with a totalitarian system equally tyrannical but less stable. Echoing Bataille's analysis of a writer who is omnipotent and unaccountable in his own text, Mayné explains that Miller's transgression is predicated on destructive, reactionary motives rather than a desire to improve the world.

Although this correctly highlights something of the antihumanist/humanist reversal that takes place in Miller's work, I argue that the connections to Pound, Hulme, and their radical conservative beliefs do not imply a genuine "totalitarian" bent, much less an affiliation with political fascism. Indeed, when reading Miller's 1930s writings it is useful to keep in mind Orwell's chastisement in 1941 of the "pert...orthodoxy-sniffers" who sifted through author's works for evidence of their fascist affiliations.[39] What the crossover between Miller and these staunchly antihumanist writers does indicate is an incongruous but inescapable conservatism at the root of his otherwise subversively progressive project. In the quest to assert *Cancer* as an alternative to literature "in the ordinary sense of the word" (2) and to offer his narrative persona as a moral "tonic" to the insipid, bourgeois norm (HMW, 155), Miller assimilated much of the aggressive, absolutist rhetoric practiced by his Anglo-American early modernist predecessors. It is productive and intriguing to consider just how dramatically at odds this language is to his wider political ideology. The vitriolic attack on a weak, cuckolded man in *Cancer*, the sadistic manipulation of a vulnerable derelict in "Max" laid the early groundwork for a moral philosophy built on a utopian and radically inclusive vision of human relations. As Miller writes in his 1945 book *Sunday After the War*, the endgame is "a totally new conception of individuality...in which for the first time since the dawn of history, men will serve one another, first out of an enlightened self-interest, and finally out of a greater conception of love" (SAW, 150). Above all, an awareness of the complex paradoxes inherent in this—between anarchy and order, Bergsonian multiplicity and absolutism, control and excess—help to dispel convenient myths about Miller either as a pernicious purveyor of harmful essentialism or, in the words of 1960s David Littlejohn, a writer who is "above or below, or beyond, or apart from our most intimate social concerns."[40]

Notes

1 Ezra Pound, "Review of *Tropic of Cancer*," in *Critical Essays on Henry Miller*, ed. Ronald Gottesman (New York: G.K. Hall & Co., 1992), 88.
2 Edmund Wilson, "Twilight of the Expatriates," *Critical Essays on Henry Miller*, ed. Ronald Gottesman (New York: G.K. Hall & Co., 1992), 92.
3 George Orwell, "Inside the Whale," in *Collected Essays*, ed. Harvill Secker (London: Secker & Warburg, 1961), 128.
4 Sarah Garland, "'The Dearest of Cemeteries:' European Intertexts in Henry Miller's *Tropic of Cancer*," *The European Journal of American Culture* 29 (2010): 198.

5   Salman Rushdie, "Outside the Whale," in *Imaginary Homelands: Essays and Criticism 1981-1991* (London: Granta Books, 1991.), 95.
6   Wyndham Lewis, "Fashion," in *Wyndham Lewis the Artist*, ed. by Wyndham Lewis (London: Laidlaw & Laidlaw, 1939), 268.
7   Pound, "Review of *Cancer*," 88.
8   Pound, "Review of *Cancer*," 87.
9   Ezra Pound, "Dr Williams' Position," *The Literary Essays of Ezra Pound*, edited and with an introduction by T.S. Eliot (London: Faber & Faber, 1954), 392.
10 Ezra Pound, "How to Read," *The Literary Essays of Ezra Pound*, ed. and with intro. by T.S. Eliot (London: Faber & Faber, 1954) 21.
11 Ezra Pound, "Ulysses," *The Literary Essays of Ezra Pound*, ed. and with an introduction by T.S. Eliot (London: Faber & Faber, 1954), 407.
12 T.E. Hulme, "Humanism and the Religious Attitude," in *Speculations—Essays on the Humanism and Philosophy of Art*, ed. by Herbert Read (London: Kegan Paul, 1924), 157.
13 Kate Millett, *Sexual Politics* (London: Rupert Hart-Davis, 1969), 295.
14 Millett, *Sexual Politics*, 295.
15 Kenneth Rexroth, "The Reality of Henry Miller," in *Critical Essays on Henry Miller*, ed. Ron Gottesman (New York: G.K. Hall, 1992), 99.
16 Lawrence Durrell, "An Interview with Lawrence Durrell," in *Lawrence Durrell: In Conversation*, ed. Earl G. Ingersoll (London: Fairleigh Dickinson University Press, 1998).
17 Georges Bataille, "The Psychological Structure of Fascism," in *Visions of Excess: Selected Writings, 1927-39*, ed. and with introduction by Allan Stoekl, translated by Allan Stoekl with Carl R. Lovit and Donald M. Leslie, Jr (Manchester: Manchester University Press, 1985), 144.
18 Georges Bataille, "La Morale de Miller," *Critique—Revue Generale des Publications Francaises et Etrangeres*, transl. by Caroline Blinder 1 (Juin 1946): 3-17. The issue also includes work by Jean Paul Sartre, Albert Camus, André Breton, and Paul Eluard.
19 Bataille, "Fascism," 142.
20 Bataille, "Fascism," 146.
21 Bataille, "Fascism," 142.
22 Bataille, "Fascism," 144.
23 Bataille, "Fascism," 146.
24 Bataille, "Fascism," 144.
25 Bataille, "Fascism," 144.
26 Henry Mead, "T.E. Hulme, Bergson, and the New Philosophy," *European Journal of English Studies* 12(2008): 245.
27 Rebecca Beasley, *Theorists of Modernist Poetry—T.S Eliot, T.E Hulme, and Ezra Pound* (London: Routledge, 2007), 26.
28 Hulme, "Humanism," 47.
29 Hulme, "Humanism," 47.
30 Hulme, "Humanism," 47-48.
31 Bataille, "La Morale de Miller," 2.
32 Ezra Pound, *Guide to Kulchur* (London: Peter Owen, 1952), 253.
33 Pound, "Review of *Cancer*," 88.
34 Ezra Pound, *Jefferson and/or Mussolini* (London: Stanley Nott, 1935), 110.
35 Ezra Pound, "Axiomata," in *Manifesto—A Century of Isms*, ed. Mary Ann Caws (London: University of Nebraska Press, 2001), 260. Originally published in *New Age*, 28 (1921).

36 Pound, *Kulchur*, 57.
37 Caroline Blinder, *A Self-Made Surrealist-Ideology and Aesthetics in the Work of Henry Miller* (London: Camden House, 2000).
38 Gilles Mayné, *Eroticism in Georges Bataille and Henry Miller* (Birmingham: Summa, 1993), 167.
39 Orwell, "Inside the Whale," 129.
40 David Littlejohn, "The Tropics of Miller" in *Three Decades of Criticism*, ed. with introduction by Edward B. Mitchell (New York: New York University Press, 1971), 104.

6

Tropic of Cancer: Word Becoming Flesh

Ondřej Skovajsa

Sit awhile wayfarer,
Here are biscuits to eat and here is milk to drink.

Leaves of Grass

The word must become flesh; the soul thirsts.
… we must search for fragments, splinters, toenails,
anything that has ore in it,
anything that is capable of resuscitating the body and soul.

Tropic of Cancer (CAN, 103)

Miller writes voice. Drawing sap from Whitman's *Leaves of Grass*, *Cancer* breaks in a radical fashion with literature ("this is not a book, in the ordinary sense of the word" (CAN, 2)) in order to question the linear and meager narrative of modernity, and to resurrect the readers' bodies, emotions, and dignity. In other words, Miller's textual *I* ventures to *kill* the reader to a more courageous and perceptive life, if the reader is willing to suspend the hermeneutics of the suspicion, and approach *Tropic of Cancer* with "hermeneutics of hunger."[1] The present chapter examines how this is achieved, drawing on linguistic, anthropological, and theological aspects of oral theory, while moving from *paratextual* level to *style*, *genesis*, *ethos*, and finally the *story* of the *I*. Terminologically, the study embraces terms appropriate to *Cancer*'s oral and kinetic theopoetics, such as "composition," "text," and "cadences."

Already at the *paratextual* level, we witness traits bringing the book close to a premodern, preprint milieu: the absence of chapters (a product of textual discourse of disciplining the text under a heading), an obscene nonliterary cover with a crab holding a female body, designed by the fourteen-year-old Maurice, the son of the Obelisk Press owner Jack Kahane, and wrapped with signs in both English and French: "NOT TO BE IMPORTED TO GREAT BRITAIN OR USA" and "*Ne doit* être *exposé* en étalage ou en vitrine," as if these were stickers on a jar of poison or a box of explosives. As premodern/preprint intention, we can also view Miller's original intention to publish the book anonymously,[2] in line with *Lyrical Ballads* (1798), *Nature* (1836), and *Leaves of Grass* (1855), initially "anonymous" publications.[3]

Regarding *stylistic* features, *Cancer* attacks by the predominant *present* tense, the *deep posteriority* and *irony* of literature and drawing near the *futurality*, *kinetism*, and *efficacy* of both the spoken word and the biblical word. The latter, according to James Nohrneberg's study, aims "outside" the text, to nourish and shape the life of the readers/believers ("Being efficacious by nature ... biblical words ... obtain a purchase upon the future ... they are kind of signposts that have a pointer at one end").[4] Parts of *Cancer*, written in the past tense, like the one in Lycée Carnot in Dijon, then symptomatically represent *I*'s "stasis of life-flow."[5] Further, prominent stylistic category is the brash first person singular, which, following Whitman's lead, communicates a message to the YOU of the reader. "Let us living ones dance about the rim of the crater, a last expiring dance. But a dance!" (CAN, 260). This differs sharply from William Wordsworth's "bucket" metaphor of the "overflow" of calmly recollected emotion. We find in *Cancer* also a plethora of questions, insults, orders, or pieces of advice to the reader, or perhaps to a beginning writer: "The thing is, never to be too anxious. Everything comes in due time" (318). Miller's lexis is colloquially American with plenty of French, italics, and from the very beginning Miller also stresses his role of a bard, who "sings" with his "mouth" and his "pair of lungs" (2).

In Miller's attempt to *write voice*, the usage of *parallelism* is crucial. Marcel Jousse (1886–1961) interprets the general function of parallelism as *mnemonic*, connected with and involving the bilateral symmetry of human body and the rhythmical breath with the span of pronouncing 15–17 syllables.[6] Jousse illustrates this on the first verses of John: "In the beginning was the Word, and the Word was with God, and the Word was God. The same was in the beginning with God (Joh. 1:1–2)," where the illiterate singer rendering the chant—while rocking from leg to leg, gesticulating, and breathing rhythmically—reminds himself of the following by *repeating* the previous.[7] Miller's "voluntary" usage of parallel structure in a text (Miller *wrote* his book, he did not *preach* on a soapbox or just *talk* like Van Norden/Wambly Bald) can thus be seen as the composition's chief structural means of rehabilitation of the body, its "pair of lungs," and the move of its "parallel" limbs. There are repetitive formulas all over *Cancer*, which always serves as a certain mnemonic function to restart with the sentence and add new information. See the incremental, lavish, and copious and joyful repetitions of forms of "singing" right in the opening cadences of the composition:[8]

> I am going to sing for you, a little off key perhaps, but I will sing. I will sing while you croak, I will dance over your dirty corpse.... To sing you must first open your mouth. You must have a pair of lungs, and a little knowledge of music. It is not necessary to have an accordion, or a guitar. The essential thing is to *want* to sing. This then is a song. I am singing.... It is to you, Tania, that I am singing. I wish that I could sing better, more melodiously, but then perhaps you would never have consented to listen to me. You have heard the others sing and they have left you cold. They sang too beautifully, or not beautifully enough. (CAN, 2)

Forms of "singing" are here repeated and always proceeded by specific, incremental chunks of words. This repetitive strategy of *parallelism*—which celebrates creation and "replicates" beauty[9]—is continued throughout *Cancer* using also much wider blocks[10] such as whole sections and paragraphs, not mere sentences. Miller thus attacks the linear, dietetic, and prudent narrative of textual modernity, being born out of the thrifty protestant work ethic. In the quoted paragraphs above, we could have observed Miller even "tasting the consonants,"[11] enjoying the melody of the "singing," and also of the rhythmical strikes of his typewriter. Miller feeds himself and others with words. Parallelism joins forces with still another stylistically oral feature: the "pedagogic" usage of obscenity that often follows a philosophical part. Its main function is "to awaken, to usher in a sense of reality. In a sense, its use by the artist may be compared to the use of miraculous by the masters" (WHO, 186). By the Rabelaisian marriage of the high and low, Miller's text makes the reader laugh and by laughing feel his or her body ("Paff, paff, paff!," CAN, 241).

As to what concerns composition's *genesis*, it was Michael Fraenkel who told Miller "Write as you talk!,"[12] and it was in August 1931 when Miller found his oral, lavish, repetitive, digressive style of writing[13] based to a large extent on incremental sewing together mnemonic formulas of parallelism. After Miller's initial "misfire" books with a plot (*Moloch, Crazy Cock, Clipped Wings*), Miller finds his signature style, his voice, and begins to sew into his newly discovered stylistic frame his previous Parisian notes, letters (especially those to Emil Schnellock), excerpts from reading, parts of his previous sketches, and adding new part to the recycled ones. "So fast and furiously am I compelled to live now that there is scarcely time to record even these fragmentary notes" (CAN, 12). *Cancer*, then, oscillates genre-wise between *journal, confession*, and *spiritual autobiography*, while none of them gains an upper hand for good. *Journal* is a relevant label, because Miller has simply no luxury of bourgeois novelistic plot, composed from the end: "The plot focuses the work in its climax and denouement: a literary work has an interior posteriority, a posterior slant from the beginning."[14] There is no space of this in *Cancer* because of the *I*'s fragmentary existence, what Russian formalists would call Miller's "byt"; his living situation penetrates into the very structure of the composition! "My spirit is dribbling away. She may come back in an hour or so and take the chair from under my ass. How the hell can a man write when he doesn't know where he's going to sit the next half-hour?... Even a bad novel requires a chair to sit on and a bit of privacy" (33). Why *confession*? We may trace here Miller's curious variation on Charles Baudelaire's disgust of bourgeois complacency. For example, in the last part of the book when the *I* virtually sends Fillmore off to America, the *I* takes 2800 francs of his. In the intersubjective world, Miller however kept 800 francs, sending the 2000 to Fillmore's never-to-be French bride.[15] If Miller much later stated, "I much prefer to show the evil side of myself" (HMC, 7), this is already very much present in the biographical tension of *Cancer*. We can also view *Cancer* as *spiritual autobiography* that tells two stories in one, namely, the tale of the author's liberation and the genesis of the book itself.[16] Miller pastes into his "human book" (CE, 161) also private things, which he mythopoetizes, such as his hemorrhoids: "... the sun bleeds like a broken rectum" (CAN, 168). In this, Miller follows Whitman's "Camerado, this is no book; /who touches this, touches a man"[17] and also shares a lot with Czech graphic artist, and a fellow "explosiviste," Vladimír Boudník (1924–1968) who would sometimes insert his sperm on his printing blocks. *Cancer* thus – in an avant-garde fashion – merges "art" and "life" and its very genesis can be viewed in analogy to the sewing formulas of guslar Demail Zogić's and Homer of the Parry-Lord theory: "An oral poem is not composed *for*, but *in* performance."[18]

Since another oral theorist, Eric Havelock, has called the compositions of *Iliad* and *Odyssey* "social encyclopedias,"[19] why don't we talk about a specific "oral" ethos of *Tropic of Cancer* that takes form of uncompromising critique? Miller's *I* diagnoses the rising cultural and social uniformity and sterility of modernity, accompanied by consumerism, industrialism, and militarism as the spreading disease of *cancer*. For Miller, the epicenter of the cultural and social "cancer" is the United States and especially New York. Miller even provides us with the exact date of the beginning of the disease: "In the four hundred years since the last devouring soul appeared, the last man to know the meaning of ecstasy, there has been a constant and steady decline of man in art, in thought, in action" (CAN, 252–253). The "last devouring soul" here is François Rabelais whose birth in 1494 or 1483 roughly matches the discovery of America and inauguration of the printing press. From America the disease of cancer spreads to the rest of the world.

As David Abram has shown, together with Whitman, *Cancer* dismisses the abstractions of "cold" Platonic ideas, which, in Havelock's footsteps, are unthinkable without the scriptural discourse.[20] For Miller, "Ideas have to be wedded into action; if there is no sex, no vitality in them, there is no action. Ideas cannot exist alone in the vacuum of the mind. Ideas are related to living: liver ideas, kidney ideas, interstitial ideas, etc."(246). Together with criticism of insular ideas—very much in the footsteps of Nietzsche—Miller aims at the constructions made out of them: science such as astronomy ("Learning, the empty breadbasket!" 278), institutional religion ("cockroach of a priest," 101), and literary classics ("I thought of the good time I had wasted reading Virgil or wading through such incomprehensible nonsense as *Hermann and Dorothea*. The insanity of it!," 277–278)[21]; political ideologies right or left ("They don't want to see sad faces in Russia; they want you to be cheerful, enthusiastic, lighthearted, optimistic. It sounded very much like America to me. I wasn't born with this kind of enthusiasm," 175); and technological optimism ("More and more the world resembles an entomologist's dream," 168). Accordingly, *Cancer* mechanization has fully penetrated the realm of human life and human relationships. Peckover and Van Norden thus manifest one of the many "martyrs of modern progress" (165). Cartesian disconnection from the "soul" results also in the "hollow," nonanimated bodies such as Van Norden's, who will "never know what it means to die; you can't die if your own proper body has been stolen" (149).

Yet, mere critical diagnosis of sick society does not suffice. In order to kill the reader's life in quiet desperation, Miller, apart from the already discussed means, offers the reader—like Whitman did before him—both the vehicle of the deictic textual *I*, and a record of "personal" example. A kind of "Look, I have come through!" in terms of D.H. Lawrence. Throughout *Cancer*, Miller's textual *I* undergoes several epiphanies and the reader—perhaps a future artist—is invited to share them.

In the *story* throughout *Cancer*, the *I* adopts the role of Christ, the artist. This anchors Henry Valentine Miller's experience (who turned 40 in 1931) onto a religious symbol, thus endowing meaning to his history of years of frustration, providing a "metaphysical grounding" and meaning to his life story[22] that perhaps was in danger of crumbling into chaos. Paris, depicted strikingly ambivalently, serves—already in *Cancer*'s theopoetics—as the very "crucifix" where the *I* gets "picked clean" of remnants of its mere "human" existence (185).

This Christ-the-Artist role is evident already in the "roadmap"[23] of the open cadences where after the first three apocalyptic paragraphs and a transitory fourth paragraph appear the famous lines:

> I have no money, no resources, no hopes. I am the happiest man alive. A year ago, six months ago, I thought that I was an artist. I no longer think about it, I *am*. Everything that was literature has fallen from me. There are no more books to be written, thank God (1–2).

We learn that the *I* does not possess what a modern person considers as absolutely necessary prerequisites for happiness: money, resources, and hopes. These ambitions died somewhere in Villa Borgese/Seurat; the new *I* was born in realizing the Nietzschean "death of the metaphysics," and of being tired of the Cartesian modernity's ontological *cogito/dubito*, the *I* does not want to "think," it affirmatively "is" ("an artist"). The "AM" appears both as a copula to syntactically link the *I* with the "artist" and as a full verb, brashly alluding both the biblical "I AM" (Ex. 3:14; Joh. 8:58),[24] and from here Quakers, Coleridge, and Whitman's "I AM." Miller's *I* shakes off the embracing of modern doubt together with modernity's print culture with the affirmation of being the "happiest man alive." The Christ-the-Artist role is reminiscent of Whitman's savage *I* arisen after his realizing "the usual mistake,"[25] of D.H. Lawrence's Christ in *The Man Who Died* (1931), and of the theologian's Dorothee Soelle's "happy" Christ, "who risked saying 'I' without support or backing."[26]

The opening cadences indeed foreshadow the crucial *epiphany* at the end of the first third of the book, after the I's humiliation at Nanantatee's (78–90) and after "young Gandhi's" hilarious accident in the bidet of the luxurious Parisian brothel (95–97). The very epiphany, however, happens inside of a cheap brothel with "pandemonium in the air" (99). The *I* suddenly perceives that

> everything was justified, supremely justified.... On the meridian of time there is no injustice: there is only the poetry of motion creating the illusion of truth and drama. If at any moment anywhere one comes face to face with the absolute, that great sympathy which makes men like Gautama and Jesus seem divine freezes away. (100)

These sentences stand at the backdrop of Nietzsche's *The Birth of Tragedy*: "Whatever exists is alike just and unjust, and equally justified in both respects,"[27] and "for only as an *aesthetic phenomenon* is existence and the world *eternally justified.*"[28] Miller's sentences can thus be viewed as the author's self-acceptance of his—possibly also deforming and "unjust" artistic involvement in the world. In contrast to early Nietzsche, whose "tragic view of human existence, both in the sense of myth and mystery and in the sense of aesthetic justification of existence, which...escaped a metaphysical grounding"[29] for Miller reality "escapes" toward a metaphysical *absolute*, which "justifies" reality, yet the absolute remains indifferent to life. In other words, *the only thing we can expect from the absolute is to expect nothing*. This joyful and vitalizing realization, which comes from "the absolute hopelessness of everything" (102)—here differing strongly from Whitman's analogous epiphany "kelson of creation is love"[30]—Miller soon confirms with a scatological image: "And so I think what a miracle it would be if this miracle which man attends eternally should turn out to be nothing more than these two enormous turds which the faithful disciple dropped in the bidet" (101). By this life-affirming "death of illusions" epiphany, the *I* feels finally relieved of his American dream he had been dreaming up to now: "...all my life I had been looking forward to something happening, some intrinsic event that would alter my life, and now suddenly, inspired by the absolute hopelessness of everything, I felt relieved, felt as though a great burden had been lifted from my shoulders" (102).

This beginning of the *via negativa* of the *I* is connected to letting go of the *ego* drives and complete passivity. *I* plunges into the embrace of the dark night of life and professes *amor* fati: "I decided...not to make the least resistance to fate, no matter in what form it presented itself...nothing had been destroyed except my illusions. I myself was intact. The world was intact" (102) and "Even if war were declared, and it were my lot to go, I would grab the bayonet and plunge it, plunge it up to the hilt" (102). With the epiphany of indifferent *absolute*, everything that is not *necessary* is left behind: that is, the *I*'s artistic ambitions, expectations from life, and utopian illusions—such as the American dream—all "die." The death of heteronymous ethics and the temporary death of sympathy follow. The *I* sums up and points the way:

> I am only spiritually dead. Physically I am alive. Morally I am free. The world which I have departed is a menagerie. The dawn is breaking on a new world, a jungle world in which the lean spirits roam with sharp claws. If I am a hyena I am a lean and hungry one: I go forth to fatten myself (103).

By claiming "spiritual death" the *I* refuses to let the scriptural "invention" of Platonic isolated ideas shape his soul, and rejects the idea of afterlife, a metaphysical solace. By insisting on being "physically alive," the *I* stresses his own animated body, which Boris, Peckover, and Van Norden lack. "Moral freedom" does not mean immorality, but a temporary suspension of outside ethics in order to find its own autonomous ethics. The *I*'s declared hunger points the course. Is the hyenic *I* here reduced to mere biological existence, like the protagonist of Knut Hamsun's *Hunger*? No, because of Miller's appropriation of John 1:14: "And the Word was made flesh, and dwelt among us."[31] This blasphemy of identification with Christ draws a direct parallel to Whitman's *Is* of "Song of Myself" whose central tenet—similarly like for Miller in *Cancer*—was the death and rebirth of sympathy. At this, crucial Miller's *I* darts to "wed" ideas into action, to "incarnate" *logos*.

What follows are pictures of the new life of the *I*, initial two scenes illustrate the death of sympathy. First is the scene of Peckover's death where the *I* refuses to pretend sympathy like the "guys upstairs" (141). For Miller's *I*, just like for D.H. Lawrence in his willful reading of Whitman, unfelt sympathy leads to morbidity and spiritual death. Peckover is for both Van Norden and the *I* "better off dead than alive" (141). Further illustration of this death of sympathy is Miller's rejoicing in his "little niche" as a proofreader of the *Chicago Tribune* he inherited after dead Peckover. The *I* is totally oblivious to the catastrophes, while relishing them: "They have a wonderful therapeutic effect upon me, these catastrophes which I proofread. Imagine a state of perfect immunity, a charmed existence, a life of absolute security in the midst of poison bacilli.... The world can blow up—I'll be here just the same to put in a comma or a semicolon" (151). By linking proofreader to God, the *I* laughs at the problematic theological attribute of divine *omniscience*,[32] suggesting God's indifference, even sadism: "A good proofreader is a little God Almighty, he's for Sundays only. Sunday is his night off. On Sundays he steps down from his pedestal and shows his ass to the faithful" (151).

Yet, after such passages soon glitter sparks of spontaneous situation ethics, when, first, the *I* speaks for the humiliated and the poor when Van Norden is involved in the machine-like sexual intercourse with a prostitute after the set deal of "fifteen francs" (147). After seeing the girl's face, the *I* "tickles Van Norden on the rump" and exhorts: "For God's sake, Joe, give it up! You'll kill the poor girl" (145). Similarly, after the proofreading hours, we see the *I* speaking in a cheap sawdust bar on behalf of the abused and othered prostitutes and pimps, exhorting the reader: "You don't think that a pimp is inhuman, I hope? A pimp has his private grief and misery, too, don't you forget" (162), and varying Whitman's famous line "And whoever walks a furlong without sympathy walks to his own funeral, dressed in his shroud"[33] with "A man who can walk through the Faubourg Montmartre at night without panting or sweating, without a prayer or a curse on his lips, a man like that has no balls, and if he has, then he ought to be castrated!" (162). This Miller's take on the "Sermon on the Mount" (Mt.5) sharply contrasts previous exulting over textual distance of punctuating catastrophes of the cancerous world in his cozy proofreader's "niche." This ethical call, of course, will be mediated by the text of *Cancer* to the reader only when the course of the text is "fixed," printed, and by the reader hermeneutically resurrected—when the written words turn to flesh in the reader's body, perception, and action.

However, even before the crucifying of the *I* occurs in the last lines of *Cancer*, we witness ambitious reflections on the theme of death and resurrection. Important is the description of the *I*'s almost fatal illness and his cure by the sailor Collins, who fed the *I* with his "yarn:" "he put it on a bit thick, for my benefit... more and more his words actually seemed to caress me" (202). Even more importantly, we see the *I*—in a way of oral "dirty dozens"—to delimit himself from other artists such as Boris/Fraenkel (13, 33), Papini (67–69), Ravel (80), Matisse and Proust (166–170), among others and to sum up his credo, strongly involving of (life-in-)death and rebirth symbolism: the artist has to die to the world, because nonartistic life is a "poor, sorry, miserable affair" (259). For Miller, the loss of ordinary human life is a *tragic* self-sacrifice, much in lines of Nietzsche's *Birth of Tragedy*. Art's roots "lie in a massacre" (252); by *dying* the artist "fecundates the masses" (CE, 108). The *I* had to die to being "human" in order to become an artist, which is a "call" with numinously divine attributes: "Once I thought that to be human was the highest aim a man could have, but I see now that it was meant to destroy me. Today I am proud to say that I am *inhuman*... I can feel the horns sprouting of my temples" (257). The (awakened) "artist" becomes a member of "another race of beings, the inhuman ones" (258). The artist's goal is, however, *humanistic*, or more precisely: Miller evokes traditional role of the artist/shaman in oral societies to heal the sick society—it is to awaken or "contaminate" people in order to restore them to *life* from the inhuman *life-in-death* discourse of modernity, to "overthrow existing values, to make of the chaos about him an order which is his own, to sow strife and ferment so that by the emotional release those who are dead may be restored to life" (256). The artists reinstate what the *I*—after Nietzsche—imagines as a full, oral, prescriptural life: "To paint a pre-Socratic being, a creature part goat, part Titan. In short, to erect a world on the basis of the *omphalos*, not an abstract idea nailed to a cross" (247). The artist achieves this emotional explosion and hereby the reader's revivification by a full *translation* of what is in the heart but "which is omitted in books" (11). Such *aesthetic* is thus for Miller the only cure of the *anesthetic* of modernity. These theoretical musings and aesthetic sermoning, lead—after a contrasting intermezzo in Dijon and dispatching of depressed Fillmore—to the final whitmanesque epiphany.

As the day and the book ends, Miller's *I participates* (see L. Lévi-Bruhl, M. Merleau-Ponty, D. Abram) with the "speaking" landscape body of more-than-human life-world of a green Parisian suburb:

> The sun is setting. I feel this river flowing through meets past, its ancient soil, the changing climate. The hills gently girdle it about: its course is fixed. (321)

The *I* identifies the Seine as his artery: the Seine waters the *I* and the *I* via the now "fixed" course of the text waters Paris and quenches the thirst of the Parisians. The previous Miller's "hyena" version of mystical journey, the *via negativa*, now turns to *via unitiva*, a "cocreation," as described by Dorothee Soelle: "To become one with what was intended in creation has the shape of cocreation; to live in God means to take an active part in the ongoing creation."[34]

Henry V. Miller, the man, is here (cruci)fixed on the tree of his text. Here dies the part of him, which has heretofore been writing, sewing, and nourishing the text, and Miller's life has now gained a "fixed course." *Tropic of Cancer*'s printed, dead words—stuccoed in mnemonic parallelisms—wait to become flesh in the pairs of lungs, arms, legs, tongues, fingertips, and acts of the readers. The I AM jumps out of the grave of the text as a lean and hungry hyena to devour the dead.[35]

Notes

1. Dorothee Soelle, *The Silent Cry: Mysticism and Resistance*, trans. Barbara and Martin Rumscheidt (Minneapolis: Fortress Press, 2001), 45–49.
2. Jay Martin, *Always Merry and Bright: The Life of Henry Miller*, (Santa Barbara: Capra Press, 1978), 227.
3. Miller's Parisian cronies, Michael Fraenkel ("Boris") and Walter Lowenfels ("Cronstadt") also published anonymously as their brochure *Anonymous* (1930).
4. James Nohrnberg, "On Literature and the Bible," *Centrum* 2, 2 (1974): 25.
5. Nesbit, *Henry*, 45.
6. Marcel Jousse, *Le style oral: rhytmique et mnémotechnique chez les verbo-moteurs* (Paris: Traveaux de Laboratorie d´anthropologie rythmo–pédagogique de Paris, 1925), 183–184.
7. Marcel Jousse *The Oral Style*, trans. Edgard Sienaért and Richard Whitaker (New York: Garland, 1990), xxii.
8. This dominant, organic, oral repetition can be seen in contrast to the calculated, deathly, mechanical repetition of the first three paragraphs of the text signifying the multiplication of the cancer germ.
9. Elaine Scarry, *On Beauty and Being Just* (Princeton: Princeton University Press, 1999), 3–8.
10. Roman Jakobson, "Grammatical Parallelism and Its Russian Facet," *Language* 42, 2 (1966): 424.
11. M.H. Abrams, *Fourth Dimension of a Poem and Other Essays* (New York: Norton, 2012), 9.
12. Martin, *Always*, 250.
13. Decker, *Henry Miller and Narrative Form*, 1–25.
14. W.J. Ong, "Maranatha: Death and Life in the Text of the Book," *Journal of the American Academy of Religion* 45, 4 (Dec., 1977): 419–449.
15. Martin, *Always*, 260.
16. Nesbit, *Henry*, 42.
17. Walt Whitman, *Leaves of Grass and Other Writings: Authoritative Texts, Other Poetry and Prose, Criticism*, ed. Michael Moon, Sculley Bradley, and Harold William Blodgett (New York: Norton, 2002), 424.
18. Albert B. Lord, *The Singer of Tales [1960]* (New York: Atheneum, 1971), 13.
19. Eric A. Havelock, *Preface to Plato* (Cambridge, MA: Harvard University Press, 1963), 31.
20. David Abram, *The Spell of the Sensuous* (New York: Vintage, 1997), 112.
21. To prove the antiliterary aim and show disdain of textual perfection in favor of oral multi-variety Miller even leaves an obvious error in *Cancer*. It is simply impossible that the *I* would not tell Fillmore that "princess has the clap" (230–231, 234). Here the *I* follows Lawrence's hatred of "perfection," which is connected to the printing press and embodied in ethics of Benjamin Franklin who, referred to his past mistakes in life as "errata."
22. Clifford Geertz, *Interpretation of Cultures* (New York: Basic Books, 2000), 131.
23. Nesbit, *Henry*, 42.
24. Nesbit, *Henry*, 44.

25 Whitman, *Leaves* (1855 edn.), 957.
26 Soelle, *Silent*, 54.
27 Friedrich Nietzsche, *The Birth of Tragedy and Other Writings*, ed. Raimond Geuss and Ronald Speirs, trans. Ronald Speirs (Cambridge: Cambridge: University Press, 1999), 51.
28 Nietzsche, *The Birth of Tragedy and Other Writings*, 33.
29 Gianni Vattimo, *Nietzsche: An Introduction*, trans. Nicholas Martin (Stanford: Stanford University Press, 2002), 24.
30 Whitman, *Leaves*, (1855 edn.), 86.
31 cf. Nesbit, *Henry*, 44.
32 Similar to the Platonic "ideas," the category of "omniscience" is unthinkable without the medium of writing. "Omniscience" is, of course, a later Greek category and alien to the original text of the Torah.
33 Whitman, *Leaves*, (1855 edn.), 1265.
34 Soelle, *Silent*, 93.
35 Coda: In Miller's work that follows *Cancer*, we can trace the *I* becoming more *literary*: more plotted and past oriented. Present tense is replaced by past tense, there occurs more textual compartmentalization (such as chapter divisions), the principle of organization of experience in the Christ symbol is strengthened and remains in Miller's opus as a whole. After the Second World War, Miller is also less apocalyptic and more humble when speaking about the artist. In the first and main line of his works (*Tropic of Capricorn* and the unfinished *Rosy Crucifixion: Sexus, Plexus, Nexus*), the *I* returns back to hated "Golgotha" of New York and re-writes Henry's and June's love-hate relationship. Second line of Miller's texts (*The Colossus of Maroussi, Big Sur and the Oranges of Hieronymus Bosch*) seems to draw on the ending of *Cancer*, and here Miller seems to reestablish the oral participatory relation with *talking* landscape and its inhabitants, and is generally more focused on the present, Greece and California, respectively. Miller's essays (*Cosmological Eye, Wisdom of the Heart, The Time of Assassins: A Study of Rimbaud, Stand Still like the Hummingbird, Books in My Life, Book of Friends*, etc.) celebrate creation in discussion of artistic and non-artistic works of fellow artists and friends.

7

"A dirty book worth reading": Henry Miller's *Tropic of Cancer* and the Feminist Backlash

Anna Lillios

Arguably, no author of the twentieth century has attracted more controversial attention from feminist critics than Henry Miller. His *Tropic of Cancer*, published in Paris in 1934 but censored in the United States until the Supreme Court declared it nonobscene in 1964, has been a litmus test of sexual mores in America as successive waves of feminists have projected their own idiosyncratic views on Miller's narrative of sexual adventures in 1930s Paris. The feminist assault on Miller, most intense during the height of the second wave of feminism in the 1960s, led Erica Jong to claim that "Miller remains among the most misunderstood of writers—seen either as a pornographer or a guru, a sexual enslaver or a sexual liberator, a prophet or a pervert."[1] If Miller's many facets were "sliced into transparent cubist pieces," as Jay Martin imagines, then critics would have interpreted his self "now this way, now that, a self existing only in its multiplicity."[2] Readers have considered Miller from extreme positions, ranging from viewing him as the embodiment of "a compendium of American sexual neuroses" (Kate Millett) to a "feminist" (Allison Palumbo). What has been missing is the middle ground, the humanist perspective on Miller, which would evaluate his work holistically, not solely on its controversial, racy parts. In *The Devil at Large*, Jong, who considered Miller a friend—or, as Jeanette Winterson says, was "an Athena to Miller's Zeus"[3]—most closely articulates this position in her assessment of *The Colossus of Maroussi*, which she claims was Miller's highest achievement: "He transcended sex and war, as we all must, man and woman both, to become entirely human."[4] This view corresponds to feminists today who believe, as Helen Vendler does, that if "feminism is to succeed it must de-idealize women" in order to celebrate the human.[5] Miller does not reach the point at which he de-idealizes women in his work; yet, he does celebrate the human connection between the sexes.

The twentieth century was the century of the woman, with three waves of feminist movements sweeping through the decades, as women struggled to attain their human rights. The first wave began in 1848 and culminated in the passage of the Nineteenth Amendment to the U.S. Constitution, establishing women's right to vote when it was ratified in 1920. Along with the vote, feminists made progress on the birth control front with the creation of the American Birth Control League in 1921, under the leadership of Margaret Sanger (although it was not until 1965 when women in all states could obtain legal contraceptives). These first-wave feminists "establish[ed] the legal policy that women are human beings and cannot be treated like property."[6] Even though *Tropic of Cancer* appeared over a decade later in 1934, after women achieved suffrage, Miller portrays their continued low position in the novel and their ongoing struggles in the social, political, and economic spheres. The second wave of feminism began after the Second World War when women demanded more rights. They had gone to work in factories and expected to be rewarded with full citizenship for their contribution to the war effort. Their goal was nothing less than "gender equality in [their] social, political, legal, and economic rights."[7] This wave, continuing up until the 1970s, overlapped with the emerging third-wave feminism, which began in the 1990s in response to the belief that feminism was defined by and limited to upper-middle-class white women. Third-wave feminists felt that the center of feminism should be "in the concerns of women of color, lower-class women, lesbians, transgendered women, 'Third World' women, all previously marginalized."[8] Today, there is a lot of debate about whether a fourth wave has emerged. If so, it is amorphous, in the process of being defined, and most likely involves the Internet as a new activist space for feminists. What is certain, though, is that social media has created a "call-out culture," "in which sexism or misogyny can be 'called out' and challenged,"[9] "facilitat[ing] the creation of a global community of feminists who use the Internet both for discussion and activism."[10] Feminists are currently debating whether this activism is leading to transformative change or even a new wave.

When Miller published *Tropic of Cancer* in Paris in September 1934, he was oblivious to the role his book would play in the subsequent evolution of women's rights. He was entirely focused on getting his new book out. He turned into a one-man publicity machine, sending out copies to leading male authors, such as Aldous Huxley, John Dos Passos, Herbert Read, Blaise Cendrars, and Louis-Ferdinand Céline.[11] He was gratified when his novel received the critical acclaim of the male modernist establishment. T.S. Eliot referred to it as "a rather magnificent piece of work"; Huxley found it "a bit terrifying, but well-done"; Dos Passos said it was "certainly interesting"; William Carlos Williams called it "a whore with her pants off for purity and candour"; and Ezra Pound called it "a dirty book worth reading."[12] Miller seemed not too concerned about the female response, sending copies to only a few female writers, such as Emma Goldman, Katherine Anne Porter, and Gertrude Stein. He knew, at least, that he had the whole-hearted approval of his lover, Anaïs Nin, who had traveled to London in search of a publisher for the book and eventually supplied 5,000 francs (about $330) for the printing costs—borrowed from her other lover, Otto Rank.[13] As far as the general female reader was concerned, Miller was only mildly curious about an "ordinary wench's reaction to [his] writing about cunt."[14]

Miller would not have been able to gauge the response of the ordinary American "wench," because censors were seizing the books at the U.S. border under the Tariff Act of 1930. Later, the book was declared obscene in a U.S. district court,[15] causing Miller to feel "frustrated by the lack of American response."[16] His friend Michael Fraenkel tried to circumvent the censors by cutting the books up and sending the pieces to eager readers in the States.[17] Unfortunately for Miller, these legal impediments impacted the sale of the novel and any possibility he had of becoming a part of the American literary canon for thirty years.

When *Tropic of Cancer* was finally released to the American public in 1961 and won its battle in the U.S. Supreme Court in 1964, it was an instant bestseller, reaching a sizable audience. Brisk book sales gave Miller a level of material success and public attention that he had never experienced before. Part of this attention was notoriety because the book appeared at the height of the second wave of American feminism in the 1960s, and, needless to say, caught the notice of feminists. Second-wave feminists in the 1960s were building on the accomplishments of the first-wave feminists and featured female writers, who used works of literature to illustrate how the female "self" had been fabricated by men, embodying "various male fears and anxieties."[18] The most famous—or outrageous, depending on one's viewpoint—of these studies was Kate Millett's *Sexual Politics*, published in 1969. In her book, Millett attacked D.H. Lawrence, Norman Mailer, Jean Genet, and Henry Miller, citing them as examples of "male writers [who] distort women by associating them with (male) deviance." Millett claimed that the "interior colonization" of women by men is "sturdier than any form of segregation," such as class, "more uniform, and certainly more enduring."[19] Focusing on Miller, Millett writes:

> What Miller did articulate was the disgust, the contempt, the hostility, the violence, and the sense of filth with which our culture, or more specifically, its masculine sensibility, surrounds sexuality. And women too, for somehow it is women upon whom this onerous burden of sexuality falls.[20]

Unfortunately, Miller—the writer and the person—became equated in the public mind with this masculine sensibility, irreparably damaging his literary reputation. Allison Palumbo in "Finding the Feminine: Rethinking Henry Miller's *Tropics* Trilogy" contends that "the literary criticism of the burgeoning second-wave feminist movement, which deemed Miller a misogynist, was responsible for discouraging critical interest in his work beyond the few, dedicated inquiries continued by his local academic readership."[21] Second-wave feminists, according to Palumbo, hated Miller's "depersonalization of women" and believed that misogynists like him missed a woman's "metaphorical complexity" when they reduced her to "body parts," which are "metonyms for expressions of the body."[22]

Palumbo, as a third-wave feminist concerned with marginalization and exclusion, attempts to redress the negative image that feminists have created around Miller's persona as an artist. She urges readers to reevaluate Miller in a new light—as a feminist. By analyzing Miller's *Tropics* trilogy—*Tropic of Cancer, Tropic of Capricorn*, and *Black Spring*—she tries to "clarify the subversive nature of Miller's writing to show how his work reflects feminist interests for the way it undermines phallocentric values by envisioning individual expression outside of social constraints."[23] She turns to Hélène Cixous's concept of *écriture féminine* to provide support for her theory. Cixous, explaining how throughout history binary oppositions, such as masculine and feminine, have privileged the masculine, refuses to eliminate these so-called masculine principles ("often stereotypically associated with values like logic, power/control, aggression/ competition, virility, discipline, etc."). Instead, she simply wants to undo or take away "the privilege afforded to those principles at the expense of various others."[24] Going further, Cixous stresses the importance of the marginalized—the "various others"— reasoning that "nothing can be privileged without something else being marginalized."[25] Women, she claims, have traditionally occupied these marginal positions in patriarchal society and know what it is like to be socially inferior. In a radical move, she broadens her definition of "women" to include anyone else who has been marginalized, "who is alienated from their culture, who lives outside the phallocentric value system either by choice or exclusion, shares the same history of subordination as women,"[26] in fact, anyone who "might struggle with conventional man."[27]

In the realm of language, feminine writing—Cixous's *écriture feminine*—has the power to break apart the binaries. When binaries are broken apart, new space is made for diversity, difference, and multiplicity. Feminine texts, which occupy this space, according to Toril Moi, "strive in the direction of difference, struggle to undermine the dominant phallogocentric logic, split open the closure of binary opposition and revel in the pleasures of open-ended textuality."[28] The effect, Cixous says, can be "volcanic."[29] When a writer uses this type of writing, then she or he creates an "impregnable language that will wreck partitions, classes, and rhetorics, regulations and codes."[30]

Palumbo applies these concepts to Miller's work and labels him a feminist writer, because of the way, "his language portrays meaning as an unpredictable and arbitrary signification of ideas."[31] Rosemary Tong agrees that his work is "full of pleasures and, perhaps more importantly, of possibilities" concerning new ways of experiencing the self.[32] He is iconoclastic, reveling in diversity, openness, and multiplicity, because he embraces contradiction as a life principle, feeling that it is an essential element of his artistry. Early in *Tropic of Capricorn*, he realizes this truth:

> Everything that happens, when it has significance, is in the nature of a contradiction. Until the one for whom this is written came along I imagined that somewhere outside, in life, as they say, lay the solution to all things. I thought, when I came upon her, that I was seizing hold of life, seizing hold of something which I could bite into. Instead I lost hold of life completely. I reached out for something to attach myself to—and I found nothing. But in reaching out, in the effort to grasp, to attach myself, left high and dry as I was, I nevertheless found something I had not looked for—*myself*. I found that what I had desired all my life was not to live— if what others are doing is called living—but to express myself. (5)

He finds a space where he can actualize himself as an artist, as he declares at the start of *Tropic of Cancer*: "A year ago, six months ago, I thought that I was an artist. I no longer think about it, I *am*" (1). No longer fearful, he knows that disorder is his friend, giving him the confidence that he has the ability to create his own type of order and land on his feet anywhere. Later on in *Tropic of Capricorn* he can say that "The labyrinth is my happy hunting ground and the deeper I burrow into the maze the more oriented I become" (217).

Sex, of course, is often the means by which Miller becomes disoriented in the labyrinth. His frank exploration of the relationship between men and women has led to the second-wave feminist view that he is a misogynist. Holly Hoffman, as most second-wave feminists would agree, claims that "Miller's greatest sin was in his consistent depersonalization of women," which is "a more subtle form of contempt against women" and is "just as damaging as open violence."[33]

To refute this argument, first of all, Miller as frequently depersonalizes male characters in his novels as he does the female. Men do not escape his scathing notice; they are ruled by their sexual appetites and greed for money (and food) just as women are. Second, sex in Miller's fiction may seem at first demeaning to women, but if read carefully can often be the means of spiritual transcendence, as the following passage from *The Tropic of Capricorn* illustrates:

> I no longer look into the eyes of the woman I hold in my arms but I swim through, head and arms and legs, and I see behind the sockets of the eyes there is a region unexplored, the world of futurity, and here there is no logic whatsoever, just the still germination of events unbroken by night and ay, by yesterday and tomorrow ... I no longer look *into* the eyes or *through* the eyes, but by the legerdemain of will swim through the eyes head and arms and legs, to explore the curve of vision. (115–116)

In fact, later in *Capricorn*, the narrator expands his concept of the female presence in nature to include the whole world. He believes that he is writing about a "New World," which is entirely ruled by this female principle:

> I was describing the New World—unfortunately a little too soon because it had not yet been discovered and nobody could be persuaded that it existed. It was an ovarian world, still hidden away in the fallopian tubes .... Sex was the last thing to be dreamed of; it was the world of Chronos and his ovicular progeny .... The ovarian world is the product of a life rhythm. (CAP, 282–283, 285)

Palumbo interprets this passage to mean that Miller "assigns [the female] body (as a form of 'everybody') nothing less than the role of everything, of possibility. She becomes a metonym for the marginal, the place in writing where there are no limits, exclusions, or constrictions to thought ... he becomes these parts and enters himself from them."[34] The narrator's incorporation of his self into the female principle implies his need for the women's body, in order to achieve this spiritual goal. Sex, thus, often begins in Miller's fiction with a gritty physical act, rising to near religious significance. James Decker explains: "Throughout [*Tropic of Cancer*] Miller dives deep within the gutters only to soar back to the heavens a moment later. Gonorrhea, shit, lice, and hunger dissolve (or explode) into music, art, philosophy, and God ... ."[35]

For this reason, Erica Jong in *The Devil at Large* calls Miller a "wisdom" writer, whose "narrative is far less important to him than the philosophical digressions."[36] She goes on to say, "He embodied in both his writings and his life the paradigm of the writer as the giver of gifts, the voyager into the underworld who comes back with a boon for humankind."[37] She calls him a "transcendentalist in the indigenous American tradition of Thoreau, Emerson, Dickinson, and Whitman."[38]

It is in the endings of Miller's novels, where the philosophical reflections are most common and meaningful. The ending of *Tropic of Cancer* is a good example of Miller's thinking on a higher plane, far from the exigencies of sexual encounters. The narrator in *Cancer*, his adventures in Paris seemingly near an end, is walking along the Seine. He thinks he has done a good deed for a friend by sending him back to America to escape a greedy lover and an equally good deed for himself by pocketing the money the friend had asked him to give to his paramour. The narrator finds himself finally living in the moment: "Everything was close and palpitant, and vibrant with the strong light" (CAN, 319). The depiction of the Seine in this scene is symbolic of a new start, after a cycle has ended, yielding wisdom and self-awareness. The narrator feels changed: "After everything had quietly sifted through my head a great peace came over me. Here, where the river gently winds through the girdle of hills ... there shimmered such a golden peace that only a neurotic could dream of turning his head away .... In the wonderful peace that fell over me it seemed as if I had climbed to the top of a high mountain ..." (CAN, 320).

In a moment of epiphany, the narrator once again imagines that his body is dissolving into nature: "I feel this river flowing through me—its past, its ancient soil, the changing climate. The hills gently girdle it about: its course is fixed" (CAN, 321). These passages are reminiscent of the ending of Eliot's *The Waste Land* (or the fishing trip in Ernest Hemingway's *The Sun Also Rises*). Like Eliot's Fisher King, Miller's narrator idles by the river as he contemplates his rebirth. He feels an overwhelming sense of "Shantih," the same kind of "peace which passeth understanding" that Eliot's narrator experiences at the end of *The Waste Land*. He too is ready to "set [his] lands in order," with the "arid plain behind [him]."

Frederick Turner in his book, *Renegade: Henry Miller and the Making of* Tropic of Cancer, also recognizes that there is a spiritual element in Miller's work. Calling *Tropic of Cancer* "an outlaw book," he says that "it might seem oxymoronic to speak of *Tropic of Cancer* as having a 'moral.' But when stripped of its rhetorical excesses, its comic boasts, its wild contradictions and coprolalia, it does have this spiritual arc."[39]

Today, Miller's reputation has not recovered from the assaults made on it by the second-wave feminists. Unfortunately, radical feminist critics overlook or simply do not want to deal with any spiritual aspect of Miller's work; they remain fixated on its purported violations against their feminist ideals. In 2012, Jeanette Winterson in "The Male Mystique of Henry Miller," reiterated the same second-wave feminist complaints against Miller. In a review of Turner's *Renegade* for the *New York Times Sunday Book Review*, Winterson goes on the attack:

> Miller the renegade wanted his body slaves like any other capitalist—and as cheaply as possible. When he could not pay, Miller the man and Miller the fictional creation worked out how to cheat women with romance. What they could not buy they stole. No connection is made between woman as commodity and the "slaughterhouse" of capitalism that Miller hates.[40]

She cannot accept Turner's judgment that Miller's *Tropic of Cancer* is a "spiritual classic that tells us 'who we are,' " because " 'we' cannot include women, unless a woman is comfortable with her identity as a half-witted 'piece of tail.' "[41] Winterson ends her essay by posing a query: "The question is not art versus pornography or sexuality versus censorship or any question about achievement. The question is: Why do men revel in the degradation of women?"[42]

Views such as the above still remain in the public consciousness, perhaps, irreparably damaging Miller's reputation. James Decker in *Guernica* reports that "Miller would for the rest of his life [after his Supreme Court victory] find himself reduced in the public imagination to a sex writer, a one-dimensional purveyor of smut."[43] Arthur Hoyle in "Remember Henry Miller? Censored Then, Forgotten Now," points out: "... more than thirty years after his death, [Miller] remains a marginalized and largely forgotten American writer."[44] Hoyle claims that, "Miller's star burned brightly and briefly in America, then burned out." Censorship and a moral backlash in this country impacted his literary reputation, causing Hoyle to conclude that "he has been denied his rightful place in the American pantheon."[45]

Hope, though, for a revival of Miller's reputation may come in the still nascent fourth wave of feminism and its emphasis on the humanity that males and females share. Contemporary men and women recognize that yes, there are biological differences between the sexes; but they are also fully aware of the social construction and permeability of sexual orientation. Sexual differences are no longer predictably self-evident in gender determinations nor do the previously marginalized need to be relegated to the category of "the other." In fact, many contemporary young men and women insist on their equality with each other and do not want to be limited by any sexual label. Guerin notes that "Today one hears that young women who have benefited from the dramatic struggles and sacrifices of their foremothers decline to use the term *feminist* to describe themselves. We hear of a backlash against feminism ... ."[46] One can only assume that this backlash is driven by the belief in the equality of the sexes, that one sex should not in any way be privileged over the other. On the scholarly front, Vendler in "Feminism and Literature," does not believe that there is a "female" type of writing or literature. Nor is she sentimental in believing that women have "special virtue," nor "that men, as a class, are base and women are moral." She concludes by stating the controversial view that "a de-idealizing of women is necessary for the women's movement." [47] Allison Palumbo would most likely add that if feminism were to de-idealize women, it must be done in favor of our humanity. Regarding Miller, she writes: "where there was once man and woman, [Miller] saw only the human, with all its complexities and possibilities, with its need to be freed to achieve a deeper, stronger humanity."[48]

In conclusion, if Miller's reputation is to be saved going forward in the twenty-first century, then I believe less attention should be placed on his supposed feminism or his sharp delineation of the sexes, in favor of his humanism. Interestingly enough, this approach may be the one most likely to appeal to the newest generation, the millennials, aged 18–29, who are 50 million strong—a number even greater than the boomers. In "The Millennials are Generation Nice," Sam Tanenhaus attempts to define this generation. According to Tanenhaus, "the millennial generation is skeptical of institutions—political and religious—and prefers to improvise solutions to the challenges of the moment."[49] Part of their skepticism has arisen from the fact that they have "weathered many public catastrophes" (and viewed them on television), such as 9-11, wars in Iraq and Afghanistan, and the recession. As a result, they are "a complex and introspective generation," according to a Pew Research Center report on the Millenials entitled "Confident. Connected. Open to Change" (2010).

The millennials' skepticism toward institutions is reminiscent of Miller's rants against American capitalism, materialism, and greed. Hoyle summarizes Miller's views:

> Miller believed that only the individual could be saved from the fate that awaited mass man, a fate that he likened to a living death in which people mechanically lived their lives in obedience to ignorant and inhuman taboos. Social movements, political revolutions, only produced more of the same. For Miller, the way to individuation was through art, and it was the role of the artist to point the way for others by being an example of how to escape the prevailing system and achieve personal freedom.[50]

Miller would probably be pleased to see how millennials shun the materialism of earlier generations in favor of their individuality and sense of freedom, as Tanenhaus explains: "Thanks to the 2008 economic crash, millennials know how fleeting wealth can be. Their solution? For many, it is to acquire not more, but less." In a Brookings Institution report, "How Millennials Could Upend Wall Street and Corporate America," Morley Winograd and Michael Hais claim that "Almost two-thirds (64 percent) of millennials said they would rather make $40,000 a year at a job they love than $100,000 a year at a job they think is boring." Instead, "Generation Nice" has "embraced its own mode of entrepreneurship, found across the broad spectrum of 'creatives,' from stylist to techies, who reject the presumed security of the corporate job and riskily pursue their own ventures ... ."[51] Like Miller, they would go to Paris to work on their art and live in poverty. But, they would also work as volunteers in the Peace Corps, AmeriCorps, or Teach for America. And, like the residents of the Villa Seurat, they support each other's artistic efforts by practicing "communalism." Tanenhaus concludes, though, that Generation Nice's communalism's "highest value isn't self-promotion, but its opposite, empathy—an open-minded and—hearted connection to others."[52] Miller, too, throughout his work, creates characters that radiate this embracing connection to others. When he portrays both women and men who are base and moral, he is simply celebrating their common humanity.

Notes

1. Erica Jong, *The Devil at Large* (New York: Turtle Bay, 1993), 3.
2. Martin, *Always*, 293.
3. Winterson, "The Male Mystique of Henry Miller," *The New York Times*.
4. Jong, *Devil*, 195.
5. Helen Vendler, "Feminism and Literature," *New York Review of Books* 31 May 1990: 23.
6. Wildred L. Guerin, et al., eds., *A Handbook of Critical Approaches to Literature*. 6th ed. (New York: Oxford University Press, 2011), 254.
7. Guerin, *Handbook*, 255.
8. Guerin, *Handbook*, 256.
9. Ealasaid Munro, "Feminism: A Fourth Wave?" *Political Studies Association (UK)*. n.pag. Web. 22 Sept. 2014.
10. Munro, "Feminism: A Fourth Wave?".
11. Mary Dearborn, *The Happiest Man Alive: A Biography of Henry Miller* (New York: Simon and Schuster, 1991), 173; Ferguson, *Henry*, 240.
12. Ferguson, *Henry*, 237, 240.
13. Ferguson, *Henry*, 229.
14. Dearborn, *Happiest*, 174.
15. Hoyle, *Unknown*, 1.
16. Dearborn, *Happiest*, 173.
17. Dearborn, *Happiest*, 173–174.
18. Guerin, *Handbook*, 255.
19. Kate Millett, *Sexual Politics* (New York: Avon, 1969), 255–256.
20. Millett, *Sexual Politics*, 295.
21. Allison Palumbo, "Finding the Feminine: Rethinking Henry Miller's *Tropics* Trilogy," *Nexus: The International Henry Miller Journal*, 7 (2010): 145.
22. Palumbo, "Finding," 168.
23. Palumbo, "Finding," 145.
24. Palumbo, "Finding," 148.
25. Palumbo, "Finding," 147.
26. Palumbo, "Finding," 149.
27. Hélène Cixous, "The Laugh of the Medusa," Trans. Keith and Paula Cohen, *Signs* 1, 4 (1976): 875.
28. Toril Moi, *Sexual/Textual Politics: Feminist Literary Theory* (London: Routledge, 1985), 108.
29. Cixous, "Laugh," 888.
30. Cixous, "Laugh," 886.
31. Palumbo, "Finding," 151.
32. Rosemarie Tong, *Feminist Thought: A Comprehensive Introduction* (Boulder: Westview, 1989), 225.
33. Holly Hoffman in Palumbo, "Finding," 168.
34. Palumbo, "Finding," 169.
35. Decker, James M. "Henry Miller's Pyrrhic Victory." *Guernica*. 3 Oct. 2012.
36. Jong, *Devil*, 237.
37. Jong, *Devil*, 47.
38. Jong, *Devil*, 47–48.

39 Frederick Turner, *Renegade: Henry Miller and the Making of* Tropic of Cancer (New Haven: Yale University Press, 2011), 210.
40 Winterson, "The Male Mystique of Henry Miller," *New York Times*.
41 Winterson, "The Male Mystique of Henry Miller," *New York Times*.
42 Winterson, "The Male Mystique of Henry Miller," *New York Times*.
43 Decker, "Henry."
44 Arthur Hoyle, "Remember Henry Miller? Censored Then, Forgotten Now." *The Huffington Post Books*. 14 May 2014.
45 Hoyle, "Remember Henry Miller?," *The Huffington Post Books*.
46 Guerin, *Handbook*, 300.
47 Vendler, "Feminism," 22–23.
48 Palumbo, "Finding," 172.
49 Sam Tanenhaus, "Generation Nice," *The New York Times*, 17 Aug. 2014, 1, 7.
50 Hoyle, *Unknown*, 10.
51 Tanenhaus, "Generation," 7.
52 Tanenhaus, "Generation," 7.

8

Henry Miller: Obscene Other of the Law

Rob Herian

Let each one turn his gaze inward and regard himself with awe and wonder, with mystery and reverence; let each one promulgate his own laws, his own theories; let each one work his own influence, his own havoc, his own miracles. Let each one as an individual, assume the roles of artist, healer, prophet, priest, king, warrior, saint.

Henry Miller (CE, 174–175)

Introduction

Ban Henry Miller!

Do it, as this might be the only way to save what is truly great about this writer. Take his books from the shelves. Put them out of the reach and the delectation of the public. Take them from the musty, dusty shelves of the bookshop. Hide Miller's books from the lustful, hungry roving eyes and the all-consuming gaze. Wrap Miller's *Tropics* and his triadic *Rosy Crucifixion* in deep circumspection. Disguise and mask if you like in the improvised jacket of the bootlegged edition, just make sure those books slip from the conscious imaginings of the many. Conceal, disavow, reject, deny, overlook, but above all let the mainstream and all those that jump on the fashion wagon once more return to a state of blissful ignorance where Miller is concerned.

But it's too late …

In bringing Miller forth from the shadows, in allowing him to cross that boundary from the dark, fetid reaches of perversion and obscenity to the (en)lightened halls of normality, have we, the judging reader subjects, lost much of the promise Miller as a writer and an artist held?

In short, do Miller's books now fall squarely into what Slavoj Žižek has provocatively called the realm of "decaffeinated belief?" A realm at once dedicated to overt and politically correct tolerance toward people and things, but equally do not hurt anyone and thus do not fully engage or commit at any level.[1] Miller's proto-punk aesthetic, his "gob of spit in the face of Art" could surely never be accused of not committing (CAN, 2). Certainly, "a kick in the pants to God," is seemingly less of a provocation today (CAN, 2). Indeed, for the legions who now consider themselves anywhere on the spectrum of (militant) atheism that "kick" is simply sport.

Are we therefore able to extrapolate anything from Miller's work to counter and render problematic this cultural sway in which, "you can enjoy everything, BUT deprived of its substance which makes it dangerous"?[2] Moreover, what responsibility or role does law have apropos the (re)*caffeine-nation* of Miller (to reverse and transform Žižek's idea into an admittedly awkward linguistic construct)?

Caffeine and law..?

Far from conjuring the type of images recognizable from classic police dramas of overworked cops guzzling cup after cup of a questionable filtered brew, the connection being made here, for the purposes of quick clarification, is that sense of full-throttle alertness that caffeine provides tempered as it is by the fetters of asceticism, prohibition, and proscription. A sense of what it means to fully commit, "up to the hilt" as Miller might have it, is the caffeine in Miller that needs to be sought out (CAN, 102). We might even search in Miller for that same counterlegal representative much in the way that his character in *Tropic of Cancer* looked about his world with flaming eyes, searching amid the damp squibs for one that would ignite:

> There is only one thing that interests me vitally now, and that is the recording of all that which is omitted in books. Nobody, so far as I can see, is making use of those elements in the air which gives direction and motivation to our lives. Only the killers seem to be extracting from life some satisfactory measure of what they are putting into it. *The age demands violence, but we are getting only abortive explosions.* (CAN, 11; my emphasis)

The following discussion centers on the law, but not from a strictly doctrinal or positivist legal perspective; far from it. Rather, this chapter will draw on those aspects born in the psychic space of the subject, as elucidated by psychoanalysis, which are in dialogue with the external sociojuridical structure called "law," and which strive to better understand affective and culturally engrained notions of obscenity.

Henry Miller, as the chapter will seek to demonstrate, occupies an ideal position in order to explore this, and the many questions which flow from it. And many do. There is no shortage of question marks here; but they do not denote a discussion that has stalled or is grasping for purchase on the sheer face of understanding. No, each of those marks is a fissure, a break in the tree line revealing another path. They are marks of pure contingency …

The justifiably obscene?

If Žižek, after Jacques Lacan, is correct in his measure of contemporary cultural products of which literature is one—that is, a degree of liberal toleration premised upon (cultural) products now containing the agent of their own containment,[3] for example, pleasure and containment bound up in a single easily consumable artifact—then where does this leave Miller, or rather his body of work?

Is Miller's work still vital in the twenty-first century precisely because within its dark recesses we may still find that which skews the agent of its own containment and bends it out of true; can his work be read from this point and still inspire through its heady blend of cosmic vulgarity; or does his work for the reader, writer, artist, or whosoever should come to it in the here-and-now, simply represent exotic dalliance with or sentimentality for a more parochial era?

Indeed, there are many questions Miller and his work still kick up. In order to address some of them, the following chapter will revisit the moment when the juridical line or *limit* apropos Miller was (re)drawn during the obscenity cases heard across the United States, up to the Supreme Court, during the middle of the twentieth century: cases in which the complainants sought to reinforce a discourse of normality as much as one of decency under the rubric of "contemporary community standards,"[4] and which decried Miller's work, among others, as obscene by virtue of it running counter to favored, legally mandated norms.

The series of landmark obscenity cases, which were bookended in the main relative to Miller by *Roth v. United States* (1957)[5] and *Jacobellis v. Ohio* (1964),[6] have during the last fifty to sixty years had an undeniable material effect upon public perceptions of media previously deemed obscene. As such some of them now also represent well-known "free-speech" narratives in their own right, notably in opposition to the perceived erosion of First Amendment rights—having been made the subject of *inter alia* contemporary films, including *The People vs Larry Flynt* (1996) and *Howl* (2010).[7]

Revisiting the challenge these cases faced, and subsequently disposed of, however, is to assess to what degree the juridical limit, defined by law but rendered *a priori* in the psychic space of the subject as a necessary limitation against the tyranny of unbridled pleasure, remains resolutely in place in spite of so-called victories against censorship or even more profoundly *the end of obscenity* altogether,[8] and whether it can ever or it is even desirable to attempt to dismiss it.

In short, as the firebrand introduction to this chapter proclaimed, in giving their seal of approval to Miller, the U.S. Supreme Court failed to recognize a certain value and importance inherent to the community of keeping Miller on the side of obscenity, and thus of ensuring that his passion was not too quickly exhausted for our benefit. Miller's work could be rebanned, but in truth that misses the point. Rather, another aim of this chapter is to understand the merits of writers and artists, such as Miller, who shine a light on the limit from beyond, so to speak, and as such serve to enrich the psychical fabric of the subjects who make up the community.

We need(ed) Miller and others like him in this avant-garde form to remain obscene, even dangerous, in order to direct the rest of us toward a better understanding of obscenity. This is a somewhat trite statement but one nevertheless possessing of a recognizable truth traceable to the foundations, at least, of Western philosophy and its relationship with art. As Iris Murdoch has suggested:

> [Art] breaks the grip of our own dull fantasy life and stirs us to the effort of true vision. Most of the time we fail to see the big wide real world at all because we are blinded by obsession, anxiety, envy, resentment, fear.... Great art is liberating, it enables us to see and take pleasure in what is not ourselves.[9]

Therefore, to invite a broader discussion on the merits of the obscene and its operatives, it may well be asked whether or not we need tension between art and law in order to approach an understanding of obscenity.[10] The suggestion being made here is that we most certainly do. But are we as a community still prone to an acceptable and healthy degree of shock, which is both transformative and redefining?

Law alone has failed in maintaining that tension. There is a degree even of which it can be said that the law is too self-aware, too quick to agree or satisfy fleeting popular mandates. Therefore, the last place we should seek definitions of obscenity is the law. Perhaps that is why the closest the community can now hope to get to the obscene are terrorist acts. This is not to condone such acts. But Miller's manifestation in *Tropic of Cancer* would and does maintain something not dissimilar; and how much has changed since those words, that world, was conceived, which makes his ideas more relevant or vital today:

> For a hundred years or more the world, *our* world, has been dying. And not one man, in these last hundred years or so, has been crazy enough to put a bomb up the asshole of creation and set it off. The world is rotting away, dying piecemeal. But it needs the *coup de grâce*, it needs to be blown to smithereens. (CAN, 27)

In the twenty-first-century U.S., a "workable" definition of obscenity still turns on the tripartite test established in *Miller v. California* (1973)[11] (no relation to Henry!), although Burger CJ in that case recognized the concern articulated by his colleague Mr. Justice Harlan in an earlier case of the "intractable obscenity problem,"[12] which in essence turned and continues to turn upon whether or not a piece of work could or should be deemed pornographic relative to the impact that it has upon the moral fabric of the community.[13] Something else is in evidence here; a certain anarchical spirit which Miller brings to the world. Rather than couching it in terms of anarchy, however, it is important to confront the notion of an intractable obscenity and see where it takes us. Hence, it is Miller as *obscene other of the law* which is favored and proposed.

In short, we need the obscene other of the law in all its artistic glory, as the two polarities, if indeed that is a suitable term, fundamentally support one another. As Žižek suggests in relation to this obscene other, it is, "the unacknowledgeable 'spectral,' fantasmatic secret history that effectively sustains the explicit symbolic tradition, but has to remain foreclosed if it is to be operative."[14] It is the issue of revealing the foreclosed, the confession of the otherwise unsaid, which marks a primary concern. Miller enacts this reveal, and does so with gusto, from his earliest work.

Welcome to the limit

Obscenity as a form of corruption of high moral values has a long history in society and thus law. Indeed, to outline societal confrontation with ideas of obscenity (*née* pornography) is well beyond the scope of this chapter, even by focusing on the United States alone.[15] There are, however, clear parallels that can be drawn relative to the form of juridical demarcation suggested above across the recent and not so recent history of Western legal thought, between Miller and the Marquis de Sade for example. After all, both were constructed by law, if not directly then certainly obliquely, as obscene and with a desire to promote their own brand of depravity.

A notable example of juridical common ground between Miller and Sade resides in them as obscene *other* to the symbolic construct of decency. While Miller himself reportedly retreated from the works of Sade,[16] and others find a substantive comparison between the two "frivolous,"[17] such a comparison nonetheless provides a useful point of reference beyond the legal for highlighting what is perhaps best referred to as the *limit*, and which inaugurates this obscene other of the law.

Indeed, in his short story, "The Mystified Magistrate",[18] Sade enacts a scene in which the obscene other to the law confronts the law directly, making its presence felt literally on the *corpus juris*:

> Without further ado the poor judge was taken and placed facedown on a narrow bench, to which he was securely tied from head to foot. The four wanton spirits each took a leather thong five feet long and, striking up a cadence among them, proceeded to let the lashes fall with all the strength their arms could muster, on every square inch of poor Fontanis's bare body.[19]

In law, it is entirely possible, in a doctrinal sense at least, to reverse and unpick the authority that paved the way from one state of legal being to the next—from the obscene to the *legally* decent for example, as demonstrated by Miller. At least that is the level of authority the law wishes for itself and in turn demands of us. Once a judge's opinion overturns what is obscene and is recorded as such, and all the more so once that opinion forms the backbone of precedence and thus shapes the law, greater distance opens up from the moment when a writer *was* obscene to when that nomination was lifted. Yet such outwardly clear and precise delineations of states of being are of course deceptive, so entangled is the law with culture—and is it not so much harder to reverse the direction of cultural fancies and the prejudices of individuals?

There is therefore a problem with casting Miller out or plunging him from whence he came unto the depths of depravity where he may live eternally as, in his own self-reflective words, "a dirty saint," and wipe the slate clean so to speak (R, 113). Miller's ascent to a degree of community acceptance and thus also the *decaffeinated realm* cannot be *un*remembered and as such cannot be undone. To be sure, communities collectively can and often do (temporarily) forget the works and lives of many writers before revisiting them or have them reemerge in unexpected and unanticipated ways.

Writers, indeed any artists, are after all subject to the vagaries of fashion: a cultural centerpiece one minute, a denizen of the bargain bin the next.

But this toing and froing from the depths of the cultural archive, which attaches to so much human endeavor, does not turn the clock back and cannot undo the initial casuistry of an artist's work. "It's out there!" as we so often hear in the troubled contemporary parlance of information and big data dissemination, rife as it is in our post-*X-Files*, WikiLeaks world. Similarly, we cannot in the here and now say therefore, with regards to Miller, that the genie has not been set free.

Miller's journey from darkness into light and from obscurity to a relative ideal of mainstream decency was conducted largely (and formally) by the hands of the law, but against a highly charged affective backdrop. Mary Kellie Munsil suggests via the reasoning of Edward S. Silver, the district attorney who wrote Brooklyn's complaint against Miller and his publisher Grove Press following the release of *Tropic of Cancer* in the United States, "For him [Silver] the danger of the book lies in its creation of unacceptable mental and emotional states in the reader."[20]

Did the law's operatives, albeit working for a self-proclaimed community good equally exemplified and underwritten by certain conservatism, not fail in their aims however? Well, yes and no. On the facts Miller *et al.* tipped a delicate balance thereby eschewing the chains restricting the artistic mind.[21] But as Roland Barthes has demonstrated in his work,[22] the author's (the artist's) perspective is but one amid a matrix which inform the artwork as such in the wider field of perception:

> We know that a text is not a line of words releasing a single "theological" meaning (the "message" of the Author-God) but a multi-dimensional space in which a variety of writings, none of them original, blend and clash. The text is a tissue of quotations drawn from the innumerable centres of culture.[23]

Thus, the groundswell of cases that played out during the mid-twentieth century redefined the limit and shifted it, seemingly, to a new libertarian location in which Miller was welcomed. Yet, this new locus, as time has indicated, would prove not to be defined relative to traditional notions of community standards—that is, so much by external, objective notions of obscenity—but rather by a transference of that regulatory agency back on to the subject, be they consumer, reader, and so on. As a result, inaugurating a new era of asceticism contrived as something wholly freeing for the subject.

In order to prevent or counteract "lecherous thoughts and desires" in those that came into contact with Miller's books,[24] Silver along with other operatives of the law attempted to reaffirm, perhaps even reconstitute, the line of juridical reasoning traceable to Scots judge Sir James Alexander Edmund Cockburn's definition of obscenity laid down in the case *R v. Hicklin* (1868)[25]; a baton picked up soon after in the United States by the *Comstock Act* (or *Law*) 1873, which as an "Act of the Suppression of Trade in, and Circulation of, Obscene Literature and Articles of Immoral Use" sought to deal with the unpalatable issue of obscene material by severing the postal supply lines, which ultimately kept those hungry for it fed.[26]

It was reasoning, one presumes, Silver hoped to rely on in order to maintain the *status quo*—that is, a community standard enforced, perhaps less by the fierce moral notions of "Comstockery" than by a resolute adherence to the dictates of the law. Those that had supposedly succumbed to the corruptible influence of Miller's ideas, of his "manifesto,"[27] would fall foul of Silver's strict legal limit, thus opening themselves first to chastisement at the hands of "the community" before subsequent return to its bosom via the suppression or rather *repression* of their prurient thoughts under the name of rehabilitation.

It was doubtless, however, a double bind for Silver: in order to achieve the (continued) suppression of obscene material, which in actuality many people either already knew about or were already engaging with—Miller's work was both lauded and available in Europe and thus had already made its way via smugglers and fans to the North American shores during this time[28]—it was necessary to expose and render conscious the underbelly, the very kernel of obscenity that signaled his complaint.

From a Foucauldian perspective this may signal a form of power that serves to generate the very excess it would censor. For Žižek, Foucault does not go far enough, as he suggests: "What it [Foucault's notion] misses is the way in which censorship not only affects the status of the marginal or subversive force that the power discourse endeavours to dominate but, at an even more radical level, splits the power discourse itself from within."[29]

How was this split evidenced in terms of Silver's case against Miller? The form of reveal alone, both exposing and exemplifying the level of obscenity he found so disconcerting, must have been troublesome enough for Silver. But perhaps, for the man who stated with resolve that there was a duty incumbent upon the people of America to grasp the importance of the administration of criminal law in their country, that it was also necessary for Silver to expose the weakness in the (criminal) laws he held in such high regard is the more notable and compelling thing. That was his radical splitting of the power discourse from within.[30]

Is this not also an interesting, further inversion of Žižek's notion of a product containing the agency of its own containment?—one which clearly demonstrates that censorship of obscene publications as such has never gone away, but has been marked by transference of censorial agency. Rather than an emphasis on the self-contained, internal agency working tirelessly against the perils of prurience as we might see today in a postobscene world—for example, the sex shops once veiled as to their contents from the street while their presence is advertised in lurid, bright neon; or the pornographic magazines, their covers veiled by opaque plastic, once present but just out of reach on the top shelf of the magazine rack[31]—there roamed from town to town *externalized* agents, picking off obscene materials one by one, their only desire/reward being *inter alia* the succor of organized religion (Comstock[32]), or the maintenance of the legal order (Silver).

Clearly, the internalized limit within each subject, which triggers, with varying degrees of success, the ability to personally gauge levels of obscenity, did not suddenly appear in order to counteract the change in the law. After all, Freud had outlined his notion of the superego—broadly speaking, as an updated notion of conscience befitting of the scientific age—many years prior to the obscenity cases, and conscience as a register of individual ethical values had been prevalent far longer still.

Therefore, in considering the limit between law and decency and its obscene other as a phenomena *simpliciter*, it is necessary to consider its relationship to agency, and more specifically to those parties as agents who stood to gain, so to speak, from the definitive internalization of the limit and the subsequent corollary of a *laissez faire* approach on the part of the law. While the question of who "stood to gain" injects a sense of the conspiratorial that will not be entertained here, the notion of agency does once again return to Žižek's *containment* thesis.

The limit in law and the psyche

Law in this context simply represents limit: nothing more, nothing less. Imagined as a slider on a scale of "decency," it is those with a firm grip on the reins of power, the guardians of community standards, who set the (symbolic) limit in place.

But it is important to contrast it with the parallel sense of the limit at work here, which is the psychoanalytical determination outlined by Freud relative to the Pleasure Principle.[33] In other words, the law is never just "law," but is, I argue, tied inexorably to unconscious psychical evaluations relative to the subject's approach toward the *thing*—the object of the subject's *desire*. The point being that the law relative to obscenity apes the actions of the limit known as the Pleasure Principle inasmuch as for the subject to surpass it, to go beyond the limit (the law) as such, invites unpleasure psychically, which in terms of community standards manifests as anxiety and disavowal at the level of the symbolic law.

Obscenity, like many other legal terms and phrases, escapes singular or rather settled definition *per se* and therefore invites contestation. But, as Charles Rembar, the erstwhile defender of free speech against this limit as such during the mid-twentieth century on behalf of *inter alia* Miller's publisher at the time Grove Press, proclaimed in a manner peculiarly sympathetic in tone to the statements of his counterpart Edward Silver: "Laws are hard to apply and enforce; this does mean we should not have them."[34]

Comprised of both action and idea, obscenity is a regulated limit we, either as individuals or as a community, dare to cross. Instead we leave it, necessarily, to the artist. It is also an exceedingly affected or affective line, or at least has been in recent history as the question of obscenity has been raised time and again, with each iteration seeking to limit different media—first literature, then theater, then film *ad infinitum*. As Rembar maintained in the late 1970s with a degree of hindsight as to his part in the obscenity trials:

> "Obscene" for legal purposes should be discarded altogether. It carries an impossible burden of passionate conviction from both sides of the question. And it diverts attention from real issues.[35]

Quite what Rembar's "real issues" are and whether they are any easier for a community to define is open to question, although at a certain level those issues are guaranteed to represent a knot of conflicting desires. Nevertheless, the limit (or "question" in Rembar's terms) at first appearance simply separates the obscene from the decent based on what passes for each of those nominations at any one period in time. But it is not a limit defined solely or simply by the binary divisions it inaugurates.

Rather, by rendering the limit and by extension the motivations of those that control it as a regulatory mechanism in, for example, the vein of Freud's superego is to color it more perverse than a mere dividing line. Instead, it is revealed as a limit that bids those that approach to cross, before hurriedly gathering the dark forces of guilt to condemn their actions. In that sense it is a psychical feedback loop as much as a legal prohibition which ensures our insatiable desire remains at a certain biting point. This is the psychical dimension that cannot be easily uncoupled from the juridical.

To return to a couple of allusions made previously: this bidding of the superego transliterates into the neon sign of the sex shop, or the opaque plastic veil of the pornographic magazine. There is a sense of temptation here in the theological mold. But, equally, there is a sign of healthy allegiance to the law of our own being, of our own desire. An allegiance analogous to that conjured by Miller as he continued to make sense of the Parisian world he moved through:

> I found God, but he is insufficient. I am spiritually dead. Physically I am alive. Morally I am free. The world which I have departed is a menagerie. The dawn is breaking on a new world, a jungle world in which the lean spirits roam with sharp claws. If I am a hyena I am a lean and hungry one: I go forth to fatten myself. (CAN, 103)

Miller's crossing

It was the line of judicial reasoning that ultimately ended with the decision in *Jacobellis v. Ohio* (1964),[36] which to all intents and purposes clothed Miller in the acceptable and protective cloth of symbolic legal decency. In that sense Miller crossed the limit from obscenity to decency, and with it his fortunes, largely fiscal in nature, were also transformed. The legal decision also transformed his fortunes to the extent that he was able to openly enjoy international recognition as an author and artist. Moreover, it even became relatively safe for the mainstream media to court Miller for the enthusiastic titillation of their audiences.

Miller surmounted the heady and treacherous heights of cultural savoir faire to become a popular icon, albeit as the reluctant "king of smut."[37] But becoming known or better known, infamous or popular even, is not the same as becoming accepted as such and Miller only remained a liminal figure as far as the mainstream and the regulated standards of the community was concerned, irrespective of any official rubber stamping of his acceptability.

Clearly, the period following Miller's *legal* acceptance was offset to a certain degree by the failure of community standards to keep in step with the changes. And the gap between the two was ripe for exploitation from a number of angles. Perhaps one of the better known being Miller's *Playboy* interview shortly after the Supreme Court ruling, in which the interviewer and Miller's friend, Bernard Wolfe, playfully suggested that having been stamped with Court's seal of approval, Miller was now "socially acceptable among all but the ladies' auxiliary tea societies."[38]

Miller, rendered unobscene, fissured so-called "standards" and exposed the tender marrow within, which would not invite plaudits from certain conservative factions, namely tea societies. The Supreme Court ruling had, to some degree and in Miller's own words, brought down barriers and shattered "the wretched molds [sic] in which we're fixed."[39] But as this chapter has sought to illustrate, the general optimism of Miller's declaration was overstated.

The various court cases that clustered between the late 1950s and the early 1960s could not ensure Miller would be accepted as a literary figure of any lasting merit—an idea he fleshed out in stark contrast to a degree of entitlement he felt toward an award of the Nobel Prize (R, 112). Rather, those cases sought only to deal with the limit of what was deemed acceptable and decent as opposed to obscene and depraved in the eyes of the law. In other words, part of Miller's work would forever remain in the dark; would forever mark him with the question of whether he was a demon or a saint (R, 113).

While Miller may have been given the Court's seal of approval, does a part of him remain beyond the limit? What use is there to the cultural landscape of elements if not whole sections of Miller's oeuvre remaining below this conscious Plimsoll line? It's as if the Supreme Court ruling opened a door to decency through which Miller passed, but that same door slammed shut too soon severing his arm (that element of Miller as a metaphor for his obscenity) and leaving it on the other side where it continued working—an image one cannot help but evoke in full consideration of Miller's great friendship and respect for the one-armed writer Blaise Cendrars, creator of his own obscene and monstrous figures, including the perverse *Moravagine*.[40]

Is this element of Miller held back in the name of obscenity that which suggests acceptability at a deeply unconscious level of desire, but that which must equally remain unacknowledgeable (unconscious) in order to ensure the continuation of a more powerful and explicit symbolic tradition engendered by all that *is* acceptable? In other words, this line of high-profile cases engaged only at the level of explicit symbolism, all the while leaving untouched the otherwise unconscious world of fantastical desire that represents the heart and soul of Miller's work.

To evoke Jacques Lacan at this point: correlation may be found between the hypothetical example of Miller's severed limb and Lacan's notion of the Real.[41] Notwithstanding, Lacan oversaw a number of iterations of the Real during the course of his life, and while developing his many concepts and their interrelatedness, there remains a continuous sense throughout that the Real is that which escapes symbolization and cuts through the imagination.

Further, Miller's severed limb is analogous to the Real because both represent a semblance of pure desire. To imagine the severed, disembodied limb furiously scribbling its chaotic and obscene reflections of the world, its hymn to vast expansive unknowns, is to imagine a *thing* more Miller than Miller. This is Miller residing beyond Freud's pleasure principle; beyond the limit, enraptured in the throes of the death drive.

In this sense Miller ceases to be obscene, in any ordinary or linear understanding of the term, and emerges, even while considered acceptable, as something of an extraordinary and traumatic intervention in the world of the symbolic—that is, the world in which the law holds sway and grants Miller approval. We cling to Miller's work precisely because he functions to disrupt the everyday and the parochial. As Žižek, again following Lacan, contends: "the Real, at its most radical, has to be totally de-substantialized. It is not an external thing that resists being caught in the symbolic network, but the fissure within the symbolic network itself."[42]

It is precisely this latter concept that needs to be grasped relative to the continued importance of Miller's work. It reveals that small but vital space between the conscious assertions of the symbolic law (Miller as saint) and the unconscious desires of the community of subjects (Miller as demon). More now than ever, the agency splitting the power from within, where once it resided in agents such as Silver, now resides in each and every subject as we (as community) traverse the cultural landscape, often unsure at which point we stray too close to the edge, to the psychical limit saving us from ourselves.

A conclusion …

Miller cannot be returned to the position he was in prior to *Jacobellis*, but it is possible to approach his work now and for future generations with the knowledge that parts of it continue to reside in the beyond of the limit as obscene other.

This may sound like an argument romanticizing a lost past of strict moral virtue, but I assure you that is not the intention. We need obscene others, or perhaps an "Enemy" to couch it the terms Miller reserved for Wyndham Lewis (CE, 188). That is the thrust of the argument here and one that has hopefully been made plain.

There can be no doubt that contemporary examples exist and indeed thrive in their own way; examples that even ape Miller such as Eric Miles Williamson.[43] Perhaps the concern underlying the argument therefore is less about the continued existence of artists such as Miller, and more about the landscape in which are propagated the ideas such artists hope to bring to the fore. After all, if all around we find only those cultural products that contain the agent of their own containment (decaffeination), something mirrored in those that create, use, abuse, and enjoy those same products, then what is the hope for diverse and challenging art in the long term?

Moreover, not everyone can do what Miller and his like have done, namely lead us, the community, to the limit, sometimes to its very edge, even challenging us to take that additional fateful step. The landscape for creativity is suggestively open and wide in the contemporary era and technologies have cemented that reality. But does that in itself not dilute the impact, and more worryingly detract from voices like Miller's?

Could someone, an artist, a writer, or a musician, in the vein of Miller make his voice heard today?

In closing, it seems only appropriate to leave the final word to Miller himself—a summing up encompassing both the need for the obscene other and its manifestation, its very encroachment, into the everyday reality of the community and the subjects who comprise it:

> The day face of the world is unbearable, it is perhaps true. But this mask which we wear, through which we look at the world of reality, who has clapped it on us? Have we not grown it ourselves? The mask is inevitable: we cannot meet the world with naked skins. We move within the grooves, formerly taboos, now conventions. Are we to throw away the mask, the lying face of the world? Could we, even if we choose? It seems to me that only the lunatic is capable of making such a gesture—and at what a price! Instead of the conventional but flexible groove, which irks more or less, he adopts the obsessional mould which clamps and imprisons. He has completely lost contact with reality, we say of the insane man. But has he liberated himself? Which is the prison—reality or anarchy? Who is the gaoler? (CE, 192)

Notes

1. Slavoj Žižek, "Passion in the Era of Decaffeinated Belief," *The Symptom*, 5, Winter 2004, http://www.lacan.com/passion.htm
2. Žižek, "Passion in the Era of Decaffeinated Belief."
3. Žižek, "Passion in the Era of Decaffeinated Belief."
4. See *Roth v. United States*, 354 U.S. 476 (1957).
5. *Roth v. United States*, 354 U.S. 476 (1957).
6. 378 U.S. 184.
7. For example, *The People vs Larry Flynt* (1996) directed by Milos Forman; *Howl* (2010) directed by Rob Epstein and Jeffrey Friedman.
8. This is the title of the book published by the lawyer who helped overturn the obscenity laws relating to literature in the United States during the mid-twentieth century. See Charles Rembar, *The End of Obscenity: The Trials of* Lady Chatterley, Tropic of Cancer and Fanny Hill (New York: Random House, 1968).
9. Iris Murdoch, *Existentialists and Mystics: Writings on Philosophy and Literature*, ed. Peter Conradi (New York: Penguin, 1999), 14.
10. While broader discussion is invited, the ideas outlined here all fall within a notional understanding of Henry Miller's work. That is, the means through which the scope of what is a vast and long-standing debate is narrowed for present purposes.
11. 413 U.S. 15.
12. *Interstate Circuit, Inc. v. City of Dallas*, 390 U.S. 676, 704 (1968) (Harlan dissenting); *Memoirs v. Massachusetts*, 383 U.S. 413, 456 (1966).
13. Clearly the "intractable obscenity problem" remains intractable as much across the media platforms of the twenty-first century, namely the Internet, as it did throughout the twentieth century in books and later videos, not to mention artworks, painting,

sculpture, and so on. For example, see Matthew Dawson, "The Intractable Obscenity Problem 2.0: The Emerging Circuit Split over the Constitutionality of 'Local Community Standards' Online," *Catholic University Law Review* 60 (2010–2011): 719–748.

14 Slavoj Žižek, "The Act and Its Vicissitudes," *The Symptom*, 6 (2005). http://www.lacan.com/symptom6_articles/zizek.html

15 A number of titles exist that deal with the issue of obscenity with law. For a good example which covers a range of materials, see Thomas C. Mackey, *Pornography on Trial: A Handbook with Cases, Laws and Documents* (Santa Barbara: ABC-CLIO, 2002).

16 George Wickes, "Henry Miller: Down and Out in Paris," *Critical Essays on Henry Miller*, ed. Ronald Gottesman, (New York: G.K. Hall, 1992), 122.

17 Kenneth Rexroth, "The Reality of Henry Miller," *Critical Essays on Henry Miller*, ed. Ronald Gottesman, (New York: G.K. Hall, 1992), 98.

18 Marquis de Sade, *The Mystified Magistrate and Other Tales*, trans. Richard Seaver (New York: Arcade, 2000).

19 Sade, *The Mystified Magistrate*, 56.

20 Mary Kellie Munsil, "The Body in the Prison-house of Language: Henry Miller, Pornography and Feminism," *Critical Essays on Henry Miller*, ed. Ronald Gottesman (New York: G.K. Hall, 1992). 286.

21 Rembar recalls that the question put to the courts during the trial of D.H. Lawrence's *Lady Chatterley's Lover* was "Should the courts chain creative minds to the dead center of convention at a given moment in time?" See Charles Rembar, "Obscenity—Forget It," *Atlantic Monthly* 1 May 1977. http://www.theatlantic.com/magazine/archive/1977/05/obscenity-forget-it/305053/

22 Roland Barthes, "The Death of the Author," *Image-Music-Text*, translated by Stephen Heath (New York: Hill and Wang, 1977), 142–148.

23 Barthes, "The Death of the Author," 146.

24 Munsil, "The Body," 286.

25 L.R. 3 Q.B. 360.

26 See: http://www.britannica.com/EBchecked/topic/130734/Comstock-Act

27 Munsil, "The Body," 286.

28 The drive to get copies of Miller's work, irrespective of its standing in the eyes of the law, was articulated by John Lennon during an interview with Howard Cosell on ABC television in 1974 and later reproduced in a poetic form under the title "On Censorship and Henry Miller," where Lennon says, "We used to go to Paris, and everybody would buy Henry Miller books because they were banned, and everybody saw them, all the students had them"; John Lennon, "On Censorship and Henry Miller," *Henry Miller: A Book of Tributes, 1931–1994*, ed. Craig Peter Standish (Orlando: Standish Books, 1994), 633.

29 Slavoj Žižek, *The Plague of Fantasies* (London: Verso, 2008), 31.

30 While Silver does not expressly deal with the issue of obscenity in his acceptance speech for the "Furtherance of Justice" Award presented to him at the National District Attorneys' Association annual meeting in 1962, he does offer his thoughts as to society's failure to attend to the mores of criminal law enforcement. His address, entitled "Public Apathy and Law Enforcement," while short, demonstrates a lawyer with a strong vocation and belief in maintaining standards within the strict

boundaries of the criminal jurisdiction. See "Notes and Announcements," *Journal of Criminal Law and Criminology* 54, 2 (1963): 198–199.
31 Both of these examples represent at least the British experience.
32 Comstock told a *Harper's Weekly* reporter: "If you allow the Devil to decorate the Chamber of Imagery in your heart with licentious and sensual things, you will find that he has practically thrown a noose about your neck and will forever exert himself to draw you away from the Lamb of God which taketh away the sins of the world." This quote was taken from: Margaret A. Blanchard and John E. Semonche, "Anthony Comstock and His Adversaries: The Mixed Legacy of this Battle for Free Speech," *Communication Law and Policy* 11, 3 (2006): 339.
33 Sigmund Freud, "Beyond the Pleasure Principle," *The Penguin Freud Reader*, ed. Adam Phillips, (London: Penguin, 2006), 132–195.
34 Rembar, "Obscenity."
35 Rembar, "Obscenity."
36 378 U.S. 184.
37 Mary V. Dearborn, *The Happiest Man Alive: A Biography of Henry Miller*, (New York: Simon & Schuster, 1991), 279.
38 Bernard Wolfe, "Playboy Interview: Henry Miller," *Playboy* September 1964, 78.
39 Wolfe, "Playboy Interview: Henry Miller," *Playboy* September 1964, 77.
40 Blaise Cendrars, *Moravagine*, trans. Alan Brown, (New York: New York Review of Books, 2004).
41 Lacan discusses the Real throughout the long gestation of his work so it is not possible to point to any particular definition. As an example, see: Jacques Lacan, *On the Names-of-the-Father*, trans. Bruce Fink, (Cambridge: Polity, 2013).
42 Slavoj Žižek, *How to Read Lacan* (New York: W.W. Norton & Company, 2007), 72.
43 For example, see Eric Miles Williamson, *Welcome to Oakland* (Hyattsville: Raw Dog Screaming Press, 2009).

9

The Ecstatic Psychotic:
Henry Miller via Jacques Lacan

Hamish Dale Mercer Jackson

*The unamable is the eternally real
Naming is the origin
of all particular things.*

~

*If you open yourself to loss,
you are at one with loss
and you accept loss completely*

~

True words seem paradoxical[1]

The form or formlessness of Miller's prose has troubled many critics; Alan Friedman complains, "Miller is extremely difficult to quote in brief" because "what most characterizes his writing ... is his interminable jamming together of formless, exuberant imagery."[2] Reading Miller can be disorienting. While the narrative is generally coherent, if not linear, there are moments when, without warning, he flings you into the surreal. As Brassaï points out, these hallucinatory passages—or epiphanies—were influenced by the surrealist movement that bloomed in Paris in the 1920s and 1930s:

> Like the Surrealists and Dadaists, Henry believed that dreams provided fertile soil for writing, and that writing did involve the struggle to bring to the surface that which is unknown, hidden, and unrealized.

Tapping into the unconscious appealed to Miller, but he preferred to employ surrealist techniques "when it felt natural and spontaneous," not so as to be "counted as one of their adherents."[3] In an interview with George Wickes, Miller confirmed this, saying he understood surrealism as "always more and more getting into the unconscious, into the unpremeditated, the instinctive ... obeying your instincts [and] subconscious impulses."[4]

Jacques Lacan's work was driven by the same impulse: to access, and analyze, the unconscious. His essay "The Agency of the Letter in the Unconscious Since Freud" begins, "As my title suggests, beyond this 'speech,' what the psychoanalytic experience discovers in the unconscious is the whole structure of language."[5] Anthony Wilden reifies the importance of this discovery: "[Lacan] has introduced us to the less than obvious fact that psychoanalysis is a theory of language."[6] As Henry Miller was interested in accessing his unconscious through language, writing copiously and often without conscious interference, he is an ideal subject for Lacanian analysis. It is my contention that in the moments where Miller's prose transcends into the surreal, we glimpse that which is hidden—his unconscious—and in this, we discover his psychosis.

I use the term "psychosis" in a strictly Lacanian sense. Lacan's conception of psychosis, laid out in Seminar III, *The Psychoses*, is based on Freud's work on the subject, particularly Daniel Schreber's case. Schreber was a successful judge who documented his own descent into psychosis in *Memoirs of My Nervous Illness*. Schreber's psychosis was characterized by "hallucinations"[7] such as God, in the form of sunlight, communicating to him: "the rays must speak"[8] and a "fragmented" sense of his body.[9] Lacan's definition of psychosis emerges as follows:

> How can one fail to see in the phenomenology of psychosis that everything from beginning to end stems from a particular relationship between the subject and this language that has suddenly been thrust into the foreground, that speaks all by itself, out loud, in its noise and furor, as well as in its neutrality? If the neurotic inhabits language, the psychotic is inhabited, possessed, by language.[10]

Lacan's definition is based entirely upon the subject's relationship with language: it possesses them. Lacan stated, "disorders at the level of language" are central to psychosis: "We must insist upon the presence of these disorders before making a diagnosis of psychosis."[11] This is what we will discover in Miller's writing: disorders of, and possession by, language.

Slave of language

> A certificate tells me that I was born. I repudiate this certificate: I am not a poet, but a poem. A poem that is being written, even if it looks like a subject.[12]

A central paradox in Miller's writing is the intention to express *himself*, as a self-realized man, despite being psychologically unsure of whom *he* is. This paradox lies behind much of the critics' confusion surrounding the reliability of his narrator. In an early review of *Cancer*, "Twilight of the Expatriates," Edmund Wilson wrote:

> The theme of *Tropic of Cancer* is the lives of a group of Americans who have more or less come to Paris with the intention of occupying themselves with literature but who have actually subsided easily into an existence almost exclusively occupied with drinking and fornication.[13]

The review offended Miller, especially the implication that his narrator was fictional. He retorted, "The theme of the book...is not at all what Mr Wilson describes: the theme is myself, and the narrator, or the hero, as your critic puts it, is also myself."[14] He is categorical; *Cancer* is about expressing "Henry Miller." A letter to Bob MacGregor shows this is not so transparent:

> [M]y aim, from the beginning, has been to give myself—totally. No evasions, no compromises, no falsifications. Distortions and exaggerations, yes! But for aesthetic reasons, to make the truth more truthful. To put it another way, I put down what comes to me in the way it is given. I don't question how it is given or by whom. I obey, I yield. I know "it" knows better than I. I am the receiving station. (HMJL, 116–117)

To begin with, this quote seems simple: he confesses to embellishing his life in Paris in order to express the "real" Henry Miller. Then, curiously, he admits to writing only what is "given" to him, by a source labeled simply as "it." Miller is not in control of his self-portrait. This mysterious "it" is our first hint of the agency of the Other.

Lacan says, "the Other is already there in the very opening, however evanescent, of the unconscious"[15] and "the unconscious is the Other's discourse."[16] The Other is a part of the subject's unconscious: it is constituted by, and mediates, language. Lacan states, "the Other must first of all be considered a locus, the locus in which speech is constituted."[17] For the psychotic, possessed by language, there is no separation between themselves and the Other. Professor of Comparative Literature and Critical Theory at the University of Missouri, Ellie Ragland explained this to me: "What the psychotic thinks is what the Other thinks. What the psychotic wants is what the Other wants: there is no distance between the subject and the Other."[18] We recognize this in "The Angel Is My Watermark!," in which Miller describes the genesis of one of his paintings, but must first appease the Other:

> I am in the hands of unseen powers. I put the typewriter away and I commence to record what is being dictated to me. Pages and pages of notes, and for each incident I am reminded of where to find the context...I am exultant and at the same time I am worried. If it continues at this rate I may have a haemorrhage. About three o'clock I decide to obey no longer. Someone is dictating to me constantly—and with no regard for my health. I tell you, the whole day passes this way, I've surrendered long ago. O.K., I say to myself. If it's *ideas* today, then it's ideas. *Princesse, a vosordres*. And I slave away, as though it were exactly what I wanted to do myself. After dinner I am quite worn out. The ideas are still inundating me, but I am so exhausted that I can lie back now and let them play over me like an electric massage....The pencil is in my hand again, the margin crammed with notes. It is midnight. I am exhilarated. The dictation has ceased. A free man again. (BS, 60–61)

The Other is an unseen power, dictating to Miller with "no regard" for his health, forcing him to embrace the surrealist impulse of automatic writing. Flooded with ideas and compelled to record them in a great rush, Miller is powerless to stop it. The process goes on for hours; at 3.00 p.m. he decides to "obey no longer," but finds himself still going at midnight. Miller is under the influence of the Other, as a scribe for it; literally a "slave of language."[19]

This is not an isolated example. In his letters to Anaïs Nin, we see the looming presence of the Other: "I know now I am truly possessed—fou [crazy]. Good Christ, how everything is boiling in me" (LP, 46). In *Cancer*, Miller says, "The only writers about me for whom I have any respect, at present, are Carl and Boris. They are possessed. They glow inwardly with a white flame. They are mad and tone deaf. They are sufferers" (CAN, 4). This sounds like a description of Miller himself. Many of Miller's characters, perhaps even all of them, exude elements of himself and function as incarnations of the Other. Moldorf is an obvious example:

> We have so many points in common that it is like looking at myself in a cracked mirror ... I have been looking over my manuscripts, pages scrawled with revisions. Pages of literature. This frightens me a little. It is so much like Moldorf ... I recall distinctly how I enjoyed my suffering. It was like taking a cub to bed with you. (CAN, 9)

Miller describes Moldorf as his doppelgänger: a *méconnaissance* (misidentification) that threatens his sense of self, especially when he also finds Moldorf in his writing. The cub metaphor is apt. Miller's mind is the bed and usually a safe haven, and while the cub is only immature, it still functions as a symbol of power and danger: "Once in a while he clawed you—and then you were really frightened" (CAN, 9). Despite the potential danger of the Other's presence within his Unconscious, he enjoys his suffering. This is indicative of Miller's psychosis. One naturally associate psychosis with danger or even criminality, but for Miller it functions primarily as a creative source. Miller ends "The Angel Is My Watermark!" with a celebration of the Other: "the angel I can't scrub out. The angel is my watermark" (BS, 79). This notion is repeated in his letter to MacGregor: "This is my 'purity' if you like. And my credo, as writer. Or—'my water-mark'" (HMJL, 116–117). The force dictating to Miller and enslaving him—the angel, or "it," or Other—is at once his muse and his captor.

The Borromean Knot and Sinthome

In order to access the surreal moments of Miller's writing—his epiphanies, an awareness of Lacan's Borromean Knot is necessary. Lacan uses the Borromean Knot as a "non metaphorical way of exploring the symbolic order and its interactions with the real and the imaginary."[20] The Real, Symbolic, and Imaginary are the three realms, orders, or realities (Lacan uses these terms interchangeably) of a subject's existence. Each order is chained to the others, as shown in Figure 9.1.[21]

Figure 9.1. Lacan's Borromean Knot

The Imaginary is a time of wholeness, when the subject feels one with its mother. The Imaginary can never be regained. Put simply, the Mirror Stage heralds the departure from the Imaginary and entrance to the Symbolic, when the subject realizes itself as a separate entity. Dylan Evans defines the Symbolic as "a set of differentiated, discrete elements called signifiers"[22] and Lacan states, the "structures of society are Symbolic"[23]. The Symbolic is the world around us; all of the laws, economies, sciences, and so on. It is everything we know, and as such is constituted by language.

Miller was preoccupied with the Imaginary, conceptualizing it in terms of the womb and locating the entry to the Symbolic at the severance of the umbilical cord:

> A fear of living separate, of staying born. The door of the womb always on the latch. Dread and longing. Deep in the blood the pull of paradise. The beyond. Always the beyond. It must have all started with the navel. They cut the umbilical cord, give you a slap on the ass, and presto! You're out in the world, adrift, a ship without a rudder. (CAN, 290)

The principal image of this section is repeated from earlier in *Cancer*, "the door of the womb always on the latch, always open" (256). This is an excellent metaphor for the Imaginary order. Miller longs for wholeness with his mother, the paradise of the womb, and is dissatisfied with being alone in the Symbolic. He decries the structures of the Symbolic, "Who that has a desperate, hungry eye can have the slightest regard for these existent governments, laws, codes, principles, ideals, ideas, totems, and taboos?" (CAN, 253). Miller's displeasure with the Symbolic is apparent in much of his work, but most virulently in *The Air Conditioned Nightmare* (1945).

The third order, the Real, is by far the trickiest of the three. In Lacan's early teachings, the Real was incomprehensible and defined as "the impossible."[24] In Seminar XXIII, Lacan added the *sinthome* to his topological model. This was "a way of unconcealing the Real," as Savaş Yazici argues in his doctoral dissertation.[25] The sinthome is a fourth ring, functioning "to repair, mend, correct, or restore a fault in the knot R.S.I."[26] The sinthome is crucial for this study because "the links between the Real, Symbolic and Imaginary are very weak in psychotic subjects"[27], and the knot "constantly threaten[s] to come undone."[28] The sinthome is the additional link, drawn on the Borromean Knot.[29]

I asked Luke Thurston, Professor of Modern Literature at Aberystwyth University, how the Real could be accessed through the Symbolic. He responded with the concept of radical foreclosure:

> Radical foreclosure is when the ego or the imaginary slips in the model of the Borromean Knot. It is the point of the slippage, where the knot comes undone ... if the ego is foreclosed then the whole possibility of meaning is eclipsed. This is in itself quite a hard concept. I mean how can you have non-meaning? But you've got this idea that for a moment, a fraction of a second, there is this complete collapse of meaning and in that moment you have a sudden flood of jouissance, of the absolute.

Figure 9.2. Sinthome

For Thurston, the absolute is synonymous with the Real. Radical foreclosure is the point at which the knot disentangles, before the sinthome intervenes to repair it. In the instant of its undoing, in that radical foreclosure, we glimpse the Real through a "flood of jouissance." Thurston asserted that "the event that is un-inscribable is somehow encoded in this later moment." By the "event," he means radical foreclosure, and by the "later moment," he refers to the process of reflection. Miller's epiphanies are those "later moments" where he tries to relate the Real that he has glimpsed in that instant of radical foreclosure, before the sinthome reties the Borromean Knot.

Epiphanies

In Seminar XXIII, Lacan applies the sinthome to James Joyce's writing, particularly focusing on Joyce's "epiphanies," to illustrate its function. Lacan argues that we can see Joyce's unconscious, when he "loses touch with language," and has what amounts to a "kind of psychotic break."[30] The epiphanies are moments when the Symbolic order is invaded by "the subject's private jouissance"[31] and "the Real forecloses meaning."[32] That is to say, Joyce managed to find a way of expressing the Real in moments of jouissance, by exposing the sinthome. Thurston describes Joyce's epiphanies as "experiences of an almost hallucinatory intensity... recorded in enigmatic, fragmentary texts."[33] This could easily be a description of Miller's surreal passages. I have chosen to analyze a few epiphanies from *Tropic of Cancer*, but this is far from exhaustive. After an introductory example, they are divided by theme: the punctured body, ecstasy, and language.

Miller builds up the first epiphany of *Cancer* with a tense, melodramatic atmosphere: "There is a sort of subdued pandemonium in the air, a note of repressed violence, as if the awaited explosion required the advent of some utterly minute detail" (CAN, 99). A simultaneous reaction takes place within Miller's body; a bomb grows while his sense of self shrinks:

> The state of tension was so finely drawn now that the introduction of a single foreign particle, even a microscopic particle, as I say, would have shattered everything. For the fraction of a second perhaps I experienced that utter clarity which the epileptic, it is said, is given to know. In that moment I lost completely the illusion of time and space: the world unfurled its drama simultaneously along a meridian which had no axis. (CAN, 99)

Miller implodes quietly and serenely, experiencing the impossible; utter clarity, a "sort of hair-trigger eternity" wherein he is "face to face with the absolute" (CAN, 100). In the Lacanian model, eternity and the absolute are synonymous with the Real, and for a fraction of a second via radical foreclosure, Miller glimpses it. Soon after, the sinthome kicks in and the Borromean Knot reties, Miller falling back, anticlimactically into the Symbolic: "no miracle comes forth, no microscopic vestige even of relief. Only ideas, pale attenuated ideas, which have to be fattened by slaughter; ideas which come forth like bile, like the guts of a pig when the carcass is ripped open" (CAN, 101).

Miller describes these "ideas" with disgust as they are in the realm of language, and in occupying his mind they are once more inscribing him in the Symbolic.

The punctured body

In her book, *Nets of Modernism*, Maud Ellman examines "Epiphany 19" from 1902, in which Joyce's mother bursts into a room to announce that his brother Georgie is hemorrhaging from the navel:

> MRS. JOYCE—There's some matter coming away from the hole in Georgie's stomach... Did you ever hear of that happening? ...
> JOYCE—I don't know... what hole?
> MRS. JOYCE—[impatient] ... The hole we all have... here [points].[34]

Ellman notes, "the deictic 'here' is un-locatable"; in other words, we cannot tell for certain which hole Mrs. Joyce is talking about, but we assume it is the navel. Ellman says the navel acts as "both seam and fissure, knot and not," which opens "a puncture in the text itself, a hole through which its meanings hemorrhage."[35] This is an excellent metaphor for the sinthome.

Miller read and appreciated Joyce, as Caroline Blinder points out; his "notebooks contain copious notes on James Joyce," and he was "highly influenced by a Joycean mimicking of thought processes."[36] In *Cancer*, Miller calls Joyce the "the great blind Milton" (260), and he quotes a large chunk of hallucinatory prose from *Finnegans Wake* (94).[37] He admires Joyce's "destruction of language" (WOL, 88), and describes the experience of reading *Ulysses* as one in which "the mind has become a recording machine: we are aware of a double world" (CE, 128). This is prescient, demonstrating Miller's attraction to the unconscious apparent in Joyce's work, and his attempt to access it through similarly destructive language.

The longest epiphany in *Cancer* springs from Miller looking into the hole women have ... 'here':

> A glance into that dark unstitched wound and a deep fissure in my brain opens up: all the images and memories that had been laboriously or absent-mindedly assorted, labelled, documented, filed, sealed and stamped break forth pell-mell like ants pouring out of a crack in the sidewalk; the world ceases to revolve, time stops, the very nexus of my dreams is broken and dissolved and my guts spill out in a grand schizophrenic rush, an evacuation that leaves me face to face with the Absolute. I see again the great sprawling mothers of Picasso, their breasts covered with spiders, their legend hidden deep in the labyrinth. And Molly Bloom lying on a dirty mattress for eternity. (CAN, 250)

Looking into that "great yawning gulf of nothingness" (CAN, 253), a crack opens up in Miller's mind, and outflow reams of memories and images. Meaning slips into surrealism as he jams together images of Molly Bloom and Picasso's mothers covered with spiders. The signifiers that have been "labelled, documented, filed, sealed and stamped" in his mind spill out, deracinated from the Symbolic, and made meaningless by their foreclosure. This is one of the moments where Miller experiences the Real: he is "face to face with the Absolute," in a moment of pure jouissance that takes eleven caterwauling pages to try to express. If I had unlimited space in this chapter, I would have reproduced these pages in full and analyzed them further, as this section is the closest Miller gets to expressing the Real. I urge you to reread them.

Ecstasy

Many of Miller's epiphanies are moments of ecstasy:

> Today I awoke from a sound sleep with curses of joy on my lips, with gibberish on my tongue, repeating to myself like a litany—'*Fay ce que vouldras! …fay ce que vouldras!*' Do anything, but let it produce joy. Do anything, but let it yield ecstasy. So much crowds into my head when I say this to myself: images, gay ones, terrible ones, maddening ones, the wolf and the goat, the spider, the crab, syphilis with her wings outstretched…. But above all, *the ecstasy!*. (CAN, 255–256)

Miller's prose has an exultant, Nietzschean tone, with the French translating as "Do what thou wilt!" He emerges from sleep with these words already on his lips, a leftover from the liminal, unconscious land of dreams. The air quivers with excitement, but only temporarily, as in his other epiphanies, and the orgasmic moment soon turns bathetic. In another epiphany, Miller dives from the jouissance of "bright, gasping orgasms" to an image of sterility, "the air itself is steady with a stagnant sperm" (CAN, 170). This transition from ecstasy to suffering is the inevitable paradox of jouissance.

Another character who Miller writes through, as an Other, is Van Norden. He mirrors Miller's aims in writing: "Some day I'll write a book about myself, about my thoughts … I'll lay myself on the operating table and I'll expose my whole guts" (CAN, 136) and also experiences the "meaning of ecstasy" (CAN, 252):

> [f]or one second like I obliterate myself… there's not even one me then… there's nothing…. It's like receiving communion. Honest, I mean that. For a few seconds afterward I have a fine spiritual glow… and maybe it would continue that way indefinitely—how can you tell?—if it weren't for the fact that there's a woman beside you and then the douche bag and the water running… all those little details that make you desperately self-conscious, desperately lonely. (CAN, 134–135)

Van Norden experiences bliss momentarily, but blames its end, and the postcoital lack he feels, on the woman beside him. Van Norden is frustrated because he cannot conceive of why his jouissance must end: in Lacanian terms, he has glimpsed the Real, and doesn't want to return to loneliness of the Symbolic order. The fundamental problem with trying to express jouissance is that, once articulated, it is lost. The frustration Miller feels stems from his ability to experience the Real, and his inability to record it.

Language

Miller repeatedly conceptualizes language as a stream spewing forth from him. We saw this in the punctured body epiphanies, as here:

> Issuing from the rotted tongue and the bloated pages of ecstasy slimed with excrement. And I join my slime, my excrement, my madness, my ecstasy to the great circuit which flows through the subterranean vaults of the flesh. All this unbidden, unwanted, drunken vomit will flow on endlessly through the minds of those to come in the inexhaustible vessel that contains the history of the race. (CAN, 258)

Words on the page flow out from his "rotten tongue" like vomit and excrement. His book is an "inexhaustible vessel" made of this morass of bodily fluids. At times, Miller's prose embodies this image, in the form of barely mediated lists of words. In *Tropic of Capricorn*, we have a spiraling list that moves from "collar buttons" to "typewriter ribbons" to "cellophane" (CAP, 92). Another example is a list I found in the Miller collection at the Charles E. Young Library. It is titled "W O R D S" and is truly monumental. Each of the eight A4 pages is packed. The words range from dilly-dally to whang-doodle, calabash to calaboos, sconce to shitepoke, anaconda to excreta …

The list evidences Miller's obsessive relationship with language, each word representing that "aha" moment of epiphany, when he felt compelled to scribble it down. In *Cancer*, Miller discusses his compulsion toward words as a "mild sort of insanity," a "neurosis" that he, half-jokingly, diagnoses as *echolalia*. *Echolalia* is the automatic repetition of words, often seen in children. Miller does not repeat deliberately, but he

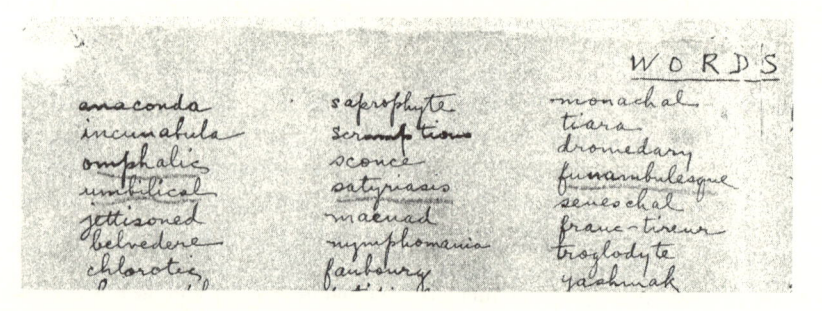

Figure 9.3. Henry Miller, word list, Charles E. Young Library

Figure 9.4. Henry Miller, word list, Charles E. Young Library

does have certain fixations. He places the same weight on all words, which is often why readers and critics raise concern with his writing: words like "cunt" or "whore" exist on the same plane as any other. Brassaï said that Miller believed any passage of his writing "could conceal the sublime," which helps explain his reluctance to edit; "the superb might have been swept up in the gutter, like a diamond in a torrent of mud and silt."[38]

In Seminar III, *The Psychoses*, Lacan attributes language disorders to the psychotic's lack of a sufficient number of *point de capiton*. *Point de capiton* are quilting points, like the buttons used in upholstery, where, "signified and signifier are knotted together."[39] Evans states that a lack of these *point de capiton* means that the "psychotic experience is characterized by a constant slippage of the signified under the signifier."[40] In Lacan's words, "there is a continual cascade of reshaping the signifier ... until the level is reached at which signifier and signified are stabilized in the delusional metaphor."[41] Language disorders are characterized by strings of signifiers that fail to reach a stable meaning or quilting point. Lacan calls this skewed relationship of the subject to the signifier "the nucleus of psychosis."[42] Miller's epiphanies embody this principle in both form and content: signifiers slip indefinitely, until, Lacan says, signification is stabilized in "delusional metaphor." We recognize these delusional metaphors, vividly displayed, in Miller's nightmares.

Miller's nightmares

Henry Miller admitted to considering suicide many times. Georges Belmont asked him where this "obsession with suicide" came from, to which he replied, "Everything was desolation, sadness.... You know, not long ago in Venice I thought about committing suicide again. From time to time it gets me" (HMC, 55). The key to understanding Miller's thoughts of suicide, which Ragland calls "another very common symptom in psychotic patients,"[43] are the dreams he suffered throughout his life. Miller's nightmares are delusional metaphors—extreme epiphanies—when the Borromean Knot slips and the sinthome fails to retie immediately. In other words, they are psychotic episodes when Miller's unconscious is accessible.

In Henry Miller: *Asleep and Awake*, a video monologue by Miller (aged 81), he tells of how his nightmares started in his early twenties, while buying a pack of Wrigley's gum in New York. Looking into the vending machine mirror, he saw a face that was not his own. He goes on to give an example of how this event affected him:

> I have veritable nightmares and it's always the same theme. I was shaving perhaps, I look in the mirror, and it's another face. I go crazy. I'm in the mental asylum. I'm in there for an interminable amount of time. I don't know what is happening. I don't know who I am: that especially. I'm just a nut like all the others. Finally I escape, it's a heroic job to jump over the walls, and then I breathe a sigh of relief, think everything is fine. I see a couple down the street and I wave and begin to talk to them, and as they look at me it's obvious that they don't know what I'm saying, what language I'm speaking. So I'm still mad. Then I usually wake up.[44]

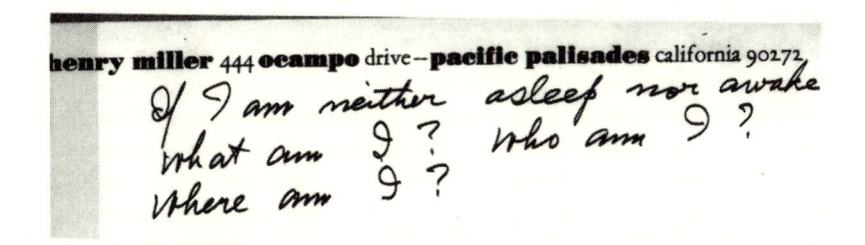

The Ecstatic Psychotic: Henry Miller via Jacques Lacan 121

> henry miller 444 ocampo drive — pacific palisades california 90272
>
> *If I am neither asleep nor awake*
> *what am I? who am I?*
> *where am I?*

Figure 9.5. Henry Miller, note, Charles E. Young Library, 404, Box 94, Folder 7

Miller fails to recognize himself in a mirror, and then completely loses his sense of self. Breaking out of the asylum he thinks he is cured, but finds to his dismay that the couple cannot understand what he is saying. In Lacanian terms, this initial terror is an upending of the mirror stage. Rather than realizing himself and entering the world of language, Miller experiences the opposite: a crisis of identification and failure to reach points of signification. These questions of identity haunted Miller throughout his life, as is apparent in the note written at his final residence.

It is in the liminal space of dreams, such as "Walking Up and Down in China," that we see Miller's paranoia played out.[45] He is walking down a Parisian street and sees a man lying on the sidewalk, "flat on his back with arms outstretched" (BS, 206). He cannot tell whether he is "dreaming or awake" but continues, "[t]he more I think of it the more I am convinced that what disturbs me is not whether I am dreaming or not but whether the man on the sidewalk, the man with arms outstretched, was myself" (BS, 207). In a surreal re-enactment, of his original hallucination in New York, the man on the ground becomes a vision of himself; his Other. Following this, Miller launches into a list of 102 places, from Quebec to Louveciennes. This chain of signifiers is another example of the Other dictating to him, signifiers slipping as the words flow freely out of him "pell-mell like ants pouring out of a crack in the sidewalk" (CAN, 250). Immediately proceeding the list, Miller says, "In each and every one of these places I left a dead body on the sidewalk with arms outstretched. Every time I bent over to take a good look at myself, to reassure myself that the body was not alive and that it was not I but myself that I was leaving behind" (BS, 208–209). The "dead selves peeled off" are all Others, each one representing a rebirth. The imperative behind this, as in Joyce's *Portrait of the Artist as a Young Man* and Ralph Ellison's *Invisible Man*, is the mercurial nature of the self. This chapter shows us that Miller struggles with his sense of self, in part, because the Other's identity is not fixed.

The only piece of writing Miller admitted was surreal, "Into the Night Life,"[46] contains a nightmarish scene explicating this further:

> There is an enormous hole in my side, a clean hole without a drop of blood showing. I can't tell anymore who I am or where I came from or how I get here .... When I raise my eyes I see a man standing at the doorsill .... He asks

my name, my address, my profession, what I am doing and where I am going and so on and so forth. He asks endless prying questions to which I am unable to respond, first because I have lost my tongue, and second because I cannot remember any longer what language I speak. 'Why don't you speak?' he says, bending over mejeeringly, and taking his light rattan stick he jabs a hole in my side. My anguish is so great that it seems I must speak even if I have no tongue, even if I know not who I am or where I come from. With my two hands I try to wrench my jaws apart, but the teeth are locked. My chin crumbles away like dry clay, leaving the jawbone exposed. 'Speak!' he says, with that cruel jeering smile and, taking his stick once again, he jabs another hole in my side. (BS, 159)

The scene begins with an eerily clean puncture in his body. Instead of signifiers pouring out of the hole, like in previous scenes, Miller experiences extreme lock jaw, with his chin crumbling to nothing—an image of the loss of language. The man's taunts are a violent representation of the structures of the Symbolic order: his question "Why don't you speak?" can be read as "Why can't you signify?" Miller's identity is fundamentally produced through language, via the action of the Other, and therefore when he loses the ability to speak, he loses a stable sense of it. The hole in the Symbolic is taken to its utmost extent. Rather than simply enacting the sinthome, this scene shows the Borromean Knot in tatters; as Ragland confirmed, "psychotics very often lose their voice and can't say anything; it's when the Real takes over the Symbolic."[47] The Real taking over the Symbolic is only possible when the Borromean Knot is untied and radical foreclosure prolonged.

Concluding words

In his essay "Narcissism" (1976), Norman Mailer insists Miller is a narcissist: "[i]t is often too simple to think of the narcissist as someone in love with himself. One can detest oneself intimately and still be a narcissist. What characterizes narcissism is the fundamental relation. It is with oneself."[48] By Mailer's definition, Miller is the archetypal narcissist, but as his fundamental relationship is with the Other, his sense of "oneself" cannot be described as such; it is not a coherent entity. What strikes me most about Miller's writing, especially in the epiphanies and more surreal sections of his prose, is the repeated questioning of his identity. In the final interview before his death, Miller shows an awareness of this, "I have to wonder if I am singing the same song in every book."[49] Brassaï conceives this compulsion as the work of the "unseen force," which "sometimes he [Miller] calls the Voice, sometimes the Dictate, sometimes the Other."[50] Brassaï observes it first-hand:

He had no choice but to get up, get a notebook, then spend hour after hour copying down the fully formed sentences that came pouring out. He was in a sort of a trance, innocent of what might be coming next. He always said that when he read those texts later on he was as flabbergasted and as shocked as any reader might be. This was how Miller's beautiful works came to life—in a rush, tumbling out of him like a "sack of coal." Creating meant tapping into a source and turning on a faucet, not agonizing about sentence structure. The process always took him by surprise—he was a transcriber, a kind of Mohammed, an adherent to the dictates of an unseen force that had seized control of his hand.[51]

The Other is dictating once more, words and even sentences coming to him in a "flood," an "avalanche," a "hemourrage."[52] In these periods, as Brassaï points out, Miller was "practicing a kind of 'automatic writing.'"[53] In one respect, the Other possessed him, which clearly worried and disturbed him, most obviously in his nightmares, but it also functioned as the creative force from which his writing flowed.

Within the act of creation, we realize a further paradox. The act of creation is one of ecstasy, of jouissance, but that which is created represents loss and lack. Miller was caught between these forces, as we can see in this letter to Nin, from the Villa Seurat, dated 21 February 1939:

> Creation is always difficult because it is an attempt to recover what is lost. To regain we must first feel abandoned. You know all the joys and terrors of creation. You have been playing God ever since you were able to talk.... It is the ark and the covenant of the lost.... You are recording the constancy of change, the eternality of metamorphoses.... You are always striving to fill the empty vessel of life.... And finally you will realize that even this is not sufficient, not effective enough.... The word was never meant to be engraved on tablets of stone nor imprisoned between the covers of a book.... Writing is life, but what is written is death.... We are trying to record the changing ego, but the Self will not be revealed thus. We are only throwing off sparks. (LAN, 154–158)

Miller realized Anaïs Nin was another sufferer and also psychotic in the Lacanian sense; she knew the joys and terrors of creation, of playing God, just as he did. Their aim was the same: to record the metamorphosis of life, the inexpressible, the absolute, the Real. Implicit in the final line of his letter to Nin is Miller's realization that he would never be able to attain the Real through the Symbolic, and that it is impossible to experience life, or truth, through words. Words were never enough for Miller. In *The Cosmological Eye*, he says, "What do I mean to infer? Just this—that art, the art of living, involves the act of creation. The work of art is nothing" (CE, 7). This is the irony at the heart of Henry Miller: he saw the act of writing as life, but the written word as dead.

Miller often conceptualizes the moment of radical foreclosure as such: "It's like a clean birth. Everything cut away. Separate, naked, alone. Bliss and agony simultaneously" (CAN, 289). Even in his nightmares all is not pain and loss; we still get a sense of his excitement at the words unfolding and his struggle to understand them. Miller repeatedly demonstrates the duality of creation—its simultaneous agony and bliss—in his work. This is an essential truth in the creation of art and applies not just to Miller but also Joyce, Dalí, Nietzsche, Mozart, Artaud, and many other artists, perhaps all artists. It certainly applies to Jacques Lacan, who, like Miller, built a web with the

Symbolic to try and access the Real, who never stopped searching for the answer, and who was unable to fill the lack he felt. Whereas Lacan ended life frustrated and tied up in his own theoretical knots, disbanding his school (Écolefreudienne) shortly before his death in 1981, Miller continued to write copiously as the scribe of the Other. He accepted the hole in himself, the lack that he could never fill, and he surrendered to it. Miller explained this to Belmont: "it's when you surrender, that miracles happen. The whole thing is knowing how to surrender" (HMC, 61). Miller also impressed the importance of this to Barbara Kraft, describing surrender as a "marvellous feeling," akin to bliss.[54] He realized that accepting the Other was his only chance to glimpse the Real.

When I described Miller's relationship with the Other—his obsessive lists, surreal prose, epiphanies, and nightmares of loss of identity and language—to Ellie Ragland, she said, "every symptom you are saying he has is a psychotic symptom."[55] Clearly, language disorders and prolonged moments of radical foreclosure are present in Miller's work. Ragland went on, "a lot of the most genius authors we have are psychotic. They use their art to make a whole. They are seeking a cure by writing."[56] We notice this throughout Miller's tremendous body of work—his books, letters, and notes were the battlefield and transcript of his internal struggle. He surrendered himself to writing and sought treatment through language, insecure in the knowledge that words were not the cure but a self-perpetuating symptom of his psychosis.

Notes

1 Lao-Tzu, *Tao Te Ching: A New English Version*, trans. Stephen Mitchell (New York: Harper & Row, 1988), 1, 23, 78.
2 Alan Friedman, "The Pitching of Love's Mansion in the Tropics of Henry Miller," *Seven Contemporary Authors* (Austin: University of Texas Press, 1966), 134.
3 Caroline Blinder, *A Self-Made Surrealist: Ideology and Aesthetics in the Work of Henry Miller* (Rochester: Camden House, 2000), 11.
4 Charles E. Young Library, Collection 404, Box 94, Folder 13.
5 Jacques Lacan, *Écrits: A Selection*, ttrans. Alan Sheridan (New York: Norton, 1977), 147.
6 Jacques Lacan and Anthony Wilden, *Speech and Language in Psychoanalysis* (Baltimore: Johns Hopkins, 1981), 81.
7 Jacques Lacan and Jacques-Alain Miller, *The Psychoses: The Seminar III of Jacques Lacan* (London: Routledge, 1993), 68.
8 D.P. Schreber, *Memoirs of My Nervous Illness*, trans. and ed. Ida Mac Alpine and Richard Hunter (Cambridge: Harvard University Press, 1988), 130.
9 Lacan, *The Psychoses*, 44.
10 Lacan, *The Psychoses*, 228.
11 Lacan, *The Psychoses*, 89.
12 Lacan, *Écrits*, viii.
13 Edmund Wilson, "Twilight of the Expatriates." *New Republic* 98.1214: 141.
14 Edmund Wilson, *The Shores of Light: A Literary Chronicle of the Twenties and Thirties* (New York: Farrar, Straus and Young, 1952), 708.

15 Jacques Lacan and Jacques-Alain Miller, *The Four Fundamental Concepts of Psychoanalysis* (London: Hogarth, 1977), 118.
16 Lacan, *Écrits*, 10.
17 Lacan, *The Psychoses*, 274.
18 Interview with Ellie Ragland, Professor of Comparative Literature and Critical Theory, University of Missouri, Thursday, 29 November 2012.
19 Lacan, *Écrits*, 148.
20 Dylan Evans, *An Introductory Dictionary of Lacanian Psychoanalysis* (London: Routledge, 1996), 18.
21 Diagram from Lacan.com, Ellie Jabour.
22 Evans, *Introductory*, 159.
23 Evans, *Introductory*, 132.
24 Lacan, *Four*, 167.
25 Savas Yazici, "Encountering with the Real: A Critical Reading of the Works of Lacan, Lacau, Žižek, and Badiou," PhD dissertation, The Graduate School of Social Sciences of Middle East Technical University, 2007, 90.
26 Ellie Ragland-Sullivan and Dragan Milovanovic, *Lacan: Topologically Speaking* (New York: Other, 2004), 373.
27 Ragland, interview.
28 Evans, *Introductory*, 89.
29 Jacques Lacan, *The Seminar of Jacques Lacan, Book XXIII–Joyce and the Sinthome–1975–1976*, trans. Cormac Gallagher. Parts 1 and 2.file:///D:/Downloads/Book-23-Joyce-and-the-Sinthome-Part-2.pdf
30 Ragland, interview.
31 Evans, *Introductory*, 190.
32 Evans, *Introductory*, 89.
33 Interview with Luke Thurston, Professor of Modern Literature, Aberystwyth University, Tuesday, 24 November 2012.
34 Scholes and Kain 1965, 29 cited in Maud Ellmann, *The Nets of Modernism: Henry James, Virginia Woolf, James Joyce, and Sigmund Freud* (Cambridge: Cambridge University Press, 2010).
35 Ellman, *Nets*, 5.
36 Blinder, *Self-Made*, 27.
37 The section from, "But what" to "a week," is taken, word for word, from *Finnegans Wake* ("Shem the Penman," Book 1, Chapter 7, 179).
38 Brassaï, *Henry Miller, the Paris Years*, trans. Timothy Bent (New York: Arcade, 1995), 154.
39 Lacan, *The Psychoses*, 268.
40 Evans, *Introductory*, 156.
41 Lacan, *Écrits*, 217.
42 Lacan, *The Psychoses*, 250.
43 Ragland, interview.
44 *Henry Miller: Asleep & Awake*, Dir. Tom Schiller, (NTSC, 2007), DVD.
45 I examine this in more detail in my article, "Henry Miller's *Black Spring* through the Looking Glass of Jacques Lacan," *Nexus: The International Henry Miller Journal*, 9 (2012), 105–123.
46 Brassaï, *Henry*, 156.

47 Ragland, interview.
48 Mailer, *Genius and Lust*, 138.
49 Barbara Kraft and Henry Miller. Interview for NPR, 26 December 1979.
50 Brassaï, *Henry*, 150.
51 Brassaï, *Henry*, 149.
52 Brassaï, *Henry*, 150.
53 Brassaï, *Henry*, 154–155.
54 Kraft, interview.
55 Ragland, interview.
56 Ragland, interview.

10

Big Sur and *Walden*: Henry Miller's Practical Transcendentalism

Eric D. Lehman

Henry Miller has long been associated with the Transcendentalist tradition in American literature, and with good reason. At the beginning of *Tropic of Cancer* he announces his own lineage by quoting Ralph Waldo Emerson, while Emerson's *Representative Men*, Henry David Thoreau's *Civil Disobedience*, and Walt Whitman's *Leaves of Grass* all make his list of one hundred influential books in *Books in My Life*. In that book he also puts the three authors in his "genealogical line," as well as in Abraham Lincoln's imaginary cabinet. (BIML, 124, 236) In fact, mentions of Whitman throughout Miller's work are abundant, with Emerson and Thoreau close behind. He has placed himself firmly in this American tradition.[1]

However, the exploration of these connections in the scholarship is thinner than it should be. In particular, by focusing on Miller's early novels many critics have missed even deeper and more profound similarities. *Big Sur and the Oranges of Hieronymus Bosch* parallels Thoreau's *Walden* in many ways, explores transcendental values, and shows where he diverges from them regarding the relationship of the individual to community. He particularly challenges the Transcendentalists' idealistic and utopian thinking, exploring the positive and negative sides of it. This inevitably leads to a struggle with his established philosophy of creative individualism, and we find him stubbornly defending his privacy, bewailing his lost relationships, and trying to answer the question—what is the relationship of the creative individual to the rest of the world?

In some ways Miller seems an unlikely heir to the Transcendentalists. Though he is certainly civilly disobedient, he does not take up a cause. He usually does not take an interest in reforming theology or government. He certainly bears little resemblance to the genteel, formal persona of Ralph Waldo Emerson. On the other hand, Miller is a clear descendent of Thoreau, Whitman, and even Emerson in the way he approached the individual. His work is full of visions, of epiphanies, and of personal realizations described in hyperbolic prose. The Transcendentalists sought to "transcend" old forms of religions, society, and ethics. Miller did, too. As critics have pointed out, Miller continues the Transcendentalist tradition of identifying with "formidable and heroic rebels," including Lucifer, Prometheus, Jesus, and Napoleon.[2]

Previous scholarship has focused primarily on connecting Miller to the "creative individualism" inherent in this tradition. For example, William Gordon's early seminal work *The Mind and Art of Henry Miller* contains the throwaway line "Miller's later work will become more transcendental, in the manner of Whitman." He follows up with a comparison to Whitman, whom he sees as a romantic interested in self-creation.[3] Others have also focused on Miller's discovery of the self, reliance on intuition, nonconformity, and rejection of society.[4] In short, Miller is a Transcendentalist because of his free, creative spirit, and staunch individualism. Of course, the same might be said for nearly every creative artist, including those who do not credit Emerson and company directly, as Miller does.

A few have gone farther. Working from the Transcendentalist side of the equation, Arnold Smithline in the *Emerson Society Quarterly* compares Emerson, Whitman, and Miller closely on several different points, including their theories of art, their optimism, their hatred of society, and their ideas of the divinity of man.[5] Smithline also mentions Miller's occasional endorsement of the unity of man and nature and feeling of universal connection, though he does not go into it in detail.[6] Another important study is Paul Jackson's "Henry Miller, Emerson, and the Divided Self," which explores the influence of the nineteenth century sage on Miller's "prophetic announcements," and more particularly on the structure of his semiautobiographical work, following the epigraph from *Tropic of Cancer*, "These novels will give way, by and by, to diaries or autobiographies—captivating books, if only a man knew how to choose among what he calls his experiences that which is really his experience, and how to record truth truly" (CAN, ii). Jackson lays out the two authors' parallel ideas about selfhood in text and in reality, through the parallel of "Osman" in Emerson's journals and "Osmanli" in *Sexus*. In doing so Jackson demonstrates not only the specific connection, but also the larger connection between the two writers.[7]

Though more work could be done to connect Miller's creative individualism with his American forebears, the most surprising oversight is *Big Sur*. Though it also includes call-outs and citations of Emerson and Whitman, in many ways it is Miller's response to Thoreau's *Walden*.[8] Miller announces his program immediately by quoting Thoreau in the epigraph: "I am convinced that to maintain one's self on this earth is not a hardship, but a pastime, if we will live simply and wisely."[9] He then uncharacteristically begins with three short sections, "chronological," "topographical," and "in the beginning," giving personal history to be sure, but also historical information on the Big Sur area, as well as a more mythological version, invoking Titans, Troglodytes, fauns, and giants, asking "From what realm of light were we shadows who darken the earth spawned?" (BSOHB, 8). In this way he makes sure to emphasize the importance of the place, both for him and for humanity. And then, in case we didn't get his point yet, he tells us clearly, "... there is a world here as full and rich, as compelling and instructive, as Thoreau found at Walden" (BSOHB, 33). He even ends the book as Thoreau might have ended, saying:

> ... here there is abiding peace, the peace of God, and the serene security created by a handful of good neighbors living at one with the creature world, with noble, ancient trees, scrub and sagebrush, wild lilac and lovely lupin, with poppies and

buzzards, eagles and humming birds, gophers and rattlesnakes, and sea and sky unending. (BSOHB, 404)

The many parallels include the structure of the two books. Miller describes his life at Big Sur, and uses it as a jumping off point for philosophical musing; Thoreau describes his life at Walden, and uses it as a jumping off point for philosophical musing. Like Thoreau, Miller alludes to various authors and thinkers, talking about those close at hand, those far off who write him letters, and those far off in time. Miller separates the ideas of solitude and loneliness (BSOHB, 34) in the same way that Thoreau does.[10] Miller also talks of the practical things, like "to get rid of your empty bottles, tin cans and other refuse, you must own a car and drive an appreciable distance to the allotted dumping ground, or else engage the professional services of Howard Welch, the man from Missouri" (BSOHB, 38). Thoreau's time is taken up with practical matters, too: "I did not read books the first summer; I hoed beans."[11]

However, *Big Sur* is not *Walden* in one important respect. Miller has passed that point of life where he needs solitude to stimulate his creative individualism. He is already a published author whose books have challenged both established literature and social mores. When you have accomplished your goal and broken tradition into a thousand pieces, how do you come back into the world? How should Miller *live*? In *Big Sur* he confronts that future, and therefore his main theme is not the relationship of the individual to nature, but the relationship of the individual to the community. To explore this, he uses his transcendental forebears as a launching pad for his own vision, which is exactly what Emerson and company would hope for.

To make sure we know his program of locating the individual and the community, the first line of the book proper is "The little community of one ..." and he continues to use the word throughout the book (BSOHB, 11, 15, et al.). He goes on to speak of the "art colony" and points out that "Artists never thrive in colonies. Ants do." What he needs, what every artist needs, is "solitude" (BSOHB, 13). He then goes on to complain about the chief problem of this model, which is the "idle visitor," a concern that he takes right through the book to the end, where he rants for many pages about the letters that arrive to which he cannot respond. Here he is partly echoing Thoreau himself, who says in *Walden* "I could easily do without the post-office" and goes on a similar, if shorter, rant about the sorry excuses for letters that people send.[12] For Miller, though, other people are not only mediocre nuisances, but also something unavoidable about the world.

Connecting the society at Big Sur to a long tradition Miller discusses the "idealist ventures" of Utopian communities, but then says "Today it is not communities or groups who seek to lead 'the good life' but isolated individuals" (BSOHB, 17). He then admits that his concern with the theme is new, saying:

Digging in at Big Sur eleven years ago, I must confess that I had not the least thought or concern about the life of the community. With a population of one hundred souls scattered over several hundred square miles, I was not even conscious of an existent "community." My community then comprised a dog, Pascal ... a few trees, the buzzards, and a seeming jungle of poison oak. (BSOHB, 19)

But neighbors arrived, and helped out this city dweller to live in this crazy place. As they did, "the community, from being at first an invisible web, gradually became most tangible, most real" (BSOHB, 20).

In fact, Miller fills most of the book with encounters with people who live in the area, or who come in from the outside. A woman from Holland berates him for "cleaning, cooking, gardening, taking care of a child, fixing cesspools, and so on" (BSOHB, 44). Instead, she thinks he should be writing. When friends show up things are even worse, and the woman is shocked that the mundanities of the real world should intrude on the solitary "sublime" life of the writer (BSOHB, 44). Another is a boy named Ralph who arrives to join the "cult of sex and anarchy" and become a writer. Miller must finally tell him that he is a "nuisance" and a "pest" and give him the boot (BSOHB, 48).

Walden, too, has an entire chapter on "Visitors," and Thoreau declares, like Miller, that he "feared the men-harriers," those visitors who would not leave him in solitude.[13] But these are interruptions from his commune with nature, whereas for Miller they seem to represent a larger society that needs to be appeased. Mothers drop children off at his house to play with his children. Disturbing notices arrive. Miller tries to ignore it all, saying, "Though not cut off, in the strict sense, Big Sur receives, as through a filter, the violent waves which agitate the world.... One can live with or without, take it or leave it, and not feel out of step with the rest of the community" (BSOHB, 145). He is trying to stay true to his Transcendentalist principles and reject society whenever he can. But there are some people that he cannot ignore.

Walden works in part because Thoreau is alone. What about children? Marriage? Miller is not a young man any more; he has responsibilities to his family, responsibilities to which he does not always attend. Throughout the book he readily admits his flaws as a husband, which lead to the dissolution of yet another marriage. His wife takes his children "ostensibly to become acquainted with their grandparents," and letters stop coming. He begins to panic, and after finally figuring out their whereabouts, notes that she had gone "home." "And then and there I realized that 'home' had come to mean some other place—for her. Now I had no way of communicating with her. I was cut off, just as sharp and neat as if by a razor blade" (BSOHB, 146–147).

The most practical problem with living the creative life is children. His two children, Val and Tony, are just like any others and need a father. To elucidate this, Miller includes a chapter called "Discipline," perhaps a call out to Emerson's identically titled chapter in *Nature*. Emerson speaks of the "moral influence of nature upon every individual."[14] However, sometimes philosophy is best in the abstract, and Miller points this out in a funny and sad chapter as "discipline" regards his children, which he cannot control. A sort of nanny tries to help, and gives up after twelve hours, saying "my kids were impossible" (BSOHB, 180). Miller and his friend Walker Winslow give it a try, and barely survive, repeating "patience" to each other as they try to nurture Val and Tony (BSOHB, 182). They entertain the children endlessly, make meals, and deal with all the usual problems of small children. Finally, it is too much for Walker, who yells, "face red as a beet, 'These kids are completely out of hand'" (BSOHB, 189). Walker convinces Miller that he is doing himself and the children a disservice by trying to keep them at Big Sur. He calls his ex-wife, and she picks them up, leaving him "heartbroken." "A dozen times a night I would wake with a start, thinking that they were calling me. There is no emptiness like the emptiness of a home which your children have flown. It was worse than death" (BSOHB, 190). He weeps and screams and curses, and knows that he has failed as a father. Creative solitude is all well and good, unless you have children to provide for. Furthermore, Miller uses his failed "discipline" of his children to show how he has failed to have the discipline necessary to be fully educated by nature. Do they lack discipline, or does he?

The biggest challenge, though, comes with Conrad Moricand, in the section of the book Miller appropriately titles "Paradise Lost." A former friend of Blaise Cendrars, an astrologer and scholar who first met Miller in Paris, Moricand "was a disturbed being, a man of nerves, caprices, and stubborn will" (BSOHB, 276). Miller helped him in Paris by getting him food and keeping him occupied doing various astrological charts. Then, shortly after Miller moves to Big Sur, he receives a letter from Moricand, asking for money and food. Miller helps him again and "letters began to fly back and forth" (BSOHB, 295), but he keeps asking for more money. But Miller doesn't have that sort of money, and "Finally, I conceived what I thought to be a brilliant idea...to invite him to come and live with us, share what we had, regard our home as his own for the rest of his days" (BSOHB, 295). His wife (still with him at this time) objects, asking practical questions, and Miller stubbornly sticks to his plan. "What she could not understand was why I felt it imperative to assume such a responsibility for one who had never really been an intimate friend" (BSOHB, 296). He tries to argue with her. "Finally, I grew ashamed of myself. Why did I have to justify myself? Why make excuses? The man was starving. He was ill. He was penniless. He was at the end of his rope. Weren't these reason enough?" (BSOHB, 296–297).

The Transcendentalists have seemingly contradictory advice when it comes to helping others. Both Thoreau and Emerson give cautions about charity.[15] Thoreau does not begrudge helping people; he assists "one real runaway slave...toward the north star." But for those who do not truly need his help, Thoreau only says that "objects of charity are not guests."[16] Emerson famously wanted as little to do with other people as he could, saying "Society is good when it does not violate me, but less when it is likest to solitude."[17] However, Emerson also wrote that although some might think that "it is better to be alone than in bad company," he asserts that is short sighted, and that "the good and wise must learn to act, to carry salvation to the combatants and demagogues in the dusty arena below."[18] So, which advice should Miller follow? He chooses in this case to try to help another human being, furnishing Moricand with his writing studio, giving up his own private creative solitude to help another person.

Once Moricand arrives, he begins asking for things. Specific things, like Yardley talcum powder. He can't use any other kind. "But of that instant I knew my wife was right, knew that I had made a grave mistake...I saw the spoiled child, the man who had never done an honest stroke of work in his life, the destitute individual who was too proud to beg openly but was not above milking a friend dry" (BSOHB, 301).

And Moricand asks for more and more as time goes by, from paper to codeine. He is portrayed as being completely antithetical to transcendental self-reliance.

Miller asks him to teach his daughter French, but that never happens. "He was utterly at a loss to understand my preoccupation with the child" (BSOHB, 312). Moricand and Miller's wife agree that Miller's values are impossible for bringing up a child. "'He believes in *freedom*,' she would say, making the idea of freedom sound like utter rubbish" (BSOHB, 314). Moricand tries to have it both ways, though, "explaining to my wife that I was a born anarchist, that my sense of freedom was a peculiarly personal one, that the very idea of discipline was abhorrent to my nature. I was a rebel and an outlaw.... My function in life was to create disturbance.... It was also fact, he had to admit, that I was too good, too kind, too gentle, too patient, too indulgent, too forbearing, too forgiving" (BSOHB, 314–315). In the mouth of Moricand these become insults, and perhaps the inclusion of this episode is self-criticism.

They argue over astrology, and Miller repeats Thoreau's dictum: "live simply and wisely" (BSOHB, 326). But Moricand cannot do that. First, he is afflicted with a terrible itch. After a doctor examines him he tells Miller in confidence to get rid of him, that "he doesn't want to get well. What he wants is sympathy, attention. He's not a man, he's a child. A spoiled child" (BSOHB, 328). All of Miller's further attempts to "pull him out of his misery" fail (BSOHB, 330). Moricand tells a pathetic story of his escape during the Second World War, in which he refuses to give up two valises of his books and manuscripts, at the risk of his own life. Miller finds this ridiculous, saying he would have thrown away the junk, that life is more important than objects. "Suddenly I no longer felt sorry for him, not for anything that had ever happened to him" (BSOHB, 341). Earlier in the memoir, Miller had echoed Emerson's dismissive views on property, saying "'My horse! My land! My kingdom!' The babble of idiots" (BSOHB, 8).[19] The episode with Moricand shows very clearly that most people cannot take this enlightened view.

But Moricand's problems go deeper than clinging to material possessions and neurotic behavior. He embodies everything negative about humans: their greed, their selfishness, and their evil appetites. When Miller's daughter Val "in a playful way... snatched the piece of bread lying beside him," Moricand snatches it back with "a look full of hatred, the look of a man so beside himself that he might even commit murder" (BSOHB, 361). Then, worse, Moricand shares a story about molesting a little girl, and "as he uttered these words I felt my hair stand on end. It was no longer Moricand I was facing but Satan himself" (BSOHB, 363). Miller hustles him out of the house soon afterwards, even when confronted with boulders blocking the highway and a broken car. Finally, after multiple problems, they carry him to the mailman's car, and take him to a hospital in Monterey, then a hotel, dealing with innumerable setbacks.

Moricand leaves for San Francisco, saying "that it was obvious I didn't wish to see him any more" (BSOHB, 373). Miller sends all his remaining belongings, "fumigates" the writing studio, and gives him travel guides to San Francisco. However, inevitably more requests for money follow. Miller arranges for him to sail to Europe, which he requested, but Moricand slips away from this arrangement, and promptly threatens his former friend with a lawsuit, scandal, and more. He is really trying to get more money out of Miller, a thousand dollars, saying that as Miller reported, "It was I who had induced him to come to America, and I had promised to take care of him." Miller is furious, and tells him that he'll cut him off if he doesn't leave the country. Moricand cannot believe this is "the same Miller" the "great compassionate heart who gave to one and all." But Miller is stubborn: "I called him a worm, a leech, a dirty blackmailer" (BSOHB, 378). At last, the insufferable Moricand is deported by the immigration authorities, solving the problem for Miller at least.

Miller sums up with, "Never, never again, would I make the mistake of trying to solve someone's problems for him. How deceptive to think that by means of a little self-sacrifice one can help another overcome his difficulties! How egotistical!" (BSOHB, 355). This echoes Emerson's negative opinion of charity; Miller says "No wonder we hang our heads in shame when we perform a simple act of charity" (BSOHB, 381). However, Miller himself spent many years living off the kindness of others, from Anaïs Nin to Alfred Perlès. So, Moricand's situation causes Miller to reflect on those poverty-stricken times when he was asking for handouts, and find the clear difference: gratitude for everything given to him (BSOHB, 381). Earlier he wrote that the people at Big Sur "behave as if it were a privilege to live here, as if it were by an act of grace they found themselves here" (BSOHB, 26). But not everyone is grateful, and not everyone is suited to live in a perfect society. In pointing this out, Miller may be echoing the tradition of the "naysayers" of Transcendentalism such as Edgar Allan Poe, Nathaniel Hawthorne, and Herman Melville. He certainly shared their concern, which was Transcendentalism's insubstantial treatment of the darker side of humanity.[20] With freedom and solitude, some men do not find a creative spirit, but instead turn to evil.

So is Moricand the snake in the garden that made Miller question his entire philosophy? Is *Big Sur* a rejection of Transcendentalism as a viable system? Not at all. It is an attempt at reconciliation. Miller gives a hint of this near the center of the book when he asks, "What is the task of genuine love?" In answer he quotes *The Millennium of Hieronymous Bosch*, "However free each may be to follow his own inclination, there remains an invisible bond holding them all together. This is the *tenderness* with which all these inhabitants of the heavenly meadows cling together in brotherly and sisterly intimacy" (BSOHB, 237). It is this love or tenderness that creates community, "and what is a nation, or a people, without a sense of community—there must be a common purpose." But at this point in the book he admits, "Even here in Big Sur, where the oranges are ready to blossom forth, there is no common purpose, no common effort. There is a remarkable neighborliness, but no community spirit." Where then is the hope he looks for? It is with the "lone travelers," who "have more real community spirit than those who talk community ... they are assisting in the creation of a new fabric, a simple, viable one, better able to stand the stress and strain, the wear and tear of time" (BSOHB, 264–265).[21]

At the end of the book he continues this discussion, with another nod to *Walden*, saying "When first I beheld this wondrous region I thought to myself.—'Here I will find peace. Here I shall find the strength to do the work I was made to do.'" And he continues:

Back of the ridge which overshadows us is a wilderness in which scarcely anyone ever sets foot. It is a great forest and game reserve intended to be set apart forever. At night one feels the silence all about, a silence which begins far back of the ridge and which creeps in with the fog and the stars, with the warm valley winds, and which carries in its folds a mystery as deep as the earth's own. A magnetic, healing ambiance.... The very looks of the land makes one long to keep it intact—the spiritual reserve of a few bright spirits. (BSOHB, 402–403)

This paean to the natural world and its "few bright spirits" might seem to indicate that Miller is finally affirming the vision and methods of Thoreau's *Walden*. But he continues, saying that he now has a "different view," and that sometimes he thinks "how wonderful will be the day when all these mountain sides are filled with habitations, when the slopes are terraced with fields, when flowers burst forth everywhere, not only wild flowers but flowers planted by human hands for human delectation." He pictures the land hundreds of years in the future with "villas dotting the slopes," "colossal stairways," "chapels and monasteries," "tables spread under brilliant awnings," and "laughter like pearling rapids, rising from thousands of jubilant throats." It is a paradise now, he says, but "*then* it will another paradise, one in which all share, all participate. The *only* paradise, after all" (BSOHB, 403–404). This is a new vision, an attempt to reconcile the transcendental tradition of individual creative spirits and a world that will and must include others. As he said earlier in the book, such a place does not exist now, but must be left for future generations.

Emerson wrote that "There is no pure Transcendentalist."[22] In *Big Sur* Miller proves this, working within and expanding the boundaries of the Transcendentalist traditions of his literary antecedents. He has concluded that the birth of each creative individual is not only an end in itself, but the first step to a better community. He resumes these musings in later volumes like *The Books in My Life*, where he makes specific reference to Walt Whitman's quote "The world will be complete for him who is himself complete." He continues, saying "There can only be government—that is, abdication of the self, of one's own inalienable rights—where there are incomplete beings. The New Jerusalem can only be made of and by emancipated individuals. That is community" (BIML, 229–230). It is a remarkably hopeful vision of the future from a man who some call nihilistic and who is concerned with the destruction of all things.

Notes

1 Some people even teach Miller as a Transcendentalist in the classroom. Doug Matus, "Teach as You Like and Die Happy: Henry Miller as High School Curriculum," *Nexus: The International Henry Miller Journal*, 7 (2010): 87–95.
2 Arnold Smithline, "Henry Miller and the Transcendental Spirit," *Emerson Society Quarterly* 2 (1966): 53. Smithline is not the only one, of course. Miller's identification with (or personification of) the rebel is well documented.
3 Gordon, *The Mind*, 98, 206–207.

4 See for example Harold McCarthy, "Henry Miller's Democratic Vistas," 221–235. Or Elet, Joost, *The Influence of American Transcendentalism on Miller via Walt Whitman.* (Ghent: Ghent University, 2009).
5 Smithline, "Henry Miller," 50–56.
6 Smithline quotes a paragraph from "The Air-Conditioned Nightmare" that only marginally deals with this, and is more of a paean to "peace." See Henry Miller, *The Air-Conditioned Nightmare* (New York: New Directions, 1945), 146–148.
7 Paul Jackson, "Henry Miller, Emerson, and the Divided Self," in *Critical Essays on Henry Miller*, ed. Ronald Gottesman (New York: G.K. Hall, 1992), 223–234.
8 In "Democratic Vistas" (above) Harold McCarthy posits that Paris was a sort of Walden Pond for Miller, but offers little textual support, focusing as so many others do on his individual creative spirit.
9 He repeats this quote on page 263.
10 Henry David Thoreau, *Walden and Other Writings*, ed. Brooks Atkinson (New York: Random House, 1950), 119.
11 Thoreau, *Walden*, 101.
12 Thoreau, *Walden*, 84–86.
13 Thoreau, *Walden*, 136–139.
14 Ralph Waldo Emerson, "Nature," in *Emerson on Transcendentalism*, ed. Edward Ericson (New York: Continuum, 1999), 22.
15 Thoreau, *Walden*, 69–70 and Ralph Waldo Emerson, "Self-Reliance," in *Emerson: Essays and Lectures*, ed. Joel Porte (New York: Library of America, 1983), 262–263.
16 Thoreau, *Walden*, 137–138.
17 Emerson, "The Transcendentalist," 94.
18 Emerson, "The Transcendentalist," 102.
19 Emerson, "Self-Reliance," 281.
20 Richard Kopley, "Naysayers: Poe, Hawthorne, and Melville," in *Oxford Handbook of Transcendentalism*, ed. Joel Myerson, Sandra Petrulionis, and Laura Walls (New York: Oxford University Press, 2010), 597–613.
21 Earlier he also writes that "These isolated individuals are bringing about a community which will one day replace the dismembered warring communities which are a disgrace to the name" (BSOHB, 35).
22 Emerson, "The Transcendentalist," 96.

11

A Surrealist Duet: Word and Image in *Into the Night Life* with Henry Miller and Bezalel Schatz

Sarah Garland

"Into the Night Life," a phantasmagoria based on notes Henry Miller kept of his dreams, was taken from *Black Spring* where it appeared in 1936, and self-published again eleven years later as a stand-alone large format limited-edition serigraph, illustrated and screen printed by the Israeli artist Bezalel Schatz.[1] The book's creation out of entirely handwritten and handprinted pages, its abstracted and symbolic images, and its attention to vivid color and expression are in keeping with a version of Miller's work which sees it as part of a continuing process of exchange with other artists and writers and which remembers his practice of beginning texts in mixed media notebooks that merged watercolors, lists, handwritten and typed notes, letters, and ephemera. As Karl Orend argues, Miller's form was taken from music; from sequences of visual images in paintings, cinema, and art historical texts like Élie Faure's, as well as the vernacular traditions of burlesque, vaudeville, and *Grand Guignol*; and from religious, pagan, and literary symbolism. And so although the brochure Miller and Schatz assembled to promote *Into the Night Life* stresses its uniqueness, both as a handmade artifact and as a collaboration between writer and artist, the book is better seen as part of an ongoing conversation with the visual arts and with visual artists. On a conceptual level, as I will argue below, Miller's work treats images as ciphers and conduits for elements of the psyche that are beyond rational control, functioning as part of his career-long investigation into the limits of verbalization and of conscious control.[2]

Although Miller's narrator's monologues are seldom given to us in the novels as fully rational or empirically realist (there is enough mention of Miller's narrator being carried away by his own flood of speech to give many scenes a marked element of echolalia, or at least something like a more realist-inflected automatic writing), there is a sense that those of Miller's works based around images, like "Into the Night Life," "Scenario," and *The Smile at the Foot of the Ladder*, are given to us as even more fully exemplifying and creating a place for the irrational.[3] In *The Waters Reglitterized*, Miller identifies painting with dreaming, with visions brought about by the abdication of will in the sleeping mind, writing that as one paints, "one should not be worrying about the degree of 'success' obtained by each and every effort, but only concentrate on maintaining the vision, keeping it pure and steady. The rest is sleight of hand work in the dark, a genuine automatic process, no less somnambulistic because accompanied by pains and aches" (WR, 27). In this chapter, I argue that in his collaboration with Schatz on the large illustrated edition of "Into the Night Life," and in a general approach to writing that in *Tropic of Cancer* he calls "collaborating with myself" (CAN, 247), Miller both draws on this idea of the image as a figure for the unconscious. He uses the idea of the image as representing a trace of ungoverned creation in conjunction with a set of symbols for death and rebirth of the self in order to resurrect the self by remaking it as other.

Bezalel Schatz, known as "Lilik," was an Israeli artist and craftsman, and a part of Miller's circle of friends in Big Sur from 1945 onward, who eventually became Miller's brother-in-law in 1953 when Miller married Eve McClure, the sister of Schatz's wife Louise.[4] Stylistically, Schatz's use of line, color, and shape position his work alongside the modernist, expressionist, and *fauve* artists Miller admired so much, and over his lifetime Schatz exhibited in group shows with Henri Matisse, Pablo Picasso, Marc Chagall, and Oscar Kokoschka.[5] Schatz appears in *Big Sur and the Oranges of Hieronymus Bosch*, *The Waters Reglitterized*, and *To Paint Is to Love Again*, as well as in *Book of Friends*, where Miller records the making of the book as "a beautiful and most unusual piece of collaboration" (CBF, 141).[6] Schatz "radiated health, vitality, optimism," Miller writes, "he was irresistible. It took him no time to persuade me to do this book with him." "It was Lilik who did the major work," he continues, "Not only did he do the illustrations and the layout, but he did all the silkscreen pages himself. I think it took him almost two years to complete the job" (CBF, 141). The collaboration, then, was both a partnership and part of a friendship. The book is now very rare; of an intended series of 800, less than 400 were eventually bound, Shifreen and Jackson state.[7] The copy of *Into the Night Life* I consulted at the British Library in London has an inscribed frontispiece by Miller that calls attention again to the joint nature of the book: "This book, a labor of love, is a duet between Bezalel Schatz and myself. It was done without money—entirely on faith."[8]

Interestingly, though, Miller's dream scenarios do not fully coincide with Schatz's imagination of that dream, neither in tone nor in content. Although it was sent to André Breton for possible inclusion in the surrealist exhibition of 1947,[9] *Into the Night Life* does not have recourse to the visually uncanny style we see in Salvador Dalí, Max Ernst, or Georges de Chirico. Instead, Schatz's work contains echoes of Chagall's evocation of something more like the marvelous, with its figures flying through the air, slanted houses and cemeteries, and wraith-like men and women wrapped around sensuous curves.

The colors of *Into the Nightlife* are beautiful and form a design element in themselves: clean, clear primaries and pastels highlight the line drawings and handwritten script in black, red, and white, working against the heavy colored paper background to produce the feeling of layering of images and forms. The layers produced by the silk screen technique evoke both evanescence and flatness, evoking the dream state by giving the impression of fragments only tentatively held together on one plane.

The handwritten script used throughout the book was produced specially for the volume by Miller and Schatz, and is used as both a design and an expressive element so that image and text combine to produce a single vivid experience.[10] The difference

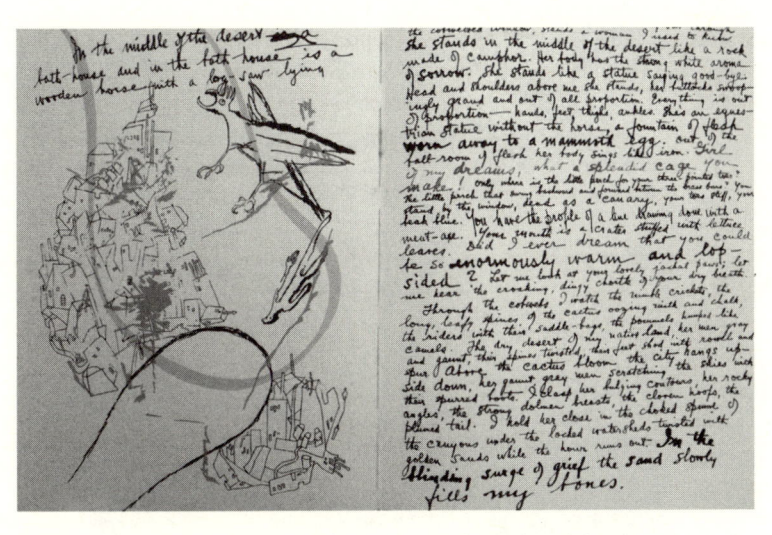

Figure 11.1. Henry Miller and Bezalel Schatz, *Into the Night Life* (n.p.)

between reading the version in Miller's handwriting and the version in typescript in *Black Spring* is one of speed and emotional stress. The variation in the letters that tell of a variation in the hand gives a greater weight to some of the words and phrases in a way that leaves them more internally differentiated than Miller's usual Whitmanesque catalogs. Handwritten, the list moves nearer to being scored, in a musical sense, for tone and for emphasis, and it gives a much slower and more modulated reading experience than typescript.

Jacques Den Hann, a Dutch critic, correspondent and advocate of Miller, writes in the prospectus for the book:

> His hand moves in the rhythm of the text, now in a quiet, almost persuasive style, steady and thin, suddenly getting thicker, angrier, rougher, with violent words—in red ink—like curses thrown in, heavily underlined. Then the waves rise, rolling over the paper on the swell of horror, grimmer, fiercer, weakening again, and occasionally ending in a desperate ink-blot. Into these movements the painter Schatz, *de sa part*, wove his lines, drew his parallel view of the essentials of the dream: the sexual symbols, the mother-womb, the embryo, the night bird of horror. Not Miller's dreams alone but their assimilated experiences gave birth to a gruesome, cruel, unequalled, colorful and authentic short-hand report of our lives behind the threshold of day. (DB, n.p.)

As Den Hann points out, Schatz's graphics and typographic layout offer an interpretation of Miller's dream narratives, illustrating what, after Freud, we might call the latent, rather than the manifest, content of the dream. Schatz's images are of figures – some female, some androgynous – cemeteries, cities tumbling off into diagonals, eyes and

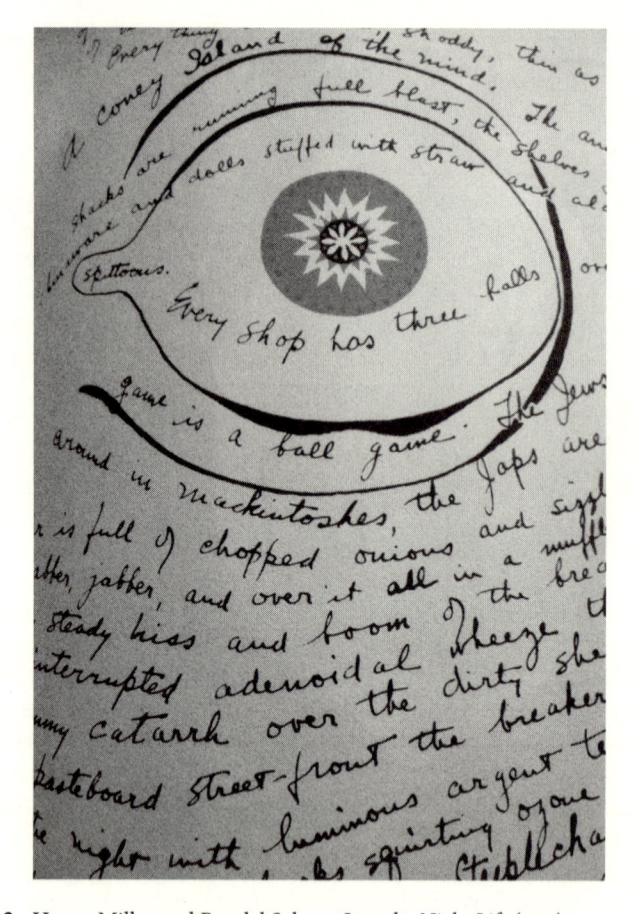

Figure 11.2. Henry Miller and Bezalel Schatz, *Into the Night Life* (n.p.)

wombs. There are abstract patches of color that counterpoint and provide dynamic backgrounds for the splattered ink around many of Miller's sentences. Schatz's images do not correspond in any easy way to the text. Often the text will write of a man but picture a woman, or a fetus will occur in a passage that does not refer to birth in any literal way, or the text will contain references to colors that the plates disregard. This relative independence of word and image acts to shift the thematic register of Miller's original quite substantially. Whereas the threat to Miller's narrator appears to come from women, Schatz's illustrations do not present the women as monsters. Instead, he transposes the figure of the terror of a nightmare into a metamorphosing sharp-toothed flying animal, creating a spectacular dog–bird–dragon–wolf composite that condenses several of the animal figures in Miller's scenario, dwarfing the text in two multicolored double page illustrations.

Reading Miller and Schatz together takes apart any gender binaries that Miller's text might set up; in one figure the dream animal appears to be pregnant, in another it

Figure 11.3. Henry Miller and Bezalel Schatz, *Into the Night Life* (n.p.)

also seems to have spiked male genitals, neither of which appear in Miller's narrative. The illustrations of women are all nudes, designated as women through their breasts and hair, but, unlike in Miller's text where the women are the active and murderous other to the narrator's frozen, speechless self. Schatz's women are much more obviously a counterpart to the outline features used to represent the dreamer and the dead. There are drawings of female genitals floating free of women's bodies, suggested by hair-like black patches, which are visible on the contortionist too, but because these generally appear with equivalent or similar visual weight to the others on the page they work to mute Miller's insistence on female genitalia in the dream sequence, and, as with the symbolic readings I outline below, work to integrate them into a more wide-ranging depiction of a personal mythology that links death, sex, rebirth, and the subconscious.[11]

In this collaboration, the book becomes even more haunting than the bare text alone, perhaps because the duet allows image and text to act as points for resistance and interpretation. As Caroline Blinder demonstrates in her analysis of the ways in which Miller learnt from André Breton's use of Brassaï's photographs in *Nadja* (1924), proposing his own image-text disjunction when using Brassaï's images for the first edition of *Quiet Days in Clichy*, Miller's conceptualization of image and text was very much—as the inscription to the copy of *Into the Night Life* that I saw suggests—a "duet." Miller wanted "the image to become an end in itself, an autonomous creation," Brassaï, writes, so that, in Blinder's words, the images "could be both an extension of the artist's vision and an independent creation."[12] Schatz's illustrations and graphic design create something other than Miller's original. The image and the text work in counterpoint, and their surreality is as much in their incommensurability as in their condensation and articulation of literary and psychoanalytic symbols. And it is this encounter with the other, particularly through images and the creators of those images, which is crucial, I will argue, to both Miller's search for recognition and to his redefinition of himself.

There is considerable evidence to suggest, as David Seed explains in *Cinematic Fictions*, that the episodic, montaged structure of "Into the Night Life" was influenced by Miller's love of cinema, in particular by what he saw in surrealist films by Germaine Dulac, Gustav Machatý, and Luis Buñuel.[13] One of Miller's first pieces of writing from his Paris years was a review of Buñuel and Salvador Dalí's *L'Age d'or*, where he wrote approvingly that the film represents "a miraculous frontier which opens up before us a dazzling new world," by giving the audience "a succession of images without sequence, the significance of which must be sought for below the threshold of consciousness" (CE, 55–56). The fact that the films Miller writes of were largely silent (set to music in their original theatrical presentations) adds further to this use of the image, and in particular the sequenced image, as a figure for the preverbal mind. His letters back to New York, to Emil Schnellock, a childhood and artist friend, speak many times of these films, and of *Un Chien Andalou*, and by the time Miller and Anaïs Nin are writing together in the early thirties at the time *Black Spring* was composed, they have translated the principle of the film scenario—that is, a series of written prompts for visual images—into a freestanding fictional form. It's worth giving Nin's journal entry for February of that year at relative length because of the way it illuminates the decisions made to differentiate this surrealist-informed writing from Miller's more discursive work: "Henry's keeping of a dream book for me became a small book (fifty pages) which he rewrote in a particularly chaotic style. We arrived at a new conclusion about the dream language. One night we clarified it well. If the films are the most successful expression of surrealism, then the scenario is what suits the surrealist stories and the dreams best."[14] "There must be a telescoping, a condensation in words" she argues:

> There was a need of getting scenes without logical, conscious explanations. I questioned, in his dream book, the discussion in the cafe before the operation of the child. I gave us an example of the silent mystery, the feeling of the dream scenes from the *Chien Andalou*, when nothing is mentioned or verbalized. A hand is lying in the street. The woman leans out of the window. The bicycle falls on the sidewalk. There is a wound in the hand. The eyes are sliced by a razor. There is no dialogue. It is a silent movie of images, as in a dream. One phrase now and then, out of a sea of sensation.[15]

Cinema has long been compared to the dream because of the sequence of images given to physically passive spectators in the dark, but in surrealist film the analogy is even closer; narrative is superseded by isolated manifestations of images that, because of their isolation, ask us to make sense of them by imaginative association or analogy, as psychoanalysis made sense of dreams, or as religious and mythical texts are interpreted.

For Miller's narrators, as well as for Miller himself, writing and painting comes from a place outside of the governance of the conscious daytime self, and it's for this reason that dreams are both generative and an enduring symbol for creation. When

George Wickes asks Miller whether surrealism is what Miller means by the phrase "Into the Night Life," Miller stresses an element of writing that comes apparently from a place not accessible through rationality:

> Yes, there it was primarily the dream. The surrealists make use of the dream, and of course that's always a marvelous fecund aspect of experience. Consciously or unconsciously, all writers employ the dream, even when they're not surrealists. The waking mind, you see, is the least serviceable in the arts. In the process of writing one is struggling to bring out what is unknown to himself.[16]

Blinder gives a thorough account of Miller's relationship with French surrealism in *A Self-Made Surrealist*. As Blinder points out, Miller shared a number of preoccupations with the surrealists, particularly their adaptation of Freudian ideas of an unconscious accessible by dreams, automatic speech, and analysis to give a source for, and material for, the creative imagination. Miller, however, dissented from Bretonian surrealism in both its political aspects and its emphasis on pure psychic automatism. For Miller the unconscious was always subject to the manipulations of the conscious, asserting, as he writes in "An Open Letters to Surrealists Everywhere" that a "stress on the Unconscious forces of man does not necessarily imply the elimination of consciousness. On the contrary it implies the expansion of consciousness" (CE, 189).[17] Jay Martin's transcriptions of Miller's original dream notebooks shows how much has been added to, and subtracted from, Miller's memories to make the final text of "Into the Night Life." The episode where a previous girlfriend has a pair of blunt scissors in "Into the Night Life" is much less compressed, and much more insistent in its sexual symbolism, in the dream book:

> As soon as I come she reaches for a pair of scissors lying on the table. It is a huge pair, very blunt, rusty, old. She is cutting the string which is attached to a condom inside her, a condom she has inserted herself without my knowing; as she cuts the string I am in a sweat for fear she will cut my penis off; in fact, as she cuts away I seem to feel it is my penis, as though the string attached to the condom were a fiber of my body, but it is dull pain, and quite bearable—simply makes me nervous.[18]

Read psychoanalytically, Martin argues that Miller's dream notebook suggests a fear of cutting the umbilical cord to the mother, as well as fear of annihilation, castration, and homosexuality.[19] In "Into the Night Life," these thematics exist as imagistic traces in the scene where an ex-girlfriend advances on the dreamer with rusty scissors, but the threat is dissolved into a more etherealized depiction of pain and loss over time, overlaid with images of a melancholy sunset. Similarly, the image of the dreamer as suffering a Christ-like wound in his side, as well as an incapacity to speak, begins in the notebook as a more elaborate scene of birth and nomination where a pronunciation that Miller has "just been born" more explicitly suggests the wound in the dreamer's side, and, I'd argue, the wound in the child's head, in "Into the Night Life" as beginning in more obviously vaginal imagery:

Looking at my clean suit of mail, I perceive that there is an enormous hole in it, as if a shell had passed through it. A horrible hole, not only through the armor, but through my body. A clean hole, without a drop of blood oozing from it. Meditatively I pass my hand over my chin and, as I do so, I see my image in the shop-front. And behold, my face is rotting away—the jaw and pieces of the palate have broken off and the pieces crumble in my hands like dry clay. In consternation I look again at the mirror. I see a young man sitting before a desk with chin in hand... "Gottlieb Leberecht Miller," says a still small voice, "you have just been born."[20]

Where the original dream notebook seems to have been more consistently frightening in terms of an attack on Miller's masculinity (his mail/male has been breached), "Into the Night Life" brings together the scenes where the dreamer is repeatedly struck dumb and powerless by strange and threatening figures, to join them in an extended fantasia where the flow from scene to scene expands into a more obvert thematization of flows, rivers, processions, and movements through time.[21] The pamphlet released in advance to promote the book asks the reader to interpret the visual and verbal images as subconscious remnants by describing them as an interlinear to Freud, an "anabasis"—that is, a military advance,—"of dream." This movement through realms is restated by Miller and Schatz in entry into the book through two transparent overlays with screen printed patterns visible as layers through each page that takes the reader's eye through partial patterns and into a large white, squared and irregular spiral on a black background. This is also played out in a playful epigram:

> The one and only life is the night life, the life of the mind, the night of night, the life, the mind, the night, the night life. This is the Coney Island of the mind, the Toboggan Slide, the Into the Into. This is the without which wherefore and however of the night's bright mind, the life and mind of night, the mind and night of night
> Or
> Into the Night Life
> with Henry Miller and Bezalel Schatz (INL, n.p.)

The image of going "Into the Into," riding through the Steeplechase ride through a "Coney Island of the mind," a pasteboard hell on the seashore at the end of a trolley car line where "everything is sliding and crumbling, everything glitters, totters, teeters, titters" (BS, 165), gives one of the figures for the flow of images that forms the written scenario. Here Miller's characteristic floods of description work to produce the centripetal movement through images Brassaï described with bemusement in *Henry Miller, Grandeur Nature*, where "the profusion in Miller's writing, rather than provide greater illumination of its subject, made it seem more distant" because Miller's narrativization of free association meant that he often meditated on one subject in order "to spawn a whole new generation of subjects."[22]

This image of figurative flow is also played out literally in "Into the Night Life's" recurrent images of rivers, oceans, streams, thaws, and trolley rides over the Montreal and Brooklyn bridges, as well as in the Eliotion flow of the dead as they carry their coffins through the dreamscape, and in the more surrealist flows of cuckoos, snakes, popcorn, and other objects in and out of people's bodies.[23] As Katy Masuga makes clear, the Brooklyn Bridge represents a source of inspiration in Miller's work, both intertextually and symbolically.[24] In *Tropic of Capricorn*, Miller's narrator crosses the bridge to Brooklyn thinking that:

> maybe, being up high between the two shores, suspended above the traffic, above life and death, on each side the high tombs, tombs blazing with dying sunlight, the river flowing heedlessly, flowing on like time itself, maybe each time I passed up there, something was tugging away at me, urging me to take it in, to announce myself; anyway each time I passed on high I was truly alone and whenever that happened the book commenced to write itself. (CAP, 44)

Interestingly, footage from the Edison company taken of the trolley journey over Brooklyn Bridge at the time when Miller was living in New York also shows what one might conceivably call a birth-like experience: the steel supports for the trolley apparatus that line the whole journey mean that Miller, travelling from Brooklyn to Manhattan and back again, would have seen a series of darkened girders moving past him to create a tunnel-like experience with only a small light visible from either end.[25]

The ease with which the kinds of isolated verbal and visual images Miller uses in the dream narrative can be divorced from their context and reread as part of symbolic structures offered a continual stimulus to both psychoanalysis and to surrealist art; in Miller's work it allows him to articulate both an account of a personal mythology and for him to integrate his work into mythic, sometimes mystical, readings of the mind of the type proposed by contemporary figures like D.H. Lawrence, Otto Rank, and Carl Jung. Mary Ann Caws argues that surrealism sought by "overturning and destroying, undoing and making a ruin of what one sees" to give "life back its passion," and to "restore the myths."[26] Like the surrealists, Miller's recourse to myth was often in the service of attempts both to access a transcendental unity and authentic impassioned experience of the self that had been obscured by modernity, and to find a poetic language for that experience: "my mind searches vainly for some remembrance which is older than any remembrance, for the myth engraved on a tablet of stone which lies buried under a mountain," he writes in *Black Spring* (BS, 168). In *Into the Night Life*, Miller and Schatz's images and text work together to create and foreground an originary myth for artistic creation and for the birth of the self that sees the unconscious as mythic incubating womb and deathly underworld.

Suitably, the phrase "Into the Night Life" that Miller attributes to Freud in the illustrated book comes not directly from Freud, but, as Masuga points out, from secondary citation: the original is in an essay by the German expressionist poet and thinker Gottfried Benn.[27] Benn's first book of poetry, *Morgue* (1912), preceded Miller's in its thematization of cancer, death, flesh, and decay; Benn himself was a doctor of venereal and skin diseases who, like Miller, read early twentieth-century culture through Nietzsche and Spengler and what Klauss Mann calls a "grim irrationalism."[28]

Miller repeats the quotation at length in *Nexus*, but the original appears in the 1932 issue of *transition*. Benn's essay linked Freud and Nietzsche, stressing the dream life as the remnants of ancestral and primal consciousness held in the self as in geological strata: "we carry the remnants and traces of former evolutionary stages in our organism, we observe how these traces are realized in the dream, in ecstasy and in certain conditions of the insane"; "when the later acquired reason is relaxed, as in the dream or in drunkenness, they emerge with their rites, their pre-logical mentality, and grant us an hour of mystic participation," Benn writes.[29] In this Benn's reading of the dream foregrounds both the modernist primitivism and archetypalism that Miller mobilized so fully throughout his work, visible in "Into the Night Life" in the return of the city to nonwhite peoples, giving a version of the dream which, as much as it might reveal desires and sexual conflicts, is also taken as a way back into an earlier evolutionary stage, both of the human race, and of the mind.

Benn's psychological atavism may have appealed to Miller while writing *Black Spring* in its confirmation of the kind of vitalism he took from Bergson's *Creative Evolution* at an early stage in his thinking and that he would have been reading about in D.H. Lawrence's work, in particular in *Fantasia of the Unconscious* and in *Apocalypse*, where underneath everyday rationality itself is a shared and self-directed "blood consciousness," present at the cellular level.[30] It may also be the case that other intellectual currents captured in Eugene Jolas's *transition* were an inspiration for "Into the Night Life," too. The November 1929 issue of *transition* contains a long section on "The Synthetist Universe, Dreams and the Cthonian Mind" where the dreams of, among others, Jolas himself, Harry Crosby, and Paul Klee are transcribed and turned into stories and scenarios. The unconscious as source of creation is an idea that also occurs throughout Jolas's *Language of the Night*, a "swell brochure" that Miller sends to his artist friend Emil Schnellock in 1932 (LE, 111).[31] In *The Language of the Night*, Jolas suggests that "since we witness in our night-mind the movement of our preconscious and inherited layers, the inherited symbols of billions of years, the poet has the task of organizing the matriarchal images transmitted to him."[32] Jolas also uses quite a few words that spice Miller's own vocabulary, such as "sexus" and "nexus," "chthonian" and "mantic," and I'd suggest that a playful combination of Benn and Jolas might also be behind Miller's parody in "Burlesk" where "by means of the dream technique" man "peels off the outer layers of his geologic mortality and comes to grips with his true mantic self, a non-stratified area of semi-liquid character" (BS, 237).

At many points in the novels Miller's narrator articulates images of mental journeys into the vagina, and onward into the womb, and allied ones where he finds things inside a woman, or pouring out of her. The passage goes both out of and into the womb, and these gynecological images in general are both ones of profusion and rebirth, but also part of a repertoire of images of death, illness, and harm—"dread and longing," as the narrator puts it (CAN, 290). For Miller's narrator in *Tropic of Cancer*, the "fear of living separate, of staying born" leaves "the door of the womb always on the latch" (CAN, 290). The image of crossing Brooklyn Bridge that I referred to earlier may also be part of this ambiguous combination of birth and death symbols. If one retains the idea of "Into the Night Life" as a "Coney Island of the mind," there are also intriguingly literal contemporary prompts for a cosmology that matches the one Miller synthesized out of the marriage of life and death he identifies with the detachment and movement of the bridge. Photographs preserved from the first half of the twentieth century show that not only was one of the Coney Island amusement parks called "Dreamland," there were rides based on Dante's visions ("End of the World"), one where the rider floated below a gigantic statue of Satan on a stream of water into the Underworld ("Hell Gate"), incubators where premature babies were shown as exhibits, a large gate supported by a thirty-foot angel labeled "Creation," where the six days of the Genesis story was meant to begin for the visitor before presenting the creation of man, as well as rollercoaster rides (including the Steeplechase that Miller refers to in his narrative) that imaginatively extended the trolley rides that joined Manhattan and Brooklyn.[33] Here too, then, going "into the into," and "Into the Night Life" is both a journey toward the source of writerly creation, as well as creation on a mythic level, but also a journey toward death, into the underworld. The flow of life the reader meets often in Miller's writing, perhaps most famously in the final third of *Tropic of Cancer* where the narrator's acceptance of his fate is resolved into the image of the Seine flowing around him, is never far from Styx-like images where the flow through a soil "saturated with the past" is also of a more ancient line of life and death (CAN, 320). Schatz's images of elongated, curved figures that echo Miller's script suggest dreaming as a kind of extrusion, reprising both flow and the multiple senses that in the night life something is being brought into, and perhaps leaving, being. (Figure 11.4).

Miller's narrator's mother figure is to be feared absolutely (and in this Anaïs Nin's summary seems right: "Henry always saw his mother immense in the scale of the universe"[34]) but in "Into the Night Life" she needs to be encountered in a series of murderous and violently threatening women, and finally in the specter of his mother herself, as a form of symbolic death that will allow him not only to go back to the womb to die there to the world as he knows it, as part of a Freudian death drive perhaps, but also in order for Miller's narrator to be able to appropriate the image of the womb for his own self-creation and rebirth. The symbolic schema for the *World of Lawrence* (written at the same time as *Black Spring* and *Tropic of Capricorn*), at the foot of a drawing labeled "tree of life and death and art, is a circle that emphasizes the words "womb=death" (WOL, 22), and in *Tropic of Capricorn* the two are part of a single resurrection image, both brought on the novel's final page in the narrator's reply to Mona: "it is like Easter Sunday. Death is behind me and birth too"; "I take you as the personification of evil, as the destroyer of the soul, as the Maharanee of the night. Tack your womb up on my wall, so that I may remember you. We must get going. Tomorrow, tomorrow …" (CAP, 345–346).

As Michael Hardin points out, Miller's narrator "associates motherhood and thus some female sexuality with male creativity" and by doing this he "has incorporated (or recorporated) the vagina and womb into his body, but not as vagina and womb; instead, it is the 'creative spirit.'"[35] This symbolic reading of creativity as a form of mortally threatening birth makes sense in terms of both the images in *Into the Night Life* of the dreamer with the hole in his side, as well as the scalping, and the girl who has a white cord, flannel, chewing gum, popcorn, and sawdust pulled out of a wound

In my heart I can feel the edelweiss blooming.

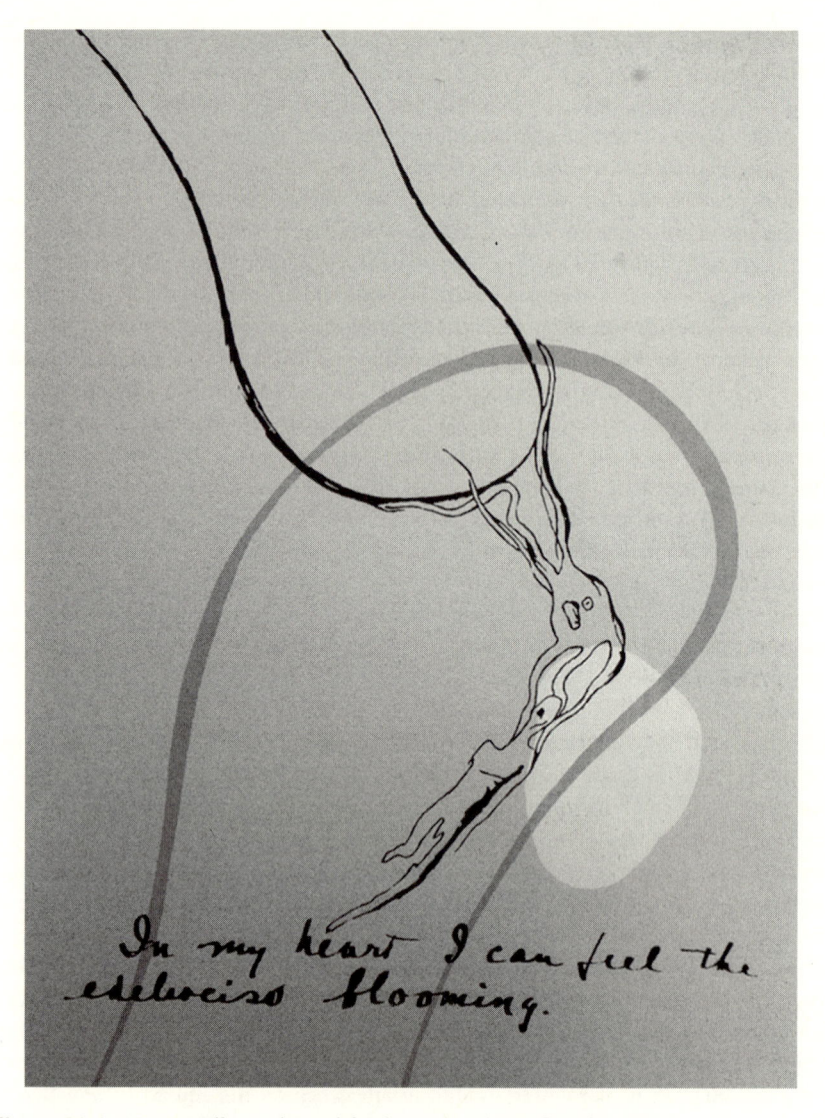

Figure 11.4. Henry Miller and Bezalel Schatz, *Into the Night Life* (n.p.)

in the side of her head, and ultimately in the idea of a fecundating cornucopia and menagerie flowing from the dreamer's mind as the witch-mother "stalking the wind" at the dream's end (BS, 185). It concurs with Jay Martin's readings of Miller's source notebooks too, as well as with the idiosyncratic terms of Miller's own readings in psychoanalysis. In 1934 Miller writes to Schnellock of *Black Spring* in terms of both the themes of the novel and the trauma of birth, making a reference to Otto Rank's book which he and Nin had both read:

> *Black Spring* has architectural dimensions. Have it all clearly charted out—and the greater part done. The *Dream* motif is like the nucleus. In each section there is a repetition of the principal motifs, each time with a new emphasis—Streets, Violence, China, etc. there were parts of the dreams I thought superb myself—the Brooklyn Bridge thing, the cock and scissors (Gertie Imhof), the edelweiss in my heart, the return to Decatur Street, etc. where I left off I had expected to explode into life—to give, in a way, a sensation thru words of the *"trauma of birth."* (LE, 150)

While Rank proposes psychoanalysis as a replaying of a universal birth trauma in "broadly, the attempt of the individual to gain freedom from dependence of any sort upon a state from which it has grown," Miller's version of analysis of the psyche, and of his own dreams, is also close to the model worked out in Rank's *Art and Artist*, a book that Nin records discussing with Miller in 1932.[36] In *Art and Artist*, the deliberate construction of the artist's personality, and then the construction of the artwork after that, leads to a birth in the form of freedom from neurotic blockages that involved privileging the creation of a safe, protected womb-like environment to allow psychic security over the urge to create, which the artist, Rank argues, knows will inevitably involve the mental and emotional dangers of conflict with society.

Night for the Miller of the novels also means the world of sexual obsession, figured most fully in *Tropic of Capricorn's* "Land of Fuck," and through the presentation of the nocturnal world of Mona/Mara and of Stasia: "We looked out of the black hole in my life into the black hole of the world. The sun was permanently blacked out, as though to aid us in our continuous internecine strife. For some we have Mars, the moon Saturn: we lived permanently in the zenith of the underworld," Miller writes in *Tropic of Capricorn* (CAP, 228). It's interesting to speculate on whether Jean Kronski, the model for Stasia, gave Miller as much of a push into becoming a self-sustaining writer as his wife June did: the description of the Kronski character in *Crazy Cock*, and the parallels Miller draws between himself, Stasia, and Rimbaud in *The Time of the Assassins*, suggest that, (along with Emil Schnellock and George Imhof) Stasia might have been one of Miller's first living models for what the life of the artist might be, as well as another manifestation of the terrifying witch he sees in both Mara and his mother.[37] In *Crazy Cock*, Miller begins the discarded novel in the mind of a young woman called Miriam who christens herself "Vanya" before moving into a full possession of and by powers that seem very like those evinced in Miller's narrator's surrealist flights:

> With bister and dried blood, with verdigris and jaundiced yellows, she pursued the rhythms and forms that consumed her vision. Orange nudes, colossal in stature, clawed at breasts dripping with slime and gore; odalisques bandaged like mummies and apostles whom not even the Christ had seen exposed their wounds, their gangrened ribs, their bloated lusts. […] Inspired by Lali and Tlaloo, she invented goddesses from whose grinning skulls reptiles issued … (CC, 5)

On one level this confluence may be attributed to early experiments in literary voice, but there are parallels in Miller's manuscripts too: in an early draft for *Tropic of Capricorn*

Miller comments explicitly on the transference of his own role and his own desires to Vanya: "How was it that I was driven to a pitch of the finest frenzy in describing the *walls* of our home, the walls which Vanya, my rival and enemy, covered with frescoes? (As a matter of fact, this was a lie; it was I who invented the frescoes, not Vanya)" (C, 233). He has Vanya meditate on Papini's phrase "taken as I am and as I shall always be, I feel that I am a force both of creation and of dissolution, that I am a real value, and have a right, a place, a mission among men," and in this early draft he reappropriates it for himself: "I said it in my novel about my enemy, but it is I to whom it applies" (C, 234). The associations Miller makes between Stasia, Vanya, and the ideas of night, and of death in life, connect through a metonymic chain to Miller's earliest efforts at working out the role of the irrational in how one might become, and how one might produce as, an artist. And, although I don't have time to fully consider it here, the role of figures that Miller's narrator defines as beyond rationality, either through madness or through their roles as fabulators—including Tante Melia, Babette, Melanie, Stasia, Mona/Mara, as well as the preacher figures, and Crazy Willie Maine—might also, in a surrealist vein, be thought of as sources for both the unhinged, fanatic, voice his narrator assumes over the course of the novels, as well as for the gentler representation of the irrational in his later clown and angel figures.

Black Spring sets up Miller's narrator's self-portrait as the last man in a wasteland of modernity, disease, war, and terrible ennui, drawing on contemporary ideas of the dissolution of Western civilization Miller found echoed in Oswald Spengler's work, throughout *transition* and in the work of Lawrence, as well as in the thinking of Michael Fraenkel, whose musings on the "universe of death" proved so influential for *Tropic of Cancer*.[38] For Miller, under the influence of contemporary ideas of the "primitive" as the uncorrupted remnant of an instinctual and psychically healthy way of being, it allows the dreamer to descend into the primal state, to be reborn again with America, retelling the American story as one where native Americans, black Americans, and an agrarian ideal replace the Spenglerian "late city man" Miller sketches in "Megalopolitan Maniac." Dreams were a "prolegomenon to the unconscious," he writes, and that unconscious was also the undoing of history (BS, 236). Couched in the imagery of wider anxieties about cultural degeneration, "Into the Night Life," and indeed *Black Spring* as a whole, presents a personal apocalypse, fixing on a moment of symbolic death and rebirth in order to play it out again and again as part of Miller's ongoing investigation into his own mental processes, and into the process of becoming a writer.

This powerlessness is figured in "Into the Night Life" both in the thematization of impotence, amputation, and helplessness, but also in these disjunctions that block the reader's access to coherent images and which bring language back as the basis of this particular dream. Crucially, for a wider reading of the beatific moments like those Miller's narrator experiences on the Japanese bridge, what *Into the Night Life* suggests is a reconciliation with a certain lack of control that is presented through a feeling of acceptance and peace in *Black Spring*'s "A Saturday Afternoon" ("I and this that passes beneath me and this that floats above me and all that surges through me, I and this, I and that joined up in one continuous movement" [BS, 41]), which parallels the flow of the Seine at the end of *Tropic of Cancer*, and the moments of transcendence throughout the *Colossus of Maroussi*, in particular. The acceptance of "flow" pictured at the repeated moment of pausing on a bridge over a dream garden, or Brooklyn Bridge, or any of the bridges named in the list in "A Saturday Afternoon," seems to be part of a larger move toward abandoning the kinds of agonized drafting and redrafting of voice Miller does on the *Crazy Cock* manuscript, toward the acceptance of more immediate, less obviously edited, vernacular forms that occur when he takes Fraenkel's advice to "write as you talk," "just sit down before the machine and let go,"[39] and when he, perhaps in response to Anaïs Nin's journals, tries to preserve the spontaneity of the letters and to notebooks in his finished novels. "Show me a man who overelaborates and I will show you a great man!," he writes in *Tropic of Cancer*, because that overelaboration shows "struggle itself with all the fibers clinging to it" and it is perhaps the imperfection inherent in struggle, as well as the inevitability of that struggle, that Miller's narrators accept (CAN, 256). The writing of a book as a form of dreaming is creation in and of itself, and, like painting, it is the activity itself, and the encounter with the medium in the process of making, that matters for Miller's narrators as much as, if not more than, what is discovered or made in the content of that writing.

This seems to be also what Miller finds in the visual arts. Reading "The Angel Is My Watermark!," "The Waters Reglitterized," and *To Paint is to Love Again*, it is striking that part of what Miller values in the experience are phenomenological encounters with the paints, or the paper, or his own creation of form, which he cannot fully explain or control. In the construction of *Into the Night Life* too, "Henry usually ended up by getting joyously angry and throwing the ink around at random—often achieving astonishing results of supreme spontaneity," Schatz writes (DB, n.p.). There are clearly parallels here with surrealist games, and with automatic production. There are phrases of Miller's that cannot be translated into mimetic visual images because they combine nouns and verbs whose coming together produces in miniature a juxtaposition of the sort that Comte de Lautréamont famously exemplified in his praise of a sixteen-year-old as beautiful "as the fortuitous encounter upon a dissecting-table of a sewing-machine and an umbrella."[40] These nonsense phrases occur throughout the text, uniting unconnected items, phrases, and registers: the "city rises up like a huge polar bear shaking off its rhododendrons," or "the butter yowsels in the mortuary" (BS, 187). A composite text like *Into the Night Life*, in asking us to compare these two moments of understanding and not understanding, problematizes both linguistic and visual apprehension in calling our attention to the incommensurability of the two. The kinds of translation and atomization one can undertake with language is not available when one views an image; as James Elkins argues in *On Pictures and the Words That Fail Them*, we can read images down to the level of the mark but the kinds of meanings generated by a mark will not always function semiotically.[41] The activities of viewing, reading, and imaginatively responding to both form and language open the conjunction of text and image us to irresolution, a creative tension between visual and verbal signals that is particularly effective in texts like *Into the Night Life* that attempt to bring us experiences of dreams, of the marvelous and the uncanny, that themselves hover on the edge of logic.

Rebirth, then, might also be figured in terms of the production of a text, as Miller did in *Tropic of Cancer*, where he writes, "The book has begun to grow inside me. I am carrying it around with me everywhere. I walk through the streets big with child"; "I am pregnant" (CAN, 27). The act of creation, of drawing form out of a womb, that, as Hardin argues, is identified with chaos[42] functions as an antidote to the powerlessness that pervades "Into the Night Life," and the descriptions of Miller's pre-Paris years more generally. Norman Mailer suggests in *Genius and Lust* that June's "maddening lack of center" leads Miller to "dive into the pit of recognizing that there may not be a geological fundament in the psyche one can call identity."[43] This "geological fundament in the psyche," especially given the context of Benn's secondhand citation from Freud, seems to be a good metaphor for both what is hoped for and what is lost in *Black Spring*. The idea of surrender to automatism is a fundamental tenet of Bretonian surrealism, which, as Hal Foster argues in *Compulsive Beauty*, estranges the mind to produce it as uncanny object, which is both itself and a machine-like collection of drives, and random thoughts that are other than itself.[44] *Into the Night Life* is a microcosm of the process of being remade through writing, and there seems to be a similar loss of agency, self, and memory in the way that the attacks and woundings in Miller's narrative present various threats to the narrator's safety, and to his self. His jaw falls off so he cannot speak, he cannot run away from the women that threaten him, he cannot answer questions posed about his name, address, or profession, and he cannot read his own book. The dreamer goes as far as to lose language, a loss that in Miller's texts is replayed again and again by those passages where he moves into, or almost into, nonsense. The fear that paralyzes him when he wonders whether he too has had his legs amputated is paralleled by the fear the narrator has of not being able to run from the women bearing down on him, and it's possible to see these moments of loss of self as parallel with others in *Black Spring*, particularly in "Walking Up and Down in China" where a recurring dream about losing identity and self[45] is translated into the death of an uncanny double:

> The more I think of it the more I am convinced that what disturbs me is not whether I am dreaming or insane but whether the man on the sidewalk, the man with arms outstretched, was myself. If it is possible to leave the body in dream, or in death, perhaps it is possible to leave the body forever, to wander endlessly unbodied, unhooked, a nameless identity, or an unidentified name, a soul unattached, indifferent to everything, a soul immortal, perhaps incorruptible, like God—who can say? (BS, 207–208)

Thomas Nesbit writes of a passage in Ludwig Lewisohn's *Expression in America* (1932) Miller marked on the literary double, and it's possible to read a doubling and splitting of self into both the dissolution of self into multiple tales and voices, and in "Into the Night Life's" multiple disjointed episodes too.[46] In terms of the mythical structure drawn in these stories, the self needs to die to both the world and to his own will in order to be born again, but it seems that the mechanism of that rebirth, the creation of an artistic self in writing, both redeems the self by creating an other that is more acceptable to it and estranges the self by making that self in a language that stands in an uncanny relation to that self.[47] The bittersweet moment of acceptance, associated in "Into the Night Life" with emotional frozenness and thaw ("an ice-blue gaiety," "sorrow gone and joy with it" [BS, 185]) and played out again and again in Miller's books, offers perhaps one way of reconciliation with this disjunction and multiplicity. The narrator's place on the bridge, above the flow of life and death, is perhaps a protective disassociation.

Surrealism magnifies the finding of the self as other in its dramatization of automatic mechanisms for the generation of speech and for consciousness, in its suggestion that the psyche can be symbolically remade by interactions with found objects, and in its rehearsal of the unmaking of the self each night in dreams. Indeed, Hal Foster writes of how the psychoanalysts around Freud and Janet disagreed profoundly with surrealist uses of automatism because they feared that automatism, rather than being a supplement for the mind, might produce a "disintegration of personality."[48] Because the moment of rebirth is also a moment where the self becomes other, the moment of redemption needs to be rehearsed over and over again in Miller's texts as both redemption and estrangement where the original self is always already irrevocably lost. This is also perhaps why Miller refers to "collaborating with himself" in *Tropic of Cancer*, and why working with real others, both with artists and with the otherness that is represented by the mediums of language and paint and collage, proved so fecundating. The figure presented by the "man cut in slices" in *Tropic of Cancer* "the same in the eyes of his mistress ... the same in the eyes of ... the same ..." (CAN, 41) is both a symbol for the estrangement of the self and the acknowledgment of that self as it is recreated again and again, in dreams, in text, in image, in interviews, and in collaged notebooks. As Mary Ann Caws argues, what is central to surrealism—and I'd suggest that this can be taken as underlying both Miller's practice as a collaborator with artists such as Schatz, and his collaboration with himself in paint, writing, and collage—is "to find ourselves, but to find ourselves *other*, and then still other."[49]

Creative rebirth is then linked to material embodiment as much as it is to speech. There is a strong argument to be made that Miller's work rests as fully in his notebooks, paintings, and holograph manuscripts as it does in the finished, published books, and there is a lot of evidence to suggest that Miller's initial notes, letters, and drafts meant much to him as objects in themselves, not least in their careful binding, preservation, and archiving. Miller's *Letters to Emil* contain first attempts at many of the passages that appear in the early books, and there are frequent requests to Schnellock to return copies of earlier letters, or to look after carbons of these early drafts. Nin had sheaves of drafts, notes, and ephemera bound for Miller as a Christmas present, and as the "Paris Notebooks," held in Yale's Beinecke Rare Book and Manuscript Library, demonstrate, Miller's thinking was as stimulated by the visual and by the tactile—by writing and watercolor painting by hand, by copying, compiling, and arranging—as it was by the purely linguistic.[50] There is clearly the intention to lay the traces for a personal mythology here, and Miller would have read in Rank's books that "the self labelling and self training of an artist is the indispensable basis of all creative work, and without it general recognition could never arise," although "needless to say, this purely internal process does not suffice to make an artist, let alone a genius," for "only the community, one's contemporaries, or posterity can do that."[51] However, this production I would suggest should also be seen in the light of Miller's need for collaboration, for contact with readers, and with art as it is manifest as an interpersonal and phenomenological experience.[52] Miller begins "The Waters Reglitterized": "This little volume, originally written by hand in a printer's dummy, was intended exclusively for my friend Emil Schnellock. It was my pleasure to write several little books in this manner, for my intimate friends," "written with the pen, and not on the typewriter, they all have a direct, intimate quality" (WR, 5). There is clearly a degree to which the offer of documentary intimacy with Miller was partly how he managed to support himself in America (in the postwar years, sale or barter of his watercolors was the sale of his fame as a taboo breaker[53]) and the handwritten manuscript acts like an autograph, as a trace of the body and of presence. The role of letters, drafts, and notebooks as intermediaries between Miller and his friends, in particular Nin, Alfred Perlès, Lawrence Durrell, and Michael Fraenkel, is evident in the collections and archives, and it's perhaps telling that Miller's greatest periods of productivity, in Paris and in Big Sur, coincide with those where he appears to be knit most firmly into communities of readers and creators. This seemed to be no less the case with Schatz. Part of Miller's attempts to stave off a repetition of the cycles of suffering, crucifixion, and death of the self he tells of in *Tropic of Capricorn* and in the *Rosy Crucifixion* can be found in the physical and mental act of making books, notebooks, and paintings as acts of "eternalisation," to use Otto Rank's term in *Art and Artist*, where both in the fixing of events in the form of a story, image, or collage and in the contact made through these artifacts with collaborators and readers, Miller is able to work with others to express and create himself in a way that looks to be denied him in the nightmare sequences captured and recreated in *Into the Night Life*.

Notes

1 Henry Miller, *Black Spring* (Paris: Obelisk, 1936; New York: Grove Press, 1963); Henry Miller and Bezalel Schatz, *Into the Night Life* (Big Sur: Henry Miller and Bezalel Schatz, 1947). I refer to the book in italics and the section of *Black Spring* in inverted commas. *Into the Night Life* is not paginated; all page numbers refer to the *Black Spring* edition.
2 Karl Orend, "The Edge of the Miraculous—First Reflections on Henry Miller and Art," *Nexus: The International Henry Miller Journal* 6 (2009): 14.
3 Henry Miller, *Black Spring* (New York: Grove Press, 1963); Henry Miller, *The Cosmological Eye* (New York: New Directions, 1939); Henry Miller, *The Smile at the Foot of the Ladder* (New York: Duell, Sloan, and Pearce, 1948).
4 Hoyle, *Unknown*, 234.
5 www.schatz.co.il (last accessed 19 Jan. 2015)
6 Henry Miller, *Big Sur and the Oranges of Hieronymus Bosch* (New York: New Directions, 1957); Henry Miller, *The Waters Reglitterized: The Subject of Water Colour in Some of Its More Liquid Phases* (London: Village Press, 1973).

7   Lawrence J. Shifreen and Roger Jackson, *Henry Miller: A Bibliography of Primary Sources* (Ann Arbor: Jackson, 1993). The book cost $100 a copy and did not sell well, and unbound pages ended up spoiling in Miller's cupboard (Hoyle, *Unknown*, 183). Copies still exist on rare book and auction sites where many of the book's images are also reproduced in color.
8   The whole inscription reads "For Pierre Sicardi/This book, a labor of love, is a duet between Bezalel Schatz and myself. It was done without money—entirely on faith. It is a narration of my dreams which are all recorded in a Dream Book at U.C.L.A./Happy reading!/Cheers!/Henry Miller/Friday the 13th of June 1975."
9   For more on Miller's involvement with surrealism, see James Gifford, "Henry Miller's Letters to Herbert Read: 1935–1958," *Nexus: The International Henry Miller Journal* 5 (2008): 3–35; James Gifford, "Surrealism's Anglo-American Afterlife: The Herbert Read and Henry Miller Network," *Nexus: The International Henry Miller Journal* 5 (2008): 36–64; Branko Aleksić, "The Unpublished Correspondence of Henry Miller & André Breton, the 'Steady Rock', 1947–1950," translated and with additional notes by Karl Orend *Nexus: The International Henry Miller Journal* 5 (2008): 150–174. For analyses of Miller's work in a surrealist context, see Caroline Blinder, *A Self-Made Surrealist: Ideology and Aesthetics in the Works of Henry Miller* (London: Camden House, 2000); Gay Louise Balliet, *Henry Miller and Surrealist Metaphor* (New York: Peter Lang, 1996); Paul Jahshan, *Henry Miller and the Surrealist Discourse of Excess: A Post-Structuralist Reading* (New York: Peter Lang, 2001); Indrek Männiste, *Henry Miller, the Inhuman Artist: A Philosophical Inquiry* (New York: Bloomsbury, 2013), 16–21.
10 The original draft manuscript of *Black Spring* from 1932–1933 at UCLA is typewritten with holograph corrections and two watercolors bound into it.
11 Jane A. Nelson's Jungian reading of Miller in *Form and Image in the Fiction of Henry Miller* (Detroit: Wayne State University Press, 1970) includes many of these images—the mother, the womb, the quest, and the rebirth—in her archetypal schema.
12 Caroline Blinder, "Images of Paris in the Work of Brassaï and Miller," in *Text and Image in Modern European Culture*, eds Natasha Grigorian, et al. (West Lafayette, Ind.: Purdue University Press, 2012), 50.
13 David Seed, *Cinematic Fictions* (Liverpool: Liverpool University Press, 2009); Branko Aleksić, "Henry Miller's Passionate Reading of Images," *Nexus: The International Henry Miller Journal* 6 (2009): 172.
14 Anaïs Nin, *The Diary of Anaïs Nin: Volume One, 1931–1934* (New York: Harvest, 1966), 307.
15 Nin, *Diary*.
16 Frank L. Kersnowski and Alice Hughes, eds, *Conversations with Henry Miller* (Jackson: University Press of Mississippi, 1994), 52.
17 Blinder, *A Self-Made Surrealist*, 18.
18 Jay Martin, "Three Stages of Dreaming: A Clinical Study of Henry Miller's Dream Book," *Journal of the American Academy of Psychoanalysis* 12, 2 (1984): 243.
19 Martin, Three Stages of Dreaming, 244.
20 Martin, Three Stages of Dreaming, 239. See Martin's article for an analysis of this dream.
21 For readings of time in Miller's work, including in "Into the Night Life," see Decker's exegesis of Miller's notion of "spiral form" in *Henry Miller and Narrative*

Form: Constructing the Self, Rejecting Modernity (New York: Routledge, 2005), and Männiste, *Henry Miller: The Inhuman Artist*, particularly Chapter 2.
22. Brassaï, *Henry*, 72.
23. See Decker, *Henry*, 85, for another analysis of the bridge motif in "Into the Night Life."
24. Katy Masuga, "Crossing Brooklyn Bridge: An Ekphrastic Correspondence between Walt Whitman, Hart Crane and Henry Miller," *Nexus: The International Henry Miller Journal* 7 (2010): 101–126. For intertextual readings of Miller's work, see Masuga, *Henry Miller and How He Got That Way* and Garland, "The Dearest of Cemeteries," 197–215.
25. http://youtube/0WA47Y6em8M (last accessed 19 Jan. 2015).
26. Mary Ann Caws, *The Surrealist Look: An Erotics of Encounter* (Cambridge, MA: MIT Press, 1999), 179.
27. This use of secondary citation is not unusual in Miller's work. For prominent examples, one might look at the quotation from Nietzsche, taken from Goethe's *Conversations with Eckermann*, in *Tropic of Cancer* (see my "Dearest of Cemeteries"), or that novel's epigraph from Emerson, taken, Thomas Nesbit argues, from Ludwig Lewisohn's *Expression in America* (1932). Thomas Nesbit, *Henry Miller and Religion* (New York: Routledge, 2007) 37.
28. Gottfried Benn, *Primal Vision: Selected Writings* (New York, New Directions Publishing, 1960), xv.
29. Gottfried Benn, "The Structure of the Personality (Outline of a Geology of the 'I')," *transition* 21 (March 1932): 200, 201, 206–214.
30. Henri Bergson, *Creative Evolution* (London: Macmillan, 1913); D.H. Lawrence, *Fantasia of the Unconscious* (London: Secker, 1930); D.H. Lawrence, *Apocalypse* (London: Secker, 1932).
31. Eugene Jolas, *The Language of Night* (The Hague: Servire Press, 1932).
32. Jolas, *The Language of Night*, 57.
33. Michael Immerso, *Coney Island: The People's Playground* (New Brunswick: Rutgers University Press, 2002), 105. For a reading of Miller's work in the context of these vernacular entertainments, see William Solomon, *Literature, Amusement, and Technology in the Great Depression* (Cambridge: Cambridge University Press, 2002).
34. Nin, *Diary*, 53.
35. Michael Hardin, "Fighting Desires: Henry Miller's Queer Tropic," *Journal of Homosexuality* 42, 3 (2002): 138.
36. Otto Rank, *Art and Artist: Creative Urge and Personality Development* (New York: Knopf, 1932), 374. Nin, *Diary*, 151.
37. For George Imhof, see *Complete Book of Friends*, 35.
38. Robert Ferguson, *Henry Miller: A Life* (New York, Norton, 1991), 153.
39. Michael Fraenkel, *The Genesis of Tropic of Cancer* (Berkeley: Bern Porter, 1946), 12–13.
40. Comte de Lautréamont, *Maldoror (Les Chants de Maldoror)* (New York: New Directions, 1965), 263. The return of language to the surface of Miller's texts is Masuga's thesis in *The Secret Violence of Henry Miller*; for Masuga what Miller's writing dramatizes is writing itself, and the incommensurability of writing with that which is outside of it.
41. James Elkins, *On Pictures and the Words That Fail Them* (Cambridge: Cambridge University Press, 1998).

42. Michael Hardin, "Fighting," 132.
43. Norman Mailer, *Genius and Lust: A Journey through the Major Writings of Henry Miller* (New York: Grove Press, 1976), 183.
44. Hal Foster, *Compulsive Beauty* (Cambridge, MA, MIT Press, 1995).
45. Martin cites Miller talking of a recurring nightmare he has where "I might be shaving myself and looking in the mirror, and certainly there is a different man: it isn't my face—is somebody else looking back at me. And then I go crazy. I don't know what I do, but I know the next thing is I'm in the insane asylum" (234), and Hamish Jackson explores Miller's moments of lost identity in what looks to be this same dream (repeated by Miller in the film *Henry Miller Asleep and Awake*) in "Henry Miller's Black Spring through the Looking Glass of Jacques Lacan," *Nexus: An International Henry Miller Journal*, (2012): 105–122.
46. Nesbit, *Religion*, 37.
47. This is a point that Rosalind Krauss makes about representation more generally in *The Optical Unconscious* (Cambridge, MA: The M.I.T. Press, 1996), 152; 174.
48. Foster, *Compulsive*, 3.
49. Caws, *Surrealist*, 22.
50. Nin, *Diary*, 158.
51. Rank, *Art*, 37.
52. I have in mind here a similar kind of reading of Miller's notebooks to that Catherine Gander suggests in "'Twenty-six Things at Once' Pragmatic Perspectives in Frank O'Hara's and Norman Bluhm's Poem-Paintings," in *Mixed Messages: American Correspondences in Visual and Verbal Practices*, eds Catherine Gander and Sarah Garland (forthcoming: Manchester: Manchester University Press, 2015).
53. Hoyle, *Unknown*, 170.

12

Cartography of the Obscene

Jeff Bursey

Current television (almost anything on HBO, or reality shows), movies (e.g., *Blue Is the Warmest Color* and *Nymphomaniac*), nude and sex selfies, contemporary music (Jarvis Cocker's "Cunts Are Still Running the World"), fiction that describes graphic sex (E.L. James' *50 Shades of Grey*, Nicholson Baker's *House of Holes*), online enjoyment of leaked sex tapes, as well as commercial soft and hard-core porn, indicate the growing acceptance of nudity, sexual activity, and profanity in Western society, while the proliferation of distribution platforms encourages easier and speedier transmission of personal and commercial images and text to a swelling community of interest. As access to such material grows exponentially, we become immune to news of the latest celebrity sex tape and the ensuing scandal and controversy; additionally, with each new addition of outrageous material (or, put another way, as old product gets replaced by a fresher entry into the marketplace) the public consciousness becomes increasingly numbed, and it becomes harder to elicit shock or even surprise. (This leaves aside things like Andres Serrano's *Piss Christ* and other art works deemed obscene for religious and other reasons.) Twenty years ago, in an article titled "The Neurobiology of the Obscene: Henry Miller and Tourette Syndrome," David B. Morris concluded that

> America no longer witnesses the epic battles over censorship that engaged modernist writers such as D.H. Lawrence and Henry Miller. The question of whether pornography constitutes or incites violence against women is certainly important, but the pornographic and the obscene (although they often overlap) are clearly not identical. Moreover, the once potent conflicts about obscenity have been transformed mostly into occasions for political posturing and bureaucratic compromise.[1]

In short, it seems it would be unlikely today that there would be a sense of urgency around the banning of a book like *Ulysses* or *Lady Chatterley's Lover*, partly due to the passage of time, and also due to the fact that, from today's viewpoint, the content, in what is perceived as an increasingly creaky medium, looks so tame.

Yet Henry Miller's *Tropic of Cancer* (1934) excites critics even today; more precisely, even talking about it disrupts critical thinking. Shortly after Frederick

Turner's *Renegade: Henry Miller and the Making of Tropic of Cancer* came out in 2011, it was reviewed in the *New York Times* by Jeanette Winterson, author of, among other notable works, *Oranges Are Not the Only Fruit* (1985), *Sexing the Cherry* (1989), and *Why Be Happy When You Could Be Normal?* (2012). The review's title, "The Male Mystique of Henry Miller," highlights the emphasis of Winterson's polemic against the narrator of *Tropic of Cancer*, Henry Miller, whom she has sport with (or shows revenge towards) by nicknaming "Hopeless Henry," "Hungry Henry," and "Heroic Henry." On the novel itself Winterson is both general and suspiciously quiet. In the first category (the least interesting for the point of this chapter, but a consideration nonetheless) she regards it as a work "so great that it takes the world nearly 30 years to face up to it."[2] In the context of the review this is not a subtle jab, and the lack of subtlety continues with misrepresentations, degree-by-degree, of the real-life figures of Miller, June Mansfield, and Anaïs Nin until, by the end of the piece, they are warped to Winterson's specifications. Those more conversant with the biographical work done on each already possess a more rounded picture, and will demur, for example, at the picture offered of Miller as a mooch on women, unable and unwilling to keep a job (his employment history is described in Turner's book and briefly mentioned in *Tropic of Cancer*), as an anti-Semite and a xenophobe, completely bypassing abundant references throughout his oeuvre to his admiration for Jewish cantors, writers, and friends, and a strong antipathy toward his ancestors. ("My people were entirely Nordic, which is to say *idiots*. Every wrong idea which has ever been expounded was theirs" [CAP, 3]). But the purpose of the review, which isn't aimed at those who know anything deep about Miller and his acquaintances, seems to be to warn people off reading Miller and to definitely not indulge an author who views women as "semihuman sex objects."[3]

To the more important aspect of Winterson's review, in her final paragraph she states: "There is beauty as well as hatred in *Cancer*, and it deserves its place on the shelf."[4] As she has said nothing positive about the novel to this point, and has been busy dodging Miller's condemnation of a capitalist society that dehumanizes everyone (as described on many pages in Turner's book), her remark is vacuous. It's as though she cannot (or is unwilling to make the effort to) bring forward either proof or an opinion that the overthrow of the obscenity ban "in 1961"—though matters did not near an end until the United States Supreme Court "indicated that to hold *Cancer* obscene was improper ..."[5] in early summer 1964—was a proper vindication of the worth of *Tropic of Cancer*. To be blunt, it's not clear if she is in favor of this ruling in Miller's case.

It may be asked in what ways Winterson's review relates to the topic of obscenity. There are two. In the last paragraph she indicates that the censorship of the 1930s and the sexual liberation of the 1960s "buried" what, for her, is the central matter: "The question is: Why do men revel in the degradation of women?"[6] Indeed, Turner's book supplies material for this argument right off when he writes: "When it was published in Paris in September 1934 by a man who dealt in what today would be called 'soft pornography,' it completely fulfilled the bravado of Miller's proclamation [to dispense with convention] ...,"[7] thereby associating *Tropic of Cancer* with smutty works.

Huw Nesbitt, in an attempt to assess Miller's first book and Louis-Ferdinand Céline's *Journey to the End of the Night* (1932), travels much the same path as Winterson when he states that Miller's work is "misogynistic... transgressive... [and contains] pornographic elements... [that were] undoubtedly the result of Miller's second career writing sex novels to make ends meet."[8] We see an almost querulous tone about Miller when Nesbitt is considering the "overwrought" language of *Tropic of Cancer*, an apparently common fault often found in those who have "the characteristic enthusiasm of a new writer desperate to appear literary."[9] In the wake of minimalist writing, which eschewed the richness of adverbs and adjectives, and the temperament of the 1980s and 1990s, which steeped readers in a disengaged irony, when someone who is aware of the potential delights of the English language bursts forth in exuberance then it's not so unexpected that a commentator is taken aback (one who is already made uncomfortable by the "pornographic element") and finds the problem not in him but in the writer under discussion. It probably doesn't help that the narrator of Miller's first book is grateful for his "really superb health" when, in an English novel, his condition would be the cause of self-embarrassment and misery. Desperate, Nesbitt resorts to the absurd judgment that Miller is "merely mimicking" Rimbaud's writing. Anyone familiar with Miller's writing knows better. It is as if Nesbitt had chosen an easy route, to fault Miller for his (lack of) plot and the characters, and his treatment of women, as that would be easier than engaging with the bulk of the text that deals with living in poverty, the importance of art, fellowship among his disreputable friends, and his love for Mona. These features either escape Nesbitt, or else he is unable to understand their importance. He chooses, instead, to make shallow remarks about the power of Miller's language and the control he exercises over it. Both must be found wanting.

Nesbitt and Winterson, in their stances, appear to implicitly agree on these matters: despite court rulings, the opinions of well-known authors (such as Nin, Edmund Wilson, George Orwell, and Erica Jong) who spoke out in favor of his work, and his widespread popularity among the reading public, and as if all of today's popular culture did not exist, Miller is morally at fault for his opinions about women and the words chosen to describe them, and therefore still guilty of obscenity. In their own ways, and couching themselves in current terms, each is trying to redefine what obscenity is, and to do this they must choose not to take into account that *Tropic of Cancer* contains more than what some have deemed obscene or pornographic. This novel is the measure of a man who has disreputable motives he does not hide, who expresses astringent and slashing criticisms of his male friends (while relying on them for food and lodging), and who speaks what he thinks, without reservation or concern for the feelings of others. It may be that the new obscene, for these commentators, is the freedom to say ugly things. Most women don't want to have their clitoris likened to a depository for "two franc pieces" (CAN, 6). Most men don't want their male friends to regard them as having a heart that's "dry" (CAN, 40) and sterile (as the narrator classifies Boris's). People are as within their rights to find those opinions distasteful, oppressive, misogynistic, and many other things, as Miller is within his rights to use such language. It is this poetic use that, for readers of Miller's first book, and the ones to come, makes them living, breathing documents that amuse, astonish, unsettle, and provoke.

That *Tropic of Cancer* remains a lightning rod for dissent along predictable lines is not news, but if the lines seem predictable, then why do people go over the same old arguments when the battle was won many years ago? That people carry on as if history didn't exist and social change has not occurred indicates that present in Miller's work, generally, are elements that cause controversy in a far more permissive climate (unimaginably so, it might seem, from when he wrote in the 1930s), and where reading seems to take up less of our free time when compared to competing media. Is what was once viewed as obscene what is, now, truly obscene? Not according to the courts; not according to public opinion; and, in comparison to what can be listened to, read, or watched so easily, it is almost laughable to consider this or that word found on any page of *Tropic of Cancer* or *Sexus* as potentially more offensive than the average episode of *Deadwood* or *Girls*. Perhaps the center of what is "the obscene" has drifted, thanks to the tides of time and taste, to a new location.

***

As many commentators have noted, in Miller's work surrealist and realist streams branch into and out of each other with ease. Where surrealist techniques, in George Orwell's mind, gave rise to a "Mickey Mouse universe"[10] wherein rationality and realism were absent, realist devices open the door for the authorities to enter the premises of literature with writs in hand. Miller's books contain (though are not limited to) realism of detail (such as street scenes in New York and Paris, and the Big Sur environment) and speech. His use of realism may come from an early admiration for Theodore Dreiser. Early on in his writing life, Miller showed sensitivity to the fact that Dreiser's style sprang from his personality and suited his subject matter, and wrote, justifying an aspect of *An American Tragedy*, that Dreiser "uses language, consciously or not, in the manner which modern writers, notably Joyce, use deliberately; that is, he identifies his language with the consciousness of his characters" (TNR, 302). This can lead readers into confusing the author with the reality depicted, and Miller rejected just such a befuddlement in the mind of a Dreiser critic that the elder writer's habit of "mixing slang with poetic archaisms, reveling in the cheap, trite and florid," indicates that Dreiser was "correspondingly muddled, banal and tawdry" (306).

Printed in 1926, one year after the publication of *An American Tragedy*, that opinion can be seen almost as a foretelling of Miller's own defense against charges leveled at his fiction. Miller provided, joyfully (though not always showing joy), graphic descriptions of acts and anatomies expressed in language that can be lyrical, demotic, salty, or corrosive. It is here where we find the porous line separating what we commonly term realism and what some categorize as obscenity. Naturally, he regarded it in another way entirely in a later essay, "Obscenity in Literature": "Deceit and hypocrisy, such as are prevalent in our time, have a way of provoking honest men to explosive language, to shocking language. They, however, who welcome truth, who believe in life, find nothing loathsome in such language… If our daily life is full of ugliness it is inevitable that men will arise to describe it and reveal it in all its manifold details"

(HMW, 197). To Frank Kermode, this will not do, and he judges Miller's chosen terms as the province of "men without women: sailors, for example or possibly men in heavy industry," and limited to "half of the population."[11] Most of the terms that critics like Kermode find objectionable relate to sexual organs and the objectification of women, and this shows a blind spot in their reading. No one who approaches *Tropic of Cancer* in an attentive manner can fail to see that Miller's rhapsody over Tania's cunt (CAN, 5–6) is balanced by, for example, Van Norden failing to orgasm when with a prostitute, and the resulting mechanical repetition of his actions (144–149). The lushness of the rhapsody, its self-contained (one might say masturbatory) pleasure at the cascade of images, as well as the exaggerations present within, leap well beyond what might excite most discerning readers, barring the passage from the domains of eroticism or pornography; as for the machine-like nature of Van Norden, his humanity is removed but the woman gives Miller "a despairing look" (148). Neither of these scenes provides endearing portraits of Tania, Van Norden, or Miller.

Frequently, sex passages are narrated in such a lengthy way as to forestall the tension that might lead to tumescence. In some passages they are part of a larger design. As Leon Lewis put it: "The desperate sexuality of Miller and his friends in *Cancer*, *Capricorn* and *Sexus* is both an expression of the twisted, inhuman attitudes toward sex which society encouraged by repression and ignorance, and an example of Miller overreacting to this repression in an excess of self-indulgence."[12] At other times their exaggeration (here one thinks most immediately of *Sexus*, [1949]) can only undercut the potential for prurience. Katy Masuga makes this point as well: "The prevalence of sexual encounters with women indicates an acutely self-conscious mode of writing, where the absurdity, the overabundance, and the persistent indefatigability of the sexual encounters promote this very incapturability of the woman-object in Miller."[13] There is playfulness in some of the sex scenes in his novels that may be missed due to their intensity or duration.

In "Astrological Fricassee," Miller plays with his reputation as the author of dirty books when asked by an actress at a party what he writes:

"Naughty books," I said, trying to blush deeply.
"What kind of naughty books? Naughty-naughty—or just dirt?"
"Just dirt, I guess."
"You mean Lady Chatterby, or Chattersley, or whatever the hell it is? Not that sort of swill you don't mean, do you?"
I laughed. "No, not that sort ... just straight obscenity. You know—duck, chit, kiss, trick, punt ..." (RTR, 226)

In Miller's work, sex and obscenity take on a classical and European flavor—we think of Rabelais and de Sade, and, as Sir Herbert Read pointed out, there are echoes of "Catullus, Petronius, Boccaccio"[14]—but the engine of his expression is a United Statesian rambunctiousness that Turner, viewing it from his own historical context, calls "that unconquerable wildness beating in American's heart ... [that] made the nation coarse, uncouth, and at times even disgusting"[15] to someone like Thoreau.

The entrance of formerly off-limit terms—as one critic reminds us, "obscenities are among the most common features of human speech"[16]—introduces a radical disturbance to the conventions of the novel, enough to set the teeth of propriety on edge, but which is needed in order to capture the alienation and isolation that the narrators of Miller's novels experience. Modernism, of which Miller is a part, is to an extent antiart when it confronts established and respected aesthetic and societal conventions.

In *What Ever Happened to Modernism?* Gabriel Josipovici comments on *Don Quixote*:

> Don Quixote's madness dramatizes for us the hidden madness in every realist novel, the fact that the hero of every such novel is given a name merely in order to persuade us of his reality, and that he has giants created for him to do battle with and Dulcineas for him to fall in love with simply to satisfy the demands of the narrative. And it dramatizes the way we as readers collude in this narrative game because we want, for the duration of our reading, to be part of a realised world, a world full of meaning and adventure, an *enchanted world* ... We need enchantment and are prepared to pay good money to get at least a dose of it.[17]

We can say that the madness Miller exposes through his wild flights of prose and the brutal imagery that dismantle our expectations of what is proper is one singled out by both Josipovici and, in a negative sense, Kermode. In *Tropic of Cancer* men are called Joe, a uniformly bland name that means nothing too specific—"a pleasant reminder not to take yourself too seriously" (CAN, 107)—while it serves to depersonalize everyone. Individual characteristics remain (a beard, a philosophy, a position on art, an occupation), but the impetus is not egalitarian or democratic, that would be a ridiculous claim, and not a goal any of the figures would aim for. Yet it is not meant to undercut anyone. (The narrator has other ways of doing that.) It is an attempt, a "pleasant" one, both to keep anyone from succumbing to an inflated ego and to build camaraderie against the despair generated by unhappiness. Flipping it over, it can also be seen as a way to remove ethnicity and class distinctions and to objectify the male characters by viewing them in a very United Statesian way: "Joe" makes everyone a regular guy, it is a name that levels all. With no one in charge—and though it can be argued that the narrator is in a position of power due to this being his tale, he also states "I call him [Van Norden] Joe because he calls me Joe. When Carl is with us he is Joe too" (CAN, 107)—this is more homogeneity than hegemon.

The interchangeable units called Joe or Henry, or Sylvester, share a form of speech filled with curses and slang, which reflects how people talk within their own group, herd, or tribe. Miller is showing the world as it exists, not as some want it to be, and that ran afoul of the law. In *The Unknown Henry Miller*, Hoyle writes of Huntington Cairns, the United States censor, that he defined as "the essential characteristic of obscenity its quality of being hidden. Under this definition a work is obscene because it brings into public view 'sexual stimulants' that, according to common standards of decency, should remain private. Of course, bringing out into the open what society wants to hide was exactly Miller's purpose in writing his banned books."[18] It may not be hard to see why a wartime sailor turned literary critic would wish to cordon off Miller's works from the manners of general society. That men refer to women in certain ways is a truth that's as hard for Kermode to accept as for those who confronted Miller's works before him, and we can see the same refusal operating in Winterson and Nesbitt. ("Those who are shocked, pained, wounded or horrified by these written symbols are not unfamiliar with them in speech... But why should literature be more sacrosanct than speech?" [HMW, 195]) This denial of reality is only a variety of the "madness" Josipovici describes, for a kind of magical thinking is going on—that we are better than we are, that allowing the language of "men in heavy industry" to be set down will encourage the worst kind of thinking, and that Miller's form of direct address, because it attacks decorum and relegates women to a level where they are called whores or cunts, is corrosive and worth attacking for not being respectful; it isn't what some people would prefer to be the proper mode of discourse or, in a word, it's not civilized.

It is worth being reminded what life was like in the Western world during the Depression years. Speaking about France specifically, Turner states that it "had suffered about a million-and-a-half fatalities in the war and another 740,000 severely wounded. Here was a deeper damage to the infrastructure than bridges and rail liners, because it would take a generation and more to repair."[19] Miller left New York in 1930 amid a collapsing economy and a dying marriage, and the new environment proved difficult to make his way through because of his lack of French (at first) and not having working papers. The Paris of 1934, then, was far from an enchanted world. In the mind of the narrator of Miller's first book it can be a cold place populated by bare trees that call to mind "T.S. Eliot's verse" (CAN, 40); it can be "... a menagerie. The dawn is breaking on a new world, a jungle world in which the lean spirits roam with sharp claws" (103); and, on rare occasions, it is welcoming, as when, at the novel's end, the Seine is described as "always there, quiet and unobtrusive, like a great artery running through the human body" (320). Its aspects are always perilously close to changing, and not often for the better.

The only "dose" that occurs in this world is the clap, as nicely portrayed in a scene with Miller, Macha, Fillmore, and some towels (237). Men and women don't always hesitate from having sex due to the fear of venereal disease. While experience shows that caution is wise—"That's how one gets acquainted in Paris—genito-urinary friendships" (239)—everyone lives in the hope that nothing will be transmitted. Madness and sickness required a particularly robust vocabulary for the literature of the time—the emblematic nature of the astrological sign of Cancer combines with the "cancer of time [that] is eating us away" (1), and "cancer" functions as an umbrella term for the assorted physical and spiritual malaises afflicting the characters—that disrupted the politeness demanded by upholders of mores and legal frameworks.

***

It would be of some use to determine, as much as we can, what Miller regarded as obscene. In a letter to Miller dated 21 November 1962, amid court challenges in various states to the publication of *Tropic of Cancer* based on its alleged obscenity, with judges leaning one way or another, one of Miller's lawyers, Elmer Gertz, wrote: "This in itself is preposterous. Either the book is, or is not, obscene. It is not that much a matter of geography."[20] We might find that sentiment sensible, and wonder to ourselves why one location would view things differently than another. But if we take the remark out of its original context, tease its potential meaning a bit, and insert it into the ongoing debate, it may show us something more productive than ill-informed knee-jerk reactions or stale polemics that, with seeming obliviousness, smack of the conservatism of the 1930s through the early 1960s, bear the marks of the censor, and betray a tendency to believe that free speech in theory is all right, but in actuality there should be limits. As the need exists, we once more must repeat Miller's own perspective to help clear up where, exactly, he would find the obscene, and see if it exists on a map that is, for some reason, seldom consulted by certain commentators. We may even extend its parameters.

One of Miller's best-known essays on the matter is "Obscenity and the Law of Reflection." In it he states: "When obscenity crops out in art, literature more particularly, it usually functions as a technical device; the element of the deliberate which is there has nothing to do with sexual excitation, as in pornography. If there is an ulterior motive at work it is one which goes far beyond sex. Its purpose is to awaken, to usher in a sense of reality" (HMW, 196). There is nothing intrinsically arousing, in his opinion, in the sexual escapades found in his works. Obscenity is a device, like foreshadowing, and has a specific function: to help an author get at what is real.

Considering the use of obscenity and the role of women in Miller's novels, Masuga concludes that he "forces the presence of the text as a work of writing on the reader, and the reader attempts to find confirmation of what he or she is reading in the 'real.'" (It is worthwhile bearing in mind the suspension of disbelief that occurs when fiction is well done, and how early critics like Kingsley Widmer and Gore Vidal seemed to forget this and subsequently were flummoxed by *Sexus* especially.) "The reader wants to jump *hors texte* to confirm what is being read, with Miller luring him or her into that state and then denying the fulfillment of that desire by revealing its inadequacy. The desire is misdirected and needs to be placated through a reconsideration of the role and effects of a text."[21] Frustration of desire casts readers back onto their own devices. Josipovici makes a useful point when, in his examination of British novelists, he says that the "smooth chain of [their] sentences gives us a sense of security, of comfort even, precisely because it denies the openness, the 'trembling' of life itself …"[22] What is this trembling but a version of Miller's ushering in a sense of reality?

What Miller finds obscene is multifold: "Fear, guilt and murder—these constitute the real triumvirate which rules our world. *What is obscene then?* The whole fabric of life as we know it today." He states himself even more explicitly late in the same essay: "If there is anything which deserves to be called 'obscene' it is this oblique, glancing confrontation with the mysteries of vertigo and yet refusing to yield to the spell of the unknown" (HMW, 189). Masuga, Josipovici, and Miller stress the unknown, the contingent, the potential of life and not its closure through a preference for neat rationalizing, and the great desire to get to the next level of awareness. They want the reader to come along with them, but some who write on Miller balk at this. They would do well to read further in "Obscenity and the Law of Reflection," particularly the end where he advises those who view him with distaste for using profane language—"It is my honest conviction that the fear and dread which the obscene inspires, particularly in modern times, spring from the language employed rather than the thought. It is very much as if we were dealing here with primitive taboos" (195)—to consider that once the obscene "is recognized and accepted, whether as a figment of the imagination or as an integral part of human reality, it inspires no more dread or revulsion than could be ascribed to the flowering lotus which sends its roots down into the mud of the stream on which it is borne" (189).

When *Sexus* became the subject of a "1957 censorship trial"[23] in Norway, a lawyer, Trygve Hirsch, asked Miller for input. A letter dated February 1959 lays out Miller's case, and its final paragraph reads:

> But it is not something evil, nor something poisonous, which this book *Sexus* offers the Norwegian reader. It is a dose of life which I administered to myself first, and which I not only survived but thrived on. Certainly I would not recommend it to infants, but then neither would I offer a child a bottle of *aqua vite*. I can say one thing for it unblushingly—compared to the atom bomb, it is full of life-giving qualities. (HMW, 216)

Recent commentary indicates that we are far from being able to accept the "life-giving qualities" of Miller's works. As Gina Frangello put it in a 2013 piece that dealt with portraying sex in U.S. fiction, "to write about the messy interplay between bodies and psychology is a risky business, and in my humble opinion, why we are *here*."[24] It is one reason, and a compelling one, but I venture that there are other messy interplays Miller had in mind that might be considered the new obscene.

***

> I think it was the Fourth of July when they took the chair from under my ass again. Not a word of warning. One of the big muck-a-mucks from the other side of the water had decided to make economies; cutting down on proofreaders and helpless little *dactylos* enabled him to pay the expenses of his trips back and forth and the palatial quarters he occupied at the Ritz. (CAN, 191)

In *Tropic of Cancer, Tropic of Capricorn*, and the *Rosy Crucifixion*, Miller regularly condemns the meager economic prospects open to him, his friends, and the people he comes across. "At a time when others were getting comfortable berths I was taking one miserable job after another," the narrator of *Tropic of Capricorn* complains, "and never enough in it to keep body and soul together. Almost as quickly as I was hired I was fired. I had plenty of intelligence but I inspired distrust. Wherever I went I fomented discord—not because I was idealistic but because I was like a searchlight exposing the stupidity and futility of everything" (CAP, 8). In 1920, Miller landed a position at

Western Union that, some time after meeting June, he leaves in order to write full time, even though from this time he rarely brought in money except for that begged from or given by friends and strangers, a pittance that barely supplemented what his new wife earned: "she began to 'gold-dig'—a thin euphemism for whoring—bringing home to [Miller] cash from her various 'admirers.'"[25] Time spent at the "Cosmodemonic Telephone Company" supplied Miller, via its ethos, personnel, and organizational structure, a view of corporate life in the United States that he had had no access to previously. As a manager he became aware of the personal attributes of the messengers, and their status: "Men were walking the streets of New York in that bloody, degrading outfit, the despised, the lowest of the low ... and many a one was fit to govern the world, to write the greatest book ever written" (CAP, 25). In *Tropic of Cancer* he arrives at almost the lowest level he can reach, and we as readers are more surprised that the job at the newspaper referred to above lasts any length of time than that the chair is removed from under him. Financial security does not become him, in a manner of speaking, nor does it become anyone we see in this novel or his later ones.

William Vollmann, whose work in many ways deals with some of the same classes and topics as Miller (prostitutes, the down-and-out, precarity, freedom of thought, speech, and act), and who also shares mixed feelings about the United States, in a review of several books by John O'Hara, wrote:

> John O'Hara's themes are alcoholism, infidelity, rape, perversion, child molestation, the yearning for power and financial security (many who knew the author believed this to be his own basic preoccupation), the instability of love and passion, the effects of economic substructures on the superstructures of private life (in method, if certainly not in ideology, he resembles a Marxist), boardroom and statehouse politics, and the secret corruptions of families. In many respects he is a cruel writer; not only does he portray quotidian cruelty unblinkingly and intimately, but his portrayals themselves can be cruel.[26]

There is an overlap of elements in O'Hara's fiction with what Miller depicted from his life in New York, Paris, and Big Sur, from *Tropic of Cancer* through *The Devil in Paradise* (1956) to *Nexus* (1965). In these recessionary times—agitation over the one percent, the echoes of the Occupy movement, banking crises occurring on both sides of the Atlantic balanced by extravagant bonuses to a handful of banking executives, the degradation of living conditions in many countries, and the disparity between the rich and the poor—we cannot help but notice that there is a universal chair being yanked from under our collective asses and our independence being revoked as irrevocably as was Miller's. "If [*Tropic of Cancer*] was not a pleasant, conventional or decorous piece of literature it was at least normal and natural, given the circumstances which made its birth inevitable" (HMW, 191), and we need only to look around to see the values of Vollmann and Larry Fondation as spokesmen for the destitute and the marginal.

Miller's scarce resources in Paris, a throwback to New York and also not very different from the long stretch of poverty to come in Big Sur, are only occasionally augmented by odd jobs as a writer, but he is not alone in his worries. Van Norden complains that he's "grinding my balls off on that job, and it doesn't even give me a clean shirt" (CAN, 112), while another friend, Carl, is fearful of losing a position it took him "a year to land ..." (54). A Hindu businessman first met in New York is waiting for the pearl business to return to life: "The pearls will sell again some day, maybe five years hence, maybe twenty ..." (87). Recalling his life in New York, the narrator talks about Forty-second Street: "You can walk along with your hands put out and they'll put cinders in your cap" (71). "But I don't ask to go back to America, to be put in double harness again, to work the treadmill. No, I prefer to be a poor man of Europe" (73). No one is at ease in this depressed environment and no one rests on a firm foundation except those who can order changes from afar while dining at the Ritz.

In "Obscenity and the Law of Reflection," Miller expresses his belief that " ... [n]othing would be regarded as obscene, I feel, if men were living out their inmost desires" (HMW, 183), and we can see in Paris the impossibility of doing this for the narrator and his friends, just as we will see in later works that few can do this in the New York of *Tropic of Capricorn* and the *Rosy Crucifixion*. Approximate conditions apply today, for how do the ninety-nine percent live out their desires and wishes when the one percent is entrenched? While Miller's work is not a pure indictment of the capitalist system, it does often contain a set of charges against the system ("I am against the *status quo* both *before* and *after* the revolution," [CE, 160]) that makes it an appropriate set of works to study now.

A recent article by Curtis White pointed out that working conditions, wherever they can be found now, have not improved for many in the United States:

> Most work in the United States is an expression of contempt for the people who must perform it. Most work is humiliating, stripped of worthy skills, destructive, and tedious. Even the most sought after jobs are places of real human misery: boredom.
>
> The despair of work, because it is a despair that all oligarchs depend on, is never seriously addressed by liberalism. Even for unions, it's off the table. If it weren't, they'd never have gotten a seat at the table in the first place. Instead, we hear: "You're lucky to have a job." In the meantime, what Karl Marx's son-in-law, Paul Lafargue, called the "dogma of work" makes its way, physically and spiritually impoverishing those who kneel before it.[27]

Things are not much better in the United Kingdom, as Ivor Southwood describes it:

> Work is no longer a secure base, but rather a source of anxiety and indignity, both a matter of life and death and utterly meaningless, overwhelming and yet so insubstantial it could run through our fingers. It is normal to feel under threat and undervalued, to feel snivellingly grateful to have a job, any job. We must be sure not to take work for granted and yet be willing to be taken for granted ourselves.[28]

This era of despair, fatigue, fear, and self-loathing is the "spirit of an age [that] is the crucible in which, through one means or another, certain vital and mysterious forces seek expression" (HMW, 180). Desperation is visible everywhere. Even succeeding as a writer, what Miller sought for much of his life, is fraught and flawed for some: "Becoming a novelist, earning money easily, provoking as much repulsion as fascination: the public shame is comparable to that of the whore."[29] We have crossed over unknowingly, or not fully consciously, I tentatively suggest, into a new "sense of reality," a terrain of the obscene that the opening lines of "Obscenity and the Law of Reflection" help chart: "To discuss the nature and meaning of obscenity is almost as difficult as to talk about God" (HMW, 175).

Even the most general survey of what is obscene would discover that it is a topic that contains competing definitions, distinctions, biases, and judgments. What would also be evident is that what the obscene is cannot ever be decided, and that to keep to a narrow remit is confining. Literature loses when discussion is closed off because of indignation and repulsion. James Decker offers this summary: "the notoriety [Miller] gained first as an 'obscene' writer and later as an exemplar of sexist values continues to color the reception of his work …,"[30] which echoes what Lewis wrote thirty years ago: "As Kate Millett's sometimes devastating critique of Miller suggests, it is still easier for most critics to see Miller as a limited, single-issue author, but this continuing practice has kept the field of Miller criticism rather narrow in scope."[31]

Winterson's rhetorical question—"Why do men revel in the degradation of women?"—is insufficient when it comes to furthering a discussion of what Miller meant or may yet come to mean, and it can be argued that her question is posed so as to close off a search for potential and alternate interpretations of *Tropic of Cancer* or any other work by Miller. As Masuga underlines, "Miller has sustained an unwarranted and undying reputation as a writer of ill repute. It is also the most unfortunate categorization of Miller in that, with an eye solely on the negativity of sexual content, this category fails to critically examine Miller's work in any way."[32]

Those opening lines of "Obscenity and the Law of Reflection" equate obscenity and God, hinting that these are two universals that can never be explained with certitude by everyone or for all time. The "nature and meaning of obscenity" is so complex as to discourage any one meaning (such as: Miller hates women and is therefore hateful) and must, through its ramifications, by who we were in the 1930s and the 1960s, and who we are today, simultaneously bring to our apprehension the fact that consideration of what is obscene will be inexhaustible while positively encouraging further exploration. Going in a direction Miller might not have anticipated, we can choose to regard Miller's first fiction (as well as certain of his other ones, especially *Tropic of Capricorn*) as profitable for alternate as well as complementary interpretations of "the obscene," allowing for its shifting meaning over time and its deepening importance to whatever audience it reaches at any historical time. Its multiform nature is made evident in the two Miller essays quoted herein, in Morris's peculiar slant on Miller's mind, in Masuga's criticism, in specific criticism by others, and more broadly in the general public, and it is not much of a stretch to allow it to encompass economics as well as language, imagery, and gender issues. This essay can only hope to advocate for the expansion of the definition of obscenity and to locate it, and *Tropic of Cancer* (as an example), in the current worldwide fiscal situation.

The last pages of Hoyle's biography feature comments by university literature teachers. Among them is fiction writer Tobias Wolff, who says:

> Miller was so influential, it's hard to think of his books not being taught, but the truth is I don't think they are, certainly not to my knowledge here at Stanford. Maybe that's not such a bad thing—to discover Miller is to feel one-self caught up in defiance, subversion, outrageous unrespectable frankness and revolutionary humor. Can you sustain these feelings if they are blessed by sober institutional authority? Is that not a sort of counter-subversion? (italics removed)[33]

We come full circle to Winterson and Nesbitt here, and the counterargument is strong, that "unrespectable frankness" is always worth preserving, especially in times of hardship.

Notes

1. David B. Morris, "The Neurobiology of the Obscene: Henry Miller and Tourette Syndrome," *Literature and Medicine* 12, 2 (1993): 195.
2. Jeanette Winterson, "The Male Mystique of Henry Miller," *New York Times*, 26 January 2012. There is a certain irony in the fact that excerpts from Miller and Winterson are included in *The Naughty Bits: The Steamiest and Most Scandalous Sex Scenes from the World's Great Books*, by Jack Murnighan (New York: Broadway Books, 2001).
3. Winterson, "The Male Mystique of Henry Miller."
4. Winterson, "The Male Mystique of Henry Miller."
5. Elmer Gertz and Felice Flannery Lewis, eds, *Henry Miller: Years of Trial & Triumph, 1962–1964* (Carbondale: Southern Illinois University Press, 1978), 318, n 2.
6. Winterson, "The Male Mystique of Henry Miller."
7. Turner, *Renegade*, 3.
8. Huw Nesbitt, "Why Henry Miller and Louis-Ferdinand Céline Deserve Success as well as Scandal," in *Guardian*, 19 February 2014. http://www.theguardian.com/books/booksblog/2014/feb/19/henry-miller-louis-ferdinand-celine-scandal
9. Nesbitt, "Why Henry Miller and Louis-Ferdinand Céline Deserve Success as well as Scandal."
10. George Orwell, "Review," in *An Age Like This: 1920–1940, Vol. 1 of The Collected Essays, Journalism and Letters of George Orwell*, eds. Sonia Orwell and Ian Angus (New York: Harcourt, Brace and World, Inc., 1968), 231.
11. Frank Kermode, *Continuities* (London: Routledge, 1968), 158.
12. Lewis, *Major Writings*, 27.
13. Katy Masuga, *The Secret Violence of Henry Miller* (Rochester: Camden House, 2011), 67.
14. Sir Herbert Read, *The Tenth Muse* (Freeport: Books for Libraries Press, 1969), 253.
15. Turner, *Renegade*, 44.
16. Morris, "Neurobiology," 194–214.
17. Gabriel Josipovici, *What Ever Happened to Modernism*? (New Haven: Yale University Press, 2010), 34.
18. Hoyle, *Unknown*, 142–143.

19 Turner, *Renegade*, 125–126.
20 Gertz and Lewis, *Trial & Triumph*, 134.
21 Masuga, *Secret Violence*, 66.
22 Josipovici, *Modernism*, 164.
23 Hoyle, *Unknown*, 228.
24 Gina Frangello, "State of the (Literary/Sexual) Union," *American Book Review* 34, 6 (2013): 18.
25 Turner, *Renegade*, 106.
26 William T. Vollmann, "Decently Downward," *The Baffler* 24 (2014) http://thebaffler.com/past/decently_downward (last accessed 19 Jan. 2015).
27 Curtis White, "Managing Despair," *big other* 8 (2012) http://bigother.com/2012/03/08/27085/
28 Ivor Southwood, *Non-stop Inertia* (Alresford, Hants: Zero Books, 2011), 76.
29 Virginie Despentes, *King Kong Theory*, trans. Stéphanie Benson (New York: The Feminist Press, 2010), 79.
30 Decker, *Henry*, 2.
31 Lewis, *Major Writings*, 4.
32 Masuga, *Secret Violence*, 20.
33 Hoyle, *Unknown*, 327.

13

Dispossessed Sexual Politics: Henry Miller's Anarchism *Qua* Kate Millett and Ursula K. Le Guin

James Gifford

> *The age we live in is the age which suits us: its is we who make it, not God, not Capitalism, not this or that, call it by any name you like. The evil is in us... When at last each man realizes that nothing is to be expected from God, or society, or friends, or benevolent tyrants, or democratic governments, or saints, or saviours, or even from the holiest of holies, education, when each man realizes that he must work with his own hands to save himself, and that he need expect no mercy, perhaps then... No god is coming to save us. No system of government, no belief will provide us with that liberty and justice which men whistle for with the death-rattle.*
>
> The Cosmological Eye (154–155)

In a surprising but very real sense, when Kate Millett's *Sexual Politics* first appeared in 1968 with an extensive critique of misogyny in *Tropic of Cancer*, it fulfilled Henry Miller's anarchist praxis for writing. Although Millett disapproves of Miller, her spirited response to his works is much in the spirit of their composition and reflects a major part of Miller's larger anarchist praxis. Miller indicates this antiauthoritarian position in his letters to her when he writes, "I believe in the freedom of the reader as well as the writer" (LKM, 157). This is to say, Millett's reading against Miller, despite its desire to convert the reader to a way of understanding the text and world, follows from the anarchic paradigm set up for his work when Miller argued in his 1938 essay "An Open Letter to Surrealists Everywhere" that "I am fatuous enough to believe that in living my own life in my own way I am more apt to give life to others (though even that is not my chief concern)" (CE, 157). Miller's works, even while provoking readerly engagements through the text, never proscribe the interpretive freedom of Millett's own explosively responsive writing. Nonetheless, this is putting the cart before the horse, or more aptly, the reactionary before the provocateur. The problem, however, is that contrary to easy assumptions, Miller is the anarchic provocateur and Millett, the reactionary progressive, the former antiauthoritarian and the latter propaganda by either the deed or the pen (even if one agrees with its spirit and aims). This nexus of confused engagements becomes clearer when Miller's ostensibly fatuous belief in living and provoking proves reasonable and modest five years after giving life to Millett's *Sexual Politics* when Ursula Le Guin's *The Dispossessed* allusively adapts the same passage as Millett critiques. This sequence of works illustrates both Miller's sexual politics and his relational anarchism, or his sexual anarchism and relational politics, although the horse and cart, provocateur and reactionary, must be reordered for intelligibility: Miller as anarchist, Miller as provocateur *qua* Millett and Le Guin, and the anarchist ethos of Miller's writing.

Miller as anarchist

Miller, it should be acknowledged, often espoused an "anarchic life" (CE, 151). However, he did not explicitly identify himself or his politics as anarchist. Instead, he made it implicitly clear and affiliated himself both deeply and broadly with global anarchist networks of authors for the majority of his writing career.[1] There is no doubt about Miller's anarchism,[2] although it is equally clear that Miller deliberately avoided voicing explicit political anarchist affiliations, most likely for both ideological reasons that avoid influencing the views of others and for personal reasons that avoid the persecutions of anarchists across the 1920s, 1930s, and then across the century as a whole. In parallel to how David Weir has argued with regard to anarchism and literature more generally across the twentieth century,[3] but with a very different paradigm than his Jamesonian *Anarchism and Culture* (1997), Miller's anarchism migrated from a social moment in which anarchism was principally expressed in social action or activism to a largely formal artistic expression. However, Miller's emphasis on the "anarchic life" marks the vital distinction by linking both the "anarchic" and "life"— for Miller the formal and stylistic expression of anarchist politics, while eschewing explicit anarchist activism and propaganda, includes not only anarchism but also lived experience and quotidian praxis. In a different phrasing, Miller's migration of activism to artistic form centers on praxis and lived experience, which is an expansion beyond purely aesthetic matters. In this, he is both very much like Weir's analysis of the migration of anarchism from action for form and also very much unlike it for valuing form *as* political praxis.

This combination of formal concerns and lived praxis is implicit in Miller's indirect references to the anarchic life again and again. In the first instance, Miller distinguishes his own role as provocateur against that of the proselytizer. He makes his understanding of conversion and movements clear, as well as his anarchist politics, in two statements in "An Open Letter to Surrealists Everywhere": "To get men to rally round a cause, a belief, an idea, is always easier than to persuade them to lead their own lives" (CE, 156). This praxis-oriented emphasis on living one's own life runs contrary to the conversion-focused language of "a cause, a belief, an idea" and more generally the position of leadership implicit in this relationship between reader and text. By extension, Miller disparages this proselytizing or leadership capacity in artistic creation. Nonetheless, this does not mean that Miller supports only a purely aesthetic text, and even this prioritization of personal experience is, for Miller, a profoundly political intervention. Miller extends this specific reference to persuasion and conversion to offer an alternative that provokes without leading the reader:

> I am fatuous enough to believe that in living my own life in my own way I am more apt to give life to others (though even that is not my chief concern) than I would if I simply followed somebody else's idea of how to live my life and thus become a man among men. It seems to me that this struggle for liberty and justice is a confession or admission on the part of all those engaging in such a struggle that they have failed to live their own lives. (157)

To this he adds, if anyone could have missed the anarchist context of his comments, "I am against revolutions because they always involve a return to the status quo. I am against the status quo both before and after revolutions. I don't want to wear a black shirt or a red shirt. I want to wear the shirt that suits my taste" (160). However, while Miller's pacifism led him to critique George Orwell for participating in the Spanish Civil War, Orwell went regardless but while wearing Miller's coat. Although they disagreed on matters of direct political activism, they found much in each other to admire, particularly their antiauthoritarian visions. But this leads to the more specific matter at hand, more visible in their contemporary context than our modern paradigm. Miller's "black shirt or a red shirt" refers to the same conflict in Spain, though his paradigm is much the same as George Barker's black, red, and brown in his major poem "Elegy on Spain" (the proxy actors: the red Russian communists, the brown German *Sturmabteilung*, and the black Italian *camice nere*). The black and red are not symbols of the anarchists in the conflict who were defeated by the time Miller wrote the "Open Letter" but rather the black shirts of the fascists and the red communists, both in an authoritarian struggle for supremacy, and both refuting the significant antiauthoritarian and antigovernmental voices in the conflict. The fascists and the communists both recognized their common foe in the antiauthoritarian anarchist movement based in Barcelona.

This would appear to be an overt gesture, and it stands among many others in Miller's works as he writes about or refers to various anarchist figures ranging from Henry David Thoreau to Emma Goldman. Despite this, Miller is largely regarded as apolitical and out of touch with his contemporary political circumstances, particularly those of the Second World War, the Spanish Civil War, and the Munich Crisis. While Miller scholarship has repeatedly shown otherwise, Patrick von Richthofen in particular, the casual interpretation from scholarly readers of the majority Left and Right without an antiauthoritarian vertical axis stubbornly looks to Miller as dangerously counterrevolutionary or destructively libidinal. Despite this false dualism, the contemporary commentary from his colleagues and friends, distinct from the work of critics, tends to return to the same indirect anarchic affiliations and radical praxis espoused by Miller. Apart from Miller's own repeated statements of preference for the "anarchic," his correspondent Wallace Fowlie notes,

> He has always been the pure singer of individual freedom who was a-political because he believed that to give up a capitalistic regime for a socialistic regime was simply to change masters. His personal creed may be attached in part to the European utopia of the noble savage, and in part to the American tradition of

return to nature we read in Thoreau and Whitman. His sense of anarchy is partly that of Thoreau and partly that of the Beat Generation.[4]

The indirect movement from individual freedom contra the conflicting masters of a "capitalistic regime" versus "a socialistic regime" only anticipates Fowlie's ambiguous gesture to "anarchy," albeit quieted in this rendering of the concept rather than the noun "anarchism." While this does not expressly identify Miller as anarchist, the confluence is striking, especially since it recurs so very frequently in Miller's own works and those of his friends writing about him. As Alfred Perlès notes, the club that sponsored the Villa Seurat's journal "The Booster" thought "it was highly immoral and dangerously anarchic,"[5] and he repeats the "anarchic" description of Miller and the Villa Seurat's activities more generally. Perlès then also self-identifies as an anarchist in his own later works.[6] Alternatively, in his ostensibly apolitical book on a pacifist culture on Crete, written during its occupation by the Nazis during the Second World War, Miller says, "I like... the anarchic character of the landscape" (COM, 41). Anent the same, when Miller writes of Henry David Thoreau, he describes him as "nearer to being an anarchist than a democrat, socialist, or communist... [I]f there were more of his kind, [it] would soon cause governments to become non-existent... And that is why I have unbounded respect and admiration for Thoreau."[7]. The anarchism runs thick here, ubiquitous yet ambiguous.

In the same essay, the ostensibly unread and unpolitical Miller notes the importance of Thoreau for Gandhi's Satyagraha movement in India and the continuing importance of Thoreau's actions in relation to racism and slavery to the contemporary American political scene. In contrast to the seeming inspiration of this "great men" tradition, and as with "An Open Letter to Surrealists Everywhere," when modern readers *follow* Whitman, Emerson, or Thoreau, they "flout their wisdom. We have become victims of the times; we look backward with longing and regret."[8] It is as much as to say, when we follow these past voices rather than be provoked by them to our own actions, we fail to maintain fidelity to their praxis. Fidelity to their revolutionary politics lies not in following their own actions but rather in living in one's own way, and only thereby being revolutionary. The turn, again and again across the chapter, is Miller's emphasis on the ethical and relational importance of social communities, which also avoids the rising tide of the All-American "objectivist" libertarianism of Ayn Rand that elides community and reifies capitalism as a natural object in the world, or the social activism of Objectivist poetics through Louis Zukofsky, Lorine Niedecker, and George Oppen.

Miller as provocateur *qua* Millett and Le Guin

Miller's description of his anarchism, set in contrast against the Marxism of the Surrealists in "An Open Letter to Surrealists Everywhere," emphasizes his focus on doing his own work in his own way in the belief that this will encourage others to pursue their own ends as well, but not to follow his own path prescriptively nor with this as an aim or goal. In short, by pursuing his own ends, Miller provokes rather than leads, and this peculiar balance enacts his antiauthoritarian politics: to enliven but not to foster. Lawrence Durrell is perhaps the most adroit reader of Miller in this respect, recognizing the importance of Miller's letter that states "My books represent *germination* in all its phases"[7] and thereby Durrell's interpretation:

> "Germination," the word is a key to many of the intentions of Miller in his writings; it is the key to what Miller feels himself to be—a fecundating force expressing itself through writing, not a "literary man" or an "artist." The distinction is worth underlining for the shape and colour of this writer's work is dictated by his attitude to art.[8]

Miller's various provocations are widespread, ranging from the young Durrell finding *Tropic of Cancer* and setting out on a new direction in his own writing, Erica Jong's turn in *Fear of Flying* (1973), or the innumerable authors of the San Francisco Renaissance and Beats who were startled by his works into creative production. In most instances, these provocations also resulted in epistemologically and formally "open" texts that do not resolve ambiguity. For Durrell this could be leaving the reader on a blank page and thereby his or her own interpretive ingenuity, for Robert Duncan an unresolved "then" to follow "if" or "when," and so forth. However, Miller as provocateur is, here with Millett and Le Guin, focused on a single scene in *Tropic of Cancer* at the very end of the first section of the novel.

Miller's narrator describes remembering an evening out in Paris with Mona and Boris. This act of remembrance of a thing past is critical to how Miller casts the scene in contrast to the present moment of the narrative. Following an extended and beautiful observation of Paris at night, which attends in detail to class and gender by recuperating the downtrodden of the city, Miller sets his meaning-rich and fecund present moment against the meaninglessness of his failed relationship with Mona and the sterility of his writing: "St. Sulpice not meaning much to me then... tired of seeing so many people jabbering away about nothing... the notebooks I never touched, the manuscripts lying cold and dead" (CAN, 17). The scene that follows is complex and allusively linked to the opening of the novel with two men nude, picking lice off each other (CAN, 1) as well as a later scene with two men touching each other while attempting to hire a prostitute (CAN, 144–149)—it is a series of inebriated images around which other parts of the novel orbit, its drunkenness symptomatic of the human failures that comprise its theme:

> We wriggle into the cabinet and there I stand her up, slap up against the wall, and I try to get it into her but it won't work and so we sit down on the seat and try it that way but it won't work either. No matter how we try it, it won't work. And all the while she's got hold of my prick, she's clutching it like a lifesaver, but it's no use, we're too hot, too eager. The music is still playing and so we waltz out of the cabinet into the vestibule again and as we're dancing there in the shithouse I come all over her beautiful gown and she's sore as hell about it... When we get back to the hotel I vomit all over the place, in the bed, in the washbowl, over the suits and gowns and

the galoshes and canes and the notebooks I never touched and the manuscripts lying cold and dead. (CAN, 18)

For the close reader, the repeated "it won't work" marks the lack of penetration and connection in the scene and the corruption of the relations between man and woman (and equally between man and man). Yet, this is only a beginning to the complexities with the woman clutching his "prick...like a lifesaver," which also marks the peculiarity of the failed engagement—her sexual desire is a substitute, perhaps for protection from a fear or loss. This failure leaves her "sore as hell," and after the entire transaction Miller's eponymous narrator is left only with the abjection of vomiting across his room and creative process. Mixed with both is the "cabinet," the toilet, or later "the shithouse" closing the passage with the word "dead" just as the section as a whole opened with in the first quotations above, and indeed the novel itself in its first scene (CAN, 1). This image of shit also stitches the scene into a relationship with the later image of culture as the same shit on a silver platter (CAN, 101) and the shit-filled *bidet* from "Gandhi's man" in the novel and Miller's implicit skepticism over the efficacy of the politically active anarchism of the Satyagraha movement, which he links to "disciples" round their "master" (CAN, 97). Like the sterile opening of the novel, in which everyone is "dead" (CAN, 1), this passage lays out the failures of human engagement based on the insidiously necrotizing effects of capital and its substitutional logics on human relations, such that the phallus becomes protection from something else, and because of this substitutional logic, "it won't work" and he is impotent, which reflects coercive and power-laden human relations generally. Rather than a depiction of sexual conquest and masculine virility, the scene depicts a profoundly impoverished gender dynamic in failures of *inter*course, failures to relate, and a deadly sterility. At the textual level, this is the series of relations that emerge in the seminal passage, and it exemplifies Miller's sexual politics and relational anarchism, or relational political and sexual anarchism.

With these complexities in mind, it is no surprise to find the same scene attracting some of Millett's most careful textual attention in *Sexual Politics*. When Millett considers this complexity, she focuses on the failed relations between Miller's narrator and the anonymous woman in the cabinet:

He finds he can't "get it into her." With his never-failing ingenuity, he next tries sitting on the toilet seat. This won't do either, so, in a burst of hostility posing as passion, he reports: "I come all over her beautiful gown and she's sore as hell about it." In the *Tropic of Capricorn* he repeats the stunt; in *Sexus* too. It is a performance that nicely combines defecation with orgasm... What he really wants to do is shit on her.[9]

In contrast to Millett, my attention is turned to Miller's comment that "I try to get it into her but *it won't work*" (CAN, 18; emphasis mine), which is an anticipation of Van Norden's mechanized scene where he "almost got it in that time" (CAN, 148), but the "machinery" likewise did not work, which is to say neither man could maintain an erection with the woman, or for its thematic import, the patriarchal and capitalist exchange relations are enervating such that they leave all involved sterile and failing to connect. The explicit theme is failure.[10] *Tropic of Cancer* was Miller's most carefully composed and revised text, so the fact of repetition bears emphasis and suggests this is not a casually created link between scenes. In both cases, physical penetration seems less the issue than the anonymity of the sex and the faulty machinery, with its textual bond to excrement. The latter two make the former metaphorical.

Furthermore, Millett is right to point out how this scene "nicely combines defecation with orgasm,"[11] but she does not follow this up with Miller's more pointed and extensive description of shit as a thematic and certainly metaphorical image in the same book. Given the direct repetition, this would not seem to be a chance combination of defecation and orgasm, although shit, semen, death, and failures to connect are already replete in the scene and the book as a whole. Miller's view of the excremental world is solidified when he takes "one of Gandhi's men" (CAN, 94) to a brothel. In the ensuing scene, "The five of them are standing there looking at the *bidet*. There are two enormous turds floating in the water" (CAN, 96) and the Madame is berating "Gandhi's man" (CAN, 96) ferociously. As the problem is resolved, Miller muses:

> ...I think what a miracle it would be if this miracle which man attends eternally should turn out to be nothing more than two enormous turds which the faithful disciple dropped in the *bidet*. What if at the last moment, when the banquet table is set and the cymbals clash, there should appear suddenly, and wholly without warning, a silver platter on which even the blind could see that there is nothing more, and nothing less, than two enormous lumps of shit. That, I believe would be more miraculous than anything which man has looked forward to. (CAN, 101)

Despite the number of pages between the scenes, it is clear that "the faithful disciple" (CAN, 101) at least nominally refers to "Gandhi's man" (CAN, 94) and that the "two enormous" (CAN, 96, 101) lumps of shit are the same in both descriptions. However, the paragraph immediately preceding the "miracle of shit" does not refer to Gandhi, but rather to "Gautama and Jesus" (CAN, 100). This links the creation of the disciple and master to disillusionment with two dominant worldviews (lumps of shit) and belief systems that double as means to identification through submission to conversion and proselytizing. The close blurring of the excremental and the orgasmic is surely no accident, but it is also thick with connections to the failures Miller identifies and the abjection of social failures that his novel recounts. The language of "disciples" marks Miller's worries over the authoritarian turn in convincing, converting, and leading rather than an anarchist provocation.

As with Millet's linking of sex and defecation, the silver platter and bidet scenes take place in a brothel and anticipate copulation, but the orgasm–defecation elision is not as narrow as she presents it. It is preceded and followed by a number of blendings of the sublime and the defecatory. As with the woman whose gown Miller soils with sperm (CAN, 18), the defecation of the young Indian (Gandhi's man) is closely tied to the relation between people and sex. Furthermore, if the reader accepts the expansion of defecation in a brothel's bidet to a critique of social relations, then the excretions in the nightclub's cabinet equally point to the coercive function of capitalist and patriarchal transactions. I read against Millett's argument that "What [Miller] really wants to do is shit on her,"[12] and instead suggest that the metaphoric shit of their meeting indicates the same rotting flaw that Miller finds in structures such as religion. If the "miracle of shit" applies to the "miracle which man attends eternally" (CAN, 101) as a false pedestal of projected desire and the false patriarchal promise of protection by service to the master, then the revelation of the defecatory nature of exploitative power relations may be a miracle indeed. They are equally undermined, and this is a meeting point where Millett may actually have found common ground with Miller. Millett's point is who gets shat on while Miller's is that patriarchal power, religious power, capitalist exploitation, and gender stereotypes contribute to the same problem. The marked contrast between Millett and Miller here is their aim to shape the reader's response. Miller provokes but rejects the master–disciple relationship; Millett, no matter how much we may agree with her social aims, seeks to convert the reader.

A greater surprise, however, is to find Ursula K. Le Guin's radical science fiction novel *The Dispossessed: An Ambiguous Utopia* alluding to the same scene only five years after Millett's *Sexual Politics*. Le Guin's novel is, as with Miller's works, anarchist in both its ambitions and its understanding of form and style. Le Guin's protagonist, Shevek (an anarchist from a anarchist moon colony orbiting a patriarchal capitalist and Marxist planet Uras), is drunk at a party in very much the same circumstances as Miller in the scene in *Tropic of Cancer*: "He now felt his face was very pale, and the dizziness did not pass; he hoped she was taking him to the washroom, or to a window where he could breathe fresh air. But the room they came into was large and dimly lit."[13] In the ensuing failed sexual consummation, the protagonist Shevek is "confused by her sudden high tone of fear and her struggle; but he could not stop, her resistance excited him further. He gripped her to him, and his semen spurted out against the white silk of her dress."[14] Le Guin's use of the allusion is very much in the spirit of Miller's original scene—the function is to draw attention to the sterility of the interaction, the invidious nature of capitalism's reshaping of human intimacies, and the "death" and "shit" it brings to human creative activities. The toilet, the drunken failure, and the enervating impact of capital and patriarchy on human relations are common to both Miller and Le Guin.

Much as Miller was answered by Millett, Le Guin was answered by Samuel R. Delany, who's "To Read *The Dispossessed*" takes issue with this specific scene as well. For both Miller and Le Guin, the proselytizing reading that will lead the reader cannot "get it in" or cannot recognize the anarchist praxis at work. Delany first complains "alcohol in large quantities is an orgasmic inhibitor in men."[15] Hence, the scene is unrealistic and does not adhere to reality, but also more importantly for him, "the scene as written—with rampant, primitive lust completely failing to make contact with sophisticated flirtation and coyness—is all 'literature'. That the scene also manages to contravene a general law of metabolism and male plumbing is just one emblem of its overall lack of psychological veracity."[16] He goes on to outline how he sees the failed copulation as unlikely and a genuine meeting of the minds in the fictional patriarchal society of A-io a more plausibly leading to "some sort of conversation in which they gave each other the very real benefit of their mutually alien views."[17] Delany's extensive "attack"[18] on Le Guin's work may open with a speculation on a very unlikely allusion to T.S. Eliot's *Four Quartets* (1943), yet this strongest of allusions in her novel to Miller's *Tropic of Cancer* slips past his reading eye in "To Read *The Dispossessed*." As a consequence, Delany reduced the complex literary work on the scene to a demand for realism in science fiction. In context, Le Guin's allusion to Miller's cabinet scene links her own depiction of the failure of sexual relations in a fictional patriarchal society to Miller's earlier depiction of the same in a realist mode forty years earlier.

Apart from demonstrating the literary provocations of Miller's cabinet scene from Millett to Le Guin, this example and the conflicts around it return attention to Miller's anarchist writing practice. This first becomes clear by recognizing Delany's critique of Le Guin as a reflection of the Marxist orientation of science fiction studies, particularly the conflict over deterministic conceptualizations of culture and consciousness, which is most visible in Delany's close alignment with Fredric Jameson and Darko Suvin in the founding of the journal *Science Fiction Studies* and its rapid disengagement from Le Guin's anarchism. Jameson's animosity toward Le Guin has manifested in a continuous critique over nearly forty years. Delany quickly followed suit, and the quarrelousness of some of his critiques in "To Read *The Dispossessed*" in particular, and his Marxist reimagining of Le Guin's works in his own novel *Triton*, as well as his rethinking of several themes from Le Guin's Earthsea series in his own Nevèrÿon, show clearly the personal as well as critical entanglements of the dispute. For her part, Le Guin's response to the critique is very much the same as Miller's disagreement with Millett: silence for commentary and an absence of critique over the different directions taken by their respective literary progeny. The sum, however, is the tired return of the authority/determinism dispute between anarchism and Marxism, first rehearsed between Marx and Mikhail Bakunin but still alive and well between Miller and Millett, and Le Guin and Delany or Jameson.

Robert Duncan notes precisely the same conflict in his early assessment of Miller during his time on James Cooney's colony in Woodstock where he assisted in the production of the journal *Phoenix*, with which Miller engaged extensively. In his own *Experimental Review* from the same period, Duncan writes (writing under his adoptive family's name Symmes) not only of Miller's anarchism but also of the ideological conflict it would entail:

> From the meridian of Dada Miller has moved into the free world. He is a revolutionist who holds no betrayal, for he has no desire to replace the prison which he has destroyed with another prison which he likes better. Politically he has no politics. Having come at last into the real world he is an anarchist. Anyone reading over the foregoing passage will see clearly why the Marxist Surrealists are afraid of Miller.[19]

Miller addressed the same matter the year prior in "An Open Letter to Surrealists Everywhere" and earlier still in his correspondence with Herbert Read following on the

1936 London International Surrealist Exhibition.[20] In both, Miller directly recognizes his conflict with the Marxist components of French Surrealism and in particular the proselytizing function of its critical works and the implicit leadership function of a professionalized revolutionary party. The conflict between anarchism and Marxism originates in Bakunin's rejection of Marx's belief in the necessity of violent revolutionary change and the dictatorship of the proletariat in the First International. Miller's and Read's discussion follows after the communist betrayal of their anarchist colleagues during the Spanish Civil War in which they had sided against the fascists, and Miller's works as noted by Duncan carry forward this same distinction: the antiauthoritarian nature of anarchism cannot comfortably sit with the party politics and impoverished understanding of culture and consciousness in 1930s Marxism.

Hence, the anarchist praxis of Miller's work plays out in its provocations rather than its guidance. It provokes but does not foster. That is, insofar as Das Cabinet des Doktor Millett works as a new direction uniquely Millett's own despite being provoked by Miller's expression of his own creative interests, it is remarkably in line with how Miller saw his work ideally operating—as such, it is also very much a living project in Miller's paradigm. The only difficulty is that Millett's responsive, lively provocation seeks to lead the reader to a specific outcome, a specific revolutionary ambition, and much like a professional organization, directs the spontaneous revolution of the proletariat. In contrast, Le Guin's allusive renovation and expansion of Miller's cabinet scene is likewise provocative and in her own terms "ambiguous" in its call for responses from readers. As with Millett's response to Miller, the ambiguity and readerly freedom in Le Guin's text elicited the same provocation and difficulty from Delany, eager to lead the potentially free ranging and spontaneous reader to a professionally organized critique and specific political intervention for revolutionary political consciousness.

The anarchist ethos of Miller's writing

Miller's letter to Millett calls attention to the key word "freedom" as a marker of his stance. Rather than the colloquial ambiguities of the term, when set in the longer context of Miller's body of works, "freedom" associates with the anarchist and anti-Marxist Art and Freedom post-Surrealist group in Egypt, whose work he had supported during the war in his aid to publishing Albert Cossery in America. The term is also deployed contrary to the widespread notion of "bourgeois freedom" in discourses of the Left, where the anarchist privileging of the notion is equated with a system of control via the disruption of solidarity and the fragmentation of the working class into serialized individuals. Miller's stance is a refutation of the Marxist understanding of freedom in this sense. Finally, in Miller's specific context of "the freedom of the reader as well as the writer" (LKM, 157), the notion implies the antiauthoritarian *text* that provokes rather than leads and that remains open rather than collapsing meaning or ambiguity. These notions are evident in the ambiguities of the open ending of *Tropic of Cancer* that places complex interpretive responsibility on the reader, the kinetic nature of the provocative and libidinal text (without a definite objective) that works contrary to James Joyce's theory of the epiphany in *Portrait of the Artist as a Young Man*[21] by provoking without proselytizing, or arguably the reverse in Joyce, and finally Miller's unstable dealings with subjectivity that ambivalently hesitate between the autonomy and the incoherence of the subject.

A specific element of Miller's anarchist praxis and indirect allusive gestures in his discussions of other anarchist notions appears in the close of his essay about Thoreau, cited above. For Miller, "We should not strive to become like Thoreau ... but to become what we are in truth and in essence."[22] This is the active agenda in Miller's works and the parallel he emphasizes between himself and Thoreau. It is also the aforementioned praxis he envisions for his writing again and again across his lengthy career: not to foster but to provoke, not to become *like* but to enter becom*ing*, and thereby to concentrate attention on autonomous self-possession. However, this position also makes visible the in-between position of his writing, which operates in the shadow of rational humanism and at the dawn of poststructuralist destabilizations of grand narratives and the Enlightenment subject. That is to say, Miller's corpus sits uncomfortably between nineteenth-century articulations of the self that can call up complexities such as "freedom" through the rational hypothesis of the unethical nature of foreclosing choice for rational subjects in possession of reason and thereby capable of making self-determining choices. This is in contrast to the subsequent poststructuralist turn now identified as post-anarchism. The first notion fits handily with Robert Paul Wolff's articulation of anarchism:

> The defining mark of the state is authority, the right to rule. The primary obligation of man is autonomy, the refusal to be ruled. It would seem, then, that there can be no resolution of the conflict between the autonomy of the individual and the putative authority of the state. Insofar as a man fulfills his obligation to make himself the author of his decisions, he will resist the state's claim to have authority over him.[22]

This position relies ostensibly on the notion of the self in its Enlightenment sense (albeit self-possession and thereby autonomy are not necessarily equated with self-comprehension nor even stability since a protean subject may be self-possessed regardless of its protean nature). In post-anarchism, which seeks to set aside the Enlightenment subject while retaining the anarchist understandings of power and authority, Todd May[23] outlined the engagement between poststructuralism, particularly poststructuralist understandings of subjectivity, and anarchism's emphasis on the self-possession of the individual. Saul Newman[24] expanded the concept through a social constructivist paradigm, and Lewis Call[25] focused attention on the conflict between the Enlightenment subject that sits behind the conceptual paradigms for liberalism and Nietzsche's cause creating drive that disentangles consciousness from the self.

The difficulty for Miller is to reconcile his Enlightenment anarchist emphasis on autonomy that could lead to the statement "If the self were not imperishable, the 'I' I write about would have been destroyed long ago" (CAP, 5) in contrast to the inhuman and protean self that is continuously disrupting his texts through eruptions of the unconscious and narratives of self-transformation. The notion of continuous becoming recurs in Miller's *Hamlet* letters with Michael Fraenkel in a passage taken up later by Deleuze and Guattari:[26]

> ...why revert to myth?... This ideational rubbish out of which our world has erected its cultural edifice is now, by a critical irony, being given its poetic immolation, its mythos, through a kind of writing which, because it is *of* the disease and therefore *beyond*, clears the ground for fresh superstructures. (In my own mind the thought of "fresh superstructures" is abhorrent, but this is merely the awareness of a process and not the process itself.) Actually, in process, I believe with each line I write that I am scouring the womb. Behind this process lies the idea not of "edifice" and "superstructure," which is culture and hence false, but of continuous birth, renewal, life, life... In myth there is no life for us. Only the myth lives in myth. (HAM, 89–91)

The inhuman in Miller's sense, here, of the womb makes a clear and quick appeal to Deleuze and Guattari, as does his linkage of such concepts to the state, state thought, and the abstract machine in "superstructure." The problem for Miller is reconciling the autonomy of the self and the unbinding of the self as a protean construction of the cause creating drive that orients itself toward power. Thereby, we see Miller's career-spanning construction of the self as a quintessentially anarchist act deriving from Enlightenment rationality and the problematic liberal conceptualization of selfhood, while at the same time a poststructuralist anarchism also thrives in Miller's prioritization of the unconscious, the instinctual, the inhuman, and the transformative that gives the lie to stable notions of identity.

This argument does not offer closure, much as Miller's works remain open and ambiguous. Tellingly, the close of *Tropic of Cancer* moves not to introspection but to the social. In the gesture toward a mountaintop sage focused on self-discovery and guru-like introspection, Miller begins to close with "In the wonderful peace that fell over me it seemed as if I had climbed to the top of a high mountain" in a moment replete with the comprehension of "meaning" (CAN, 320). However, rather than self-discovery or introspection, the textual aporia that follows leaves a visible gap in the page prior to the penultimate fragment: "Human beings make a strange fauna and flora. From a distance they appear negligible; close up they are apt to appear ugly and malicious. More than anything they need to be surrounded with sufficient space—space even more than time" (CAN, 320). The various allegorical and mystical interpretations possible here may attract attention, but the tension between the anarchist fauna capable of choice and the Marxist flora determined in social consciousness by the material mode of production stands out: the mindful and the mindless. Also visible is Miller's self-implication in the appearance of his persona as being "ugly and malicious." Nonetheless, gaps on the page before and after this passage signal its limitedness. The temptation-filled mountaintop observation Miller offers in his Christ-like closing contrasts the impossibility of a position of judgment since distance grants negligibility and closeness revulsion, yet the book itself has delighted in glorifying the beauty of the repulsive closeness of humanity without pretense over its beastly brutality and operations of power. The closing ethic of space to leave the self to its own resources, whatever they may be, is only tempered in the end by a shift outward from the self to, not the social, but landscape and a river, the path it flows, and its way. There is no external authority in Miller to which one may appeal for protection or meaning without the capitalist substitutional logic of authority, just as the "liberty and justice" wished for with the "death rattle" quoted at the outset of this chapter will fail Millett's implicitly neoliberal ethos of equality imposed by appeal to ethical validity rather than self-determination in a world bent on perverse limitation. Like Le Guin's Odonians on the "odos" or road or way, the antiauthoritarian quasi-Taoist movement out from social determinism to a discovery of self in the ecological world in Miller signals the vitality of self-possession amid the ineluctable self floating between earth and heaven as a manner of process, as a path, with a fixed course absent of the authoritarian dictates of the superego or the chastisements of the unjust state he finds himself surprisingly in.

Notes

1   This international network has been explored in more detail in my *Personal Modernisms* (Edmonton, AB: University of Alberta Press, 2014).
2   Karl Orend, "Fucking Your Way to Paradise," *Nexus: The International Henry Miller Journal* 6 (2009): 44–77; Gifford, "Surrealism's Anglo-American Afterlife," 36–64; Gifford, *Personal Modernisms*.
3   For example, see David Weir's comment that "the failure of anarchism assured the success of modernism; that is, the politics of anarchism was transformed into the culture of modernism by a number of artists who gave aesthetic expression to political principles" in *Anarchy and Culture: The Aesthetic Politics of Modernism* (Amherst: University of Massachusetts Press, 1997), 158.
4   Wallace Fowlie, "Introduction," in *Letters of Henry Miller and Wallace Fowlie 1943–72* (New York: Grove Press, 1975), 16.
5   Alfred Perlès, *My Friend Henry Miller* (New York: Belmont Books, 1962), 139.
6   Alfred Perlès, *Round Trip* (London: Dennis Dobson, 1946), 115–119.
7   Lawrence Durrell, "Studies in Genius VIII—Henry Miller," *Horizon* 20 (July 1949): 45.
8   Durrell, "Studies in Genius VIII—Henry Miller."
9   Kate Millett, *Sexual Politics* (1969. London: Virago, 1981), 309.
10 See James Gifford, "Reading Miller's 'Numinous Cock': Heterosexist Presumption and Queerings of the Censored Text," *ESC: English Studies in Canada* 34, 2–3 (2009): 49–70.
11 Millett, *Sexual Politics*, 309.
12 Millett, *Sexual Politics*, 309.
13 Ursula K. Le Guin, *The Dispossessed: An Ambiguous Utopia* (New York: Harper Voyager, 1994), 270.
14 Le Guin, *The Dispossessed*, 271.
15 Samuel R. Delany, "To Read the Dispossessed," in *The Jewel-Hinged Jaw: Notes on the Language of Science Fiction* (Middletown: Wesleyan University Press, 2009), 116–117.

16 Delany, "To Read," 117.
17 Delany, "To Read," 117.
18 Delany, "To Read," 113.
19 Robert Symmes, "An Embryo for God," *Experimental Review* 2 (1940): 78–79.
20 Henry Miller, "Henry Miller's Letters to Herbert Read: 1935–1958," *Nexus: The International Henry Miller Journal* 5 (2008): 3–35.
21 James Joyce, *A Portrait of the Artist as a Young Man* (New York: W.W. Norton, 2006), 180–182, 186–188.
22 Robert Paul Wolff, *In Defense of Anarchism* (New York: Harper & Row, 1970), 18.
23 Todd May, *The Political Philosophy of Poststructuralist Anarchism* (University Park: Pennsylvania State University Press, 1994).
24 Saul Newman, *From Bakunin to Lacan: Anti-authoritarianism and the Dislocation of Power* (Lanham: Lexington Books, 2001).
25 Lewis Call, *Postmodern Anarchism* (Lanham: Lexington Books, 2002).
26 Deleuze and Guattari, *Capitalism and Schizophrenia*, 298–299.

14

Miller's Paris

Finn Jensen

Perhaps the most overwhelming experience in the developed world in the late nineteenth century was the chaos and the bombardment of the senses in the new metropolis. In these perplexing surroundings it became evident that all the rules and values of the traditional rural society were under serious threat: the social community, the rules of the family, the authorities, the meaningfulness of work in close contact with nature, religion, traditions, security; but also the strict control over the individual, the narrow-mindedness of the traditions and social rules, the formal social structures, poverty, and boredom. Instead, in the modern metropolis, like London, you would discover the shocking new feeling of anonymity and insecurity, but also of individual freedom and the possibilities of the social change. All this was part of a whole new life—of modernity—and the fundamental changes are reflected in art and literature. However, two of the following, and very different interpretations, emerged. The first view was influenced by the spectacular progress of modern science and technology, by capitalism and positivism, which saw the modern metropolis as a reflection of the modern, rational way of thinking; as a scene set for the triumphs of modern man: the liberation of the individual, freedom from religion and superstition, man's definitive domination over nature, and the ability to plan on a big scale. The Great Exhibition in Crystal Palace in London in 1851 was a grand performance of this worldview. Here, in the words of Prince Albert, man's rational achievements could be seen as reflections of a divine order. Civilization was close to achieving a complete fulfillment of a sacred mission.[1]

In stark contrast to this optimism, a great variety of intellectuals, artists, and politicians saw the new enormous city as a chaotic hell-like place, plagued by disease, crime, hopeless poverty, and fundamental loneliness. For Marx and Engels, this city, with its desperate population, was the cradle of the socialist revolution, and the bourgeoisie watched with anxiety that, as they established all the new factories and horrible slums, they, at the same time, created a dangerous revolutionary situation. The socialist Paris Commune in 1872 proved them right. While Edgar Allan Poe reflected in his "The Man of the Crowd" (1840) upon the criminal perspectives of the modern anonymity, Baudelaire saw in the new surroundings, where the old values were in a deep crisis, the possibilities for the new excitement and nerve-impulses in the modern city, where the *flâneur* could move freely and anonymously around and enjoy and gather all the impressions. For Nietzsche, and later for Spengler, the modern city was simply the most evident proof of a culture on the brink of total collapse.

In Miller's writing, the modern cities of New York and Paris play important roles. He usually sees them as places of degradation and destruction, but there are variations, and especially Paris can play very different roles for Miller. Fundamentally, it seems as if Miller in general, like the romanticists and Emerson, dislikes the city and sees it as a destroyer of the fundamental link between man and the vital forces of nature. It is characteristic that the places where he felt most inspired and uplifted were far away from cities, for example, Epidaurus in Greece and Big Sur in California. However, Paris is an exception: he did most of his best writing here; it was here he found his voice and identity, because the city provided him with the right kind of intellectual companionship and an easygoing lifestyle. And it was in Paris, he experienced the most important love affair in his life. But it is obvious that when he directly expresses joy of being in the city itself, it is mostly in the village-like neighborhood of the Latin Quarter around St. Germaine, Villa Seurat in Montparnasse, and, of course, Clichy, the most amazing little paradise in his universe.

In the larger perspective, we can establish at least four important stations in Miller's universe: first the all-important axis between New York and Paris. New York is almost constantly seen in a negative light as the embodiment of the evil forces of American capitalism and industrialism. It was his city of constant sufferings in all aspects of his life: family, work, love, writing, and money. The only brief exception is the early childhood in Brooklyn before the devastating invasion of the immigrants from Europe that ruined the last elements of a traditional society in his life (see his "The Fourteenth Ward"). New York is the place in his universe where he is most convinced of the immediate collapse of the Western civilization. In Paris he can see the same signs of degeneration and disease, but it is above all a place of inspiration and creativity and community with people who understand him. The third station is Greece, as described in *The Colossus of Maroussi*, where he discovered the places of revelation and myth, which would change his life forever. The fourth is Big Sur, where he could finally settle down after the traumatic and forced return to the United States after Greece. It is typical that he had to travel all the way across the continent to a completely remote and isolated spot before he could find his voice again.

The four stations, two American and two European, two modern cities and two remote places, one mythical and one in pure nature, are the four fixed points in Miller's universe, and it is obvious that Paris is of enormous importance as the place where he could finally develop himself as a writer and a man. But as we shall see, the different aspects of Paris play very different roles in his writing. On the basic level we find the elementary present-day Paris as he came to experience it in March 1930, when he arrived (he described it excitingly in his letters to his friend Emil Schnellock who stayed in New York). But in an immediate contact with this physical and "real" Paris was the historic, classical Paris, with all its different layers of culture, literature, and dramatic events. And in contrast to New York, these two layers were closely connected here. This gave the city a whole new perspective as he discovered it among other places in his various guidebooks.² In Paris, he discovered that the French name streets after writers, they erect statues for them, and he can meet writers and others artists on the famous terraces on Montparnasse. In Paris, he can be inspired by the present and just by looking around, he can go thousands of years back in history:

> How vastly different from New York! What eloquent surprises at every turn of the street. To get lost here is an adventure extraordinary. The streets sing, the stones talk. The houses drip history, glory, romance. (LE, 18)

But there is a third layer, which plays the main role in *Tropic of Cancer*, which I would like to call the *symbolic* or *mythological* Paris. It is a city where the vital forces are still alive and moving as symbolized by the river Seine, which runs constantly through the book, but it is also a city where the death forces are visible everywhere as a threat to everyone. As always in Miller's universe, the starting point, and the forces behind the destruction, is the American modern way of life and capitalism, and after his arrival in Paris, this is more and more confirmed, as he expresses it in an early letter to Schnellock:

> I feel deeply this day how pernicious is the influence of our country. I see its paralyzing, stultifying effects. We are dead and Europe is moribund. Somewhere a new people must arise, with vitality, with original ideas. (30)

In *Tropic of Cancer*, he often expresses that his own city of sufferings, New York, is at the center of the death forces. In Paris, even the poorest beggars can feel proud, whereas in New York, the richest feel their lack of importance:

> New York is cold, glittering, malign. The buildings dominate. There is a sort of atomic frenzy to the activity going on; the more furious the pace, the more diminished the spirit... A whole city erected over a hollow pit of nothingness. Meaningless. Absolutely meaningless. (CAN, 70)

Because Paris is not yet totally destroyed, because its population is still alive, and the vital forces, as well as the historic perspectives, are still visible, this city becomes an important inspiration for Miller: the place on earth, where he could find his voice and develop his style. In Paris, the drama and struggle between life and death is constantly going on before his eyes, and this gives him the unique possibility to express himself through projections—one of the most important features of his new and personal style. He becomes himself the center of his writing, and just by walking through the city, he explores himself, his sentiments, and interpretations. As in the letters to Schnellock, he discovers that by putting himself in the center as both narrator and "fictive" person, everything falls into place, and that he has achieved a new and very effective artistic freedom. In an important passage in *Tropic of Cancer*, he dwells on the similarities between himself and one of his important role models, August Strindberg, who had used Paris in much the same way. He has just visited the Pension Orfila, where

Strindberg suffered his "Inferno" crisis, and he understands the meaning of his (and his own!) pilgrimage to this city:

> ... the heroic descent to the very bowels of the earth, the dark and fearsome sojourn in the belly of the whale, the bloody struggle to liberate himself, to emerge clean of the past, a bright, gory sun god cast up on an alien shore. It was no mystery to me any longer why he and others (Dante, Rabelais, Van Gogh, etc., etc.) had made their pilgrimage to Paris. I understood then why it is that Paris attracts the tortured, the hallucinated, the great maniacs of love... One walks the streets knowing that he is mad, possessed, because it is only too obvious that these cold indifferent faces are the visages of one's keepers. Here all boundaries fade away and the world reveals itself for the mad slaughterhouse that it is. (CAN, 185)

When Miller visited Paris for the first time in 1928 with his wife June, he had none of these feelings and the city simply did not open up to him then. He only saw it from the outside, and although he made a few contacts via June, like the sculptor Ossip Zadkine, he was mostly a disappointed tourist: "The life of the boulevardier in the cafés and ateliers is as stupid here as anywhere else," he wrote to his friend Emil Conason in New York.[3] But in fact, what he witnessed here, were the last movements of the great feast of the 1920s in Paris, and when he returned alone in 1930, the party was mostly over (although he could make the few contacts he needed).

In the beginning of the twentieth century, Paris was undeniably the intellectual capital of the Western world. Many factors contributed to this role: the French open-mindedness toward strangers and their great respect for the arts, the lack of censorship, the free morality, the joy of pleasures of all kind: food, wine, feasts, talks, sex, the favorable exchange rates (which made even poor Americans rich), and perhaps most importantly, the Parisian terraces! These famous meeting places like Cafè du Dôme, Le Select, and La Rotonde, all in the center of Montparnasse, were the unintended results of Baron Hausmann's drastic modernization of Paris in the nineteenth century, when he tore down old and derelict quarters and built the new fashionable boulevards with the characteristic new houses with cast-iron balconies. The wide breadth of these boulevards had the consequence that you could expand the restaurants outside on the pavements, resulting in terraces with their informal atmosphere, a perfect scene for meetings and intellectual exchanges. If one wanted contact of whatever sort, one could just be at the terrace, and someone would turn up! Many of the guests were Americans, fleeing from the prohibition and puritanical atmosphere back home and enjoying the inspirational company of each other.

In Paris one could live on many levels at the same time: one could enjoy the intimate feeling of the village-like Parisian neighborhood in the small shops, hotels, and cafés, or, one could join the cosmopolitans at the terraces. And, of course, one could also throw oneself into the fantastic nightlife of the city.

Perhaps no one else was better equipped to show Miller the "real" Paris, the essence of Paris, than the brilliant photographer Brassaï, whom Miller met at the terraces; the same way he had met his most important helper, and friend, Alfred Perlès. Brassaï was able to open the city up for Miller. In the essay, "The Eye of Paris" Miller salutes Brassaï for being able to display the city, the streets, and the people for what they really were, and not in any mythical light. Especially the famous night pictures were revelation to Miller, which he discovered, when visiting the photographer in his primitive studio in the Hôtel des Terresses on Montparnasse.

He was astonished to find what seemed to be illustrations for his books:

> I beheld to my astonishment a thousand replicas of all the scenes, all the streets, all the walls, all the fragments of that Paris wherein I died and was born again. (WOH, 179)

Brassaï was also able to detect Miller's role, which he eventually developed for himself: the Parisian bohemian. It was also he, who drew the famous picture of that role to go with the article that Miller wrote himself in *Chicago Tribune* in 1930:

An early example of Miller's use of the Parisian streets, which shows both an inspiration from Brassaï and the technique he developed of projecting his own feelings into the picture, is the street scene he wrote (instead of Alfred Perlès) for *Chicago Tribune* called "Rue Lourmel in Fog." Here, the insignificant, and rather unknown, street of Paris grows from the realistic presence into a nightmarish image of total decay:

> Cerebrally and emotionally, dislocated, like a man coming out of an anesthetic, I perceived then that the street was swimming in fog. The street lamps shed a narcotic glow over the pavement and from the houses there was exuded a damp, fetid odour, as of wet plaster and rotting vegetables... In the livid gleam of the street, in this air which was heavy and almost too oppressive for the lungs, I felt the city palpitating, beating with an impalpable beat, as though it were a heart just removed from a warm body.[4]

Miller had arrived.

Miller's life in Paris from 1930 to 1939 can be divided into at least four periods, which transformed him from a failure as an artist and man to an accomplished and self-conscious writer in touch with his time and himself. The first period is after the arrival in March 1930, when he still had money left from June, which allowed him to stay in small hotels and stroll around the city. The letters to Schnellock express his joy, when he systematically studied the city on endless walks, guided by maps and guidebooks. But already in November he fell out of luck and was on the brink of returning home. The second period, which is most of the year of 1931, he was literally saved by his new friends, especially Richard Osborn and Alfred Perlès, who put him up in their lodgings and provided him with small sums. This gave Miller certain peace of mind and an opportunity to write, since he was still working on the manuscripts he had brought with him from the United States. This let him on to the new contacts, which made him able to move on to the next phase—the third phase, where he finally met the people who were able to inspire him on the more fundamental level, and, at the same time, provide him with a new self-consciousness. These people were Walter Lowenfels and Michael Fraenkel, and later in 1931, Anaïs Nin. His moving together with Alfred Perlès, in their apartment on Avenue Anatole France in Clichy in March 1932, marks the fourth, and final, phase. This marks the beginning of a period of frenetic and inspired writing. Most importantly, he discards his old manuscripts and starts writing what would become *Tropic of Cancer*. Miller had now found his voice and completed the transformation. In 1934, he moved to Villa Seurat on Montparnasse and his first book was published. He was now officially the writer Henry Miller.

What really had happened was this: he had developed into an accomplished modernistic writer and had found a new identity—both as an artist and a man. He established a new style, completely his own, and adopted a worldview, where his personal sufferings, so evident in the New York, now could be seen as a part of a total crisis of the Western civilization. Miller dared now to give up the traditional plot of the psychological and sociological novels; instead, the text dissolved into a group of fragments without hierarchical order, where only the subjective *I*, expressing itself, was the constant factor binding the text together. Now he was able to say:

> Everything that was literature has fallen from me. There are no more books to be written, thank God. This then? This is not a book. This is libel, slander, defamation of character. This is not a book, in the ordinary sense of the word. No, this is a prolonged insult, a gob of spit in the face of Art, a kick in the pants to God, Man, Destiny, Time, Love, Beauty... what you will. (CAN, 1-2)

In a declining world, where all the values were dissolving before his eyes, he could no longer be confined within the laws of bourgeois morality. Instead, like the Dadaists and Surrealists before him, he felt free to write exactly as he wanted. In *Tropic of Cancer*, *The Cosmological Eye*, *Black Spring*, and finally, in *Tropic of Capricorn*, he established himself completely in his new role as a freely expressing and experimenting modernist; it took him only two years to make this transition. It is difficult to imagine that this could have been possible in any other place than Paris at that moment in history. This was Miller's lucky moment. In my view, he was only a few steps away from being a complete failure. If he had followed an impulse to return to the United States in November 1930 (as he expressed it to Schnellock), his personal disaster would have been total.

What was it about Paris that made all this possible? It was mainly the people he was lucky to meet in Paris precisely at that moment but also the artistic and literary environment that still existed here. The Surrealists were still very active, as was the group around the magazine called *transition*; but also "classical" modernists like James Joyce and lots of other minor groups (like Lowenfels and Fraenkel). All of them were more or less receiving and transmitting impulses from Nietzsche, D.H. Lawrence, Spengler, and to some extent Freud. All of them were seriously critical of the development of the Western culture with its focus on industrial power and materialism. The enormous disaster of the First World War was still very much in the background and a fair amount of cripples could be seen in the streets of Paris. It is important to remember just how widespread and profound the eschatological feelings were, and how this affected art and literature, as well as the new political movements, not the least communism and fascism.

In the stimulating company, and in the endless discussions with Lowenfels and Fraenkel, Miller developed a new confidence and could now put the critical view on society, which he had brought with him from New York, into a larger framework. He had finally met the intellectual stimulus he had been yearning for so long. But they couldn't teach him to write, and the letters to Schnellock and others show that they didn't have to. But they could, as Fraenkel later claimed, show him that he already had a style and a voice—he didn't have to search for a special literary one. Once he could combine the personal, natural voice with his view of the chaos of the world, he had transformed himself into an authentic modernist writer. In Fraenkel's words:

> He would not seek to interpret and define this chaos; he would seek only to give it utterance. In this utterance lay his salvation; in this utterance was life. He would leave it to others to reveal the meaning of this chaos—the death. He would stick to his task. His was not to understand and reflect, but to witness and report. His life was chaos and the world was chaos, and he would reflect the chaos of his life and the chaos of the world.[5]

It would take a special study to establish which part of his literary luggage from New York Miller was able to transform in Paris. Instead, I will restrict myself to a brief study of how he could use Paris in this new and inspired period of his life. First of all, he was able to use the concrete, real city as a symbolic world by lifting his trivial movements up to an almost mythological level and also by projecting his feelings and emotions into the cityscape. And as everything else in *Tropic of Cancer*, this is established by and around the all-dominating *I*, the narrator calling himself "Henry Miller."

In the real life, as he often described to Schnellock in his letters, much of his early period in Paris was spent on futile walks across the town to the American Express office in rue Scribe opposite the Opera. In the novel, these walks take on a new shape. By repeating them, he turns them into a "leitmotif"; they are lifted up from practical information into symbols of his sufferings and the hopelessness of his situation. In these situations, the city, with its endless streets and the distances he has to cover, becomes a place of suffering. The technique of leitmotifs was very much used by Joyce in *Ulysses* as a means to establish some kind of coherence in a fragmented world. Another example in *Tropic of Cancer* with a very different meaning is the recurrent images of the river Seine flowing through the city:

> The river is still swollen, muddy, streaked with lights. I don't know what it is rushes up in me at the sight of this dark, swift-moving current, but a great exultation lifts me up, affirms the deep wish that is in me never to leave this land. (CAN, 70)

And the quote continues, characteristically, with the contrasting image of his walks to the American Express. This is not just the river; this is the essential life force running through the dissolving city with its unhappy citizens—the vital force that they are unable to get in contact with. Here, Miller speaks as an eschatological vitalist; a modernist who believes that the real values of life are still intact underneath the destruction and, normally, out of reach. He construed his surroundings the way Nietzsche had done in his *Also Sprach Zarathustra*, and as Eugene Jolas had seen in his articles in *transition*. So, the movement of the river and of the ever-walking narrator are the two extremes within the same picture of the "real" city.

Miller's sufferings are the world's sufferings, and he can learn about it just by observing the city. He is the opposite of Baudelaire's *flâneur*; he is not walking around just to give himself up to all the impulses of the modern city as he moves about in anonymity. In contrast, he is moving about looking at himself, reading himself into the cityscape, just as Strindberg had done in his Swedenborgian "madness," when he believed that he was the object of a cosmic conspiracy. And Miller is very much aware of the similarities:

> Just as Strindberg in his madness had recognized omens and portents in the very flagging of the Pension Orfila, so, as I wandered aimlessly through this muddy lane bespattered with blood, fragments of the past detached themselves and floated listlessly before my eyes, taunting me with the direst forebodings. I saw my own blood being spilled... My world of human beings had perished; I was utterly alone in the world and for friends I had the streets, and the streets spoke to me in that sad, bitter language compounded of human misery, yearning, regret, failure, wasted effort. (CAN, 187)

In these images, culminating in the repeated views of all the signs of cancer and syphilis (189), the "real" Paris is transformed into an image of a world on the brink of the total disaster—the eschatological perspective.

Later, after having returned to the United States due to the outbreak of the Second World War, Miller's images of Paris seem to undergo a transformation. He no longer needs the city to describe the cultural nightmare; the war does more than enough to prove that point. Instead, he now dwells on his life in the idyllic, village-like quarters like Clichy and Villa Seurat, where he had felt settled down and where his writing had taken an inspiration. But the fact remains that this Paris was no less a construction than that of the horrible signs of decay. The idyllic village, with its cozy bars and the honest, and almost loving, prostitutes of *Quiet Days in Clichy*, is just another kind of projection; this time of his dreams of an authentic world untouched by the disasters of the war. As Eric Lehman has noted, many of the passages correspond to the images the classical idyll, where life is simple in an atmosphere of peace and fulfillment.[6] In the classical pastoral life, young shepherds lived apart from the great cities and in a state of union with nature. Their main occupation seemed to be making love and poetry and they could perform this lifestyle without the restrictions of bourgeois morality. These pastoral idylls were able to uphold their charm and popularity from the classical Roman writers up to the seventeenth century, through the rococo, and the Victorian period up to the present days, not least in delicate porcelain figures.

In Miller's world, it all comes down to food, sex, and inspiration. In *Remember to Remember*, he formulates it like this when he talks of his life in Clichy with Perlès:

> The three principal questions we put to each other every time we were: (1) Is there food? (2) Was it a good lay? (3) Are you writing? Everything centered around these exigencies... It's such a simple efficacious way of living, I wonder it isn't tried out on a universal scale. (RTR, 192)

Money is important only as a means to acquire these essentials. This constructed idyll is the pure vitalism of Miller, and Paris is perfect for this purpose. Here he can live *en marge*; outside of the "real" society, with all of its political and social conflicts—and the real Paris of the 1930s was full of dramatic demonstrations, strikes, and manifestations, completely unnoticed by Miller and his friends. It is typical of Miller that he deals only with the extremes: either with the demonic decay of the city or the harmonic fantasy. Like the romanticists of the nineteenth century, he writes of the bourgeois middle classes with their dull, normal lives, only as caricature or nightmare, a form of nonlife. As an eschatological vitalist, he constantly deals with death—life's duality, and his writing, always seems to go to the extremes. On another level, in real life, Miller lived in Paris as in a bubble: he lived among expatriates like himself with very little contact with ordinary Frenchmen (except waiters and prostitutes) or, for that matter, French intellectuals. He lived and worked in his own little tight group, which he detested, having been labeled as "The Villa Seurat"—cult, but which nevertheless was very well defined and quite isolated both in France and elsewhere.

An important part of his construction of the Parisian idyll is that it is living on borrowed time, it will soon be absorbed by the destructive powers of the American capitalist culture, the one he has just escaped from. In *Remember to Remember* he dwells once more on the contrasts between the America he left, and the France that took him in:

> I was so desperately hungry not only for the physical and the sensual, for human warmth and understanding, but also for inspiration and illumination. During the dark years in Paris all these needs were answered. (RTR, 157)

In order to make the most of the contrast between the American "death-culture," both body and soul are killed (158); he is not afraid of delivering all the clichés of the life of the intellectual in Paris:

> Walking the streets of Paris the book shops and art galleries never cease to remind one of the heritage of the past and the fever of the present. A random jaunt through one little quarter is sufficient often to create such a glut of emotions that one is paralyzed with conflicting impulses and desires. The atmosphere is saturated with creation. One has to make an effort to avoid being over-stimulated. After a day's work one can always find recreation. It costs almost nothing, the price of a coffee

merely. Just sit and watch the passing throng, this is a form of recreation almost unknown in America. (171)

Writing in this way of the days in Clichy with Perlès, and later in Villa Seurat with Lawrence Durrell, Hans Reichel, David Edgar, Michael Fraenkel, Perlès, and others, he is writing about a world, which must have seemed lost to him in the United States in the 1940s. Not only had they been lost in the war, but also lost to him personally. He may have dreamed of returning to the happy life, but it stayed a dream. And when he got the chance and the money (made off his books published in Paris during the war), he was bound by his new family and a strong sense of hesitation. His Paris did not exist any more because all his friends had scattered all over the world. He led a very different life in California now; his new idyllic life was far away from the great cities, and the nine years in Paris seemed like a closed chapter. A world frozen in time, it seemed. If one visited the unchanged Villa Seurat (as I did a few months ago), one could still imagine Miller and Anaïs opening the door in no.18 to step out in a city, they now could hardly recognize. But Paris had not forgotten him, as he experienced on his first visit after the war in 1953, where he received a great reception. In 1946, when he was translated, these were the French intellectuals, who defended him and prevented the censorship to step in. Even today, French philosophers who hold him in great regard, frequently quote him.

But there is an aspect of his Parisian life, which he never wrote about in his published works, although it was one of the deepest experiences of his whole life and a determinant factor from December 1931 until he left Paris in the fall of 1939: his love affair with Anaïs Nin. They had early on made a pact of not using their love as the material for their work (a promise she promptly broke). Miller, however, left it untouched although it must have been a dramatic inspiration in his life. She was a vital aid for his ability to stay on and work in Paris; she supported him financially (with money from her husband) and she almost lived with him in periods in both Clichy and Villa Seurat, but also at her home in Louveciennes, outside of Paris, which became a paradise for him too, and the inspiration behind the final scene in *Tropic of Cancer*, where he finally leaves the city, so the life forces and the flowing river can have the final word:

> So quietly flows the Seine that one hardly notices its presence. It is always there, quiet and unobtrusive, like a great artery running through the human body. In the wonderful peace that fell over me it seemed as if I had climbed to the top of a high mountain; for a little while I would be able to look around me, to take in the meaning of the landscape. (CAN, 320)

With Anaïs Nin, Miller's life in Paris became complete although he could never make her leave her husband (who fortunately traveled a lot!). She inspired him, she was an intellectual match, which he had never experienced before, she had contacts, she opened up the city even more to him, and she was the love of his life. To Miller's readers she remained the secret ingredient in the idyll. But she was not one to hold on to, and he lost her as he lost his Paris.

Miller's known addresses in Paris

1. St. Germain quarter. Rue Bonarparte (6.). Miller lived with June in 1928 and later in 1930 in Grand Hotel de la France, no. 24. After his arrival in 1930 he lived in Hotel Saint Germain, no. 36.
2. Boulevard Montparnasse (6. and 14.). The four great cafés on Montparnasse:
   Le Select, no. 99
   La Coupole, no. 102
   La Rotonde, no. 105
   Café du Dôme, no. 108
3. 2, rue Auguste Bartholdi (15.). Richard Osborn's flat, where Miller stayed from November 1930 to March 1931.
4. 16, Avenue Denfert Rochereau (14.). Walter Lowenfels's flat, where Miller met with his circle.
5. 18, Villa Seurat (14.). Miller stayed with Fraenkel on the ground floor in 1931 and on the first floor from 1934–1939.
6. 1 bis, rue de Maine (14.). Hotel Central, Miller lived here in a room shared with Alfred Perlès in several periods in 1931 and 1932.
7. 4. Avenue Anatole France, Clichy (18.). Miller and Perlès shared an apartment from 1932 to 1934.
8. 29–31 rue Vavin (6.), Chez les Vikings. Scandinavian style café, where Miller and Anaïs Nin often met.
9. 230–234, Avenue du Maine (14.), Zeyer. Café where Miller, Fraenkel and Perlès often met.
10. 14, Place Clichy (18.), Le Wepler. Miller's favorite café in Clichy.
11. 2 bis, rue Montbuisson, Louveciennes, outside of Paris. Anaïs Nin lived here with her husband Hugh Guiler from 1930 to 1936.

Notes

1 Prince Albert's speech at a banquet at the Mansion House, 21. March, 1849.
2 See Kreg Wallace, "Henry Miller's Paris Guidebooks," *Nexus: The International Henry Miller Journal* 7 (2010): 79–86.
3 Quoted from Martin, *Always*, 156.
4 Quoted from Perlès, *My Friend Henry Miller*, 26.
5 Fraenkel, *The Genesis of Tropic of Cancer*, 26.
6 Eric Lehman, "Quiet Days in Clichy: Henry Miller's Urban Idyll," *Nexus: The International Henry Miller Journal* 9 (2012): 81–89.

15

Henry Miller's Titillating Words

Katy Masuga

Miller found his place on the fringe of modernist literature for a variety of reasons, not least of which is his so-called obscenity, or, in Miller's own words, writing that is "a gob of spit in the face of Art" (CAN, 2). Often misunderstood, this most memorable quality demands renewed attention. This chapter argues that Miller's lifetime of writing relies on a use of the erotic that is oriented toward greater ends—to explore the limits of language[1]—than usually recognized in his work. His work requires and admits no defense, but his readers might perhaps consider a new orientation for approaching it. In *The Work of Fire* [*La part du feu*], Blanchot writes:

> Miller's motivation is neither cruelty nor hatred but insurrection and defiance, a rebellion for ambiguous truth, because it asserts itself against constraints of very different natures, in the name of an instinct for freedom that does not know exactly what it is or what threatens it.[2]

Miller uses the erotic experience as one of the most crucial gestures for attempting to express the interminable chaos that exists beyond the borders of cultural complacency.

Part of Miller's audience often mistakes his brazen descriptions as pornographic exclamations of a revolutionary call against moralized conventional social standards. Indeed, such a commonplace reading is, according to Foucault, the result of a centuries-old, culturally self-imposed conviction in a hypothesis of the repression of sexuality that itself is already complicit in the active formulation of sexuality as a concept and field. Interested in what motivates the hypothesis, in *The History of Sexuality* [*Histoire de la sexualité*], Foucault writes:

> All these negative elements—defenses, censorships, denials—which the repressive hypothesis groups together in one great central mechanism destined to say no, are doubtless only component parts that have a local and tactical role to play in a transformation into discourse, a technology of power, and a will to knowledge that are far from being reducible to the former.[3]

Not denying sexual repression itself but rather the origins of its theoretical basis, Foucault explores the development of a "science of the sexual" [*science du sexuel*],[4] which in turn not only affects the regulation of discourse on sex but, more primarily, also establishes the very concept of sex in discourse.

Miller targets this *science du sexuel*: "To trace the history of man's attitude towards sex is like threading a labyrinth whose heart is situated in an unknown planet" (HMW, 184). Both Foucault and Miller observe that, despite its illusory and precarious nature, the *science du sexuel* defines boundaries on sexual expression. Through an understanding of this mode of sexual discourse then, Miller is consequently regarded, on the negative side, as obscene, and on the positive, liberating. Lamenting censorship, Miller feels literature in particular is treated even less fairly than the other arts because of the dual role of language. He writes:

> Parenthetically it is curious to observe that painters, however unapproachable their work may be, are seldom subjected to the same meddling interference as writers. Language, because it also serves as a means of communication, tends to bring about weird obfuscations.... With books even the butcher and the plumber seem to feel that they have a right to an opinion, especially if the book happens to be what is called a filthy or disgusting one. (HMW, 184)

Miller wants to link up the power of language with the power of the erotic but repeatedly finds it a trap. His oeuvre is an endless cycle of that ruse, wherein he recognizes that the gesture toward writing the erotic invariably comes out as obscenity, as something flat in the very moment it is set in relation to the discourse of the world.

On the affirmative side of a reading via the *science du sexuel*, Miller is considered a hero of "sexual liberation" and the "bad boy progeny" of code breakers like D.H. Lawrence,[5] propagating a kind of literature that readers envision as capturing "real" life on the streets, thus releasing them (and the entire world by proxy) into a freer, more expressive and "natural" state of being. In "The Prisoner of Sex" Norman Mailer writes: "Miller was a true American spirit, he knew that in a nation of transplants and weeds the best was always next to the worst, and right after shit comes Shinola."[6] Miller is consequently the godfather of figures like the Beats and writers of sexually explicit, or otherwise "liberated," prose. This kind of analysis unfortunately results in a superficial exploration of Miller's writerly effects.

As condemning on one hand, and gloriously emancipating on the other, as these approaches might seem, they both miss the literary and deeply ontological import of Miller's writing. There is something far more interesting to Miller's form of explicit prose that moves beyond any cultural critique of sexuality and enters directly into the fissures of language, more precisely, of literary language and its paradoxical boundaries that encourage absolute expression while necessarily inhibiting that absolutism through its own elusively mitigated form. In *Sexus*, Miller writes:

> Words, sentences, ideas, no matter how subtle or ingenious, the maddest flights of poetry, the most profound dreams, the most hallucinating visions, are but crude

hieroglyphs chiselled in pain and sorrow to commemorate an event which is intransmissable. (SEX, 19-20)

One immediately notes here the teetering irony in the last tenet of Wittgenstein's *Tractatus* (1921): "What can't be spoken about must be passed over in silence."[7] Upon close reading, it becomes evident that Miller's endeavors express something more imperative regarding these questions of language and writing than they do of human experience.

Miller's literary innovations do not proceed from moral shock but from the shock of undercutting the medium of writing. He identifies this very distinction as existing culturally between Americans and Europeans, suggesting that "When [the Europeans] are shocked, to take another example, it is because of the language itself, what has been done to it and with it by the author, not by the moral or immoral implications of this language" (HMW, 138). Though his prose may not always be extraordinary,[8] Miller's efforts to push and examine language through modes of the erotic are essential examples of the unexpected results when literature tries to address the absurdity of metaphysical inquiry of itself. Gilles Mayné confirms this paradox of the writerly pursuit: "if one wants to represent in writing the great intensity of the erotic experience without losing anything of such an intensity, one faces unfathomable—and indeed epistemological—problems."[9] As part of a critical juncture of such developments in philosophy at the start of the twentieth century, the projects of modernist writers like Miller have at their core a deliberate attempt to write *the impossible*.

Miller's oeuvre tackles in various ways the problem of language attempting to speak beyond language, fulfilling Wittgenstein's claim: "The limit [of thought] will therefore only be drawn in language, and what lies beyond the limit will simply be nonsense."[10] When language attempts to express its own logical structure, the fallout enters into metaphysics and other extra-linguistic realms, the erotic included. How this translates into discourse is through absence or struggle, as Ihab Hassan says of Beckett and Miller: "For the human tongue is speechless in fright and ecstasy."[11] These language webs in philosophical and aesthetic exploration constitute the precarious space of which writers like Miller are wary, precisely due to their attraction toward it.

Concerning Bataille and Miller, Mayné writes: "The writer, being aware of such an impossibility, faces an enhanced challenge: the necessity to reach, through words, what Bataille calls, in many instances, 'l'absence de poésie,' and in so doing, to give access to an experience equivalent in intensity to that of the erotic experience."[12] Miller's subject becomes the paradox of writing as containing both its own possibility and impossibility of the supposed transgression of that system. Of "a great work of art" in *Sexus* Miller writes: "Whatever it purports to be it is not: it is always something more for which the last word will never be said" (9). Like Blanchot's own work on the endless circularity of writing, Miller takes up writing to express *life*, but which instead becomes a creation unto itself; disconnected from its source, namely the reality that haunts it and drives it onward.

The writer rearranges the grey matter in his noodle. He makes a beginning and an end—the very opposite of creation!—and in between, where he shuffles around, or more properly is shuffled around, there is born the imitation of reality: a book. Some writers have altered the face of the world. Re-arrangement, nothing more. (NEX, 245)

Yet, somehow still forced to take up the occupation, for Miller this paradox notably leads his work into the erotic in order to push against these limits in literary language.

As the erotic is a revelatory experience permitting a momentary release of self, its appearance in language for Miller would be the most immediate mode for arriving at expression itself. In *Tropic of Cancer*, he writes:

Everything that was literature has fallen from me. There are no more books to be written, thank God. This then? This is not a book. This is libel, slander, defamation of character. This not a book, in the ordinary sense of the word. No, this is a prolonged insult, a gob of spit in the face of Art, a kick in the pants to God, Man, Destiny, Time, Love, Beauty ... what you will. I am going to sing for you. I will sing while you croak, I will dance over your dirty corpse ... (1–2)

Confirming what John Parkin calls "the therapeutic quality of laughter"[13] of sexual expression, Miller's desire to write about the erotic experience through play is a gesture to write away Literature.

Bringing the above cited abstract trance into everyday reality, Miller subsequently announces that he is singing to Tania followed by several pages of an explicit, imaginary sexual encounter with her. This daydream as a whole is also interrupted by an abstract, colorful reverie: "Twilight hour. Indian blue, water of glass, trees glistening and liquescent" (4). The basic narrative continues, followed by more of the daydream, which ends with the following: "I will bite into your clitoris and spit out two franc pieces" (6). Another unexpected and metaphor-rich reverie follows this claim that begins: "Indigo sky swept clear of fleecy clouds, gaunt trees infinitely extended, their black boughs gesticulating like a sleepwalker" (6). Arriving at surprising junctures, the erotic experience that Miller moves toward is a rebellious and seemingly subversive gesture not because it explores the so-called forbidden, but because it seeks to access the unattainable in language.

The case with Miller is an attempt to tackle both the expression of the erotic and expression in general. In *Plexus*, he writes: "I wanted to describe the world I knew and be in it at the same time" (52). Writing as a move toward this same desire of a union, expressed in the erotic, seeks to locate meaning in words; to validate and concretize a moment of existence or thought through its literary expression. Blanchot writes:

If language and, in particular, literary language did not constantly hurl itself eagerly at its death, it would not be possible, since it is this movement toward its impossibility that is its nature and its foundation; it is this movement that, by anticipating its nothingness, determines its potential to be this nothingness without actualizing it. In other words, language is real because it can project itself toward non-language, which it is and does not actualize.[14]

Writing becomes a tool for getting at the unspeakable, and yet every word precipitates its own annihilation. What can the writer do, Miller asks, but indulge this paradox with full abandon toward a gesture of complete expression?

Plagued by his need to write, Miller perpetually commits himself to ever-greater efforts, both aware and unaware of the cyclical puzzle of the literary gesture. In *Sexus*, he rhetorically asks: "If it is a world of truth, beauty and magic that [the writer] desires to create, why does he put millions of words between himself and the reality of that world" (18)? His own answer is that the writerly pursuit consists not in saying something final but in surrendering to the paradox of writing and heralding the fantasies of creation that are produced through it. "'Books are human actions in death,' said Balzac. Yet, having perceived the truth, he deliberately surrendered his angel to the demon which possessed him" (18). And so Miller turns to obscenity and sexual language to get closer to his goal.

Miller uses multiple modes to work out this desire in the text, which involve both successful and deliberate failed attempts at the erotic, as though he is searching for any possible outcome to fulfill the space left open by writing itself. Comparing Miller and the Surrealists, Paul Jahshan writes: "It is the *moment* when the *seams* are glanced which constitutes the erotic instant."[15] Miller sometimes appears aware of the impossibility of this fulfillment and sometimes not. In *Tropic of Capricorn*, he writes: "In the womb nails formed on every finger, every toe; you could stop right there, at the toenail, the tiniest toenail imaginable and you could break your head over it, trying to figure it out" (45). Miller thus appears on occasion to be searching in earnest, a position assumed ultimately at the base of his chosen writerly platform, but he searches most often in a discombobulating combination between jest and sincerity.

Of Miller's work on the whole, Blanchot writes: "Humor here is the threat of a complete *metamorphosis* of language that would change the meaning not into an absence of meaning but into a thing, a mirage in the face of which any correct reading is soon transformed into stupor."[16] This combination of humor and sincerity is Miller's tool for disrupting and transforming the text *toward* lack but *into* it—the result is an electrifying, mesmerizing alertness of the text in its simultaneous gesture of meaning and nonmeaning. In the face of writing into this ecstatic abyss, Miller is also perpetually aware of an imminent failure: "We write, knowing we are licked before we start. Every day we beg for fresh torment.... And when all these 'creations' have been finally read and digested men will still be buggering one another. No author, not even the greatest, has been able to get around that hard, cold fact" (NEX, 245–246). Therefore, each of Miller's modes provides a different approach to the erotic, divided here into three groups: 1) the playful, 2) the disgusting and mechanical via a *science du sexuel*, and 3) through abstraction. The rest of this chapter analyzes each group in turn.

Through each mode, the reader detects that Miller is either not wholly interested, or is not capable as Mayné argues, of rendering the erotic "successfully." Mayné suggests the following: "Miller (consciously or not) betrays himself as he betrays his initial movement of revolt by developing a kind of writing, which, in spite of what it says, does not allow the least loss of control."[17] Yet Mayné also admits the illogic of fulfilling the erotic in words: "Every word is one word too many, one more sign pointing to a firm object of knowledge which, as such, aims at making the erotic charge an object, when such a charge cannot be seized as an object."[18] Where I differ from Mayné's analysis of Miller's bad erotic writing is in the belief that Miller ever sought more than to be a "man of comedy"[19] or that this moniker is in itself a limitation. Miller "fails" at the erotic because he cannot reconcile its futility with any value. As such, he fluctuates between enjoying the attempt to express it and being crushed and diverted by the elusive and imposing gravity that the erotic seems to demand. Thus, the most obvious and widely cited form for Miller is the playful.

While addressing Bataille's critique of Miller on the subject of puerile language, Caroline Blinder implies that, like the child, Miller is deliberately "non-serious, humorously inefficient."[20] Explicitly, Bataille himself writes,

> He knows that sooner or later he has to humiliate himself (which the pejorative sense of the word game demonstrates). It does happen, however, that one man in a thousand persists, rebels and refuses to accept this. Such is the case for those who prefer art, which is nothing but a game, over real work.[21]

In Miller, everything usually comes out as an experience of the failure of writing the erotic or a clowning-around, and yet he maintains his exacting critique of literary language without falling entirely into either absurdity or obscenity.[22]

In *Nexus*, Miller writes: "... all these lovely dementia praecox cases, these star rovers, these diamond-backed logicians, these battle-scarred epileptics, thieves, pimps, whores, defrocked priests and students of the Talmud, the Cabala and the Sacred Books of the East? Novels! As if one could write about such matters, such specimens, in a novel" (221). Miller wants to use writing as a way for getting at the particular essences of figures, the supreme and sublime experiences of life, and is consumed by the limitations. Mayné suggests: "The only way one could try to speak of [what lovers do] is 'from within,' by making oneself the erotic experience, *being* one of these lovers. But as one lives such an experience fully, one cannot find the words for it."[23] Without the right words, Miller finds playful substitutions, often creating his greatest points on the difficulty of erotic expression in literary language as the man of comedy.

In *Tropic of Cancer*, Miller applies a playful erotic tone to an otherwise innocent encounter while opening a bottle of champagne. "I have a bottle between my legs and I'm shoving the corkscrew in. Mrs. Wren has her mouth parted expectantly. The wine is splashing between my legs, the sun is splashing through the bay window, and inside my veins there is a bubble and splash of a thousand crazy things that commence to gush out of me now pell-mell" (14). When Miller chooses to portray the splendor of an otherwise inexpressible moment of bliss, he chooses not the overtly sexual— that is reserved for a different transmission. He delivers instead an eroticized image through seemingly careless innuendo. Simple gestures in an otherwise ordinary scene are elevated by a hint of the erotic, which itself does not produce the same loss of self through sexual bliss, but instead joins in the playful while providing an edge of uneasiness, reflecting something more powerful beneath. This unexpected site of the erotic initiates the minor, exalting release brought on by laughter or perhaps by a moment of joyful, apprehensive expectancy in words that lead out of themselves.

Because Miller is not going for the grand gestures in these instances, he can best express his own need to write the world, while not entirely sacrificing it to impossibility. In such passages Miller points toward something simpler than the erotic, but it nevertheless touches on a ghostly presence of the erotic by drawing attention from the border of the controlled experience, conspicuously hinting at the other side. The erotic itself, as Mayné argues, must "maintain an essential distance" from the discourses of the "purely informational, rational or generally 'poetical' discourses."[24] In a curious turn, by staying within the bounds of the "'poetical' discourse," Miller provides a liminal experience of the erotic, as though it were on the tip of his tongue.

Miller's playful renderings that lean toward the erotic conjure a delicate desperation or anxiety in the reader, creating a sensitivity to its subtle evocation—a sense of psychological saturation—that such lightly titillating prose can produce. After a very extensive and graphic description in *Sexus* of an intense sexual encounter with his ex-wife, Miller's narrator comes down from the literary climax and provides a peculiar description of Melanie, his ex-wife's maid, who has absent-mindedly been wandering around the apartment during Miller's tryst (occasionally stumbling upon the pair without any expected embarrassment).

> She was always there, like a fleshy tumor. Something bestial and angelic about her. Always limping along, dragging her words, droning, drooling, her enormous melancholy eyes hanging like hot coals in their sockets. She was one of those beautiful hypochondriacs who, in becoming [sic] unsexed, take on the mysterious sensual qualities of the creatures which fill the apocalyptic menagerie of William Blake. (230)

The description is peculiar as it is both casually tangible and abstract. The vision of Melanie is awkward; she is repulsive but sexual as "unsexed" and dehumanized. Strangely, she becomes *textual* both through the Blakean caricature and the impossible description of her in relation to how she carries her language: "dragging her words" and expressing herself in gibberish. Miller has used her here to eroticize the text as a whole, in that the reader's mental image of Melanie touches on the vulgar, sexual and linguistic without ever being able to rest on any of those points, but instead remaining both alert and anticipatory as well as confused and subdued by the incomplete and elusive language of the description.

Miller goes on to explain how Melanie who was "old and had white hair" would walk around naked, oblivious to any distinction between her sexual and nonsexual anatomy and would also stare at him equally innocently while he bathed. "Naturally," he explains, "now and then I got an erection lying there in the tub with her looking on unabashed and talking utter gibberish" (231). The reader can sense the erotic slipping away, as Miller wipes out any semblance of it as anticipated by the reader, providing instead its impossibility through an absurd flatness of text.

The passage continues until it moves from the anomalous to the abstract. Describing Melanie's room, Miller's tone finally turns toward a sober effort at writing the impossible: "A room filled with shrill barks, with squawks punctuated by caressing murmurs, coaxings, cooings, jumbled phrases, squeals of affection" (231). The word collages are a regular technique of Miller's, creating a sense of speed and motion, hence a loss of control or orientation for the reader, once again hinting at the full erotic experience of loss of self.[25] The content itself subtly highlights the erotic, but again through the conjunction with language and loss of language through various forms of nonverbal speaking (i.e., sexual and animal sounds).

Another thoroughly obscene description with his ex-wife follows the above, also including the most unexpected interjections of humor. Along with long passages including such dialogue as "Put it in!" and "fuck your guts out!" Miller includes: "It hardly seemed to be a prick any more; it was like an instrument I had attached, an erection made flesh" (241). Yet the overt toilet humor is not what it seems ("full of unprintable words," Orwell writes.[26]); the reader immediately notes Miller's use of "erection" as a replacement for the biblical "Word," linking once again the erotic with language—both as the supposed means for getting at an expression of pure experience and repeatedly succumbing to limitation.

Descriptions of the overtly sexual can frequently take on a mechanical quality, evoking Foucault's *science du sexuel*, which is the second approach in the outline of Miller writing the erotic. This mode is paired with disgust because Miller often uses them together to imply that a sexological approach toward bodies results in an unsavory perception of the physical acts themselves, stripping them of their otherwise "natural" or erotic possibilities. Read metaphorically, this mode of writing about sexuality suggests Miller is critiquing language's attempt to move beyond logic through its own indisputably mechanical form.

In a well-known episode from *Tropic of Cancer*, Henry and Van Norden encounter a young, broken spirited prostitute, who is cold, hungry, and "goes about her preparations mechanically" (145). Themselves utterly down and out, tired and defeated, the men try to muster interest in the situation, likened to a state of war: "she's got her mind set on the fifteen francs and if I don't want to fight about it she's going to make me fight" (146–147). However, Henry can't fight, calling himself cowardly, but Van Norden goes ahead, even though "the fifteen francs are lost, whether we succeed or not" (147). The idea of pairing "success" with paying a prostitute for her services already creates an unexpected atmosphere for the reader, since suddenly the event is no longer viewed as a desired exchange but instead as an unhappy struggle to properly bring that exchange into being.

Miller overtly and immediately treats the scene as a metaphor for meaning in action and inaction, applied in the novel to life, to war, to "that spark of passion" (147), but it is even more directly applicable toward the task of writing. It is no accident that Miller uses the sexual act to despair over lack of meaning. The activities of sex and writing are both deeply tied to an attempt to produce a hidden essence by direct exposure, yet this exposure paradoxically removes that essence completely. The writing, like the mechanical sex, continues endlessly, never achieving its purpose.

Watching the pair, Miller observes, "it seems to me that I'm looking at a machine whose cogs have slipped" (147). He likens their act to "one of those crazy machines which throw the newspaper out, millions and billions and trillions of them with their meaningless headlines" (148). Comparing their sexual act directly with the printing of words invokes the futility of language directly, applied across life as stripping away "that spark of passion" (147), reducing all acts to an equal state of meaninglessness. "I wouldn't be able to differentiate between this phenomenon and the rain falling or a volcano erupting" (148). Watching the pathetic performance lacking in "human significance" (148), with each detail compiling to build a stranger and more detached environment, Miller moves away mentally leading the reader toward a long reverie on the violent machine-like and unhuman side of life.

Because he is working as a proofreader at the time, Miller explains how he is "absolutely immune" to such "catastrophes" perpetually erupting around him. If the logic is again missing, it is because Miller is once more equating language with meaning. As proofreader, Miller sees himself outside the nightmare of reason. "A good proof-reader is a little like God Almighty, he's in the world but not of it" (151). Miller's role is to observe and feign to correct. "The world can blow up—I'll be here just the same to put in a comma or a semicolon" (151). Beginning with a desperate attempt at fulfillment with the prostitute, ending with the laborious, dead and mechanical in language, newspapers and proofreading, Miller turns horror into fascination, which then turns into laughter. Mayné writes: "In other terms, only to the extent that the lovers repeatedly butt against the impossibility of transgressing a taboo can the possibility of the transgression of this taboo become, at a certain point, fascinating."[27] Eroticism is a sustaining of that laughter that Miller provides indirectly in bursts, reminding the reader that this sustaining, in Miller's estimation or at least ability, is not only difficult but also paradoxical under the restraints of language.

Miller continues to use humor, disgust, and mechanical imagery in so many of his "false" efforts at the erotic. It is as though he is searching out the crudest possibilities that violate his real attempt at writing literature but which, because of the irony, manage to keep him from being simply obscene. Always the "hero" of such excesses, Miller, or Henry the narrator, makes himself—as everyman—the butt of the joke. It is evident that these sexual extravagances do not depict anything real in the life of the author but, on the contrary, profoundly demonstrate the gap between writing and living. In "Obscenity and the Law of Reflection," Miller writes:

> When obscenity crops out in art, in literature more particularly, it usually functions as a technical device; the element of the deliberate which is there has nothing to do with sexual excitation, as in pornography. If there is an ulterior motive at work it is one which goes far beyond sex. Its purpose is to awaken, to usher in a sense of reality. (HMW, 186)

The straightforward and abrasive narration of his prose hints at Miller's resignation to the dullness with which words depict the sexual (or any) encounter. In *Nexus*, Miller painfully declares: "Words can't render the reality of it. What I'm telling you is nothing. I'm talking because I can't help it, but it's only a talking *about*. What happened I couldn't possibly tell you ..." (77). Such passages as the erection one above deliberately evade invoking the intriguing impossibility of the erotic in order instead to invoke the absurdity and peculiarity of setting the possible everydayness of sexuality in words.

Miller claims to find it impossible to write, in any satisfactory complete sense, about the very physicality of bodies and of sexual expression. In *Nexus* he laments:

> *Novels*! As if one could write about such matters, such specimens, in a novel. Where, in such a work, would one place the heart, the liver, the optic nerve, the pancreas or the gall bladder? They were not fictitious, they were alive, every one of them and, besides being riddled with disease, they ate and drank every day, they made water, they defecated, fornicated, robbed, murdered, gave false testimony, betrayed their fellow-men, put their children out to work, their sisters to whoring, their mothers to begging, their fathers to peddle shoe laces or collar buttons and to bring home cigarette butts, old newspapers and a few coppers from the blind man's tin cup. What place is there in a novel for such goings on? (221)

This lamentation is disingenuous, inasmuch as Miller is constantly writing about it. Yet, he does so in a way that uses language to criticize how bodies, sexual bodies in particular, are removed from "natural" expression. Paradoxically, it is both necessary to fill the pages with the most overt expressions of bodies and counterproductive to Miller's greatest desire to diminish them as he does, by expressing them dulled and fragmented.[28]

It is this *science du sexuel* itself that Miller prods—the transforming of bodily functions into a classified system of cause and effect, purpose and meaning, right and wrong. What is the connection between viewing intercourse as mechanical and what does it do to the expression or perception of humanity? The result is the depressing removal, again, of the "spark of passion" or the erotic element that otherwise occupies the physical events. Most sexual episodes have not much evident erotic content at all but are a mockery of the attempt at the erotic, of the very pitfall of writing as an effort toward something so elusive. Hence, these are the episodes that do appear flagrantly obscene. Miller is unapologetic and perhaps destructive in the fallout of his effort to pen the erotic experience, to pen anything to its extreme limit.

For Miller, the erotic comes out as lifeless once it is set in discourse, which leads him to aims beyond the margins. Throughout his work there are numerous examples of what appear as half-hearted attempts—a criticism often wielded by his critics— and yet that abandonment to bad eroticism is precisely Miller's point. In *Tropic of Cancer*, Miller befriends the crippled character Nanantatee (jokingly called "Mr. Nonentity") who is "fixed now on the 'fucking business'" and casually describes how he is "not a very good fucker" (92) anymore. This is followed by his detailed story of how Nanantee's sister died in childbirth after being given at the age of ten to an "aged gorilla," "who had already buried five wives" (93), and whose last words were: "I am tired of this fucking... I don't want to fuck any more, doctor" (93). The passage immediately moves into an exclamatory Hindu chat followed by a lengthy yet uncited reference to *Finnegans Wake*.[29] This series of shifts in the passage arouse again both the limits of language and the desperate attempts to move beyond them, yet communicating an equal gesture of not caring either way.[30]

If there is a history of prohibitions in language, then Miller is not looking for ways to violate the prohibition so much as unravel what those limitations are doing in literature. In *Tropic of Cancer* he announces: "There is only one thing which interests me vitally now, and that is the recording of all that which is omitted in books" (11). Miller comes closest to a fuller expression of the erotic in the mode of abstraction, because only here does he attempt to transcend literary limits without also trying simultaneously to assess those limits.[31] We subsequently find Miller's most earnest passages in this third form.

Tropic of Capricorn has several of the most prominent renderings of the erotic through abstraction. The following passage is interjected among the usual episodes in Miller's work of crude everyday life: Henry bumming a living and trying to keep tabs on Mona, the elusive taxi dancer. He waits for her at the dance hall, but she never arrives, with the text quickly jumping from basic explanation to abstract description.

> We taxi from one perfect female to another seeking the vulnerable defect, but they are flawless and impermeable in the impeccable lunar consistency. This is the icy white maidenhead of love's logic, the web of the ebbed tide, the fringe of absolute vacuity... the night too grows like an electrical plant, shooting white-hot buds into velvet black space. I am the black space of the night in which the buds break with anguish, a starfish swimming on the frozen dew of the moon... I no longer look into the eyes of the woman I hold in my arms but I swim through, head and arms and legs, and I see that behind the sockets of the eyes there is a region unexplored, the world of futurity, and here there is no logic whatever, just the still germination of events unbroken by night and day, by yesterday and tomorrow... I must shatter the walls and windows, the last shell of the lost body, if I am to rejoin the present. That is why I no longer look into the eyes or through the eyes, but by the legerdemain of will swim through the eyes, head and arms and legs to explore the curve of vision. (115–116)

Like Proust's "thin spiritual edge" [*mince liseré spirituel*] and "zone of evaporation" [*zone d'évaporation*] that separate the narrator of *A La Recherché du Temps perdu* from connecting to "an external object" [*un objet extérieur*] in the world,[32] Miller's encounter is an attempt to become one with the foreign body, in the mode here of the erotic experience, and yet this merging necessarily moves beyond what bodies are even physically capable of (e.g., to "swim through the eyes"). The ache of Proust and Miller's experience comes from the desire to unite but the impossibility of doing so without corrupting the original bodies.[33]

In breaking down at the level of language, this encounter necessarily morphs into an abstracted description that invokes the eroticism through its abstruse imagery. However, it is not merely a symbolic or metaphorical rendering, but one that operates instead by displacing expectations through words that summon unanticipated sensory perceptions, particularly among shapes and movements.[34] The resulting images ingested by the reader are left open, if also concretized yet in absolute abstraction (or at least pleasurably alienating vocabulary): "impeccable lunar consistency," "icy white maidenhead," "web of the ebbed tide," "electrical plant," "white-hot buds," "velvet black space," "starfish swimming," "frozen dew of the moon." These textual phrases are then followed by a series of nearly unimaginable (in their collective form) yet provocative actions or states of being: "swim through [the eyes of the woman]," "see ... behind the sockets of the eyes," "a region unexplored," "the world of futurity," "the still germination of events unbroken," "shatter the walls and windows," "rejoin the present," "explore the curve of vision." The reader is fulfilled—or even filled—by them, yet the encounter is also left necessarily incomplete through the manner by which expected language is replaced with the unexpected, if also familiar, and left *expectant*, moving toward this momentary release of the self in the erotic experience.

Earlier in *Tropic of Capricorn*, Henry describes his arrival at the dance hall. He looks over all the girls and says: "Into each and every one of them, as I shuffle about, I throw an imaginary fuck" (97). This declaration comes hot on the heels of a fast-paced tirade on the frenetic, decrepit, and absurd state of the world, where the immediate decision he has to make is either to sit down and write a book or to run away to a new life; both choices terrifying him. Throughout Miller's oeuvre the fear of writing "the book" is perpetual and yet perpetually enacted. Miller's pace in this particular episode is dizzying, as he makes evident the distinction between writing and living through the dance hall scene. " ... Just while I was studying a juicy ass, I had a relapse. I almost went into a trance again. I was thinking, Christ help me, that maybe I ought to beat it and go home and begin the book. A terrifying thought! ... Better not to sit down. Better to keep circulating" (98). This anxious mode of living involves keeping his mind on the dance hall and each "imaginary fuck," instead of on writing so that he is able to exist in the experience itself. He is hyperconscious of how writing not only removes him from life, destroying its own pleasures, but also how it overwhelms him in his attraction toward it as a means for capturing those very experiences.

Following this anxiety-laden spell, Miller quickly moves into a style that is similar to the abstract erotic description some pages later, analyzed previously. He begins describing one of the dancers:

> She has the loose, jaunty swing and perch of the double-barrelled sex, all her movements radiating from the groin, always in equilibrium, always ready to flow, to wind and twist, and clutch, the eyes going tic-toe, the toes twitching and twinkling, the flesh rippling like a lake furrowed by a breeze.... This is the incarnation of the hallucination of sex, the sea nymph squirming in the maniac's arms.... Between the dangling tentacles the music shimmers and flashes, now breaks in a cascade of sperm and rose water, forms again into an oily spout, a column standing erect without feet, collapses again like chalk, leaving the upper part of the leg phosphorescent, a zebra standing in a pool of golden marshmallow, one leg striped, the other molten. A golden marshmallow octopus with rubber hinges and molten hooves, its sex undone and twisted into a knot ... Laura the nympho is doing the rhumba, her sex exfoliated and twisted like a cow's tail. (100–101)

In the same way as the other abstract passage previously, the unexpected word pairs and phrases is what builds and sustains the erotic experience by suspending the reader in a liminal state of both understanding and unknowing. It is as Barthes says: " ... It is this flash which seduces, or rather: the staging of an appearance-as-disappearance."[35] The erotic is found in this combination of the anticipated as it is immediately paired with the unknown or, as Barthes says, at the "edge" [*bord*] of their meeting.

A long, three-page unbroken description on the above is suddenly interrupted: "And then crash! Like pulling a switch the music suddenly stops and with the stoppage the dancers come apart, arms and legs intact, like tea leaves dropping to the bottom of the cup. Now the air is blue with words, a slow sizzle as of fish on the griddle" (CAP, 101). With the end of the music and the sexualized dance floor scene, the atmosphere returns to logic and language where the "air is blue with words," which also permeate the air through an appetizing aural experience; edible words floating about. However, the passage carries on for another full page before returning to the narrator's everyday reality, and in that page Miller attempts repeatedly to connect language to the erotic experience, referring, for example, to Laura's lips in a double entendre: "Hunky-dory is the word on her lips. The heavy fluted lips of the sea-shell, Laura's lips, the lips of lost Uranian love" (CAP, 102). Laura's lips that speak words are described like the lips of her sexual organs but in another metaphor that itself slips into an erotic evocation. If "Hunky-dory" is the word on her lips, then what follows can only be commonplace—a contradiction in the text. With that, Miller jolts the reader back into reality but, even more clearly, a reality continually trying to express the unspeakable, or perhaps a reference to that which is spoken is only ever banalities and never the actual sensory experience of the lips themselves.

In the center of *Tropic of Capricorn* Miller places an "interlude," where he introduces the "Land of Fuck" (176, 189, 192). This alleged interlude, which is in fact a large section of the entire book itself, is, as described by James Decker, "a lyrically organized potpourri—part fantasy, part realism—of anecdotes and interior scenes."[36] Completely without plot or story, the "Land of Fuck" delivers up diatribes, endless sexual escapades, fantasies, plays on words, insults, abstract explanations, surreal imagery, and any number of other literary creations. Indeed, collectively, it is a stream of thoughts that combine all of Miller's approaches to the erotic: the playful, the disgusting and mechanical and the abstract. Getting at the heart of it, he writes:

> What is unmentionable is pure fuck and pure cunt; it must be mentioned only in deluxe editions, otherwise the world will fall apart. What holds the world together, as I have learned from bitter experience, is sexual intercourse. But *fuck*, the real thing, *cunt*, the real thing, seems to contain some unidentified element which is far more dangerous than nitroglycerine. (CAP, 187)

It seems, in this instance, that Miller is directing an attack not only toward censorship, taboo, and repression but also toward logic and language itself. The impossibility of a complete attainment of the erotic in writing could not be clearer. With the endless, both earnest and satirical meanderings in the "Land of the Fuck," Miller demonstrates for the reader how the text achieves and never achieves its own fulfillment. Lurking behind the moment of the erotic ("the real thing") is something powerful yet inexpressible.

Miller finds his best means of expression in the erotic or, at least, in the attempt itself to express the erotic. For it is only here at the site of ecstasy—the joy of a deliberate unknowing and the undoing of self and language—that writing becomes most titillating. Miller entices the reader through this risk of loss and is equally driven to express it in words, at the same time, knowing both of its futility and necessity. Aiming nevertheless at language and its logical, but also cultural, limitations, Miller uses the erotic experience—the otherwise unspeakable—to attempt access beyond them, through fissures in logic, style, and material. It is not a question of breaking taboo but of seeking to enter realms that absurdly encourage a truth beyond words, or a truth beyond what words permit. Miller wants to know how (or if) experience *at all* can be rendered in words, pressing at the heart of rapture in his effort. Sometimes confident, as in passages of abstraction, sometimes disillusioned, as in passages of mechanism, and sometimes reconciled, as in passages of play, Miller's body of work elicits both strong reactions and strong effects. Let's hope more of the strong, personal reactions will come to investigate his less explored, yet strong and innovative effects.

Notes

1. For an in-depth analysis of Miller's misunderstood and highly innovative language in general, see my work *The Secret Violence of Henry Miller* (Rochester: Camden House, 2011).
2. Maurice Blanchot, *The Work of Fire*, trans. by Charlotte Mandell (Stanford: Stanford University Press, 1995), 168.
3. Michel Foucault, *The History of Sexuality, Volume I: An Introduction*, trans. by Robert Hurley (New York: Pantheon Books, 1978), 16.
4. Michel Foucault, *Histoire de la sexualité I: La volonté de savoir* (Paris: Gallimard, 1976), 94. My translation.
5. From Kingsley Widmer's, "Lawrence's American Bad Boy Progeny: Henry Miller and Norman Mailer," in *D.H. Lawrence's Literary Inheritors*, eds Keith Cushman and Dennis Jackson (New York: St Martin's Press, 1991), 89–108.
6. Norman Mailer, "The Prisoner of Sex," *Harper's Magazine* (March 1971), 63.
7. Ludwig Wittgenstein, *Tractatus Logico-Philosophicus* (London: Kegan Paul, 1922), §7. My translation.
8. George Orwell suggests Miller writes books that "leave a flavour behind them," which, though complimentary, isn't necessarily to suggest Miller's are good books, but rather "they may be good bad books." George Orwell, "Inside the Whale," in *Three Decades of Criticism*, ed. Edward B. Mitchell (New York: New York University Press, 1971), 8.
9. Mayné, *Eroticism*, 6.
10. Wittgenstein, *Tractatus*, Vorwort. My translation.
11. Hassan, *The Literature of Silence*, 8.
12. Mayné, *Eroticism*, 6.

13 Parkin, *Henry Miller*, 3.
14 Blanchot, *Fire*, 20.
15 Jahshan, *Henry Miller and the Surrealist Discourse of Excess*, 148.
16 Blanchot, *Fire*, 174.
17 Mayné, *Eroticism*, 186.
18 Mayné, *Eroticism*, 41.
19 Mayné, *Eroticism*, 106.
20 Blinder, *A Self-Made*, 112.
21 Georges Bataille, "La Morale de Miller," in *Oeuvres complètes XI: Articles I 1944–1949*, ed. Edward B. Mitchell (Paris: Gallimard, 1988), 45. My translation.
22 Even George Wickes writes: "Perhaps the best way to view him is as a writer of satire." George Wickes, *Henry Miller* (St Paul: University of Minnesota Press, 1966), 8.
23 Mayné, *Eroticism*, 20.
24 Mayné, *Eroticism*, 65.
25 See *The Secret Violence of Henry Miller* for more on motion and speed in Miller.
26 Orwell, "Whale," 7.
27 Mayné, *Eroticism*, 13.
28 Jane Nelson, *Form and Image in the Fiction of Henry Miller* (Detroit: Wayne State University Press, 1970) examines Miller's use of fragmentation as a literary technique in great detail through a Jungian analysis of his work.
29 See *The Secret Violence of Henry Miller* for a thorough examination of this Joyce reference.
30 This brings to mind Beckett's expression of this very exhaustion of language: "il faut continuer, je ne peux pas continuer, je vais continuer." Samuel Beckett, *L'innommable* (Paris: Éditions de Minuit, 1979), 213. ("I must go on, I can't go on, I'll go on." Samuel Beckett, *The Unnamable* (London: Faber and Faber, 2010), 176.) And: "'Alors, on y va?' 'Allons-y.' Ils ne bougent pas." Samuel Beckett, *En attendant Godot* (Paris: Minuit, 1952), 133–134. ("Well? Shall we go?" "Yes, let's go." [They do not move.] Samuel Beckett, "*Waiting for Godot*," in *The Complete Dramatic Works* (London: Faber and Faber, 2006), 88.
31 Indirectly related to this development in Miller is Blinder's article on the debate between Bataille and Sartre of the possibility of "real" transgression in literature. For Sartre, Bataille (and perhaps now Miller too) cannot place his own writing above its announced limitations. Blinder writes: "Because Bataille considers language, by the nature of its structural arrangement and its cultural significance, to be inherently defective, he is forced, according to Sartre, to defend his literary position from a set of mystical propositions rather than through any rational explanations." Caroline Blinder, "La revolte enfantine: on Georges Bataille's 'La Morale de Miller' and Jean-Paul Sartre's 'Un Nouveau Mystique,' " *Critique* 40 (1998), 41.
32 Marcel Proust, *A la recherche du temps perdu I: Du côté de chez Swann* (Paris: Gallimard, 1987), 83.
33 For an in-depth look at the influence of Proust and other writers on Miller, see my book *Henry Miller and How He Got That Way* (Edinburgh: Edinburgh University Press, 2011).
34 Bertrand Mathieu compares Miller with Rimbaud in relation, in part, to Rimbaud's interest in "*assigning arbitrary meanings to words* in his desire to create bizarre and

mysterious effects" (Mathieu's italics). *Orpheus in Brooklyn: Orphism, Rimbaud, and Henry Miller* (The Hague, Paris: Mouton, 1976), 180. Mathieu also writes: "If they are pronounced with due reverence and 'purity of heart,' they can reveal to those who make use of them a clearer sense not of objective truth but of subjective identity. The purpose of magic—and of 'magical' poetry like Rilke's and Rimbaud's—lies in pure process; it is a consecration." (183).

35 Roland Barthes, *The Pleasure of the Text*, trans. by Richard Miller (New York: Hill and Wang, 1975), 10.
36 Decker, *Henry*, 8.

Bibliography

Abram, David. *The Spell of the Sensuous*. New York: Vintage, 1997.
Abrams, M.H. *Fourth Dimension of a Poem and Other Essays*. New York: Norton, 2012.
Adler Nanci, and Selma Leydesdorff, eds. *Tapestry of Memory: Evidence and Testimony in Life-Story Narratives*. New Brunswick: Transaction, 2013.
Aleksić, Branko. "The Unpublished Correspondence of Henry Miller & André Breton, the 'Steady Rock,' 1947–50." Translated and with additional notes by Karl Orend. *Nexus: The International Henry Miller Journal* 5 (2008): 150–174.
———. "Henry Miller's Passionate Reading of Images." *Nexus: The International Henry Miller Journal* 6 (2009): 169–183.
Balliet, Gay Louise. *Henry Miller and Surrealist Metaphor*. New York: Peter Lang, 1996.
Barthes, Roland. *The Pleasure of the Text*. Translated by Richard Miller. New York: Hill and Wang, 1975.
———. "The Death of the Author." *Image-Music-Text*. Translated by Stephen Heath. New York: Hill and Wang, 1977. 142–148.
Bataille, Georges. "La Morale de Miller." *Critique—Revue Generale des Publications Francaises et Etrangeres* 1 (1946): 3–17.
———. *Visions of Excess: Selected Writings, 1927–39*. Edited and with introduction by Allan Stoekl. Translated by Allan Stoekl with Carl R. Lovit and Donald M. Leslie, Jr. Manchester: Manchester University Press, 1985.
———. "La Morale de Miller" *Oeuvres Complètes XI: Articles I 1944–1949*. Paris: Gallimard, 1988.
Beasley, Rebecca. *Theorists of Modernist Poetry—T.S Eliot, T.E Hulme and Ezra Pound*. London: Routledge, 2007.
Beckett, Samuel. *En attendant Godot*. Paris: Minuit, 1952.
———. *L'innommable*. Paris: Éditions de Minuit, 1979.
———. *Waiting for Godot. The Complete Dramatic Works*. London: Faber and Faber, 2006. 7–88.
———. *The Unnamable*. London: Faber and Faber, 2010.
Bell, Michael. *D.H. Lawrence: Language and Being*. Cambridge: Cambridge University Press, 1991.
Benn, Gottfried. "The Structure of the Personality (Outline of a Geology of the 'I')." *transition* 21 (1932): 206–214.
———. *Primal Vision: Selected Writings*. New York: New Directions, 1960.
Bergson, Henri. *Creative Evolution*. London: Macmillan, 1913.
Blanchard, Margaret A., and John E. Semonche. "Anthony Comstock and His Adversaries: The Mixed Legacy of This Battle for Free Speech." *Communication Law and Policy* 11, 3 (2006): 317–366.
Blanchot, Maurice. *The Work of Fire*. Translated by Charlotte Mandell. Stanford: Stanford University Press, 1995.
Blinder, Caroline. "La revolte enfantine: on Georges Bataille's 'La Morale de Miller' and Jean-Paul Sartre's 'Un Nouveau Mystique.'" *Critique* 40 (1998): 39–47.

———. *A Self-Made Surrealist: Ideology and Aesthetics in the Work of Henry Miller.* Rochester: Camden House, 2000.

———. "Images of Paris in the Work of Brassaï and Miller." in *Text and Image in Modern European Culture.* Edited by Natasha Grigorianeds et al. West Lafayette: Purdue University Press, 2012. 48–59.

Bloshteyn, Maria. *The Making of a Counter-Culture Icon: Henry Miller's Dostoevsky.* Toronto: Toronto University Press, 2007.

Bradbury, Malcolm. "The Name and Nature of Modernism." *Modernism: 1890–1930.* Edited by James Walter McFarlane and Malcolm Bradbury. New York: Penguin, 1976.

Brassaï. *Henry Miller, the Paris Years.* Translated by Timothy Bent. New York: Arcade, 1995.

Brown, J.D. *Henry Miller.* New York: Ungar, 1986.

Bury, John Bagnell. *The Idea of Progress: An Inquiry into Its Origin and Growth.* Charleston: Bibliobazaar, 2007.

Call, Lewis. *Postmodern Anarchism.* Lanham: Lexington Books, 2002.

Calonne, "Euphoria in Paris: Henry Miller Meets D.H. Lawrence." *Library Chronicle of the University of Texas* 34 (1986): 88–98.

Caws, Mary Ann. *The Surrealist Look: An Erotics of Encounter.* Cambridge, MA: MIT Press, 1999.

Cendrars, Blaise. *Moravagine.* Translated by Alan Brown. New York: New York Review of Books, 2004.

Cixous, Hélène. "The Laugh of the Medusa." Translated by Keith and Paula Cohen. *Signs* 1, 4 (1976): 875–894.

Dawson, Matthew. "The Intractable Obscenity Problem 2.0: The Emerging Circuit Split over the Constitutionality of 'Local Community Standards' Online." *Catholic University Law Review* 60 (2010–2011): 719–748.

Dearborn, Mary. *The Happiest Man Alive: A Biography of Henry Miller.* New York: Simon and Schuster, 1991.

Decker, James M. "'Choking on My Own Saliva: Henry Miller's Bourgeois Family Christmas in *Nexus*.'" *Style* 31 (1997): 270–289.

———. *Henry Miller and Narrative Form: Constructing the Self, Rejecting Modernity.* New York: Routledge, 2005.

———. "Literary Text, Cinematic 'Edition': Adaptation, Textual Authority, and the Filming of '*Tropic of Cancer*.'" *College Literature* 34, 3 (2007): 140–160.

———. "Henry Miller's Pyrrhic Victory." *Guernica.* 3 Oct. 2012. https://www.guernicamag.com/daily/james-m-decker-henry-millers-pyrrhic-victory/

Delany, Samuel R. "To Read *the Dispossessed*." *The Jewel-Hinged Jaw: Notes on the Language of Science Fiction.* Middletown: Wesleyan University Press, 2009.

Deleuze, Gilles, and Félix Guattari. *Anti-Oedipus: Capitalism and Schizophrenia.* Translated by Robert Hurley, et al. Minneapolis: University of Minnesota Press, 1983.

———. *A Thousand Plateaus: Capitalism and Schizophrenia.* Translated by Brian Massumi. Minneapolis: University of Minnesota Press, 1987.

Despentes, Virginie. *King Kong Theory.* Translated by Stéphanie Benson. New York: The Feminist Press, 2010.

Dorsey, Peter A. *Sacred Estrangement: The Rhetoric of Conversion in Modern Autobiography.* University Park: Pennsylvania State University Press, 1993.

Durrell, Lawrence. "Studies in Genius VIII—Henry Miller." *Horizon* 20 July (1949): 45–61.

———. *Lawrence Durrell: In Conversation.* Edited by Earl G. Ingersoll. London: Fairleigh Dickinson University Press, 1998.

Elkins, James. *On Pictures and the Words That Fail Them*. Cambridge: Cambridge University Press, 1998.
Ellmann, Maud. *The Nets of Modernism: Henry James, Virginia Woolf, James Joyce, and Sigmund Freud*. Cambridge: Cambridge University Press, 2010.
Emerson, Ralph Waldo. *Emerson: Essays and Lectures*. New York: Library of America, 1983.
———. *Emerson on Transcendentalism*. Edited by Edward Ericson. New York: Continuum, 1999.
Evans, Dylan. *An Introductory Dictionary of Lacanian Psychoanalysis*. London: Routledge, 1996.
Ferguson, Robert. *Henry Miller: A Life*. New York: Norton, 1991.
Flaxman, Amy M. *New Anatomies: Tracing Emotions in Henry Miller's Writings*. Belfast, ME: Bern Porter, 2000.
Foster, Hal. *Compulsive Beauty*. Cambridge, MA: MIT Press, 1995.
Foster, Steven. "A Critical Appraisal of Henry Miller's *Tropic of Cancer*." *Twentieth Century Literature* 9, 4 (1964): 196–208.
Foucault, Michel. *Madness and Civilization: A History of Insanity in the Age of Reason*. Translated by Richard Howard. New York: Vintage, 1965.
———. *Histoire de la sexualité I: La volonté de savoir*. Paris: Gallimard, 1976.
———. *The History of Sexuality, Volume I: An Introduction*. Translated by Robert Hurley. New York: Pantheon Books, 1978.
Fowlie, Wallace. "Henry Miller as a Visionary." *Critical Essays on Henry Miller*. Edited by Ronald Gottesman. New York: G.K. Hall, 1992. 185–190.
Fraenkel, Michael. *The Genesis of Tropic of Cancer*. Berkeley: Bern Porter, 1946.
Frangello, Gina. "State of the (Literary/Sexual) Union." *American Book Review* 34, 6 (2013): 4–18.
Freeman, Mark. "Too Late: The Temporality of Memory and the Challenge of a Moral Life." *Journal für Psychologie* 11 (2003): 69–70.
Freud, Sigmund. "Beyond the Pleasure Principle." *The Penguin Freud Reader*. Edited by Adam Phillips. London: Penguin, 2006. 132–195.
Friedman, Alan. "The Pitching of Love's Mansion in the Tropics of Henry Miller." *Seven Contemporary Authors*. Edited by Thomas B. Whitbread Austin: University of Texas Press, 1966. 23–48.
Gander, Catherine. "'Twenty-six things at once' Pragmatic Perspectives in Frank O'Hara's and Norman Bluhm's *Poem-Paintings*." *Mixed Messages: American Correspondences in Visual and Verbal Practices*. Edited by Gander and Sarah Garland. (Forthcoming: Manchester, Manchester University Press, 2015)
Garland, Sarah. "'The Dearest of Cemeteries': European Intertexts in Henry *Miller's Tropic of Cancer*." *The European Journal of American Studies* 23, 3 (2010): 197–215.
Geertz, Clifford. *Interpretation of Cultures*. New York: Basic Books, 2000.
Gertz, Elmer, and Felice Flanery Lewis, eds. *Henry Miller: Years of Trial & Triumph, 1962–1964*. Carbondale: Southern Illinois University Press, 1978.
Gifford, James, ed. "Henry Miller's Letters to Herbert Read: 1935–1958." *Nexus: The International Henry Miller Journal* 5 (2008a): 3–35.
———. "Surrealism's Anglo-American Afterlife: The Herbert Read and Henry Miller Network." *Nexus: The International Henry Miller Journal* 5 (2008b): 36–64.
———. "Reading Miller's 'Numinous Cock': Heterosexist Presumption and Queerings of the Censored Text." *ESC: English Studies in Canada* 34, 2–3 (2009): 49–70.

———. *Personal Modernisms: Anarchist Networks and the Later Avant-Gardes*. Edmonton: University of Alberta Press, 2014.
Gilmore, Leigh. *The Limits of Autobiography: Trauma and Testimony*. Ithaca: Cornell University Press, 2001.
Gordon, William A. *The Mind and Art of Henry Miller*. Baton Rouge: Louisiana State University Press, 1967.
Gottesman, Ronald, ed. *Critical Essays on Henry Miller*. New York: G.K. Hall, 1992.
Guedet, Stephanie. "Transformations of Self: Narrating Conversions, Constructing Identities." Unpublished MS.
Guerin, Wildred L., et al. *A Handbook of Critical Approaches to Literature*. 6th ed. New York: Oxford University Press, 2011.
Gwynn, Frederick L., and Joseph Blotner, eds. *Faulkner in the University*. Charlottesville: University of Virginia Press, 1959.
Hardin, Michael. "Fighting Desires: Henry Miller's Queer Tropic." *Journal of Homosexuality* 42, 3 (2002): 129–150.
Hassan, Ihab. *The Literature of Silence: Henry Miller and Samuel Beckett*. New York: Knopf, 1967.
Havelock, Eric A. *Preface to Plato*. Cambridge, MA: Harvard University Press, 1963.
Heidegger, Martin. *An Introduction to Metaphysics*. Translated by Ralph Manhein. New Haven: Yale University Press, 1959.
Henry Miller: Asleep & Awake. Directed by Tom Schiller. NTSC, 2007. DVD.
Hindmarsh, D. Bruce. *The Evangelical Conversion Narrative: Spiritual Autobiography in Early Modern England*. Oxford: Oxford University Press, 2005.
Hölderlin, Friedrich. "Brot und Wein." *Sämtliche Gedichte und Hyperion*. Edited by Jochen Schmidt. Berlin: Insel-Verlag, 1999.
Hoy, David Couzens. *The Times of Our Lives: A Critical History of Temporality*. Cambridge, MA: MIT Press, 2009.
Hoyle, Arthur. "Remember Henry Miller? Censored Then, Forgotten Now." *The Huffington Post Books*. 14 May 2014. http://www.huffingtonpost.com/arthur-hoyle/remember-henry-miller_b_5320782.html
———. *The Unknown Henry Miller: A Seeker in Big Sur*. New York: Arcade, 2014.
Hulme, T.E. "Humanism and the Religious Attitude." *Speculations—Essays on the Humanism and Philosophy of Art*. London: Kegan Paul, 1924.
Hutchinson, Earl. R. *Tropic of Cancer on Trial: A Case Study of Censorship*. New York: Grove Press, 1968.
Immerso, Michael. *Coney Island: The People's Playground*. New Brunswick: Rutgers University Press, 2002.
Jackson, Hamish. "Henry Miller's *Black Spring* through the Looking Glass of Jacques Lacan." *Nexus: The International Henry Miller Journal* 9 (2012): 105–23.
Jackson, Paul. "Henry Miller, Emerson, and the Divided Self." *Critical Essays on Henry Miller*. Edited by Ronald Gottesman. New York: G.K. Hall, 1992. 223–234.
Jaeckle, Dominic. "Thoreau Was an Atlas, or Responding to the Hummingbird: Antagonizing a Diurnal Real in Henry Miller's Literary Reflections." Unpublished MS.
Jahshan, Paul. *Henry Miller and the Surrealist Discourse of Excess: A Post-Structuralist Reading*. New York: Peter Lang, 2001.
Jakobson, Roman. "Grammatical Parallelism and Its Russian Facet." *Language* 42, 2 (1966): 399–429.
Jolas, Eugene. *The Language of Night*. The Hague: Servire Press, 1932.

Jong, Erica. *The Devil at Large*. New York: Turtle Bay, 1993.
Joost, Elet. "The Influence of American Transcendentalism on Miller via Walt Whitman." MA thesis. Ghent University, 2009.
Josipovici, Gabriel. *What Ever Happened to Modernism?* New Haven: Yale University Press, 2010.
Jousse, Marcel. *Le style oral: rhytmique et mnémotechnique chez les verbo–moteurs*. Paris: Traveaux de Laboratorie d´anthropologie rythmo–pédagogique de Paris, 1925.
———. *The Oral Style*. Translated by Edgard Sienaert and Richard Whitaker. New York: Garland, 1990.
Joyce, James. *A Portrait of the Artist as a Young Man*. New York: Norton, 2006.
Jung, Carl Gustav. *Modern Man in Search of a Soul*. London: Routledge, 1961.
Kermode, Frank. *Continuities*. London: Routledge, 1968.
———. *Lawrence*. London: Fontana/Collins, 1973.
Kersnowski, Frank L., and Alice Hughes, eds. *Conversations with Henry Miller*. Jackson: University Press of Mississippi, 1994.
Kleine, Don. "Innocence Forbidden: Henry Miller in the Tropics." *Prairie Schooner* 33, 2 (1959): 125–130.
Kopley, Richard. "Naysayers: Poe, Hawthorne, and Melville." *Oxford Handbook of Transcendentalism*. Edited by Joel Myerson, Sandra Petrulionis, and Laura Walls. New York: Oxford University Press, 2010. 597–613.
Krauss, Rosalind. *Optical Unconscious*. Cambridge, MA: M.I.T. Press, 1996.
Laanes, Eneken. "Anecdotalization of Memory in Jaan Kross's *Paigallend*." *Haunted Narratives: Life Writing in an Age of Trauma*. Edited by Gabrielle Rippl, et al. Toronto: University of Toronto Press, 2013. 187–202.
Lacan, Jacques. *Écrits: A Selection*. Translated by Alan Sheridan. New York: Norton, 1977.
———. *On the Names-of-the-Father*. Translated by Bruce Fink. Cambridge: Polity, 2013.
———. *The Seminar of Jacques Lacan, Book XXIII-Joyce and the Sinthome-1975–1976*. Translated by Cormac Gallagher. Parts 1 and 2. file:///D:/Downloads/Book-23-Joyce-and-the-Sinthome-Part-2.pdf
Lacan, Jacques, and Jacques-Alain Miller. *The Four Fundamental Concepts of Psychoanalysis*. London: Hogarth, 1977.
———. *The Psychoses: The Seminar III of Jacques Lacan*. London: Routledge, 1993.
Lacan, Jacques, and Anthony Wilden. *Speech and Language in Psychoanalysis*. Baltimore: Johns Hopkins, 1981.
Lao-Tzu. *Tao Te Ching: A New English Version*. Translated by Stephen Mitchell. New York: Harper & Row, 1988.
Lautréamont, Comte de. *Maldoror [Les Chants de Maldoror]*. New York: New Directions, 1965.
Lawrence, D.H. *Fantasia of the Unconscious*. London: Secker, 1930.
———. *Apocalypse*. London: Secker, 1932.
———. "The Novel." in *Complete Works of D.H. Lawrence* [Kindle Edition] Delphi Classics, 2011.
Le Guin, Ursula K. *The Dispossessed: An Ambiguous Utopia*. New York: Harper Voyager, 1994.
Lehman, Eric. "*Quiet Days in Clichy*: Henry Miller's Urban Idyll." *Nexus: The International Henry Miller Journal* 9 (2012): 81–89.
Lennon, John. "On Censorship and Henry Miller." *Henry Miller: A Book of Tributes, 1931–1994*. Edited by Craig Peter Standish. Orlando: Standish Books, 1994. 633–634.

Lévi-Strauss, Claude. *The Savage Mind*. Chicago: University of Chicago Press, 1966.
Lewis, Leon. *Henry Miller: The Major Writings*. New York: Schocken, 1986.
Lewis, Wyndham. *Wyndham Lewis the Artist*. London: Laidlaw & Laidlaw, 1939.
Lord, Albert B. *The Singer of Tales* [1960] New York: Atheneum, 1971.
Mackey, Thomas C. *Pornography on Trial: A Handbook with Cases, Laws and Documents*.Santa Barbara: ABC-CLIO, 2002.
Mailer, Norman. "The Prisoner of Sex." *Harper's Magazine* (March 1971): 41–92.
———. *Genius and Lust: A Journey through the Major Writings of Henry Miller*. New York: Grove, 1976.
Männiste, Indrek. *Henry Miller: The Inhuman Artist, a Philosophical Inquiry*. New York: Bloomsbury, 2013.
Martin, Jay. *Always Merry and Bright: The Life of Henry Miller*. Santa Barbara: Capra, 1978.
———. "Three Stages of Dreaming: A Clinical Study of Henry Miller's Dream Book." *Journal of the American Academy of Psychoanalysis* 12, 2 (1984): 233–251.
Masuga, Katy. "Crossing Brooklyn Bridge: An Ekphrastic Correspondence between Walt Whitman, Hart Crane, and Henry Miller." *Nexus: The International Henry Miller Journal* 7 (2010a): 101–26.
———. "Henry Miller and the Book of Life." *Texas Studies in Literature and Language* 52, 2 (2010b): 181–202.
———. *Henry Miller and How He Got That Way*. Edinburgh: Edinburgh University Press, 2011a.
———. *The Secret Violence of Henry Miller*. Rochester: Camden House, 2011b.
Mathieu, Bertrand. *Orpheus in Brooklyn: Orphism, Rimbaud, and Henry Miller*. The Hague, Paris: Mouton, 1976.
Matus, Doug. "Teach as You Like and Die Happy: Henry Miller as High School Curriculum." *Nexus: The International Henry Miller Journal*, 7 (2010): 87–95.
May, Todd. *The Political Philosophy of Poststructuralist Anarchism*. University Park: Pennsylvania State University Press, 1994.
Mayné, Gilles. *Eroticism in Georges Bataille and Henry Miller*. Birmingham: Summa, 1993.
McCarthy, Harold T. "Henry Miller's Democratic Vistas." *American Quarterly* 23, 2 (1971): 221–235.
Mead, Henry. "T.E Hulme, Bergson, and the New Philosophy." *European Journal of English Studies* 12 (2008): 245–260.
Milosz, Czeslaw, and Richard Lourie. "Henry Miller." *Grand Street* 1, 3 (1982): 123–126.
Millett, Kate. *Sexual Politics*. 1969. London: Virago, 1981.
Mitchell, Edward B. "Artists and Artists: The 'Aesthetics' of Henry Miller." *Texas Studies in Literature and Language* 8, 1 (1966): 103–115.
———, ed. *Henry Miller: Three Decades of Criticism*. New York: New York University Press, 1971.
Moi, Toril. *Sexual/Textual Politics: Feminist Literary Theory*. London: Routledge, 1985.
Morris, David B. "The Neurobiology of the Obscene: Henry Miller and Tourette Syndrome." *Literature and Medicine* 12, 2 (1993): 194–214.
Munsil, Mary Kellie. "The Body in the Prison-house of Language: Henry Miller, Pornography and Feminism." *Critical Essays on Henry Miller*. Edited by Ronald Gottesman. New York: G.K. Hall, 1992. 285–296.
Murdoch, Iris. *Existentialists and Mystics: Writings on Philosophy and Literature*. Edited by Peter Conradi. New York: Penguin, 1999.

Murnighan, Jack. *The Naughty Bits: The Steamiest and Most Scandalous Sex Scenes from the World's Great Books*. New York: Broadway Books, 2001.

Nelson, Jane A. *Form and Image in the Fiction of Henry Miller*. Detroit: Wayne State University Press, 1970.

Nesbit, Thomas. *Henry Miller and Religion*. New York: Routledge, 2007.

Nesbitt, Huw. "Why Henry Miller and Louis-Ferdinand Céline Deserve Success as well as Scandal." *The Guardian* 19 Feb. 2014. http://www.theguardian.com/books/booksblog/2014/feb/19/henry-miller-louis-ferdinand-celine-scandal

Newman, Saul. *From Bakunin to Lacan: Anti-Authoritarianism and the Dislocation of Power* Lanham: Lexington Books, 2001.

Nietzsche, Friedrich. *The Birth of Tragedy and Other Writings*. Edited by Raimond Geuss and Ronald Speirs. Translated by Speirs. Cambridge: Cambridge University Press, 1999.

Nin, Anaïs. *The Diary of Anaïs Nin: Volume One, 1931–1934*. New York: Harvest, 1966.

Nohrnberg, James. "On Literature and the Bible." *Centrum* 2, 2 (1974): 5–43.

"Notes and Announcements." *Journal of Criminal Law and Criminology* 54, 2, (1963): 198–199.

Ong, Walter J. *Orality and Literacy*. London: Routledge, 1977.

Orend, Karl. *Brotherhood of Fools and Simpletons: Gods and Devils in Henry Miller's Utopia*. Paris: Alyscamps, 2005.

———. "The Edge of the Miraculous—First Reflections on Henry Miller and Art." *Nexus: The International Henry Miller Journal* 6 (2009a): 11–38.

———. "Fucking Your Way to Paradise." *Nexus: The International Henry Miller Journal* 6 (2009b): 44–77.

Orwell, George. "Inside the Whale." *Collected Essays*. Edited by Sonia Orwell London: Secker and Warburg, 1961.

———. "Review." *An Age Like This: 1920–1940, Vol. 1 of the Collected Essays, Journalism and Letters of George Orwell*. Edited by Sonia Orwell and Ian Angus. New York: Harcourt, Brace and World, 1968.

Palumbo, Allison. "Finding the Feminine: Rethinking Henry Miller's *Tropics* Trilogy." *Nexus: The International Henry Miller Journal* 7 (2010): 145–76.

Parkin, John. *Henry Miller: The Modern Rabelais*. Lewiston: Edwin Mellen Press, 1990.

Perlès, Alfred. *My Friend Henry Miller*. New York: Belmont Books, 1962.

———. *Round Trip*. London: Dennis Dobson, 1946.

Peters, Gerald. *The Mutilating God: Authorship and Authority in the Narrative of Conversion*. Amherst: Amherst University Press, 1993.

Pound, Ezra. *Jefferson and/or Mussolini*. London: Stanley Nott, 1935.

———. *Guide to Kulchur*. London: Peter Owen, 1952.

———. *The Literary Essays of Ezra Pound*. Edited and with an introduction by T.S. Eliot. London: Faber & Faber, 1954.

———. "Review of *Tropic of Cancer*." *Critical Essays on Henry Miller*. Edited by Ronald Gottesman. New York: G.K. Hall, 1992. 87–89.

———. "Axiomata." *Manifesto—A Century of Isms*. Edited by Mary Ann Caws. London: University of Nebraska Press, 2001.

Proust, Marcel. *A la recherche du temps perdu I: Du côté de chez Swann*. Paris: Gallimard, 1987.

Ragland-Sullivan, Ellie, and Dragan Milovanovic. *Lacan: Topologically Speaking*. New York: Other, 2004.

Rank, Otto. *Art and Artist: Creative Urge and Personality Development*. New York: Knopf, 1932.

Read, Herbert. *The Tenth Muse*. Freeport: Books for Libraries Press, 1969.
Rembar, Charles. *The End of Obscenity: The Trials of* Lady Chatterley, Tropic of Cancer and Fanny Hill. New York: Random House, 1968.
———. "Obscenity—Forget It." *Atlantic Monthly* 1 May 1977. http://www.theatlantic.com/magazine/archive/1977/05/obscenity-forget-it/305053/
Rexroth, Kenneth. "The Reality of Henry Miller." *Critical Essays on Henry Miller*. Edited by Ronald Gottesman. New York: G.K. Hall, 1992. 95–102.
Ricoeur, Paul. *The Symbolism of Evil*. Boston: Beacon Press, 1986.
Riley, Patrick. *Character and Conversion in Autobiography*. Charlottesville: University of Virginia Press, 2004.
Roy, Srila. "On Testimony: The Pain of Speaking and the Speaking of Pain." *Tapestry of Memory: Evidence and Testimony in Life-Story Narratives*. Edited by Nanci Adler and Sema Leydesdorff. New Brunswick: Transaction, 2013. 97–110.
Rungo, Laraine. "'Between Ideas and Living': A Foucaultian Reading of Henry Miller." *Nexus: The International Henry Miller Journal* 5 (2008): 215–239.
Rushdie, Salman. "Outside the Whale." *Imaginary Homelands: Essays and Criticism 1981–1991*. London: Granta Books, 1991.
Sade, Marquis de. *The Mystified Magistrate and Other Tales*. Translated by Richard Seaver. New York: Arcade, 2000.
Said, Edward W. *Orientalism: Western Conceptions of the Orient*. London: Penguin, 1995.
Scarry, Elaine. *On Beauty and Being Just*. Princeton: Princeton University Press, 1999.
Schreber, D.P. *Memoirs of My Nervous Illness*. Translated and edited by Ida MacAlpine and Richard Hunter. Cambridge: Harvard University Press, 1988.
Seed, David. *Cinematic Fictions*. Liverpool: Liverpool University Press, 2009.
Shapiro, Karl. "The Greatest Living Author." *Tropic of Cancer* by Henry Miller. New York: Grove, 1961. v–xxx.
Shifreen, Lawrence J., and Roger Jackson. *Henry Miller: A Bibliography of Primary Sources*. Ann Arbor: Jackson, 1993.
Smithline, Arnold. "Henry Miller and the Transcendental Spirit." *Emerson Society Quarterly* 2 (1966): 50–56.
Soelle, Dorothee. *The Silent Cry: Mysticism and Resistance*. Translated by Barbara and Martin Rumscheidt. Minneapolis: Fortress Press, 2001.
Solomon, William. *Literature, Amusement, and Technology in the Great Depression*. Cambridge: Cambridge University Press, 2002.
Southwood, Ivor. *Non-Stop Inertia*. Alresford, Hants: Zero Books, 2011.
Spengler, Oswald. *The Decline of the West*. Translated by Charles Francis Atkinson. New York: Knopf, 1926.
Straub, Julia. "Richard Wollheim's *Germs*: Life Writing as Therapy, Despite Theory." Edited by Gabrielle Rippl, et al. *Haunted Narratives: Life Writing in an Age of Trauma*. Toronto: Toronto University Press, 2013. 85–100.
Symmes, Robert. "An Embryo for God." *Experimental Review* 2 (1940): 78–80.
Tanenhaus, Sam. "Generation Nice." *The New York Times*. Sunday Styles. 17 Aug. 2014. 1, 7.
Thoreau, Henry David. *Life Without Principles: Three Essays*. Stanford: J. L. Delkin, 1946.
———. *Walden and Other Writings*. Edited by Brooks Atkinson. New York: Random House, 1950.
———. *A Week on the Concord and Merrimack Rivers*. A Penn State Electronic Classics Series Publication, edited by Jim Manis. State College: Pennsylvania State University Press, 2003.

Tong, Rosemarie. *Feminist Thought: A Comprehensive Introduction.* Boulder: Westview, 1989.
Turner, Frederick. *Renegade: Henry Miller and the Making of* Tropic of Cancer. New Haven: Yale University Press, 2011.
Ullman, Chana. *The Transformed Self: The Psychology of Religious Conversion.* New York: Plenum, 1989.
Vattimo, Gianni. *Nietzsche: An Introduction.* Translated by Nicholas Martin. Stanford: Stanford University Press, 2002.
Vendler, Helen. "Feminism and Literature." *New York Review of Books.* 31 May 1990: 19–25.
Vollmann, William T. "Decently Downward." *The Baffler* 24 (2014) http://thebaffler.com/past/decently_downward
Wallace, Kreg. "Henry Miller's Paris Guidebooks." *Nexus: The International Henry Miller Journal* 7 (2010): 79–86.
Wallace, Rob. *Improvisation and the Making of American Literary Modernism.* New York: Continuum, 2010.
Ward, Koral. *Augenblick: The Concept of the 'Decisive Moment' in 19th- and 20th-Century Western Philosophy.* Burlington: Ashgate, 2008.
Weir, David. *The Aesthetic Politics of Modernism.* Amherst: University of Massachusetts Press, 1997.
White, Curtis. "Managing Despair." *big other* 8 (2012) http://bigother.com/2012/03/08/27085/
Whitman, Walt. *Leaves of Grass and Other Writings: Authoritative Texts, Other Poetry and Prose, Criticism.* Edited by Michael Moon, Sculley Bradley, and Harold William Blodgett. New York: Norton, 2002.
Wickes, George. "Henry Miller, the Art of Fiction No. 28." *Paris Review* (1962): 1–33. http://typeofwords.com/wp-content/uploads/2010/09/4597_MILLER_H.pdf
———. ed. *Henry Miller and the Critics.* Carbondale: Southern Illinois University Press, 1963,
———. *Henry Miller.* St. Paul: University of Minnesota Press, 1966.
———. "Henry Miller: Down and Out in Paris." *Critical Essays on Henry Miller.* Edited by Ronald Gottesman. New York: G.K. Hall, 1992. 103–128.
Widmer, Kingsley. *Henry Miller.* Revised edition. Boston: Twayne, 1990.
———. "Lawrence's American Bad Boy Progeny: Henry Miller and Norman Mailer." *D. H. Lawrence's Literary Inheritors.* Edited by Keith Cushman and Dennis Jackson. New York: St Martin's Press, 1991. 89–108.
Williams, Raymond. *Marxism and Literature.* Oxford: Oxford University Press, 1977.
Williamson, Eric Miles. *Welcome to Oakland*, Hyattsville: Raw Dog Screaming Press, 2009.
Wilson, Edmund. *The Shores of Light; A Literary Chronicle of the Twenties and Thirties* New York: Farrar, Straus and Young, 1952.
———. "Twilight of the Expatriates." *New Republic* 94 (9 March 1938).
Winterson, Jeanette. "The Male Mystique of Henry Miller." Review of *Renegade: Henry Miller and the Making of* Tropic of Cancer. *The New York Times Sunday Book Review.* 26 Jan. 2012. http://www.nytimes.com/2012/01/29/books/review/renegade-henry-miller-and-the-making-of-tropic-of-cancer-by-frederick-turner-bookreview.html?pagewanted=all&_r=0
Wittgenstein, Ludwig. *Tractatus Logico-Philosophicus.* Translated by Frank P. Ramsey and C.K. Ogden. London: Kegan Paul, 1922.

Wolfe, Bernard. "Playboy Interview: Henry Miller." *Playboy* September 1964: 77–90.
Wolff, Roberl Paul. *In Defense of Anarchism*. New York: Harper & Row, 1970.
Yazici, Savas. "Encountering with the Real: A Critical Reading of the Works of Lacan Lacau, Žižek, and Badiou." Ph.D. Dissertation. The Graduate School of Social Sciences of Middle East Technical University, 2007.
Yeats, William Butler. "The Song of the Happy Shepherd." *Collected Poems of W.B. Yeats*. London: Macmillan, 1958. 7.
Young, Julian. *Heidegger's Philosophy of Art*. Cambridge: Cambridge University Press, 2011.
Žižek, Slavoj. "The Act and Its Vicissitudes." *The Symptom* 6 (2005). http://www.lacan.com/symptom6_articles/zizek.html
———. *How to Read Lacan*. New York: Norton, 2007.
———. "Passion in the Era of Decaffeinated Belief." *The Symptom* 5 (2004). http://www.lacan.com/passion.htm
———. *The Plague of Fantasies*. London: Verso, 2008.

Index

Note: Locators followed by the letter "n" refer to notes.

Abplanalp, Edward 4, 45
Abram, David 78, 82, 83n. 20
Abrams, M.H. 83n. 11
Adler, Nanci 25, 30nn. 26, 31
The Air-Conditioned Nightmare 12, 21, 39, 41–3, 114, 135n. 6
"The Air-Conditioned Nightmare" 135n. 6
Albert, Prince Consort 187, 197n. 1
Aleksić, Branko 155nn. 9, 13
altruism 68
anarchism 5, 52, 173–6, 178, 181–4, 185n. 3, 186nn. 22–3, 25
"The Angel Is My Watermark!" 111–12, 151
Anthony, St 15–16, 18
anti-Semitism 11, 47, 160
Aquinas, Thomas 45–6, 49
Artaud, Antonin 123
asceticism 96, 100
"Astrological Fricassee" 163
astrology 4, 45, 53, 131, 132, 165
Augustine, St 22, 29n. 7, 46
automatic writing (concept of) 26, 30n. 34, 111, 123, 137, 143, 151, 153
avant-garde (movement of) 22, 50, 71, 97

Baker, Nicholson 159
Bakunin, Mikhail 181–2
Balliet, Gay Louise 155n. 9
Barker, George 175
Barthes, Roland 100, 107nn. 22–3, 211, 214n. 35
Bataille, George 4, 64, 66–9, 71–2, 73nn. 17–25, 31, 74n. 38, 201, 204, 213nn. 21, 31
Baudelaire, Charles 77, 187, 194

Beat Movement 176–7, 200
Beckett, Samuel 201, 213n. 30
Beelzebub 15–16, 18
Bell, Michael 19n. 4
Belmont, Georges 120, 124
Benn, Gottfried 145–6, 152, 156nn. 28–9
Bergson, Henri 9, 50–1, 53, 68–72, 73n. 26, 146, 156n. 30
The Best of Henry Miller 66
Bible 4, 45, 49, 52–3, 59–60, 83n. 4
Big Sur 4–5, 6n. 2, 40, 42, 84n. 35, 127–31, 133–5, 138, 154, 154n. 1, 162, 168, 188
Big Sur and the Oranges of Hieronymus Bosch 5, 18, 37, 42, 84n. 35, 127–34, 138, 154n. 6
Black Spring 14–18, 23–4, 26, 34, 36, 38, 49, 52, 87, 111–12, 121–2, 137, 139, 142, 144–53, 154nn. 1, 3, 155n. 10, 192
Blake, William 205
Blanchot, Maurice 10, 199, 201–3, 212n. 2, 213nn. 14, 16
Blinder, Caroline 23, 29n. 17, 30n. 34, 63, 68, 71, 73n. 18, 74n. 37, 116, 124n. 3, 125n. 36, 141, 143, 155nn. 9, 12, 17, 204, 213nn. 20, 31
Bloshteyn, Maria 23, 29n. 16
Bobo, Roshi 33
Boccaccio, Giovanni 163
Bonaparte, Napoleon 127
The Book of Friends 84n. 35, 138, 156n. 37
The Books in My Life 3, 22, 25–6, 29n. 7, 30n. 37, 50, 84n. 35, 127, 134
"The Booster" 176
Borromean Knot 112–5, 120, 122

Bosch, Hieronymus 5, 33, 35n. 84, 127, 133, 138, 154n. 6
Boudník, Vladimir 77
Bradbury, Michael 19n. 9
Brassaï 109, 120, 122–3, 125nn. 38, 46, 126nn. 50–53, 141, 144, 156n. 22, 190–1
Breton, André 138, 141, 143, 152
Brooklyn 29n. 11, 33, 35–6, 48, 59, 66, 145–7, 149, 151, 156n. 24, 188, 214n. 34
Brown, J.D. 16, 20n. 26
Buddhism 48, 50, 53, 57, 60
Buñuel, Luis 142
"Burlesk" 146
Bursey, Jeff 5, 159
Bury, John Bagnell 19n. 12

Cairns, Huntington 164
Call, Lewis 183, 186n. 25
Calonne, David Stephen 20n. 21
Cambodia 33
capitalism (ideas of) 64, 90, 92, 160, 169, 173, 175–6, 178–80, 185, 186n. 26, 187–9, 195
Capricorne 150
Catullus 163
Caws, Mary Ann 145, 153, 156n. 26, 157n. 49
Céline, Lois-Ferdinand 6n. 3, 86, 161, 171n. 8
Cendrars, Blaise 33, 50, 53, 86, 104, 108n. 40, 131
Chagall, Marc 138
Chicago Tribune 81, 191
China (concept of) 10, 15–19, 26–7, 35, 40, 121, 149, 152
Chirico, Georges de 138
Christ, Jesus 47, 56–7, 59, 78–80, 84n. 35, 127, 143, 184
Christianity 48, 50, 52, 56
Chronos 13, 89
Cixous, Hélène 87–8, 93nn. 27, 29–30
Clipped Wings 27, 77
Cockburn, Edmund Alexander 100
Coker, Jarvis 159
Coleridge, Samuel Taylor 79

collaboration 5, 137–8, 141, 153
The Colossus of Maroussi 40–1, 50–1, 77–8, 84n. 35, 85, 151, 176, 188
communism 175, 182, 193
Comte, Auguste 11
Conason, Emil 190
Conversations with Henry Miller 155n. 16
conversion (concept of) 3, 21–9, 30n. 41, 31n. 43, 47, 70, 174, 179–80
Cooney, James 181
The Cosmological Eye 25, 46, 55–6, 58, 66, 68, 77, 82, 84n. 35, 95, 105–6, 116, 123, 142, 154n. 3, 169, 173–5, 192
Cossery, Albert 182
Crazy Cock 77, 149, 151
"Creative Death" 49, 55–7
creativity (concept of) 5, 14, 17–18, 21, 41, 55, 58–9, 68, 76, 123, 127–9, 134, 134n. 8, 142, 147, 149, 151, 178, 180, 203
Crosby, Harry 146
crucifixion (ideas of) 4, 45, 55–6, 58, 60, 154

Dadaism 46, 109, 181, 192
Dalí, Salvador 123, 138, 142
Dante (Alighieri) 147
Dawkins, Richard 45
Dearborn, Mary 93nn. 11, 14, 16–17, 108n. 37
Decker, James, M. 3, 40, 42, 44nn. 11, 14, 46, 61nn. 1, 14, 63, 66, 89, 91, 93n. 35, 94n. 43, 155n. 21, 156n. 23, 170, 172n. 30, 211, 214n. 36
The Decline of the West 19nn. 11, 14, 16, 20n. 20, 37
dehumanization 37
Delany, Samuel R. 180–1, 185n. 15, 186nn. 16–18
Deleuze, Gilles 10, 184, 186n. 26
Den Hann, Jacques 139
Dennett, Daniel 45
De Sade, Marquis 99, 107n. 18, 163
Despentes, Virginia 172n. 29
The Devil in Paradise 168
Dickinson, Emily 90
Dionysian (properties of) 48, 56

Index

Dorsey, Peter A. 21–4, 26–7, 28n. 3, 29nn. 12, 14, 30nn. 25, 33, 41, 31nn. 43, 45
Dos Passos, John 86
Dostoevsky, Fyodor 23, 29n. 16, 36, 54
"A Dream of a Book" 139, 151
dreams 17, 109, 117, 120–1, 137–46, 150–3
Dreiser, Theodore 23, 27, 162
Dulac, Germaine 142
Dumont, Santos 34
Duncan, Robert 177, 181–2
Durrell, Lawrence 16, 40, 53, 66, 73n. 16, 154, 177, 185nn. 7, 8, 196

echolalia 118, 137
ecstasy 115, 117, 123, 146, 203, 212
Edgar, David 196
Elet, Joost 134n. 4
Eliot, Thomas Stearns 73nn. 9, 27, 86, 90, 145, 165, 181
Elkins, James 151, 156n. 41
Ellis, Havelock 16, 19
Ellison, Ralph 121
Ellman, Maude 116, 125nn. 34–5
Emerson, Ralph Waldo 27, 90, 127–34, 135nn. 14, 17–19, 22, 156n. 27, 176, 188
Engels, Friedrich 187
Enlightenment (ideas of) 11–13, 22, 183–4
"The Enormous Womb" 58
epiphany 30n. 41, 112, 115–8, 120, 122, 124, 127
Ernst, Max 138
erotic 199–205, 207–12
Eschatology 192, 194–5
Evans, Dylan 113, 125nn. 20, 22–3, 28, 31–2, 40
Experimental Review 181
Expressionism 138, 145

fascism 64, 71–2, 175, 182, 193
Faure, Élie 137
Fauvism 138
feminism 85–7, 91, 93n. 5, 94n. 47, 107n. 20
Ferguson, Robert 16, 20n. 24, 93nn. 11–13, 156n. 38

First World War 4, 64, 192
flâneur 42, 188, 194
Flaxman, Amy M. 21, 28n. 2
Fondation, Larry 168
Foster, Hal 152–3, 157nn. 44, 48
Foster, Steven 33, 44n. 3
Foucault, Michel 23–4, 29nn. 18–21, 101, 199–200, 206, 212nn. 3–4
"The Fourteenth Ward" 23, 188
Fowlie, Wallace 10, 19n. 10, 175–6, 185n. 4
Fraenkel, Michael 2, 12–13, 16–17, 77, 81, 83n. 3, 86, 150–1, 154, 156n. 39, 184, 192–3, 196–7, 197n. 5
France (country of) 4, 34, 38–40, 50, 165, 192, 195
France, Anotole 192, 197n. 7
Frangello, Gina 167, 172n. 24
Freeman, Mark 25, 30n. 29
Freud, Sigmund 101–3, 105, 108n. 33, 109–10, 125n. 34, 139, 143–7, 152–3, 192
Friedman, Alan 109, 124n. 2
full present (concept of) 3, 10, 13–19, 28

Gander, Catherine 157n. 52
Gandhi, Mahatma (Mohandas) 176, 179
Garland, Sarah 5, 23, 29n. 13, 63–4, 68, 72n. 4, 137, 156n. 24, 157n. 52
Geertz, Clifford 83n. 22
Gertz, Elmer 166, 171n. 5, 172n. 20
Gifford, James 5, 31n. 46, 155n. 9, 173, 185nn. 2, 10
Gilmore, Leigh 25, 30n. 28
God 4, 6n. 5, 21–3, 29nn. 7, 9, 40, 43, 45–56, 59–60, 65–6, 69, 76, 79, 81–2, 89, 95, 100, 103, 108n. 32, 110, 123, 128, 152, 170, 173, 186n. 19, 190, 192, 202, 207
Goethe, Johann Wolfgang von 156n. 27
Goldman, Emma 86, 175
Goldsmiths (college of) 2
Gordon, William A. 16, 20n. 25, 45, 55, 61nn. 24, 27, 127–8, 134n. 3
Gottesman, Ronald 7n. 16, 19n. 10, 72n. 1, 73n. 15, 107nn. 16–17, 20, 135n. 7

Greece 4, 34, 40–1, 84, 188
The Guardian 1, 6n. 3, 171n. 8
Guattari, Félix 6n. 7, 10, 184, 186n. 26
Guedet, Stephanie 27, 30n. 42
Guerin, Wildred L. 91, 93nn. 6–8, 18, 94n. 46
Guiler, Hugh 197

Hamlet 12–13, 16, 18, 25, 29n. 7, 184
Hardin, Michael 147, 152, 156n. 35, 157n. 42
Harris, Sam 45
Hassan, Ihab 1, 6n. 7, 201, 212n. 11
Hausmann, Georges-Eugène 190
Havelock, Eric A. 78, 83n. 19
Hawthorne, Nathaniel 133
Hegel, Friedrich 11
Heidegger, Martin 19nn. 2, 5
Hemingway, Ernest 90
Henry Miller: Asleep and Awake 33, 120, 125n. 44, 157
Henry Miller in Conversation 30n. 30, 77, 120, 124
Henry Miller and James Laughlin: Selected Letters 111–12
Henry Miller: Letters to Anaïs Nin 123
"Henry Miller's Letters to Herbert Read" 186n. 20
Henry Miller on Writing 47, 57, 72, 162, 165–70, 200–1, 207
Herian, Rob 4, 95
Hesse, Herman 33
Hindmarsh, Bruce D. 24, 26, 30nn. 22, 40
Hindusim 47, 50–1, 53, 60
Hirsch, Trygve 167
Hitchens, Christopher 45
Hoffman, Holly 89, 93n. 33
Hölderlin, Friedrich 10, 19n. 11
Hoy, David Couzens 12, 19n. 15
Hoyle, Arthur 1–2, 6n. 2, 91–2, 93n. 15, 94nn. 44, 45, 50, 154n. 4, 155n. 7, 157n. 53, 164, 171, 171n. 18, 172nn. 23, 33
The Huffington Post 2, 94n. 44
Hughes, Alice 155n. 16

Hulme, T.E. 64–5, 69, 71–2, 73nn. 12, 26–30
Hutchinson, Earl R. 6n. 9
Huxley, Aldous 86

identity 3, 22, 25, 27, 34, 49, 51, 53, 55, 58, 60, 91, 121–2, 124, 152, 157n. 45, 184, 188, 192, 214n. 34
Imaginary (concept of) 112–4
Imhof, George 149
Immerso, Michael 156n. 33
individualism (ideas of) 5, 127–9
inhuman (concept of) 3, 10, 14–19, 42, 58, 60, 81–2, 92, 163, 183–4
intertextuality (concept of) 23, 145, 156n. 24
"Into the Night Life" 5, 121, 137–8, 142–4, 147, 150, 152–3
Into the Night Life 5, 137–54, 154n. 1

Jabour, Ellie 125n. 21
Jackson, Hamish 4, 157n. 45
Jackson, Paul 128, 135n. 7
Jackson, Roger 138, 155n. 7
Jaeckle, Dominic 30n. 39
Jahshan, Paul 4, 27, 33, 71, 155n. 9, 203, 213n. 15
Jakobson, Roman 83n. 10
James, E.L. 159
James, William 69
Jameson, Fredric 174, 181
Janet, Pierre 153
Jensen, Finn 5, 187
Jew(s) 35–7, 45, 50, 57, 160
Jolas, Eugene 146, 156nn. 31–2, 194
Jong, Erica 85, 89, 93nn. 1, 4, 36–8, 161, 177
Josipovici, Gabriel 164–6, 171n. 17, 172n. 22
jouissance 114–5, 117–8, 123
Jousse, Marcel 76, 83nn. 6–7
Joyce, James 13, 55–6, 115–16, 121, 123, 125nn. 29, 34, 162, 183, 186n. 21, 192–3, 213n. 29
Jung, Carl Gustav 13, 20nn. 18–19, 33, 50, 145, 155n. 11, 213n. 28

Kahane, Jack 75
Katsimbalis, George 40
Kermode, Frank 19, 163–5, 171n. 11
Kerouac, Jack 2
Kersnowski, Frank L. 155n. 16
Keyserling, Count von 10
Kierkegaarde, Søren 52
Klee, Paul 146
Kleine, Don 33, 44n. 2
Kokoschka, Oscar 138
Kopley, Richard 135n. 20
Kraft, Barbara 124, 126nn. 49, 54
Krauss, Rosalind 157n. 47
Kronski, Jean 149

Laanes, Eneken 28, 31nn. 49, 50
Lacan, Jacques 96, 104–5, 108nn. 41–2, 109–15, 117, 119–21, 123, 124nn. 5–7, 9–12, 125nn. 15–17, 19, 21, 24–6, 29, 39, 41–2, 45, 157n. 45, 186n. 24
"Land of Fuck" 149, 211
Lane, William 45
language (concept of) 2–3, 5, 22, 26, 34, 36, 64, 72, 88, 110, 115–16, 118, 121–2, 124, 145, 151–3, 161–2, 165, 167, 199–212, 213n. 31
Lao-tzu 9, 16, 54, 124n. 1
last man (concept of) 15, 59, 150
Laughlin, James 71
Lautréamont, Comte de 151, 156n. 40
Lawrence, David Herbert 9–10, 17, 19nn. 1, 8, 20n. 21, 49, 55–6, 78–9, 81, 83n. 21, 87, 107n. 21, 145–7, 150, 156n. 30, 159, 192, 200, 212n. 5
lebensphilosophie 9
lebenswelt 10
Le Guin, Ursula K. 5, 173–4, 176–7, 180–2, 185, 185nn. 13–14
Lehman, Eric D. 4–5, 127, 194, 197n. 6
"Letter to the Editor [re: Dreiser's style]" 162
"Letter to Kate Millett" 173, 182
Letters to Emil 2, 149, 153, 189
Lévi-Bruhl, Lucien 86
Lévi-Strauss, Claude 3, 7nn. 13–15, 40

Lewis, Felice Flannery 171n. 5, 172n. 20
Lewis, Leon 16, 20n. 23, 163, 170, 171n. 12, 172n. 31
Lewis, Wyndham 64, 73n. 6, 105
Lewisohn, Ludwig 152, 156n. 27
Leydesdorff, Selma 25, 30nn. 26, 30
Lillios, Anna 4, 85
Lincoln, Abraham 127
literary criticism (theory of) 1, 87
A Literate Passion 9, 30n. 30, 70, 112
Littlejohn, David 72, 77n. 40
Lord, Albert B. 83n. 18
Lorraine, Clade de 38–9
Lowenfels, Walter 191–3, 197

MacGregor, Bob 111–2
Machatý, Gustav 142
Mailer, Norman 1, 6n. 1, 87, 122, 152, 157n. 43, 200, 212nn. 5, 6
Mann, Klauss 145
Männiste, Indrek 3, 9, 28, 31nn. 47–8, 34, 42, 44nn. 6, 10, 13, 63, 155n. 9, 156n. 21
Mansfield, June *see* Miller, June
Mark, Karl 182, 187
Martin, Jay 19n. 6, 83n. 2, 85, 143, 148, 155nn. 18–20, 197n. 3
Marxism 64, 168, 176, 180–2, 184
masculinity 144
Masuga, Katy 1, 5, 6n. 6, 19n. 7, 22–3, 26, 27, 29nn. 6, 13, 30n. 38, 31n. 44, 36, 44n. 8, 63, 145, 156nn. 24, 40, 163, 166, 170, 171n. 13, 172nn. 21, 32
materialism 2, 25, 37, 92, 192
Mathieu, Bertrand 66, 213–14n. 34
Matisse, Henri 81, 138
Matus, Doug 134n. 1
"Max" 65–6, 68–70
Max and the White Phagocytes 72
May, Todd 183, 186n. 23
Mayné, Gilles 66, 71–2, 74n. 38, 201, 203–5, 207, 212nn. 9, 12, 213nn. 17–19, 23–4, 27
McCarthy, Harold T. 33, 44n. 1, 135nn. 4, 8
McClure, Eve *see* Eve Miller
McFarlane, James Walter 19n. 9

Mead, Henry 69, 73n. 26
"Megapolitan Maniac" 150
Melville, Herman 133
Merleau-Ponty, Maurice 82
metaphysics 9–11, 19n. 5, 79, 201
Miller, Eve 138
Miller, Hoki Tokuda 33
Miller, June 84n. 35, 149, 160, 168, 190–1, 197
Miller, Tony 130
Miller, Valentine 130, 132
Millett, Kate 5, 65, 85, 87, 93nn. 19–20, 170, 173–4, 176–82, 185nn. 9, 11–12
Milosz, Czeslaw 34, 44nn. 4–5
Milovanovic, Dragan 125n. 26
minimalism 161
mirror stage 121
misogyny 2, 5, 86, 161, 173
Mitchell, Edward B. 7n. 16, 42, 44n. 12
modernism 1, 26, 64, 69, 72, 86, 138, 146, 159, 164, 185n. 3, 192–4, 199, 201
modernity 3–4, 10–11, 15, 21, 23–6, 29n. 20, 75, 77–9, 82, 145, 150, 187
Moi, Toril 88, 93n. 28
Moloch, or This Gentile World 27, 29n. 7, 77
"Money and How It Gets that Way" 49
morality 4, 52, 58, 63–5, 67, 69–71, 190, 192, 194
Moricand, Conrad 131–3
Morris, David B. 159, 170, 171nn. 1, 16
Mozart, Wolfgang Amadeus 123
Munro, Ealasaid 93nn. 9–10
Munsil, Mary Kellie 100, 107nn. 20, 24, 27
Murdoch, Iris 97, 106n. 9
Muslim(s) 45, 48, 50, 53, 57

Nelson, Jane A. 155n. 11, 213n. 28
neoliberalism 185
Nesbit, Thomas 45, 61nn. 7–10, 12, 63, 152, 156n. 27
Nesbitt, Huw 6n. 3, 161, 165, 171, 171nn. 8–9

"The New Instinctivism" 47, 52–3
Newman, Saul 183, 186n. 24
New York (city of) 24, 34–7, 39, 41, 43, 44n. 9, 59, 65, 78, 84n. 35, 120–1, 142, 145, 162, 165, 168–9, 188–90, 192–3
Nexus 22, 24–5, 30n. 41, 34–5, 37–8, 43, 58, 84n. 35, 146, 168, 201–4, 207–8
Niedecker, Lorine 176
Nietzsche, Friedrich 9, 11, 15, 20nn. 18, 22, 23, 34, 50–2, 56, 58, 78–9, 82, 84nn. 27–9, 117, 123, 145–6, 183, 188, 192, 194
Nin, Anaïs 2, 6n. 8, 70, 86, 112, 123, 133, 142, 147, 151, 155n. 14, 160, 192, 196–7
Nohrnberg, James 83n. 4

Objectivist 176
obscenity 4–6, 67, 77, 86, 95–105, 106n. 13, 107nn. 15, 30, 160–7, 170, 199–200, 203–4, 206–7
"Obscenity and the Law of Reflection" 47, 166–7, 169–70, 207
"Obscenity in Literature" 162
O'Hara, John 168
"An Open Letter to Surrealists Everywhere" 143, 173–6, 181
"Open Sesame" 57
Oppen, George 176
oral theory 4, 75
Orend, Karl 1, 6n. 5, 22, 29n. 10, 45, 48, 50, 51, 53, 59, 61nn. 4, 11, 13, 19–23, 30, 137, 154n. 2, 155n. 9, 185n. 2
Orwell, George 63, 65, 72n. 3, 74n. 39, 161–2, 171n. 10, 175, 206, 212n. 8, 213n. 26
Osborn, Richard 191, 197
Other (concept of) 111–12, 117, 121–4

pacifism 175–6
painting 106n. 13, 137, 142, 151, 153
Palumbo, Allison 85, 87–9, 91, 93nn. 21–6, 31, 34, 94n. 48
parallelism (concept of) 76–7, 82, 83n. 11

Index

Paris (city of) 5, 17–18, 20n. 21, 22, 33, 36, 38–9, 43, 51, 58, 65–6, 77, 79, 82, 83n. 3, 85–6, 90, 92, 103, 107nn. 16, 28, 109–11, 121, 125n. 38, 131, 135n. 8, 142, 152–4, 155n. 12, 160, 162, 165, 168–9, 177, 187–9, 197n. 2
Parkin, John 19n. 3, 202, 213n. 13
Pascal, Blaise 45, 130
patriarchy 88, 179–80
Perlès, Alfred 133, 154, 176, 185nn. 5–6, 190–2, 195–7, 197n. 4
Peters, Gerald 22, 29n. 9
Petronius 163
philogyny 2
philo-Semitism 2
Phoenix 181
Picasso 117, 138
Plantinga, Alvin 45
Plato 42
Plexus 34–7, 43, 51, 84n. 35, 202
Poe, Edgar Allan 133, 187
Porter, Katherine Anne 86
positivism 187
post-anarchism 183
poststructuralism 183–4
Pound, Ezra 4, 61n. 4, 63–4, 69, 71, 72nn. 1, 7–11, 73nn. 27, 34–5, 86
praxis 2, 5, 173–6, 180, 182–3
progress (ideas of) 3, 11–13, 18, 19nn. 12–13, 23–6, 46, 49, 69, 71, 78
Proust, Marcel 209, 213n. 32
psychoanalysis 4, 96, 110, 124n. 6, 125nn. 15, 20, 142, 145, 148–9, 155n. 18
psychosis 4, 110–2, 114–5, 120, 122–4
Pynchon, Thomas 2

Quiet Days in Clichy 141, 194

Rabelais, François 19n. 3, 77–8, 163, 190
Ragland (Ragland-Sullivan), Ellie 54–5, 111, 120, 122, 124, 125nn. 18, 26–7, 30, 43, 126n. 47
Rand, Ayn 176
Rank, Otto 145, 148–9, 153–4, 156n. 36
Read, Herbert 163, 181–2

Real (concept of) 104–105, 108, 112, 114–15, 117–18, 122–4
realism 3, 25, 30n. 30, 137, 162, 181, 211
rebirth (concept of) 3–5, 24, 26–8, 45, 56, 58, 80, 90, 121, 138, 141, 146–7, 150, 152–3, 155n. 11
Reflections 99, 104
Reichel, Hans 18–19, 196
religion 4, 45–8, 50–3, 57, 60, 61nn. 7–10, 12, 15, 18, 25–6, 28–9, 63, 68, 70, 78, 83n. 14, 101, 127, 156n. 27, 157n. 46, 180, 187
Rembar, Charles 102–3, 106n. 8, 107n. 21, 108nn. 34–5
Remember to Remember 47, 163, 195–6
Renza, Louis 2
"Reunion in Brooklyn" 29n. 11, 48
Rexroth, Kenneth 65–6, 73n. 15, 107n. 17
Richthofen, Patrick von 175
Riley, Patrick 22, 25, 27, 29n. 8, 30n. 32, 31n. 46
Rilke, Rainer Maria 214n. 34
Rimbaud, Arthur 23, 84n. 35, 149, 161, 213–14n. 34
Roberts, Colette 53
Romanticism (ideas of) 6n. 4, 188, 195
Rosy Crucifixion 26, 48, 84n. 35, 154, 167, 169
Roth, Philip 2
Rushdie, Salman 64, 73n. 5

Sade, Marquis de 163
Said, Edward 35
salvation (ideas of) 4, 14, 45, 48–9, 53, 56–7, 60, 131, 193
San Francisco Renaissance 177
Sanger, Margaret 85
Sartre, Jean-Paul 213n. 31
"A Saturday Afternoon" 150–1
Satyagraha 176, 178
Scarry, Elaine 83n. 9
"Scenario" 137
Schatz, Bezalel 5, 137–41, 143–5, 147–9, 151, 153–4, 154nn. 1, 5, 155n. 8
Schatz, Louise 138
Schiller, Tom 33, 125n. 44

Schnellock, Emil 2, 77, 142, 146, 148–9, 153–4, 188–9, 191–3
Schreber, Daniel 110, 124n. 8
Science Fiction Studies 181
Second World War 84n. 35, 86, 132, 175–6, 194
Seed, David 142, 155n. 13
self (concept of) 4, 11, 17, 22, 25–6, 28, 31n. 46, 50–1, 54, 60, 71, 85, 87–9, 112, 121, 128, 134, 138, 142, 145–6, 152–4, 183–5, 202, 204, 206, 210, 212
self-liberation (ideas of) 1, 48–9, 51, 54–60, 64
Serrano, Andres 159
sex/sexuality 1–2, 47–8, 60, 63–6, 85, 87, 89, 91, 141, 147, 163, 178, 199–200, 204, 206–7
Sexual Politics 5, 73nn. 13–14, 87, 93nn. 19–20, 173, 178–80, 185nn. 9–12
Sexus 26–7, 30n. 27, 37–8, 84n. 35, 128, 162–3, 166–7, 178, 200–1, 203, 205
Shapiro, Karl 3, 6n. 12, 46, 61nn. 2–3, 16, 66
Shifreen, Lawrence J. 138, 155n. 7
Silver, Edward 100–2, 105, 107n. 30
Sinthome 114, 115, 120, 122
Skovajsa, Ondrej 4, 75
The Smile at the Foot of the Ladder 137, 154n. 3
Smithline, Arnold 128, 134n. 2, 135nn. 5–6
socialism 175, 187
Soelle, Dorothee 79, 82, 83n. 1, 84nn. 26, 34
Solomon, William 156n. 33
Southwood, Ivor 169, 172n. 28
Spencer, Herbert 50
Spengler, Oswald 9–14, 19nn. 11, 14, 16, 20n. 20, 23, 37, 145, 150, 188, 192
spiral form (concept of) 22–3, 26, 46, 155n. 21
Srila, Roy 25, 30n. 26
Stand Still Like the Hummingbird 25, 49, 53–4, 57, 84n. 35
Stein, Gertrude 86
Steiner, Floriano 33
Stevenson, Guy 4, 63
Stirner, Max 11

Straub, Julia 26, 30n. 35
Strindberg, August 189–90, 194
Sunday After the War 28, 29n. 11, 48, 64, 72
Supreme Court (ruling of) 104
surrealism 5, 16, 29n. 17, 36, 40, 46, 63–4, 109, 117, 142–3, 145, 152–3, 155n. 9, 182, 185n. 2, 192, 203
Suvin, Darko 181
Swift, Jonathan 66
Symbolic (concept of) 112–18, 122–4
Symmes, Robert 186n. 19

Tanenhaus, Sam 92, 94nn. 49, 51–2
Tanizaki, Junichiro 33
Taoism 16, 185
Thoreau, Henry David xiiinn. 5, 6, 90, 127–34, 135nn. 10–13, 15–16, 163, 175–6, 183
Thurston, Luke 114, 115, 125n. 33
Tibet 4, 33, 35, 37, 39, 41, 43
Time of the Assassins 26, 28, 84n. 35, 149
Tong, Rosemary 93n. 32
To Paint Is to Love Again 138, 151
traditional present (concept of) 3, 10, 13–19, 28, 42
Transcendentalism 5, 6n. 4, 127–34, 135nn. 4, 14, 20
transition 146, 150, 156n. 29, 192, 194
trauma (concept of) 3, 21, 24–6, 28, 105, 148–9
Tropic of Cancer 2, 4–6, 6n. 9, 11, 14–15, 24, 26–8, 28n. 1, 29nn. 13, 20, 30n. 41, 36–9, 42–3, 44nn. 3, 14, 47–8, 50–3, 58, 63–8, 70–2, 72nn. 1, 4, 73nn. 7–8, 33, 75–82, 83n. 21, 84n. 35, 85–91, 94n. 39, 95–6, 98, 100, 103, 106n. 8, 110–18, 121, 123, 127–8, 138, 146–7, 150–3, 156n. 27, 159–70, 173, 177–82, 184, 189–90, 192–4, 196, 199, 202, 204, 208–9
Tropic of Capricorn 11, 15–16, 24–8, 29n. 7, 33–6, 38–9, 43, 45, 48, 53, 55–6, 58–60, 65, 67, 69, 71, 84n. 35, 87–9, 95, 118, 145, 147, 149, 160, 163, 167–70, 178, 183, 192, 203, 209–11

Turner, Frederick 90–1, 94n. 39, 159–60, 163, 165, 171nn. 7, 15, 172nn. 19, 25

Ullman, Chana 23–4, 29n. 15, 30n. 23
unconscious(ness) 4–5, 17–18, 102, 104–5, 109–12, 115–7, 120, 138, 143, 145–6, 150, 156n. 30, 157n. 47, 184
"The Universe of Death" 46, 55, 57
U.S. Constitution 85

Vattimo, Gianni 84n. 29
Vendler, Helen 85, 91, 93n. 5, 94n. 47
Vidal, Gore 166
Virgil 78
Vollman, William 168, 172n. 26

Walden 4–5, 127–31, 133–4, 135nn. 8, 10–13, 15–16
"Walking Up and Down in China" 16–17, 121, 152
Wallace, Kreg 197n. 2
Wallace, Rob 26, 30n. 34
Ward, Koral 29n. 11
The Waters Reglitterized 137–8, 151, 154, 154n. 6
Weir, David 174, 185n. 3
Weiss, Paul 10
Welch, Howard 42, 129
White, Curtis 169, 172n. 27
Whitman, Walt 14, 37, 43, 57, 75, 77–81, 83n. 17, 90, 127, 134, 135n. 4, 139, 156n. 24
Wickes, George 109, 143, 213n. 22
Widmer, Kingsley 3, 6n. 10, 26, 30n. 36, 61nn. 5, 17, 166, 212n. 5
Wilden, Anthony 110, 124n. 6

Williams, Raymond 22, 28n. 5
Williams, William Carlos 86
Williamsburg 35
Williamson, Eric Miles 105, 108n. 43
Wilson, Edmund 63, 72n. 2, 102, 110–11, 124nn. 13–14, 161
Winslow, Walker 130
Winterson, Jeanette 3, 5, 6n. 11, 85, 90–1, 93n. 3, 94nn. 40–2, 160–1, 165, 170, 171nn. 2–4, 6
The Wisdom of The Heart 18, 49, 56–8, 84n. 35, 191
Wittgenstein, Ludwig 201, 212n. 7
Wolfe, Bernard 104, 108nn. 38–9
Wolff, Robert Paul 183, 186n. 22
Wolff, Tobias 171
womb 45, 58–60, 113–14, 140, 145–7, 152, 155n. 11, 184
Wordsworth, William 76
The World of Lawrence 14, 17, 116, 147
The World of Sex 21–2, 24, 46–9, 54, 57–8
writing (concept of) 5, 27–8, 77, 87–8, 123–4, 142, 147, 152, 156n. 40, 200–4, 208, 210–12

Yannopoulos 40
Yazici, Savaş 114, 125n. 25
Yeats, William Butler 19n. 17
Yoma, Tony 33
Young, Julian 19n. 2

Zadkine, Ossip 190
Žižek, Slavoj 4, 95–6, 98, 101–2, 105, 106nn. 1–3, 107nn. 14, 29, 108n. 42, 125n. 25
Zukofsky, Louis 176